T R A V E L E R ' S

SOUTH AFRICA

C O M P A N I O N

The 2001–2002 Traveler's Companions
ARGENTINA • AUSTRALIA • BALI • CALIFORNIA • CANADA • CHILI • CHINA •
COSTA RICA • CUBA • EASTERN CANADA • ECUADOR • FLORIDA • HAWAII •
HONG KONG • INDIA • INDONESIA • IRELAND • JAPAN • KENYA •
MALAYSIA & SINGAPORE • MEDITERRANEAN FRANCE • MEXICO • NEPAL •
NEW ENGLAND • NEW ZEALAND • NORTHERN ITALY • PERU • PHILIPPINES •
PORTUGAL • RUSSIA • SOUTH AFRICA • SOUTHERN ENGLAND • SPAIN • THAILAND •
TURKEY • VENEZUELA • VIETNAM, LAOS AND CAMBODIA • WESTERN CANADA

Traveler's SOUTH AFRICA Companion
First published 2001
All rights reserved
© 2001 by The Globe Pequot Press
246 Goose Lane, PO Box 480
Guilford, CT 06437 USA
www.globe-pequot.com

© 2000 The Globe Pequot Press, Guilford CT, USA

Distributed in the European Union by
World Leisure Marketing Ltd, Unit 11
Newmarket Court, Newmarket Drive,
Derby, DE24 8NW, United Kingdom
www.map-guides.com

ISBN: 0-7627-0728-3

Created, edited and produced by
Allan Amsel Publishing, 53, rue Beaudouin
27700 Les Andelys, France.
E-mail: Allan.Amsel@wanadoo.fr
Editor in Chief: Allan Amsel
Editor: Anne Trager
Original design concept: Hon Bing-wah
Picture editor and designer: David Henry
© by The Globe Pequot Press

Printed by Samwha Printing Co. Ltd., Seoul, South Korea

TRAVELER'S
SOUTH AFRICA
COMPANION

by Jack Barker

photographs by Alain Evrard

The
Globe
Pequot
Press

GUILFORD
CONNECTICUT

Contents

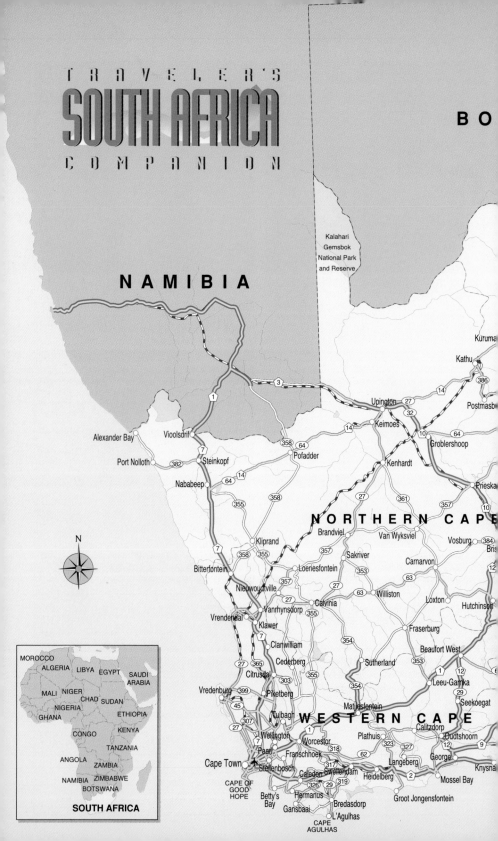

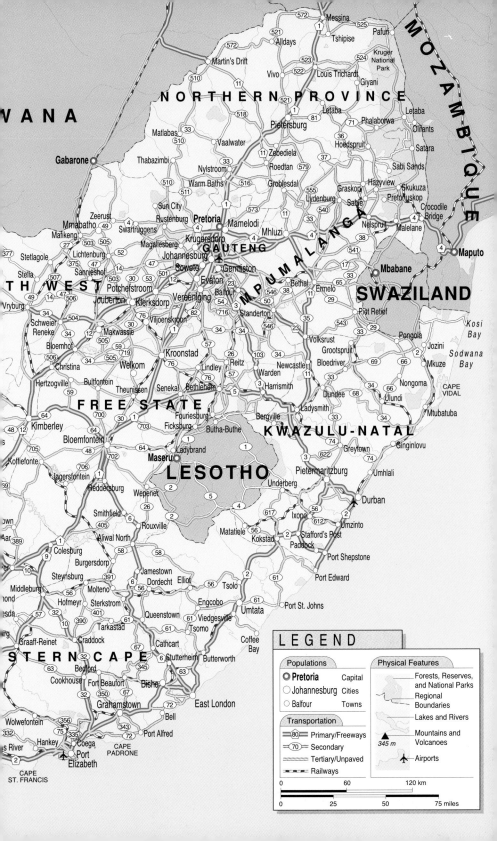

TOP SPOTS

Train to be a Ranger

HALFWAY THROUGH THE RANGER TRAINING COURSE A LARGE ELEPHANT TUSKED ITS WAY UP FROM THE RIVERBED THROUGH THE THICK RIVERINE FOREST. Mammal identification had been covered the previous day: "Oh look, it's an elephant," I thought. But as he stumbled startled onto the path 10 m (about 30 ft) ahead he suddenly noticed us, far closer than he — or I — liked.

I'd been told how to recognize the first signs of elephant anger and now I saw them. High above the elephant was shaking its head, ears flapping large and tusks cleaving the air.

Walking amongst Africa's largest wildlife is one of the most rewarding of all South Africa's travel experiences. To add a thin veneer of education onto the wildlife experience I signed up for a three-day ranger-training course on a private reserve, in theory learning the basics of looking after clients in the bush.

At the precise moment of being charged by an elephant we were midway through our survival module. However we had been concentrating on digging for water in sand rivers and how to theoretically spear warthogs in imagined emergencies. This real emergency took us rather by surprise. One thing we hadn't learned was what to do when faced with three tons of angry elephant. But the procedure turned out to be simple. "Walk away, walk away," murmured Ed, our instructor, quietly and urgently, and we reversed our walk as if someone had pressed fast rewind. But the elephant started to charge. "Run away, run away," Ed upgraded his instructions and we turned and scattered. I sprinted fast for a few yards and, puffed, took shelter behind a slender sapling and turned to meet my fate. Thankfully my fate had been postponed. The elephant had already lost interest and was shouldering a new trail through the thorns. Even though the training course had, in theory, covered tracking, I didn't feel the slightest temptation to follow.

This was one memorable highlight of a weekend course of ranger training at Sabi Sabi, a private unfenced reserve on the borders of South Africa's Kruger National Park. However the adventure of walking in the bush among Africa's wildest residents is offered by several of the more adventurous private reserves and even, if you book well ahead, by South Africa's Parks Board.

Getting close to animals on foot is always memorable, but running away is rarely recommended. Even a half-fit mongoose will easily outpace most humans, and the most worrying predators are much faster. If photography is your aim, the best way to

OPPOSITE: The giraffe's high viewpoint means, for the zebra, early warning of predators. ABOVE: An elephant is distracted from lunch in Shamwari.

get really close to animals is by car. Confused by the scent of diesel and habituated (in the private reserves at least) to the shape of safari vehicles, most of the animals will completely ignore a Landrover, even when it's decked out with tiered cinema seating and crowded with visitors letting off their cameras. A Landrover can also accelerate quickly out of trouble and keep driving longer than most animals care to chase.

The best game-viewing areas are in the private reserves of the Sabi Sands and Timbavati areas, with a less expensive option being self-drive in the park itself. However there are other areas where game-viewing is very rewarding. The Waterbergs, northwest of Johannesburg, contain a number of private farms now being restocked with game, and KwaZulu-Natal gives plenty of chances for spotting big game in the parks of Itala, Hluhluwe-Umfolozi, and Phinda. If your visit is restricted to the south of the country Addo, has elephant, and Shamwari can offer the Big Five (leopard, lion, buffalo, elephant, and rhino) in areas free of malaria, although their determination to offer a sighting of each species does, at times, make it feel something like a visit to a zoo.

The safari experience will depend on whether you go to a private reserve or the public-sector national parks and reserves. The private reserves will offer almost

universally high standards of accommodation, cuisine, and service. The conventional way to see animals is through morning and evening game-drives, with tiered seats offering a good vantage point and drinks being served at sundown and tea at dawn. Usually private reserves offer night-drives and will also head off-road to get close to animals. Be warned, the Kruger is very cold at night and you'll need warm clothes for the open vehicles.

Within the state sector things become much cheaper and rather more basic. You'll usually be driving yourself, relying on spotting your own game and from the lower vantage point of a saloon, and will not be able to leave the road to track close, nor leave the car. Accommodation in the national parks tends to be in villages of self-catering chalets, usually but not always intelligently sited over waterholes or salt-licks where you can expect to see animals as you eat.

Ranger Training is offered in the Kruger by Sabi Sabi ((011) 483 3939 FAX (011) 483 3799 E-MAIL com@sabisabi.com WEB SITE www.sabisabi.com, Box 52665, Saxonwold 2132, with three-day courses costing R4,500. Courses are also offered by Vectra Ventures (/FAX (013) 744 9629 or (083) 626 7194, Box 12585, Steiltes 1200, Nelspruit, ranging from quick introductions to longer training. Private reserves and national parks are listed in their appropriate areas in the touring chapters.

Sing out Vaudeville

I WAS ONE OF TWO WHITE FACES IN A CROWD OF 1,000. It was midnight and I was in a place I had been emphatically told to avoid at night: Durban city center, in the Beatrice Street Hostel for migrant workers, where Zulu migrant workers hold their weekly singing competition. Isicathamiya singing has its origins in the Zulu singing messengers that spread the oral history from one generation to another, the traditional Ingoma dances from the villages, molded by a big burst of influence from American vaudeville songs of the early 1900s. Every Saturday night, except Christmas and Easter, Durban's Beatrice Street Hostel lays on a display and anyone can go.

The evening so far had been spent practicing. The performances started on the street. Groups of 20, dressed in matching clothes, sang in unison, following the chants of their singing leader. Two-by-two the groups would swing into the hall, following a precise dance routine as they threaded through the crowds, working their way past a table of judges to ascend the raised stage. Then they would spread out in a wide crescent, against a background of trees and mountains left over from the last dramatic performance, and blast out a disciplined harmony of baritone, tenor, and bass.

As the night went on the standards got higher. And not just the singing: the whole performance is judged and the dress is also a factor. Each group, all male, were dressed in identical clothes, from shirts, ties and pants, to belts and shoes. Some had matching hats, bowler or top. For their entrance, jackets were always carried, neatly folded in the left hand, to be donned with a flourish during the band's first number. Of course, the jackets matched. Some groups had tuxedos, others white butcher's coats, smoking jackets or tails.

Its formative years in the single-sex working hostels have shaped the development of this musical form. Firstly, with one exception, the singers are male. The traditional stamping dance has been adapted for performance and practice in communal settings where other hostel residents might be trying to sleep: every stamping dance step ends suddenly, silently, the foot stopping just above the floor, descending with eerie precision to land quietly. Even clapping movements are half-mimed, restrained.

The changing bands sang a medley of songs, mainly Gospel, but also of their distant homes, and the trees they missed in their lives in the city. One by one bands came and performed. The High Stars, the Zulu Messengers and the New Happy Singers, black shirts with white ties, polka-dots, pinstripes and blazers. In between numbers, one performer made a phone call and put their

---

OPPOSITE: Zebra stripes are designed to confuse predators in the heat of the chase. ABOVE: Dancing and singing falls in line on Beatrice Street in Durban.

portable phone on the floor, the choral music heading through the ether to a distant relative.

Some bands were supported by groupies, huge middle-aged women in stately hats who swayed and danced at the side of the hall; relatives and friends. Younger fans gently flirted with band members, expressive arm and hand movements replacing words and phrases in a culture where language is not the only means of communication.

In between bands other competitions filled the gaps. Fashion shows, less about beauty or style and more concerned with sheer number of clothing items. Middle-aged men strutted to the stage in three-piece suits, festooned with breast-pocket handkerchiefs, watch-chains and cuff-links. With no exposure to the catwalks of the West they'd learned their poses from catalogues selling mail-order clothes, freezing in position, lifting a trouser-leg to prove their socks matched, and fixing the audience with a knowing, commercial stare. Women sailed on like battleships, tightly-wrapped in billowing dresses or freshly-laundered pinafores, lavish hats shading makeup the depth of face-packs and ringed and braceletted hands clutching stylish, empty handbags.

The show was to go on to dawn. Although I hadn't sat right at the front, the seats had been cleared away to ensure I had the best view. As I squeezed through the crowds to leave strangers shook my hands and contestants smiled. I'd been nervous about walking into the dark street in the middle of the night, but it was patrolled. Not by armed cars or police vans but by tight circles of uniformed singers, practicing quietly their repertoires in the pooled light of street-lamps. As I climbed into my car and drove away the low sound of expert singing faded into the night.

It is easy to visit the weekly Saturday Isicathamiya show, but as no tour operators know it even happens you'll need to make your own way. A lowly official from the tourist board wanted to impose punctuality and sophistication on the show, destroying its natural charm, before being prepared to promote it. It's easiest to drive there yourself. Cruise past to make sure that there's something going on — you won't miss the practicing groups from 11 PM onwards — and park. Beatrice Street is known to most taxi drivers but they probably won't know about the weekend concerts. Don't pay off the taxi before making sure the performance is going ahead and, most importantly, make sure that your driver will come back to collect you, and wait if necessary. You don't find cruising taxis in Durban, and although the busy area outside the hostel is safe, the streets and alleys surrounding it are not.

Climb Table Mountain

CLIMBING TABLE MOUNTAIN IS THE SINGLE MUST-DO ACTIVITY FOR ALL VISITORS TO CAPE TOWN. The easiest way to reach the top is by cable car, which offers on every side views of the mountain's sheer slopes and the city below, and the ranging mountains and bays of one of the world's most beautiful coastlines.

From the base station twin cables snake up in a gentle parabola, curving to the vertical as they latch onto the flat, lost-world peak of Table Mountain. The two cable cars, which pass in mid-stage, rotate 360 degrees on the journey, so there's no point jostling for space by the two open windows: they'll move.

At the top of the mountain, a network of concrete paths thread through the stunted *fynbos*, or indigenous plants, that cling to rocky life. Hyraxes hop around the boulders spilling down the sheer slopes of the mountain's face and marked paths set out strolls varying from "20 minutes, very easy" to "40 minutes, easy."

Armchair travelers who take the cable car will view Cape Bay, the Apostles, the town, and the waterfront. But there is plenty they will miss. Table Mountain alone has more plant species than the British Isles, and the best way to appreciate its beauties is on foot. The Pipe Track route leaves from the base of the cable car and follows the mountain contours for seven kilometers (just over four miles) below the lowering bulk of the Twelve Apostles, with a number of ravines giving access up to the flat peak of the mountain. Clambering to the top is not the only thing to do when faced with a big mountain, and this is a rewarding walk with little climbing involved.

To climb to the top of the mountain it's not necessary to be outstandingly fit, but you do need to be agile. The obvious, and the safest, way to ascend is to follow the line of the Aerial Cableway and then turn off to climb up Platteklip Gorge to the summit. A path proceeds from the lower station for a 15-minute hike up the mountain's lower shoulder. This reaches the upper contour path, which is clearly signposted, and then zigzags up through Platteklip Gorge, the largest cleavage in the mountain and the route chosen, sensibly enough, by the first recorded climber, the Portuguese sailor Antonio de Saldanha in 1503. It's a natural route to take,

The Swiss-built cable car is the easy way up Table Mountain.

particularly if you've just found out that the Cableway is closed on some pretext, and is safe enough, but it's a tough and not especially interesting climb: three hours of steady clambering slog.

For those who prefer a pleasant walk rather than a conquering walk a better option is to take the service road, following the irrigation pipes that take water from the mountain reservoirs to Kloof Nek.

The best routes up the mountain are Nursery Ravine and Skeleton Gorge, which start from Kirstenbosch Botanical Gardens, themselves a highlight of Cape Town. The fit can ascend by one route and return by another, making a full day out with about five hours of hiking. Skeleton Gorge is the easier ascent. Stone steps and wooden ladders make the quickest way to the top of the mountain, although it can be tricky for a rainy descent. The path starts off neat and cultivated, with indigenous *fynbos* plants lining the trail, before it enters a lush foliage tunnel of deep greens, trickling streams, and the spongy feel of moss. There are several false summits before you reach the peak, and the sight of cable-car potatoes straying down can inspire sudden desperate jealousy. Once out of the gorge it is an easy level walk across the top of Table Mountain to the Cableway; or turn right and follow signs to Nursery Ravine for a steep but safe descent back to Kirstenbosch.

Each year climbers die on Table Mountain, almost always because they've ignored basic safety caveats. The 1,087-m (3,566-ft) bulk of rock is the first land encountered by weather blowing north from the Antarctic, and conditions can change quickly — often for the worse. On the same day a hat can be needed against the heat of the sun and — later — waterproofs against sheeting rain. Good footwear is essential, preferably boots or running shoes, and always carry water and clothes. If you do get into trouble wait for help rather than try to find a new way down: steep cliffs can become suddenly sheer. Tell someone when you're going and by which route.

Finally, never climb alone. This might seem easier advice to give than enact, especially for a traveler whose partner prefers the simpler pleasures of sunbathing and shopping, but there are a number of organizations that make it easier to find climbing companions. Perhaps the best is Cape Union Mart, the hiking equipment chain with outlets all over the country, but particularly in Cape Town's Victoria and Alfred Waterfront, who arrange hikes up the mountain through the Cape Union Mart Hiking Club ((021) 419 0019 TOLL-FREE (0800) 034 000. It is also possible to get in touch with well-informed and enthusiastic hikers through the Botanical Society of South Africa (Kirstenbosch) ((021) 671 5468, during office hours. The Mountain Club of South Africa ((021) 465 3412 FAX (021) 461 8456 organizes weekend walks, hikes and climbs, perhaps best discussed through their open social evenings on Fridays at 6 PM in their Clubhouse at 97 Hatfield Street.

On foot or by cable car, the golden rule for travelers on short schedules is to take the first opportunity to go up Table Mountain. The "Tablecloth" cloud that spills from the top can appear without notice, and if the weather turns nasty the cable car will be closed. Many visitors to Cape Town spend their first day admiring the view of Table Mountain and planning their trip to the summit, only to see the weather close in for the rest of their stay.

Dive with a Great White

STRAPPING ON A MASK AND GRABBING A TUBE LINKED TO AIR-TANKS I DROPPED INTO THE CLEAR BLUE WATERS OFF MOSSELL BAY. As the water surface rippled up the glass my view opened up into the blue of the underwater world, fading opaque after about 30 m (100 ft). Then, in the gloom, a shape approached: the huge gray threat of a great white shark, one of the world's largest and certainly the most dangerous of all sharks. Drawn by a hanging bundle of meat, it flipped its way closer, effortlessly closing, inspecting and circling, the most efficient ocean killer powering towards me. Suddenly the strips of metal that made up my viewing cage seemed very fragile and I tried to avoid eye contact.

Successfully. Like a solicited stranger in the subway it flipped away. It had been circling the boat for 20 minutes assessing our value as entertainment, and my floundering, caged body was obviously the last straw. We never saw that shark again and it was hard not to take it personally.

The shark-rich waters off Africa's southern tip are the best place to meet the great white, and the world's most effective predator, top feeder in the ocean food-chain, is best seen from the comfort of a cage. Cage-diving with sharks is the most dramatic way to glimpse South Africa's oceanic life, although there are plenty of other methods that offer sightings of a greater range of species.

The biggest feeding frenzy of shark-dive operators happens in Gansbaai, a small fishing village shot to celebrity less by the regularity of shark sightings than its proximity to Cape Town. With a variety of boats it rides the wave of a boom industry with a selection of home-welded cages and jealously-guarded secret techniques for attracting elusive sharks. Despite government threats to regulate and license shark-diving operators, the competing billboards that line Gansbaai's high street leave many visitors feeling a bit of a shy shark themselves. Sightings are never guaranteed and you need a diving license to wallow out in homemade cages amongst these ocean predators.

An alternative is to flip 80 km (50 miles) up the road to Mossel Bay. Despite being a larger town — with statistically rather more sharks — there is only one shark-dive operator, and his shark cage, fixed on the stern of a yacht, can be used by people without scuba qualifications. From the wooden deck of the *Infanté* ketch sailing along Mossel Bay's bathing beaches, the matchstick figures of swimmers show black against the white sands. I wondered if they realized we were about to start siphoning out blood and guts in a 16-km (10-mile) trail across the ocean to tease and tempt an underwaterworld danger into paying us a visit. The specially designed cage, large enough to hold two divers, is pivoted down at the stern of the boat and two diving mouthpieces, attached to a tank by long rubber tubes, dangle overboard in anticipation. Some roving shark would be sure to investigate.

No operator will guarantee seeing a shark, and frenzied feeding seen from close quarters is, at best, occasional. Of all South Africa's wildlife the great white is the least understood and most elusive.

The pleasures of my day seeking shark had been more in the quieter information picked up through a day on the water: about transmitting shark deterrents for surfers, and the long research project identifying

OPPOSITE: Views of Cape Town's Atlantic seaboard.
ABOVE: The Sentinel, viewed from Chapman's Peak.

individuals and mapping this efficient killer's little-understood behavior. To go cage diving, the *Infanté* Great White Shark Experience (082 455 2438 FAX (044) 691 3796 E-MAIL Infante@pixie.co.za Box 2979, Mossel Bay, is among the best shark-dive operators, charging R450 for a day-long yacht cruise. Which may, or may not, include a sighting.

South Africa's coast, however, harbors other ocean creatures for sighting. In season, whales school off the coast east of Cape Town, where the whole area is known as the "Whale Coast." They are best spotted from on high, and most towns with any sort of cliff over the sea will claim a good whale-sighting record. The town of Hermanus takes whale-spotting to a new level, employing a town crier who keeps up-to-date with the latest sightings by mobile phone.

The most commonly seen species is the southern right whale, so called because of its high oil content and the useful (to whalers) trait of floating when dead. They begin to come inshore to calve in June and some will stay around until December, but the best time to spot them is from August to October. To find the latest sighting information in season, call the Whale Hotline ((083) 910 1028 or (083) 212 1074 (direct line to the whale crier).

Apart from whales you also have the chance to see plenty of bottlenose dolphins who play in the surf, and sometimes the rare Indo-Pacific humpback dolphin, or Bryde's and humpback whales. Occasionally there are sightings of minke and pygmy sperm whales. Polarized sunglasses make it easier to see through the water surface.

To correctly identify species it helps to have a knowledgeable guide — and a boat. In Plettenberg Bay the original pioneer of boat-based ecotourism is Ocean Adventures (/FAX (044) 533 5083 or (083) 701 3583 E-MAIL info@oceanadventures.co.za WEB SITE www.plettbay.co.za/oceanadventures, Box 1812, Plettenberg Bay 6600, run by the hugely knowledgeable Dave Rissik. Boat trips from two to three hours cost R200 to R270 per person depending on season, with space for up to 12 passengers and longer expeditions arranged on request.

An even surer way of spotting whales is to take to the air. From a height the waters are more transparent and huge distances can be surveyed. African Ramble ((044) 533 9006 or (083) 375 6514 FAX (044) 533 9012 E-MAIL aframble@cis.co.za WEB SITE www.aframble .co.za, Box 736, Knysna 6570, charge from R280 for a 30-minute flight, price per person with a minimum of two.

Relive South Africa's Battles of Birth

IT'S USUALLY QUITE HARD TO MAKE ME CRY. The death of a dog, even if not mine, will do it, but not much else. So as I was surprised, as I heard about a battle 120 years ago, to find myself fighting back tears. I looked away. It wouldn't do to show emotion.

Partly it was the setting. Remember the film *Zulu*? I was sitting by the low stone buildings of Rorke's Drift, at the very place where Michael Caine fought off hordes of Zulus, "black as hell and thick as grass," watching the sun set as it had on that night when 139 British soldiers had fought off 4,000 Zulu warriors. The ghosts, once celluloid, had come to life, brought back from the past by David Rattray, entomologist by training, historian by practice, and showman by vocation, bringing every stage of the battle vividly to life.

David Rattray, a regular speaker at London's Royal Geographical Society, has with his skill and passion single-handedly sparked off a boom in battlefield tourism in South Africa. His lodge, Fugitives' Drift, is in the midst of the Zulu war-zones of KwaZulu-Natal, and for the past 10 years he has been enthusing his guests with the area's history.

To have David as a guide should be the ideal for every visitor, but obviously he can't always be available to take tours. A good substitute is his set of five cassette tapes, which retails for R300. This is a huge sum by South African standards, and it is a tribute to him that most guests buy a set. Playing over the speakers of a car stereo, they recreate much of his magic and add to the rolling landscapes the treacherous tale of the British Empire's conquests that mix victory with disaster. For further details contact David Rattray, Fugitives Drift Lodge ((034) 642 1843 FAX (034) 271 8053, Box 3016, Rorke's Drift.

Other historians explain the tactics and history of local battles. The fight at Rorke's Drift was but a sideshow to the major battle that took place the previous day, Isandlwana. This British defeat, as overwhelming as unexpected, saw the dreams of an easy conquest of Africa washed away with blood. I went to Isandlwana with Rob Gerrard, an ex-British army officer, clipped accents recalling the tiered power structure of the army that fell

ABOVE and RIGHT: Traditional dances bring back the days when Zulu warriors defeated the British.

to the unintelligible discipline of the Zulu forces.

The drive to the battlefield at Isandlwana was spent filling in the political context of the battle using one of David Rattray's tapes. Then we ran through the sequence of the battle from the vantage point used by the Zulu general, and moved to the battlefield itself to recreate the final few moments of conflict, where the exhausted survivors fought to the death. The bloody fight dragged on, the last remaining soldiers, identified by name, fighting on a square at the top of the *kjoppe* (rocky outcrop).

The Zulu War wasn't the only conflict in the birth of this nation. For plenty of South Africans the vivid memories are of the Boer Wars fought between the British Authorities and the Boer settlers. The fighting of the Boer Wars took place all across South Africa, but KwaZulu-Natal has the most developed network of professional guides. To visit the battlefield of Spioenkop I called local historian Elizabeth Spire't ((036) 637 7702, who arrived armed with a well-thumbed reference book bound with an extra clingfilm cover. We drove across the short grass plains, burned yellow by the sun, along roads that arrowed endless across a huge country. On a gentle hill I relived Spioenkop, where a company of British soldiers were crowded into a killing field that shook the empire.

While it took a historian to bring the sunsoaked field to bloodsoaked life, the town of Ladysmith still revels in its past, with field-guns outside the city hall that date back to the 120-day siege, now more than 100 years old in the past. In October 1899 a garrison of 12,500 British soldiers were pinned down in this town by Boer forces who controlled the encircling hills. It was a long-distance war: from the town center the hills look impossibly distant, innocuous, and low. In the company of a local guide, Vusi Dayile ((036) 631 7081, I drove out to the edge of the escarpment and clambered up to a Boer battery, where the long and demanding uphill struggle over broken ground brought home the realities of armed conflict in a beautiful but unforgiving landscape.

While the siege has been lifted, where once Boer snipers had hidden in the hills there are now African townships, banished by apartheid into huge sprawling shanties. Vusi took me round to a house that belonged to a local policeman and served as a dressmaking factory and occasional restaurant while he was out upholding law and order. Three substantial women cut and sewed at one end of the living room while I was sat at the other.

While Vusi helped me dissect a cold side of mutton I was provided with plenty of entertainment. As "Mama Fashion" was born on the other side of the room, a local radio station played Western hits through two huge speakers while a wide-screen television showed an episode of *The Bold and the Beautiful*, volume turned high. I reflected as I ate that the rich drama of South Africa's early years would need another blockbusting movie to recapture the imagination of a new generation.

Saddle up a Leggy Bird

IN THE LATE EIGHTEENTH CENTURY OSTRICH FEATHERS WERE WORTH MORE, BY WEIGHT, THAN GOLD. Fortunes were made, and there are still large ostrich farms in South Africa, especially in the Little Karoo town of Oudtshoorn, and uniquely, many offer visitors the chance to ride these strange animals.

The arid fields around this desert town are still filled with herds of large, flightless birds, but nowadays ostrich breeders have more of a struggle. The feathers are still good for dusters, but there's only so much dusting the world can do and synthetic substitutes are cheaper. Eggs are fairly decorative, especially when glazed and painted, but if you want an ostrich egg for breakfast, at one and a half kilos (over three pounds) it takes an hour and a half to boil and would feed a rugby team. Although ostrich meat is low in cholesterol and high in protein, it has little international appeal. So the ostrich barons of old are, like English aristocracy fallen on hard times, forced to start taking in paying guests.

At Highgate my guide, Donna, showed me round the hatchery. "You can give a mother lots of chicks to look after and she'll assume they're all hers," I learned, "but what you can't do is give chicks to an ostrich who hasn't had an egg. They're not that stupid." As we walked over to where a pair of ostrich were guarding a small nest of eggs Donna handed me a thorny branch. "They don't usually attack but can get possessive. A thorn will scare them off. I hope." Our group had picked up a mother and two young children (human), who were also given branches. Under a small A-frame shelter we found the eggs, still warm from being incubated, and we were encouraged to pick them up and tempted to try standing on one. "It's quite safe" said Donna, but, worried about the egg — and my shoes — I held back.

We proceeded through to a small wooden *kraal* where fifteen adult birds milled around.

They were tall, sneering down their noses at their prospective jockeys and bouncing skittishly with a faintly comic, high-stepping gait. Donna's laid-back commentary acquired a certain urgency as a light cloth sock was slipped over a large ostrich's head. Still and nervous, he froze, and I started to feel sorry for him. After all, I'd lied about my weight to get the chance to clamber on his back. I hoped his spindly legs wouldn't break. Then he was backed into a wooden structure with steps to help me mount. And my concern for his legs shifted, from whether they might break to whether they might kick. I started to concentrate on his sharp, powerful toes. I'd heard that a kick from an angry ostrich can disembowel a man.

Donna led me to the mounting block. "Hold on to his wings; don't grab his neck. You'll throttle him and ostrich necks break easily." As two farm-workers held the bird securely I gingerly settled my weight on his back and grabbed nervously with my knees. I was clinging and, I realized, sliding down a perilous slope. Letting go of the wooden rails I grabbed hard at two wings, firm and strong

LEFT: A troupe of ostriches with their progeny.
BELOW: European fashions made ostrich feathers, for a time, more valuable than gold.

through the feathers. The hood was removed and my ostrich bounded from the mounting block with all the enthusiasm of a rodeo horse. As the farm-workers tried to catch up, ready to catch me, the ostrich, in a strangely silent panic, scattered his friends as he tracked two fast circles around the *kraal* in search of escape. Hunched over and clenching with all four limbs, I knew the moment I took my hands from the wings I would fall off. Then the farm-workers were either side, calming the bird — interestingly, by grabbing its neck — and helping me off. The ostrich stalked off fast and bouncy without a vengeful backward glance and was soon lost, anonymous, among his friends.

My personal bravery was soon dispelled by the two young children who went next, supported either side by handlers. It has to be said their experience was far calmer. They walked sedately around the *kraal*, smiling hugely to their mother's video camera, with farm workers on either side.

It was with mixed feelings that I set about lunch, later, at the restaurant. To start, ostrich pâté, followed by ostrich egg, and ostrich biltong snack. The main course was ostrich fillet and I just didn't ask about the cheese.

As I drove out of the Highgate Ostrich Farm on my way to Cango Caves I thought about one thing I'd learned. Ostrich don't, when threatened, hide their heads in the sand. They just lower their heads to look more like a rock. Quite an effective deception. Because I'd learned two other things. They don't ride like rocks and they don't taste like rock.

The South African Ostrich Capital is Oudtshoorn, in the heart of the Klein Karoo. The original place to try riding ostrich is the Highgate Ostrich Show Farm ((044) 272 7115 FAX (044) 272 7111 E-MAIL highgate1@pixie.co.za,

off the R328 to Mossel Bay, Box 94, Oudtshoorn 6620, whose tours cost R20 and lasts about an hour. Highgate opened to the public in 1937 but the other farmers in the area have quickly caught up. One of the rival operators is the Cango Ostrich and Butterfly Farm ((044) 272 4623 FAX (044) 272 8241, on the road to the Cango Caves. There are other ostrich farms dotted round the country but Oudtshoorn is where the boom started.

Dig Deep for Diamonds

TO GO DOWN A DIAMOND MINE IS TO UNDERSTAND THE SECRET THAT HAS TRANSFORMED SOUTH AFRICA. It was the discovery of diamonds that attracted the attention of the colonial powers and transformed South Africa from sleepy pastoral poverty into a world-class economic power. And what really changed the future of the young, raw colony were the volcanic pipes at Kimberley that plugged tubes of diamond-bearing silica into the surface of the earth. In 1866 a teenager found an 83.4-carat pebble on the banks of a river, and in a frantic rush the diamonds were scraped from the ground, leaving a man-made crater more than a kilometer (over a half a mile) deep and a mountain of tailings. The days when such wealth lay on the surface have long gone, and now the precious stones are only found in shaft-mines tunneling deep into the earth. There are a few places in the country, including Gold Reef City in Johannesburg and the gold fields near Pilgrims Rest, that preserve the past in restored conditions, but there is only one place to experience the reality of a working deep-shaft diamond mine. That is the place that first sparked off Africa's diamond rush, and where some of the world's great fortunes were made: in the heart of the Karoo desert, the historic town of Kimberley.

Ten of us were herded into an office where we paid over our fee and signed disclaimers. A wiry and energetic miner introduced himself as Bill and ushered us through into twin changing rooms. "They're not so much overalls as overnothings," Bill apologized as we slipped out of our home clothes and into blue mining uniforms, stepping finally into simple black work shoes racked by size. Then we were sat in tiers for a brief introductory chat. "If you find a diamond, let me know" he said. "We'll pay you 15% of its value." This was a good offer. On the black market you'd be lucky to get eight percent of an uncut diamond's international worth. Then Bill set off at a cracking pace to the minehead, where we buckled up battery packs, helmets, and headlights. For most of us it was to be our first experience of going so far underground.

There were nervous laughs as what passes for an elevator arrived at the surface. There are no shiny buttons on the transport suspended far below the mine's headgear: it's called a cage because that is exactly what it looks like. As our group shuffled awkwardly into the mesh box we were joined by a couple of miners carrying electrical equipment and a box of detonators. They smiled and heaved at trailing wires that pulled shut the heavy wire gate. The bright desert light was cut by the ground as we dropped into a cushion of cold air, rattling and rocking in a long descent. Our eyes adapted to the light of a flickering bulb as walls of gray silica slid past, with brief gloomy vistas of abandoned tunnels of worked-out levels. The two miners chatted in Afrikaans, defusing the tension as seconds lengthened into minutes, and we continued to descend. Finally the cage slowed to a halt 800 m (over 2,600 ft) below the surface.

With a heave Bill slid open the heavy gate and we stepped out into the underground world, walls of rough-hewn rock and roaring pipes carrying pressurized water and fresh surface air to the working mine-faces. Charges drilled into diamond-bearing rock blew out new surfaces, and mechanized diggers working in tunnels dragged out the rubble to be loaded into bogeys set on rails. Toy railways then carried the ore, three tons per truck, to the central shaft and the mechanized crushers. When enough rock had accumulated a miner would heave on a series of levers and in a huge cacophony of dust and drama the boulders were ground to pebbles for the long lift back to the surface.

Far from the cramped conditions of early mines, the Bultfontein mine has plenty of headroom; it's more underground cathedral than tunnel. Stumbling on the wet, broken floor our group, too busy getting around this strange subterranean environment to look seriously for a glitter of diamond, clambered back up long metal stairways fixed onto the rock that led back to the central shaft. In the distance the muted sounds of explosives signified a new fall of diamond-bearing silica.

While the underground mine represents an impressive human achievement, it is on the surface that most of the clever stuff happens. Although a huge pebble sparked off the diamond rush, most of the diamonds that built the country's wealth are far smaller. While the excavated rock that has been dug in the area would build a mountain to rival Everest, the entire diamond output of the

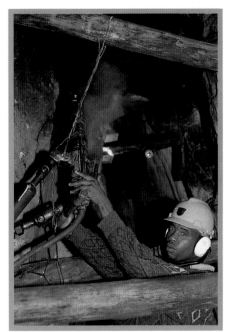

Kimberley fields, cut and polished, would fit into the back of a large automobile. It takes an endless, fascinating process of washing the mine's grit over grease-covered beds and x-ray photography to glean out the small, glittering jewels of incomparable value. We walked along conveyor belts thick with the black sand of Kimberlite, but despite my most careful attention no diamonds were visible.

Elsewhere in Kimberley the diamond-rush days still live on, vivid and fresh in the clear desert light. The "Big Hole" itself, dug by spade and wheelbarrow, winch and pulley, gapes with all the grandeur of a natural canyon, and the iron buildings of the settler town, rebuilt at the edge of this man-made chasm, have been refurbished to relive the early frontier days. The memories are strongest in the wood-paneled bar of the Kimberley Club, where the modest luxuries once enjoyed by early millionaires live on in tattered glory.

Underground tours of the Bultfontein Diamond Mine take place Mondays, Wednesdays, Thursdays and Fridays at 8 AM, and at 9:30 AM on Tuesdays; R60. Tours of the surface operations take place at 9 AM and 11 AM every weekday; R10. For further information contact the Bultfontein Mine ((053) 842 1321, Molyneux Road, Kimberley.

OPPOSITE: An ostrich kick can disembowel. Only in South Africa can you ride them — for fun.
ABOVE: South Africa's wealth was built by its miners.

Explore the Wine Routes

THE PROBLEM WITH TOURING SOUTH AFRICA'S WINELANDS IS NOT USUALLY GETTING FROM A TO B, BUT FROM B TO HOME. In a masterly stroke I had, so I thought, protected the integrity of my driving license by clambering on the back of a horse called Roschina, and riding out with Ray-Anne, owner of the Mont Rochelle Equestrian Center ((083) 300 4368 FAX (021) 876 2362.

South Africa's wines are internationally famous, but for the visitor it is perhaps more important that the vineyards are set in some of the most beautiful countryside in the world. For either amateurs or connoisseurs, they have been linked into more than a dozen wine routes with guided tours of some of South Africa's most prestigious wine cellars and a selection of the country's best restaurants. Signposted circuits of the best vineyards give visitors the chance to taste and buy wines and enjoy the very best of South Africa's cuisine. Stellenbosch and Paarl are the best-known wine producing areas, but for the wineland experience my favorite is the smaller, friendlier circuit of vineyards around Franschhoek.

The first vineyard on our horseback tour was Rickety Bridge. A young woman came out laden with bottles and presented me with three glasses of white and two of red. I'd barely climbed from my horse before the first glass, filled with three fingers of dry white wine, was pressed into my hand, accompanied by a breathless spiel. "Three years in oak and two years in the barrel…" The rest of the details spilled past as I gulped at the wine. It seemed rude to spit. I swallowed. "This one is less oaked…," another glass down. The third glass, sensibly, I spat into the graveled hedgerow, but my hostess looked affronted and asked if I'd prefer to try the red. I croaked out a yes and was immediately assaulted with two generous tastings, previewed by an explanation, precisely poured, with my satisfactory consumption minutely observed.

Roschina, I was starting to think, was a hell of a horse. Hell of a big horse, anyway. But Ray-Anne led her round to a low wall, a whitewashed mounting post for sending horseback tasters off on their way. I tottered to the top and fell into the saddle.

Just over three kilometers (two miles) later I slid out of the saddle at the second vineyard, Haute Provence. Ray-Anne left me holding the horses while she raced indoors to summon up some service, and another young South African girl appeared from her cellars, quilled like a porcupine with a range of prime vintages. "I'll just stick to the red," I managed, which still left me to gulp intelligently at three different grape varieties spread over a couple of years. I wobbled up the mounting parapet and lurched back onto my mount.

Franschhoek Valley is one of the most beautiful places in the world. On every side, sheer mountains ranged, sheltering a flat valley floor neatly latticed with vineyards. The final drop-off was at the Mont Rochelle vineyard, where an irresistible selection of dry reds and a filling plateful of locally produced cheeses rounded off my horseback experience. Daylight faded from the valley, lights flicked on along a high street lined with restaurants and antique shops, and the comfortable beds of a guest house beckoned.

The most famous wine areas are Stellenbosch, Franschhoek, and Paarl in the Western Cape province, less than an hour's drive from Cape Town, but there are plenty of smaller, more specialized wine routes. Even tiny Upington, far to the north, has a small wine route of its own that hugs the banks of Orange River, and the Little Karoo town of Calitzdorp manages a pretty, dizzying Port Route. No trip to the south of the country is complete without a tour of some of the most dynamic and visitor-friendly wineries. Most go out of their way to entertain visitors, with picnics and horseback riding among the activities that help make it a rewarding day out for South African citizens and visitors alike.

There are operators who run tours of the wineries, but the best idea is to base yourself for a night or two in the winelands and explore using your own vehicle, preferably in groups with designated drivers. The austral summer is the best time to visit, when the days are longer and the vines laden with grapes, but the area is worth a visit at any time of year. For the most up-to-date information about the state of the wineries, the monthly *Wine* magazine, available at all newsstands in South Africa, contains a full diary of events, as well as restaurant and wine reviews.

Take on a Township

THROUGH THE YEARS OF RESISTANCE TO APARTHEID, THE TOWNSHIP OF SOWETO, built to house black workers at a safe distance from Johannesburg, shot to prominence in the world's headlines through riots and shootings. Televisions followed the Soweto cast of armored cars and stone-throwing demonstrators. It came to symbolize the most brutal repression of that unhappy era and is now a place of pilgrimage for visitors who spent their student days demonstrating against apartheid. Even though established merely by the forced removal of migrant workers, which started in 1923, with a population of four million Soweto is now the largest city in South Africa.

It still has a fearsome reputation. Few white South Africans have visited this — or indeed any other — township. To confuse the security forces, street signs were removed and few have been replaced, so even finding your way around is difficult, and white faces, rarely seen, stand out. The only way to see Soweto easily is to take an organized tour, leaving from Pretoria or (nearer) Johannesburg.

Our tour maneuvered past the endless, graffiti-covered, walls, threading eventually down through the matchbox dwellings of Soweto's poor. We drove through Cliptown, the favorite squatter camp for visiting television crews, and into a large open space where several games of soccer were in progress. An itinerant preacher had parked his pickup truck and set up speakers to bring the word of God to a small crowd of scruffy, shoeless children, and we parked up to watch from a distance. One of my companion tourists had a bar of chocolate and gave a piece to a lone child straying close to our vehicle. Whether by telepathy or some faint scent, the prospect of free chocolate quickly spread across 200 m (650 ft) of waste ground, and the preacher's audience — and half the soccer-playing population of Soweto — tore towards us, jostling gently around the open window of our van. The unlucky faded,

OPPOSITE: White-painted settler mansions, now restored, in the Winelands. ABOVE: Nelson Mandela's modest bedroom in his Soweto home.

resigned, as the chocolate ran out and we continued to more conventional places of interest.

Nelson Mandela's old home is now a museum, including his prison shoes and small bed, covered with a bedspread made from black-backed jackal. Another museum, stuffed into a parking lot of open truck containers, exhibits pictures of the township's most troubled years and includes a memorial to Hans Peterson, the schoolboy shot by security forces whose picture, the next day, adorned the front pages of newspapers worldwide.

Soweto has respectable suburbs, where lie the high walls of Desmond Tutu's house and Winnie Mandela's, topped with razor wire; as well as slums, with serried ranks of hostels for single workers and the small patched dwellings of settlers living beyond the reach of sewage or electricity.

With just one cinema, Sowetans make their own entertainment. A hole in the wall serves liters of sorghum beer at R1.50 a time to a crowd of afternoon drinkers. As I went to get served, countless hands came out in greeting, names were exchanged as the locals expressed their surprise to find a white drinker in their midst. After a few mouthfuls of beer I was surprised too, as it wasn't very good. I handed my container over to a worthy-looking local and took my leave.

That night I returned to Soweto for a nighttime *shebeen* tour. Our first visit was almost refined: stickers on the window announced it would accept American Express, and a couple of locals in sports jackets and trilbys stood outside smoking. Opening the door, I found a long brightly-lit row of trestle tables, covered in white tablecloths, packed with customers drinking and eating. The sound was animated but sober, the atmosphere jovial but restrained. We made our way to the far end where a few seats were cleared next to the bar for our party, and I ordered drinks: Klipdrift and water and small airline-style bottles of wine. After a meal of self-service spicy stew on a bed of lettuce, we decided to visit somewhere less refined, where the clientele, I was assured, would be "clever but poor." At "Soloo" there was dancing in progress, the men lithe and fit, the women, though young, already lavishly huge, mellow and warm. The walls were tiled white and the ceiling sagging with polystyrene panels. The drink here was spirits. Even though late, there were no signs of drunkenness and I felt a cautious welcome.

Instead of the horror stories of violence and alienation spread by the white community, in Soweto I met nothing but smiles. For a city with so long a history of repression and political violence such a welcome was almost shocking.

There are several operators who offer Soweto tours, while far fewer undertake evening *shebeen* tours. One of the best is Imbizo Tours ((011) 838 2667 FAX (011) 781 1564 E-MAIL imbizo@iafrica.com WEB SITE www .backpackafrica.com, Box 25031, Ferreirasdorp 2048, with daytime tours costing R180 and evening tours costing R350. Mandy Mankanzana, who runs Imbizo, can also arrange for you to spend a night in Soweto, staying with either middle-class or poor families, as well as running special tours exploring African jazz or music. Trips out of town to Lesedi Cultural Village and Ndebele villages, or to Zulu, Xhosa, Sotho and other tribes are also on offer. Pioneer of township tours, Jimmy's Face to Face ((011) 331 6109 FAX 331 5388 E-MAIL face2face@pixie.co.za, 2nd Floor, Budget House, 130 Main Street, Johannesburg, is run by Jimmy Ntintili, who started by taking friends to visit Soweto and now has the largest operation of its sort in the city.

Kloof South Africa's Rivers

I CLIMBED DOWN 988 ROUGH STEPS, MADE OF WIRED SLATS, INTO THE STORMS RIVER GORGE, and hopped over countless boulders, clumsily using a 1.8-m (six-foot) customized inner tube with handles alternately as crutch and balance.

"*Kloofing*" is one of South Africa's most popular sports: following rivers, using the current to explore a world beyond traffic even hikers can't reach. And there's nowhere better to do this than along the Storms River, which threads through the Tsitsikamma Forest, headline attraction of the Garden Route, breaking out eventually in the most spectacular of the coast's gorges. South Africa's spectacular views are all very well, but there's nothing to compare with getting personally involved. And *kloofing* is, for many South Africans, the preferred way of exploring rivers. All you need is a bit of courage and a reinforced inner tube for stretches of gorge where you have to float. Oh, and a certain level of fitness. Which they didn't warn me about.

Easy in theory, first you leap from any handy rock, flipping the tube underneath, to land with a splashy bounce in the water, bum firmly in tube, hands free to paddle. Not so easy in reality. I jumped, landed on one side of my tube, and bounced off into water the color and temperature of iced tea. My wetsuit did

nothing to warm the original shock of cold liquid sluicing around my skin. Some clambering and an awkward twist were required to settle in the center of the tube without falling off, again. Getting from tube to land, a skill needed every time a pool ended and boulders began, offered a further challenge, groping for footholds and bouncing off the dubious buoyancy of the tube to grab support on land.

At first there was more boulder-hopping than tubing. In the depths of the gorge the Storm River rushed in narrow streams between huge rocks and trinkled over rapids while I lumbered over the broken boulders that filled the canyon floor. My legs, unused to such exertion, turned to jelly.

Unfortunate, then, that we came to a deep river pool with a choice of three launching boulders. One was almost at water level, another a ledge about a meter (three feet) higher, and the final peak three and a half meters (11 ft) clear of the water. In my weakened state it seemed a dizzying height. "You have a choice," I was told.

The guide had outlined some of the dangers on the way down. The biggest risk is hitting your head when you jump. The lightweight plastic crash-helmet strapped around my head felt frail and unconvincing as

I looked around at the African-sized rocks. "If you hit your head," my guide had said, "I'll try to get you out of the water and we'll wait till your piglets stop running around."

If I messed up the jump from the highest rock I didn't think my piglets would be running anywhere. I saw nothing wrong with leaping (bravely) from the lowest level.

But I wasn't alone. My fellow-*kloofer* was a young nurse from England, a dedicated bungee-jumper who'd been heaving herself off bridges, cranes, and bypasses for years and liked nothing better than stepping out into nothing. Just as I cleared my throat to suggest caution was the better part of valor she hopped up to the highest peak, hugged her tube to her bum and launched into the air. With a whoop and a big splash she spun off downstream. In the circumstances the shame of starting with a cowardly hop would have been unbearable.

Stifling the thought that she needed psychological help I dragged myself up in her wake and teetered my way to the edge, wobbling on rubber legs. Summoning deep and rarely-used reserves I whacked the tube into my bum, leaping forward.

A frail suspension bridge crosses the Storms River in the Garden Route's Tsitsikamma National Park.

Gravity took over. I floated, not, admittedly, much like a feather, towards the pool of water below, tube, correctly, landing first. With a bang I disappeared into my own wake before bobbing back to the surface.

Major challenge over I paddled gently with my hands and started to appreciate my surroundings. The river was a narrow thread in a gorge 100 m (330 ft) high, carved over the millennia into sheer cliffs curving overhead on either side. The black water was dappled by the midday sun shafting down through fringing bonsai trees, clinging to trace nutrients on the overhanging rock. Comfortingly my guide mentioned this gorge was called "the place of the flying bush pigs" because land mammals, high overhead, were apt to stroll across the hidden heights and plummet into the gorge below. Somehow I wasn't comforted. Planted firmly in my river-level tube I eyed the edges of the gorge for falling pigs. Fortunately I was tubing in the low season. At the height of summer, groups of up to 60 tube down this river. On the edge of winter our group size was two, just over cancellation levels. Even if the water was chill the scene was quiet and tranquil, the experience private.

Stormsriver Adventures ((042) 541 1836 FAX (042) 541 1609 E-MAIL adventure@ gardenroute.co.za WEB SITE www.stormsriver .co.za, Adventure Center, Darnel Street, Storms River, runs *kloofing* trips as well as trails through the woods, abseiling expeditions, and boat cruises.

Ride Restored Railways

IT SEEMED ONLY RIGHT TO DRESS FOR DINNER. The cabin was large and comfortable, with two armchairs looking out at a changing panorama of African landscapes rattling past outside the large picture window.

In the dining car black-tied waiters busied themselves with making me comfortable. Rippling reflected circles in a glass of one of Stellenbosch's finest wines was the only hint of movement as we traveled through the night. Then the food started to arrive: light presentations of smoked marlin flown over from the Indian Ocean, a seafood medley of crayfish, prawn, and mullet. Switching to an elegant red, I feasted on a kudu fillet before moving on to a selection of cheeses and a range of pastries.

Returning to my cabin I found it transformed. Gone were the armchairs, which had been folded out into a large and comfortable bed, clad in Egyptian cotton sheets and covered with a lush duvet. In the pooled glow of a reading lamp a flower lay on my pillowcase, while monogrammed bathrobe and slippers were laid out ready. I didn't quite see they'd be needed for the two steps to the en-suite bathroom, but my wife made the gesture worthwhile by slipping hers into her bag while I wasn't looking. Weighed down by countless calories and lulled by the gentle movement of the train I dropped into a deep sleep and dreamed of the golden age of rail travel.

South Africa never really upgraded its passenger rail service. Trains still potter around the countryside at a gentle 50 kph (30 mph). Unlike other countries, where new high-speed trains have pushed vintage steam-trains and period carriages off into the sidings, South Africa offers a huge choice of luxury or vintage trains still in regular use — 26 at the last count. The experience described above was on board the Blue Train, which is the most luxurious — and expensive — of all. It runs between Cape Town and Pretoria, as well as operating along the Garden Route, to the Victoria Falls and up to Hoedspruit near the Kruger. Prices are from R6,250 to R8,900 for a couple sharing the 26-hour journey from Cape Town to Pretoria including all food and wine — and for sheer comfort it's hard to beat. For reservations contact Blue Train ((011) 773 7631 TOLL-FREE 0800 117 715 FAX (011) 773 7643 E-MAIL bluetrain@transnet.co.za WEB SITE www.bluetrain.co.za, Box 2671, Joubert Park 2044.

Rovos Rail ((012) 323 6052 FAX (012) 323 0843 E-MAIL reservations@rovos.co.za WEB SITE www.rovos.co.za, Box 2837 Pretoria 0001, is another operator at the top end of the market. It uses restored carriages from the 1920s and 1930s to run slow safaris across the country, stopping off to go sightseeing or to eat at some of the most famous and atmospheric hotels along the way. Their routes include the Garden Route in the south of the country, as well as longer trips up to Swakopmund in Namibia, Maputo in Mozambique, Victoria Falls in Zimbabwe, and even as far as Dar es Salaam in Tanzania.

The Shongololo Express ((011) 453 3821 (011) 454 1262 E-MAIL shongo@mweb.co.za WEB SITE www.shongo.co.za, 9 Rotherfield Avenue, Essexwold, Bedfordview 2007, offers 17-day rail safaris around South Africa and beyond, with overnight travel linking some of the major sights. Accommodation is fairly basic

The beautifully restored Outeniqua Choo-Tjoe steam locomotive is the train to take from George to Knysna.

and meals and excursions cost extra, which can add significantly to the price.

For a shorter, more specialist experience, Bushveld Train Safaris ((014) 736 3025 FAX (014) 736 3027, Box 237, Warmbaths 0480, offer a range of six 48-hour weekend trips, and once a month an eight- to ten-day expedition. Best of all, they are aimed squarely at the domestic market so costs are low. Their trains do not have a restaurant carriage, as most of the meals are provided by schools and church groups, although they will stop at restaurants that are especially interesting. Trips start in Pretoria.

For those whose time, budget or inclination doesn't permit such a long train journey, there are a number of other train lines that offer the steam travel experience on day-trips; these are listed in the relevant sections of the touring chapters with contact details. The most popular with visitors include the Outeniqua Choo-Tjoe ((041) 520 2662, which runs from Knysna to George; the Banana Express ((031) 361 8095 on the Natal south coast; and the Apple Express ((041) 520 2360, which runs monthly between Port Elizabeth and Loerie. A good central source of information on vintage trains in the country is African Rail Romance ((021) 419 5002 FAX (021) 419 5021 E-MAIL vintrail@mweb.co.za, Monument Station, Old Marine Drive, Box 6327, Roggebaai 8012, Cape Town.

The conventional rail network still operates a schedule of overnight routes linking the major cities. For visitors this is a comfortable, but often very slow, way to travel around South Africa. First-class compartments sleep four people and include a shower, while second-class travel, cheaper and sometimes noisier, sleeps six in a carriage and only has a washbasin in the cabin. Sheets can be rented and tickets must be booked in advance. Third class is not really recommended. You have to be a bit careful with your possessions, as thieves do follow the train schedules carefully, but it can be an economical way to get around. For full timetables contact the local station (listed in the touring chapters) or contact Spoornet ℂ (011) 773 2944 (Johannesburg), (031) 361 7609 (Durban), (012) 315 2401 (Pretoria), (021) 405 3871 (Cape Town) for further details.

Hike the World's Largest Art Gallery

HIKING IN SOUTH AFRICA OFTEN BRINGS UNEXPECTED REWARDS. In caves and on rocks in stunning settings are poignant remnants of a long-dismissed culture: San rock art dating back to before the arrival of South Africa's European settlers. Though there's rock art to be found throughout the country, the most densely painted areas are in the Drakensberg Mountains around the Kingdom of Lesotho and north of Cape Town in the Cederbergs.

A few of the more famous rock art sites are marked on tourist maps and signed from the road, but these fragile monuments to a long-lost culture are generally not advertised. Local guides are usually needed to find the most worthwhile sites.

An exception to this is the Sevilla Trail, 36 km (22.5 miles) by dirt road from Clanwilliam, itself a two-hour highway drive north of Cape Town. Here a short walking trail on a private farm leads past nine sites you can explore with the help of a small, self-published guidebook, *Rock Art of the Western Cape*, Book 1, which marks out some of the best pictures on a hand-drawn map, with corresponding white-painted footsteps on boulders to guide you along the way. Sites one to four include some wonderful works. A fireside group, painted in black over the faint red of older figures, and a crowd scene, all heads turned towards the sky. Elephant and rhino are depicted, long extinct in the area, and zebra and eland, only now being reintroduced. Red handprints are scattered across an overhang, including the tiny prints of a small child, a wailing voice through the ages, across cultures and time.

My attention wandered before site five, as I was distracted by the sheer beauty of the scene. Under a brilliant, unforgiving blue the rugged mountains shouldered over dry river valleys, shelving over a thin cover of succulent growth, small flowers bursting out on a distant memory of some long-fallen raindrop. And as I looked around the cliffs and caves I started to see more art. Binoculars brought the indentations and sandstone ledges into sharp focus, and there, indeed, were the ochres and reds of bushman art, trance figures, fat-bottom women with baobab legs, skinny hunters and horned animals. Sometimes clear, more often they were suspicions, evanescent images that faded into natural stains on the rock, or turned out to be the white trails stained onto the cliff by small bounding *dassies* (rock hyraxes) elaborated by my imagination. While books accurately described the major sites, the pictures that live in my mind are the ones I'd spotted on my own.

The Cederbergs are one of South Africa's last frontiers, rugged semidesert homeland to Afrikaner cowboys, dirt roads and pickup trucks bumping through an unforgiving landscape where the beauty is harsh and remote. If it rains, August and September bring a riot of color as flowers blanket the rocky ground into a lavish meadow, but this doesn't happen every year. The art, on the other hand, is always there.

To hike the Sevilla Trail permission must be obtained from the local landowner, who runs the Travelers Rest ℂ/FAX (027) 482 1824. A leaflet map of the trail should be available. Better still, buy a copy of *Rock Art of the Western Cape*, Book 1, "The Sevilla Trail and Travelers Rest," from the Tourist Office in Clanwilliam at R25. Alternatively, an expert guiding service is operated by Bushman's Kloof ℂ (027) 482 2627 FAX (027) 482 1011 E-MAIL santrack@ilink.co.za WEB SITE www.bushmanskloof.co.za, who protect their own rock-art sites in a private nature reserve and will show their own guests around. Other good places to see rock art include the Drakensbergs, east of Durban and south of Johannesburg, where more than 600 sites have been identified. Accessible caves at Giant's Castle, Injusuti, and Kamberg are signed, but local guides are the best way to find other, quieter sites. *Rock Paintings of the Natal Drakensberg* by David Lewis-Williams and published by the University of Natal Press, is a thin but helpful booklet available locally.

Information about more sites can be obtained from the National Monuments Council ℂ (021) 462 4502 FAX (021) 462 4509 E-MAIL director@sahra.org.za, 111 Harrington Street, Box 4637, Cape Town 8000, which oversees provincial offices around the country.

A thick morning mist in the Cederbergs blankets some of the country's finest San rock art.

YOUR CHOICE

The Great Outdoors

In a country of South Africa's scenic diversity and beauty, outdoors is where most visitors will spend most of their time. Add to that the South African's love of all things sporting, and the most enterprising visitor will find a lifetime of activities lined up for their pleasure.

SAFARI

South Africa's early settlers found a land thick with wildlife. While the age of dinosaurs had long gone in Europe, Africa was still a land where the animals coexisted with man in primeval stasis. Even in the temperate south, rhino burst out of thickets and some travelers reported seeing more than 150 a day. Game carpeted the land in huge herds and elephant strolled in groups of more than 100. Lion were, quite literally, pests, albeit quite big and dangerous ones.

The reaction of the early settlers was quite simple: they unstrapped their guns and started shooting. As human settlements spread north from the Cape and inland from Durban, Africa's greatest herds were turned into decorative rugs, plumed hats, jackets and shoes, billiard balls, and endless strips of biltong. While the American colonies busied themselves wiping out huge herds of bison the African settlers applied themselves with equal dedication to spattering what is now their most precious resource over the landscape in huge, vulture-pecked mounds of rotting flesh. In the late 1800s a single factory in Graaff-Reinet brought a million skins to market. By the 1900s South Africa's wildlife had already retreated to a few enclaves where tsetse fly protected the land from encroaching cattle and malarial mosquitoes evened the odds between wild animals and their human predators.

At about this time a few high-profile hunting expeditions, lavishly mounted in East Africa, gave birth to the safari concept. Suddenly hunt-and-shoot holidays acquired a new glamour. Quickly looking around, the South Africans realized they'd shot their way into a corner, and took stock of the wildlife that remained.

The situation was bleak. Cattle had displaced wildlife through most of the country, with even the desert areas supporting a thin sprinkling of goats and sheep. Farmers keen to keep disease at bay had shot the remaining native animals, and the remnants of South Africa's prolific wildlife huddled in the remote northeast of the country, in the northern parks of Natal and in the Kruger.

LEFT: The Otter Trail, in Tsitsikamma National Park, is one of South Africa's most popular hikes.
ABOVE: Leopards are easiest to spot at the Sabi Sands Reserve.

Kruger grabbing the headline wildlife including elephant, leopard, lion, and cheetah. Serious naturalists will find equal satisfaction in spotting the smaller game, including Cape clawless otter along the Garden Route and the occasional serval cat clinging to a furtive life in city suburbs.

To spot the bigger game it is best to head for one of South Africa's many national parks, nature reserves and wilderness areas. Park accommodation is generally comfortable and designed for self-catering: South Africans, when they travel, usually like nothing better than to *braai* (barbecue) up some chunks of meat and eat in the outside air — just as they do when they're at home. Campsites tend to consist of power-points for camper vans and not a lot else. These public areas are much in demand and bookings must be made well in advance; the busiest season is around the December holidays, when accommodation anywhere in the country is much in demand. A much more expensive but luxurious experience is to see the countryside through the private reserves, which is how most overseas visitors experience the bush.

The largest of the national parks is the **Kruger**, stretching 350 km (219 miles) from end to end, where most of the famous African game species can be found. Game viewing here is generally best in the austral winter, when the malarial risk is also much reduced and the animals are drawn by thirst to waterholes. However the summer months, when the bush is green and teeming with animals, are still very rewarding. A number of other parks in KwaZulu-Natal also support significant numbers of animals, including the larger predators.

For many people the only aim of a wildlife safari is to see the animals grouped together as the "Big Five" by hunters. These, the five most dangerous animals to hunt, consist of lion, elephant, buffalo, rhino, and leopard. Transferred to a photographic safari the Big Five list makes less sense. To tick these all off a viewing list in a limited time span requires a certain artifice. Rhino are very, very rare and are usually only seen because they are guarded so closely that their whereabouts are known — exactly — to rangers, who are ready to shoot poachers on sight. Leopard are so shy and alert that only those habituated over many years to the smell and noise of game-viewing vehicles will ever hang about to be photographed by tourists. Without being tamed, they have at least learned to ignore the intrusion as a negligible threat.

Thanks to dedicated work by a number of conservationists, the erosion of South Africa's wildlife was halted, and as tourism has become recognized as a valuable resource game animals are acquiring a new significance — and value. Cattle farms are being turned back to bush and animals bought at game auctions are painstakingly being reintroduced into parts of the country. There are now many places where you can see a good sprinkling of herbivores, including zebra, springbok, and kudu, even though for most new private game farms, buying a hungry lion is a prohibitive investment. Meanwhile the great national parks, especially the Kruger, protect their own wildlife, and as nature takes its course numbers are, once again, increasing. As the most economically developed country in Africa, safaris here won't match East Africa for the sheer wilderness experience. Few of the old migration routes that once spanned the continent now remain, and even in the largest parks the wildlife is hemmed in, to some extent, by the requirements of their human neighbors. In recent years the situation has started to improve: the fences have come down between the Kruger National Park and many of the private reserves along its western border, and trans-frontier parks have been established with Botswana and Namibia.

The animals you can expect to see in South Africa depend on where you are, with the

Most of the major African species are found in the north of the country, above Durban and Johannesburg. For visitors who are flying in to Cape Town and only exploring the south of the country, the only easy opportunity to see the Big Five is at **Shamwari**. If this experience leaves a zoo-like taste in the mouth, the nearby **Addo Elephant Park** can provide more of a wilderness experience.

FLORA

While the animals were being hunted to extinction the settlers were simultaneously trashing the plant world.

South Africa's wildlife is what first attracts many visitors, but often the plant life leaves an equally lasting impression. To the north there is the characteristic dry bush of Africa — there are 300 species of tree in the Kruger alone. However it is in the south that the most surprising range of plant species is found. Botanists divide the world's flora, from tundra to rainforest, into "floral kingdoms," and the tiny strip of coastal land around the Cape is the smallest and richest. This sixth floral kingdom contains 8,500 plant species of which 6,000 are endemic. **Table Mountain** alone contains more plant species (1,470) than the British Isles (1,443). Many are so specialized they occur in just one valley. The collective noun for these magical arrays of plants is *fynbos*, literally "fine bush," and all are

seriously under threat. Invasive foreign plants, brought over by settlers, have displaced many indigenous plants from their specialized ecosystems, and without the "ooh" value of Africa's wildlife, conservation efforts have come late and grudgingly. Despite the few voices of conservation, loggers felled the milkwood forests that lined the southern shores and fast-growing wattles were imported from Australia. These days South Africans have learned from long experience, and careful environmental regulations have been put in place to protect the remaining patches of indigenous *fynbos*. Even so only remnants of indigenous forest survive. The germination processes of many of South Africa's plants and trees depend on regular forest fires. These don't entirely suit the suburban human residents, whose first reaction to a big bush fire is, unsurprisingly, to put it out. To complicate things further, the invader plant species burn just that bit hotter, cooking indigenous seeds and stopping them from germinating. The only untouched Cape forest that remains today are a few remnants around **Knysna** and **Tsitsikamma**.

Things are slightly less dire for the heathlike *fynbos* species. The best places to

OPPOSITE: Cathkin Peak, a high point of the Central Drakensberg. ABOVE: The Swartberg Pass was a challenge to road-builders in the pioneer years.

learn more about the indigenous southern ecosystems include Cape Town's **Kirstenbosch Gardens** and the **Cape of Good Hope Nature Reserve**, while on the southern coast a number of places are active in conservation and study, including **Reins Nature Reserve**, **De Hoop Nature Reserve**, and **Grootbos**.

Just two hours or so north of Cape Town the Great Karoo starts, arid flatlands that are home to a whole host of new, desert-adapted plant species that stretch up to the dry desert sands of Namibia. To learn more about this surprisingly colorful and diverse ecosystem the easiest place to start is the **Karoo Botanical Gardens** at Worcester, while the annual flower season in Namaqualand draws botanists and photographers from all over the world between July and August. Such is the interest in these flowers that there is even a special **flower hotline** ((021) 418 3705 to tell visitors where to find the best blooms.

HIKING

Hiking is almost a national sport, and it is well catered for by more than 200 designated long-distance trails that track most of the country's nature reserves, state forests, and even national parks filled with lion — where you're accompanied by a ranger with a gun. There are usually sturdy, if not luxurious, huts and chalets provided to make sure overnights are comfortable. Some routes, especially those in the temperate south, are known for their spectacular beauty, while others, particularly those in the parks and wilderness areas of the subtropical north, are more interesting because of the wildlife you'll see. Trails crisscross the country and run along miles of coast, and it's not unusual for South Africans take off on hikes lasting three weeks or longer, covering hundreds of miles.

There are different categories of trail. A "Backpacking Trail" will simply be an area of often fairly demanding terrain, where you find or make your own route. A "Hiking Trail" is marked out by stakes or painted footprints, and "Interpretive Trails" are short, easy paths marked with displays and signs. "Guided Wilderness Trails" are usually fairly short and easy strolls in national parks with a game ranger on hand to explain what you're seeing, and "Day Walks" are exactly what they sound like.

Unfortunately it's rare to be able to just go out and hike. While day hikes are usually reasonably flexible, overnight hikes always fall prey to some private or parastatal bureaucracy or other. Permission needs to be

sought to use the chalet — and to use the trail. Often a minimum of three people need to travel, and there is always a maximum: usually 12 or 15. While South Africa's city centers often seem to collapse into anarchy, the outdoor world is still highly regulated. To make things more confusing a program of privatization, which started in 1993, has transferred ownership of previously nationally-owned trails into the private sector. The popular trails book out months ahead in the high season and a plethora of different organizations control the various hikes, each with different terms and conditions as well as different contact numbers. South African National Parks handles the hikes in most of the national parks, while those in KwaZulu-Natal fall under the control of the KZN Nature Conservation Service, previously well-

respected as the Natal Parks Board.
The South African Forestry Company Ltd.
(SAFCOL) conduct their own tours of some
of the country's least-spoiled regions, and
tend, in the process, to provide the most
comfortable overnight chalets. Perhaps they
find the wood easier to come by.

For this reason the contact details are
listed in the chapters covering the areas
where the hike takes place. It's worth
planning ahead though. The South African
National Parks, for example, take
reservations 13 months in advance and the
coastal Otter Trail in Tsitsikamma is one that
sells out in days. SAFCOL take reservations
six months ahead, and once again, at popular
times of the year you have to be fast to book
a place. Often, however, it is still worth
checking for cancellations if your plans can
be flexible.

The equipment that will be needed
depends on how long the hike is, and where it
is. In the northern deserts the priority will be
something to keep water in; more often in the
south you'll need tents and clothes to keep it
out, while in the high Drakensberg mountains
you might have to be prepared for snow.
Don't underestimate the elements: people die
every year in the Drakensbergs and even Table
Mountain, in the heart of Cape Town, has an
impressive record of exposure fatalities.

For further information two useful contacts
are the **National Hiking Way Board** ((012) 297
3382 FAX (012) 323 4447, P/Bag X447, Pretoria
0001, and the **Hiking Federation of South
Africa** ((011) 886 6524 FAX (011) 886 6013,
Box 1420, Randburg 2125.

Waves from the Antarctic crash on South Africa's
Whale Coast.

BEACH LIFE

South Africa's coastline is ringed by beautiful beaches. However it comes as quite a shock to many visitors that the western coastline at least is invariably cold. The South Atlantic takes its temperature from the Antarctic ice, and even wetsuits are not enough to make taking a dip here a pleasant option: you'll need a dry-suit. Cape Town's beautiful beaches start to feel the warming effect of the Indian Ocean but, except between November and March, are still more useful for jogging than bathing; occasional offshore whale sightings are some consolation. It is only east of the southern tip at Point Agulhas that the water becomes warmed by the Benguela current and swimmers start to appear on the beaches, while further out to sea surfers become a common sight, joining the dolphins. The most famous surf resort is Jeffrey's Bay. From here east things just get better. By Durban the water temperature is swimmable year-round and the waters of Sodwana Bay in the far northeast are warm enough to support a full-fledged coral reef population. At all times bathers should be aware that there are rip tides and undertows all along the coast, and it is only advisable to bathe at beaches protected by lifesavers.

Sporting Spree

South Africa is a highly sporting nation, and there are excellent facilities for every sort of physical activity. What is more, the sporting facilities are often in areas of outstanding natural beauty, with golf courses enlivened by passing game and tennis courts set against stunning views.

DIVING

With the current exchange rates, South Africa is one of the world's least expensive places to take a scuba diving certification course. Most of the schools detailed below offer courses.

The best place to dive in South Africa is **Sodwana Bay**, in the north of KwaZulu-Natal, which is the only place where you'll find coral reefs to rival those of the tropics. Getting out to the dive sites is half the fun, riding the surf in rubber launches, and thanks to the steady ocean current all dives in the area are drifts. The closest reef to Sodwana is Quarter Mile, which plays host to schools of ragged-tooth sharks in January. The largest reef is Two Mile, which varies in depth from 12 to 36 m (40 to 118 ft). For hard corals, the best is Five Mile Reef, protected from being over-dived by a quota system.

The small Seven Mile Reef has the greatest diversity of life forms, while Nine Mile Reef has caves and blowholes against a background of pinnacles and buttresses.

Further south, **Protea Banks**, eight kilometers (five miles) off Margate, is among the world's best shark sites. No less than seven different species of shark visit, following the ocean currents, and there are also plenty of dolphin year-round. There is a good range of deep and shallow dives here so even when the summer rains reduce visibility there are some adrenaline-filled deep dives to enjoy.

The undeveloped Wild Coast has limited facilities for divers, but things pick up again in the seas that wash the Garden Route. **Tsitsikamma National Park** has a shore-entry dive with forest trails and varied fauna and flora. **Plettenberg Bay** has sheltered reefs and dramatic drop-offs, enlivened with the occasional pod of whale in season. The big draw at **Knysna** is an endangered sea horse found nowhere else in the world, but there are also underwater pinnacles, rainbows of cauliflower corals, and a number of wreck dives. **Mossel Bay** is sheltered and at its best from December to May, with pinnacles, caves, and overhangs bursting with marine life. This is also the only place in South Africa where unqualified divers can cage-dive with great white sharks. **Gansbaai** is more famous for great white encounters, which generally take place in Shark Alley alongside the appetizing seals of Dyer Island. Dress up warm for **Cape Town**'s great dives, with seals or penguins as well as a whole selection of wrecks dating back to the birth of the colony. There are 35 wrecks lying in between five to 40 m (16 to 130 ft) that are regularly dived.

As with most countries, there are sharks about in the dive industry. Local operators are listed under their location, but for a national dive operator with local contacts, try **Dive the Big Five** (/FAX (013) 750 1832 E-MAIL divebig5@iafrica.com, Box 2209, White River 1240. The **South African Underwater Union** ((021) 930 6549 provides impartial advice and a list of operators.

GOLF

The smug world of golf never took much notice of the sanctions that blighted much of South Africa's sports. Gary Player, David Frost, Harold Henning, John Bland, Simon Hobday, and Ernie Els all spread South Africa's reputation as a golfing nation far and wide, and it is still one of the most fervently pursued sporting activities in the country. There are plenty of exceptional golf courses in the country, including the Milnerton at Cape Town, Fancourt Country Club near George, the Durban Country Club in the heart of the city, Houghton in Johannesburg, and the Gary Player Country Club at Sun City.

Rather than give a comprehensive list of golf club contacts, I'd recommend contacting one of the centralized information networks: **Men's Golf** ((011) 442 3723 or **Women's Golf** ((011) 416 1263. The major golf events include the Vodacom Tour, the South African Open Championships, the Alfred Dunhill PG Championships, and the Sun City Million Dollar Golf Challenge. There are also a number of tour operators offering itineraries tailored to golfing fanatics. These include **Tee Golfing Safaris** (/FAX (011) 794 2727 E-MAIL glossop@golfsafaris.co.za WEB SITE www .golfsafaris.co.za, Box 1076, Honeydew 2040; **Golf Safari** ((013) 744 0195 FAX (011) 794 9002, Box 4482, Nelspruit 1200; and **Above Par** ((021) 448 4655 FAX (021) 448 4654 E-MAIL abovepar@iafrica.com WEB SITE www.abovepar.co.za, Box 53215, Kenilworth 7745.

OPPOSITE: Cold waters wash Llandudno's Sandy Bay near Cape Town. BELOW: In search of elephant in Pongola Game Reserve: tiered safari seats mean everyone gets a clear view.

FISHING

Fishing is also a popular South African pastime. Fly-fishing takes place all over the country but generally, and rather disconcertingly, in artificially stocked dams. However, there are plenty of opportunities to fish in the rivers, with the best areas being in the Drakensberg Mountains that stretch all the way from the Eastern Cape up to Mpumalanga and the Northern Province. There are about 250 species of freshwater fish but most fishing, strangely, is for trout, which was introduced to South Africa a century ago. The less common carp grow bigger — up to 20 kg (44 lb) — but the largest indigenous fish is the catfish, which can weigh more than 30 kg (66 lb). Catfish are found in the Vaal and Orange Rivers. I'm told the best sport is tiger fish, which you'll find at the Pongolapoort dam in the north of KwaZulu-Natal. Where appropriate, fishing contact details are included in the touring chapters, but for further information contact the **South African Freshwater Angling Association** ((056) 212 6707.

Game and deep-sea fishing is well catered for, with operators running fishing trips all around South Africa's shores, but the open sea is also where some of the world's most dramatic natural phenomena take place. Off KwaZulu-Natal and the Wild Coast, sardines mass and migrate in a huge shoal in June, attracting a huge concentration of snap-happy game fish. Generally, the best times of year here for marlin and sailfish are between November and April. Off the Cape, the two fish migrations that affect your catch are the tunny (tuna) run from October to May and the snoek run in autumn and winter.

If boat fishing's not your style, the coast is lined with South Africans casting into the surf; often permits are required, however, so contact the local tourist office before you cast your rod.

HUNTING

For opponents of hunting, killing wildlife is unnecessary and barbaric. Hunters, however, often see themselves as a key part of the conservation industry, contributing to the future of endangered species by the substantial amounts of money they pay for the trophies they shoot. Generally speaking, lodges and reserves that specialize in hunting are not listed in the text. However those who do want further information about hunting should get in touch with **African Connection** ((011) 468 1526 FAX (011) 702 2251, Box 781575, Sandton, Johannesburg 2146, or **SA Hunters'**

and Game Conservation Association ((012) 565 4856 FAX (012) 565 4910, Box 18108, Pretoria 0001.

HORSEBACK RIDING

"Wheelbarrow" Patterson, who opened up the gold fields at Pilgrim's Rest, might have thought horses were more trouble than they are worth, but before the arrival of the motor car the distances in South Africa would have been even more daunting without a horse. These graceful animals really came into their own in the Boer Wars, giving mobility to the small Boer commando that harried the British forces and became an important part of the South African psyche. The Johannesburg Lipizzaners and the many turf clubs in the major cities are signs of the horse's enduring popularity, but for most visitors it is the chance to ride out

across the beautiful countryside that is the motivation to saddle up. Local stables are listed throughout the touring chapters, or for further details contact the **Association of Horse Trails and Safaris of South Africa** ((011) 788 3923 FAX (011) 880 8401, 36 Twelfth Avenue, Parktown North, Johannesburg 2193.

SPECTATOR SPORTS

It's not hard to find sports games to watch in South Africa. At the sniff of an international challenge the local television and radio companies scrap all their scheduled programming to devote themselves entirely to whichever sport is being played. The top sports are cricket, rugby, and football (soccer) but in truth, South Africans would watch paint dry if it was competing with England or, even better, Australia.

Soccer is the most popular sport, especially with the colored and black population. The season runs from August to May in the Premier Soccer League. The sport has only just begun to attract serious sponsorship money and teams don't tend to have their own grounds. Even so, the teams attract passionate supporters with the two most important teams, the Kaizer Chiefs and the Orlando Pilots, both based in Soweto but supported nationwide. **Rugby** has a fanatical following, especially among Afrikaners, while **cricket** is still followed in one-day format, with the provincial season running from October to April, and provides endless ammunition for conversation.

The beginning of an idyllic camel ride in Oudtshoorn Town in the Karoo.

The Open Road

South Africa is a superb country to drive through. Fuel is relatively inexpensive, road surfaces are good, traffic light and relatively sensible, and the views superb, although of those four positive statements South Africans will generally only agree with the last. On the downside, cars represent a constant security problem, and if not car-jacked are often broken into. Most car rental companies charge — or try to charge — exorbitant mileage fees that take full advantage of the huge distances visitors often find they need to cover (see GETTING AROUND, page 252 in TRAVELERS' TIPS, for information on driving and car rental). Although some of the country is beautiful there are a lot of unremittingly flat and dull patches, especially in the inland semidesert areas, which can take some time to cover.

ITINERARIES

There are some spectacular drives in South Africa. Many of these can be predicted by the name. "Poort" as a suffix means "following the river" while "pass" means cresting the heights of a mountain range. Straight lines that fly straight across the map tend to be passing over a flat, featureless landscape, while it is the wiggly, fussy roads that enjoy the views and vistas.

They start within a few kilometers of the most common entry point into South Africa:

Cape Town. **Chapman's Peak Drive** and **Victoria Drive** are among the most beautiful drives in the world. If it's been raining — not unusual on the Cape — "road closed" signs appear, but if you're prepared to take the outside risk of a falling rock this is a good time to do the drive, as the traffic is considerably lessened. Alternatively, the roads through the **Winelands** pass the gently cultivated farmlands sheltered by some truly impressive mountain ranges. Personally, I love the yellows and greens of the farmlands spreading north of Cape Town through the Swartland country.

The **Garden Route** is the most relentlessly touted, following the N2 east from Cape Town. However, if you stick to the highway the drive is bound to disappoint. You have to drive for 400 km (250 miles) before the Garden Route starts and then the highway flits past the most spectacular roads. Turn off. The "R" roads are less pressured and more beautiful.

Some of South Africa's most spectacular landscapes are to the north of the Garden Route, soaring through passes built in the pioneering years by convict labor. The **Schoemanspoort** and the 27-km-long (17-mile) **Swartberg Pass** switchbacking through the mountains north of Oudtshoorn lead neatly on to the small town of Prince Albert for lunch, while the R407 tracks the northern foothills of the Swartberg Mountains before crossing back through **Meiringspoort**, winding for 25 km (15.6 miles) on the floor of a spectacular gorge, returning to Oudtshoorn or the coast.

Johannesburg and Pretoria are at the heart of a network of practical but uninspiring roads. The best drives from here are northeast, through the **Blyde River Canyon**. Alternatively, drop down to the southeast and the Drakensbergs. Head west and after the brief flickering attractions of the Magaliesbergs the road arrows out across trackless wastes that might as well have stayed trackless for all the interest they bring. Unfortunately these often have to be traveled, being the routes linking the major cities.

From **Durban**, the coast road to the north passes along spectacular coastal scenery missed by the highway, but the better views are from the network of roads heading inland, through the **Valley of 1000 Hills** and the sun-bleached, blood-soaked battlefields. The main Johannesburg Road, though generally fast and uninspiring, has long and very beautiful passages, especially as it tracks across **Van Reenen Pass** at about the halfway point, before it drops down into the flatland tedium that heads on into Gauteng.

Backpacking

South Africa has long been a wonderful destination for backpackers, with plenty of large, often period, houses around the country converted into dormitories and double rooms aimed at the backpacker market. These are almost always stocked with brochure racks and consistently involved in selling cut-price tours of the headline attractions. Most will also pick up travelers from the nearest station or even town, making it easy for backpackers to see the main sights without the expense or difficulty of renting a vehicle.

One change that has recently transformed the backpacking scene is the **Baz Bus (** (021) 439 2323 FAX (021) 439 2343 E-MAIL info@bazbus.com WEB SITE www.bazbus.com, 8 Rosedene Road, Sea Point, Cape Town 8005, which allows prepaid point-to-point tickets to be used on a hop-on, hop-off basis to travel all along South Africa's southern and eastern coast, with stops inland at Pretoria, Johannesburg, and the Kruger. Their Mercedes Sprinter buses head up as far as Victoria Falls to complete the experience. One-way fares from Cape Town to Johannesburg, offering unlimited stops en route, costs R830 one way via the North Drakensbergs, making this the cheapest way to get around. Baz Bus tickets gain a modest commission for the backpacker lodges that sell

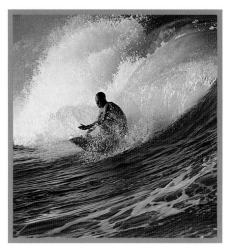

them, and few backpackers get far into a South African journey without buying a ticket for the Baz Bus route. This, in turn, tends to dictate the nature of the experience.

Although it does visit most of the most popular cities, travelers on the Baz Bus often pass through the whole experience of the country without meeting South Africans — who are not, in general, allowed to stay at backpacker lodges — and also consigns to the backpacking wilderness some of the most interesting destinations that don't feature on the Baz Bus routes.

Most lodges are sociable and friendly, offering dormitory accommodation for R35 to R50 per night and rooms for R90 to R120. These rates are not that much less than bed-and-breakfast accommodation, or even some hotels. Basic breakfasts at backpacker lodges are always extra, and guests without cars find themselves forced to buy all their food and wine from their host, especially when the lodge is in the country or — worse — in the suburbs. It is perhaps unsurprising that backpacker lodges are opening around the country at the rate of at least one a week, and far fewer seem to close down.

Few backpackers complain. Following a well-broken route, Baz Bus travelers chain through an established party scene, meeting and re-meeting friends as they drink and smoke their way around the countryside, with cut-price tours offering bungee jumps, *kloofing*, and other adventures along the way. For a fraction of the price of independent travelers they get to see the highlights, and fit in a fair few bars and nightclubs.

OPPOSITE: Chapman's Peak Drive is one of Cape Town's most spectacular roads. ABOVE: Riding the tubes of South Africa's Indian Ocean surfing culture.

Living It Up

Living it up in South Africa can take many forms. Most are covered by the world "Joll," derived from the fluid Cape dialect known as *Gamtaal,* which can refer to anything from a nice picnic to an all-night rave. South African "Jollers" head out seven days a week in cities, restraining themselves mainly to weekends in country towns, approaching their chosen pleasures with a certain dedication, inclusive and cheerful.

In the cities there is no limit to the possibilities for celebrating a special occasion. Perhaps the most logical place to start an evening celebration will be one of the countless "Action Bars" that you'll find in most city centers and suburbs. There's no need to be too scared of their title, as the nearest you'll generally find to action inside will be a screen showing live games of golf from around the world, perhaps with a bit of car racing thrown in. There will also be a range of clubs, theme pubs, night clubs and discos, with listings carried in the local papers and what's on magazines.

One form of evening relaxation you won't find at home are the *shebeens* — set up to provide drink and entertainment to the black and colored population through the years when they were banned from the white hotels and bars. Although many of these can be sleazy and forbidding, the majority are perfectly respectable and are likely to offer much better music and a warmer welcome than their counterparts in the white areas. It is not recommended to visit a *shebeen* alone, however, it is essential to take a local guide who will introduce you and, if necessary, explain what you are doing so far from your expected turf (see TAKE ON A TOWNSHIP, page 25 in TOP SPOTS).

The younger generation will find that there is a significant "rave" scene in South Africa, with most cities having occasional raves, some of which sell tickets through Computicket and are almost respectable.

If you are too old for that, the best alternative is perhaps one of South Africa's many casinos. The history of gambling in South Africa has much to do with the country's apartheid history. When the government established the nominally independent "homelands" they inadvertently opened up a loophole that allowed a truck through their 1965 Gaming Act which had banned all forms of gambling. With considerable popular support the homelands quickly welcomed the major casinos. The most famous is without doubt Sun City, in the homeland that was Bophuthatswana, but there are others. Even now the forgotten boundaries that marked the borders of the homelands of Ciskei and Transkei can be recognized by huge casino developments, sited to be in easy reach of South Africa's major cities but just beyond the reach of its upright, Calvinist legislation.

These days all such regulations have gone, and the country is gripped with gambling fever. About 40 new licenses have been issued. In Durban a temporary casino is being built to cope with demand while the main casino is being built. And while the green baize is undoubtedly a part of the appeal, for many South Africans the main activity in a casino is playing the "slots," or slot machines.

Outside the major cities the concept of living it up is quieter, centering more on good food and fine wine. There are a number of very good country hotels specializing in serving up some of the country's finest cuisine and wines, before pouring guests quietly into luxurious rooms upstairs. The exact flavor of the experience will vary with their location. In the private reserves bordering the Kruger they will be imbued with the atmosphere of the bush, in Mpumalanga they are likely to emulate the finest traditions of Victorian England, while Cape Town and the Garden Route are the places to enjoy the very latest experiments, as South Africa establishes culinary traditions to call its own. The best of these establishments are generally listed in the text under their own region.

LEFT: Relaxing after church on a Pretoria Sunday. ABOVE: At night the restaurants and bars of Cape Town's Waterfront come to life. RIGHT: Hanging out at a *shebeen* in the Fundani township in Port Elisabeth.

Family Fun

The finest restaurants, lodges and hotels tend to be a little bit too formal for the unpredictable charm of small hands and excitable voices. But take a step down and things improve dramatically. South Africa has all of Africa's attractions but backed by good healthcare, communications and facilities.

Perhaps the most enduring memories are attached to the animals children can meet, often very close up. The wild animals of the *Jungle Book* are not only found in the wild, but also tamed in parks where it is possible for children to stroke a cheetah or ride an ostrich (see RIDE A LEGGY BIRD, page 20 in TOP SPOTS). There are butterfly, bird, and game parks around all of the major cities, which all bring the natural world into easy reach. Added to which there is the outdoor world of beaches and surf, games, and other activities. Swimming pools are commonplace and although few in South Africa are heated most children quickly adapt to water too cold for their parents. Most of the major museums and aquariums make considerable effort to involve children in the learning process and are strongly aware of ways to introduce history and the natural world to young minds. Thus Cape Town's Aquarium has touch pools where children can feel the texture of our waterborne relatives, and reconstructed villages from the Victorian era make it easy for children to lend their imaginations to the life of the past. Children pay reduced fees at all South Africa's museums and aquariums.

If you are traveling in South Africa with children it is worth looking to the facilities that were set up to cater to the local market. Many of these family-friendly hotels have

very good facilities for children and you'll be hard pressed to get your kid's attention at the end of a day making new friends and discovering new sports. The large casinos, set up to wean parents away from their hard-earned dollars, are among the best at entertaining children, with structured courses and classes for children that combine full-on fun with a trace of education. Sun City has led the way on this and still offers unbeatable entertainment for all the family, albeit in a faintly sanitized, theme-park environment. South Africa's theme parks and shopping malls always provide plenty of activities and experiences for children, thus Cape Town's Ratanga Junction and Johannesburg's Randburg Waterfront are certain to make worthwhile day outings.

If, like me, you have a mild allergy to such commercialism, there's sure to be plenty to interest children in the natural world. Beaches are perhaps the best place to enjoy the summer sun, but watch out for the currents. Many of South Africa's beaches have savage rip currents that make bathing hazardous for all ages.

One thing to bear in mind is that distances can be huge, and not many children will be happy to sit quietly if your travel plans are too ambitious. It is worth stocking up with cassettes, books and games before some of the long drives that will be necessary in getting around, relying on the local attractions at your destination to grab your child's attention and give you memorable experiences to share.

Cultural Kicks

The first thing to realize about the South African culture is that it is not one single culture: instead it is a whole range, representing every level of this very stratified community. Not only have cultural traces survived intact from all South Africa's immigrants from Europe and the Far East, but traces survive of all South Africa's indigenous tribes, despite conscious suppression by the British colonial system.

Perhaps the most important cultural sights in South Africa are the oldest: the rock art left by the original inhabitants. The best places to find cave and rock paintings are in the Cederberg and the Drakensberg Mountains, though the signs of man's earliest inhabitation can be found everywhere if you know where to look.

Black cultural traditions continue in township life and rural communities, though these are only easy to experience or participate in with the help of a specialist operator taking township tours. The help of a local operator is essential because it is so easy for strangers to blunder into areas that are unsafe, and a lone white face is such a novelty in the townships that misunderstandings can ensue. By their very nature township tours are not run by national companies, but are instead small local operations with a special interest in sharing their homelands with foreign visitors, and so are listed in the cities and towns in which they operate. The best places to delve into the local communities are in Soweto, which, thanks to its international celebrity, has attracted a number of operators wishing to satisfy visitor's curiosity. Durban also has a vibrant and rewarding inner life, fired by Zulu displaced from their rural home, and the Cape Flats too, though far from safe, can provide visitors with a sometimes shocking insight into township life.

While in urban areas the tribal distinctions, first ignored then exaggerated by the apartheid regime, have lost their definition, in rural areas the nine tribes identified by the authorities still maintain distinct traditions of their own, most of which only become visible during rituals such as marriages or funerals.

Many visitors are given a taste of dancing and singing at tribal folk villages, which are found around the country, most notably Shakaland in KwaZulu-Natal, Shangana in Mpumalanga, and the Cultural Village attached to Shamwari in the Eastern Cape. These displays are rarely entirely authentic, but

are often performed with genuine enthusiasm, and are one of the few ways in which the local people can earn a little money for themselves from the tourists passing through.

Just as valid are the different traditions of grassroots architecture: the painted murals of the Sotho and Ndebele people, the round mud dwellings of the Xhosa people, or the grass beehive huts of the Zulu. These are at their most vibrant in the homelands set up under apartheid in an attempt to collect the black population into areas of limited economic activity. Freed from the constraints of zoning laws, the local dwellings grow like the fragile flowers of a threatened plant species.

The legacy of apartheid is perhaps the reason that the most lavish and accessible of South Africa's cultural achievements have come from the white community, or have been derived from European roots. The early white painters followed the Dutch school of landscape paintings, although with wide-open spaces and distinctively African subject matter. Thus most of the art galleries in the country contain endless paintings by European masters and their expatriate imitators. Through the 1950s the new movement known as Township Art, with expressive, figurative paintings by black artists, became widely accepted. Muslaba Dulibe provides a good example of this school. Through the 1970s and 1980s the growth in art accelerated, but remained mired in the all-too-dominant themes of apartheid and poverty. The lasting

OPPOSITE: South Africa's cities offer many child-friendly and educational activities. ABOVE LEFT: Dolphins on display in Port Elizabeth. RIGHT: Students at the Zulu Dance School in the Joodse Kamp township in Knysna.

university courses, with the fruits best enjoyed at al fresco concerts, including the Sunday concerts in Durban's Botanical Gardens and the summer concerts in Cape Town's Kirstenbosch. Jazz is a traditional favorite in the townships and has developed into three distinctive genres: Township Jazz, Black Jazz, and Marabi. Of these, the most popular is Marabi, using three-chord, two- or four-bar sequences with hypnotic progression. Huge Masakella, Miriam Makeba and others are classic performers of Marabi. Meanwhile, in the Zulu hostels another form of music developed: without instruments a cappella choirs grew up, using the rhythmic power of their voices to uplift homesick communities marooned in the cities. In the Cape, Malay instruments and traditions have retained the influence of their homelands despite 300 years of estrangement.

A strong literary tradition that started with Olive Shreiner's Novel *The Story of an African Farm*, first published in 1883, continued into the fairy-tale world of Rider Haggard's adventure stories. Through much of the twentieth century the focus has been on the relationship between South Africa's races, but there are works that transcend this. As always in South Africa, the published authors divide into racial strands, including members of the Congress of South African Writers (COSAW), which promotes literature in the black community; Afrikaans literature (which since its birth as a written language in 1875 has produced a number of works asserting its national identity, with the leading names being Boer and rebel André Brink); and English-language writing, which probably has no greater exponent than JM Coetzee, winner of Britain's 1999 Booker Prize.

contributions to art are primarily goods produced not as art, but as objects crafted from wire, ceramic toys, soft sculptures, and beaded blankets and necklaces. These are occasionally represented in the better museums, though most museums seem dedicated to celebrating the lifestyles of early settlers and the derivative furnishings of period dwellings. If I never see another candle-making machine again it will be too soon. To retain their government grants most have tacked on more-or-less convincing displays of the struggle for democracy.

Contemporary dance and performance arts are well represented, especially in the cities of Pretoria and Cape Town, but also in other cultural centers such as Pietermaritzburg and Grahamstown. Athol Fugard was South Africa's first internationally successful playwright, while Afrikaans theater resurged in the 1980s with plays such as *Paradise is Closing Down* and *Adapt or Die*. Experimental drama and protest theater are often given stage-space in the subsidized national theaters, including the State Theatre in Pretoria, the Nico Malan Theatre in Cape Town, Durban's Playhouse and the Sand du Plessis Theatre in Bloemfontein.

Music is an example of the range and diversity of the cultural strands of this diverse nation. Classical music, though originating in Europe, transfers comfortably to Africa, nourished by government grants and

Shop till You Drop

Since the rand was floated on the world currency markets it sank and has continued to plummet to ever-lower rates. This doesn't just mean that accommodation and meals represent great value for visitors, it also brings bargain prices for South African goods, whether bought as a souvenir or investment. Leather goods, antiques, ceramics, and curios all make good purchases. Most South Africans now shop in malls, which have sprung up in every major town and all the city suburbs. Trading hours are from 9 AM to 5 PM from Monday to Friday and 8 AM to 3 PM Saturday, with many metropolitan shops also opening from 9 AM to 1 PM on Sunday.

Meanwhile there are also plenty of flea markets around the countryside that offer a huge range of goods from all over Africa at lower prices than the shopping malls. Watch out for pickpockets, but generally you'll find flea markets are often a more rewarding place to search out those special goods that never make the mainstream retail outlets.

One reason for buying in shops is that visitors can obtain Value-Added Tax (VAT) refunds when they leave the country if they have the correct receipts. To get a VAT receipt you will need an original tax invoice, with the words "Tax Invoice" printed prominently, along with a statement of the amount of VAT included in, or added to, the purchase cost; the date of the transaction and the tax invoice number; the seller's VAT registration number; the cost of the goods in rand; the seller's name and address; a full description of the goods purchased; and the buyer's name. This sounds daunting, but most retailers are well up to the challenge. Just tell them you'll be needing to claim back the VAT. Where the shopkeepers can't help is that finally, and most importantly, the goods must be made available for inspection at the VAT refund office of your international departure airport. They will be inspected at Cape Town, Durban, or Johannesburg airports, and if they can't be produced no refund will be made. This can cause disappointment, especially for people who check their luggage through after an internal flight connecting with their flight home, and grumpy travelers are frequently found milling around the VAT refund office at the major airports. There are also VAT refund offices at the harbors of East London, Port Elizabeth, Cape Town, and Durban.

Diamonds are an obvious buy in South Africa. These carbon crystals began life 60 to 300 million years ago, crystallizing 150 km

(94 miles) below the earth's surface in the time of the dinosaurs. Three thousand years ago they were thought to be "splinters of stars" and they continue to exert a powerful appeal to the present day. Rated at 99.95% carbon, they are the only gem comprised of a single element, and are astonishingly rare. Even in the world's richest fields of Kimberley, 250 tons of dirt and rock had to be mined for every single carat (200 mg) of gem-quality diamond.

As the world's leading producer of diamonds, South Africa is a good place to buy these timeless gems, although price-fixing by the De Beers cartel means that you won't find any spectacular bargains. However, no longer are you in much danger of being seriously ripped off. In the past, it was very much buyer beware, as unscrupulous traders passed off Zircon and even glass as real diamond. Now a regulated framework of diamond traders cuts down this risk; just check that you are buying from a member of the Diamond Club of South Africa or the Jewelers Association of South Africa, whose staff are invariably qualified graders and/or gemmologists.

Two diamonds that look alike may actually vary widely in value and in quality. The assessment of a diamond depends on the "four Cs":

OPPOSITE LEFT: Reflective sculpture in the Kirstenbosch Botanical Garden, Cape Town.
LEFT: Andries Pretorius, the Boer's great leader.
ABOVE: Beads and weavings for sale on the Durban Marine Parade.

color, clarity, carat-weight, and cut. Color, ideally, should be no color. A diamond should act as a pure prism and color is a sign of impurity. Clarity, again, should be perfect, without any exterior or interior flaws or exclusions. Although small flaws do not affect the beauty or durability of the diamond they do affect the value. Carat-weight is a measurement of size, with each carat being divided into 100 "points." Bigger is not necessarily better, and you can find high-quality diamonds in all carat sizes. Finally, the cut of a diamond dictates, not its shape, but its scintillation and sparkle. Most are cut with 58 facets, so that light is reflected from one facet to another and shines out through the top of the stone. The six most popular shapes are Brilliant, Marquise, Pear, Emerald, Oval, and Heart.

Gold is another of South Africa's major exports, and many of the world's finest jewelers are found here, working the precious metal. However many of the most vibrant aspects of the new South Africa's art and culture are better expressed less expensively. The Ndebele are known for their **copper and bronze bracelets** as well as bright, bold designs. The filigree chains of **Zulu jewelry** and **woven reed baskets** are found throughout their homeland, while in the north the Vha-Venda are known for their bright clay pots. More than 100 weekly markets take place throughout South Africa, showcasing crafts from South Africa and beyond, while the very finest work finds its way to the city shopping malls.

Short Breaks

At the southern tip of Africa, this is one country that is not immediately appropriate for a short break, although night flights from Europe help for those who can sleep on planes. However, with the strategic use of internal flights and careful planning, a weekend here can make a rewarding break.

Critical is the choice of airport. Fly into Cape Town and there is a wide choice of wonderful destinations within a short drive: the Winelands of Constantia, Stellenbosch, Franschhoek, and Paarl are all within easy reach. If two hours is your driving limit, the mountains of the Cederberg or the Whale Coast around Hermanus are also within range. An internal flight will be needed to explore the Garden Route, but flights to Port Elizabeth would bring the forests of Tsitsikamma or the game of Shamwari within range.

Fly into Johannesburg and an internal flight is the quickest way to escape the urban sprawl. Nelspruit is well-served by flights, with the Kruger National Park and several stately country house hotels within an hour's drive. Head further north to Skukuza or Hoedspruit, and the scenic beauty of the Blyde River Canyon and the animals of the Sabi Sands and Timbavati area are all close by — with the prices of the private reserves, a short break might be all you can afford.

I spent a weekend once doing a three-day ranger training course at Sabi Sabi, which was a refreshing, complete break that with night flights left the working week pretty much intact.

Durban's appeal was greater when flights from Europe still flew direct. Now that they touch down first in Johannesburg it is perhaps an hour too far. However it is blessed by a warm climate and miles of surf-washed beach, and a short flight up the coast reaches the reserves of the St. Lucia Wetlands and the Hluhluwe-Umfolozi National Park.

Festive Flings

The year starts with a blast of color at the **Cape Minstrels Carnival** in Cape Town. In February the **Dias Festival** in Mossel Bay brings a carnival of history to this small Cape port. The austral autumn is the time for Capetonians to flee inland to the sunsoaked **Klein Karoo National Arts Festival** in Oudtshoorn. Durban, warm year-round, marks their sympathy with the Cape's bad weather with their **Mardi Gras Festival**, where the streets and beachfront turn into a riot of color. In July a more intellectual tone is struck by the **Standard Bank National Arts Festival** at Grahamstown, while meanwhile on the Cape coast a more hedonistic occasion is the **Knysna Oyster Festival**, providing a perfect excuse for sampling plenty of South Africa's fine sparkling wine. In September the **Zululand Show** takes place in Eshowe. At the end of September the **International Eisteddford of South Africa** is held at Roodepoort near Johannesburg while October sees the **Jacaranda Festival** in Pretoria. Rather more convivial is the **Stellenbosch Wine Festival**, held between October and November, which witnesses a certain amount of dressing up in period costume and a huge amount of drinking wine.

These are the major festivals, recognized across the nation. However, most years, even the smallest town will stage some sort of festival, known as "*fees*," celebrating local arts and musical accomplishments.

The Rainbow Nation, blending different races and cultures, also has a number of festivals imported with the cultural influences of waves of immigrants. Diwali is celebrated

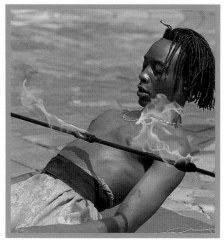

lavishly by the Indian population of Durban, while the Islamic calendar sets the structure for the Cape Muslims, and the major Jewish festivals are celebrated by the sizeable Judaic community. The Christian celebrations of Christmas and Easter are the two major events in rural areas, where religious values are important: on Sundays you can stroll unhindered onto many of the finest golf courses in many parts of the country, as the entire golfing community is in church.

A further tier of public holidays has been added by the idealistic new administration, with Freedom Day, Worker's Day, National Woman's Day, and Day of Reconciliation all being added to the roll of public holidays that can bring your travel plans to an unexpected standstill in front of the closed doors of a tourist information office or museum. Contact the local tourist information offices for up-to-date listings prior to making detailed travel plans.

OPPOSITE: Zulu culture in miniature, at Shakaland. ABOVE: High foreheads an occupational hazard if you fire limbo-dance daily. RIGHT: Rickshaws drag up Durban's Marine Parade: drivers dress to pull.

Galloping Gourmets

White South Africa was originally established to feed and water passing ships. In the 1600s, sailors disembarking after a three-month sea voyage flooded ashore to feast on fresh food. The heavy cuisine of Holland was lightened and spiced by influences from the East at the other tip of the trade route, resulting in the use of cloves, cinnamon, pimento, and anise in stews and cakes. Rice replaced potatoes and the pickles of the Orient swelled the traditional European preserves. As time went on, slaves and exiles from the furthest reaches of both Dutch and British empires blended, enriched by a new wave of immigrants from Europe, most notably France.

Surrounded by two of the world's least polluted oceans, the first European settlements on the Cape and Eastern coast quickly discovered the riches of the sea. Throughout the year mussels, oysters, crabs and crayfish are available in abundance, while between November and April the Cape's famous rock lobster comes into season prepared as thermidor, amoricaine, grilled or cold with mayonnaise, or curried in Malay style and served with rice. Among the summer visitors to the Cape most famous is snoek, named after the European pike, traditionally served fried with a jam made from honey-flavored Muscat grapes called as *korrelkonfyt*, a perfect blend of sweet and sour tastes. *Smoorsnoek* is a savory mix of onions and potatoes, also served with rice, mildly flavored with the light spices of Malaya. This fighting fish is often served in fishermen's homes, while the smarter restaurants tend to serve more exotic fare.

It's not just in climate that the eastern coast is hotter: flavored with the spices of a significant Indian community the curries here smolder with the passion of the Orient. These traditionally flavored meat and vegetable dishes are perhaps best typified by the local specialty of Durban's "Bunny Chow": a loaf of bread with the soft center removed and filled, traditionally, with curried beans. These are now available with all sorts of fillings. Meanwhile the Portuguese tastes of neighboring Mozambique flavor the prawns, calamari and langoustines of the sea and "peri-peri chicken" — which is also sold throughout the country.

Head inland, and air charters bring fresh seafood to the more expensive restaurants and lodges. However this is recent, and traditionally the Afrikaner heartlands were red-meat country, where game was killed and eaten fresh or dried into biltong. It wasn't just bloodlust that cleared the plains of buffalo and buck. South Africans have always loved the barbecue, or *braai*, charcoal cooking homemade sausages and steaks under the distinctive pattern of the Southern Cross. A whole range of cholesterol-laden cuisine prized by Afrikaners is *boerekos*, or "farmer's food." *Boerwors*, literally meaning "farmer's sausage," are chunky spiced sausages of pork and beef that can also be made from more exotic cuts of springbok, kudu, bush pig, or impala. *Potjiekos* is a stewed version of a barbecue, best cooked in a three-legged pot over an open fire. Chicken plays a lower role in the Afrikaner diet. "I don't eat poultry," I was once told, austerely, by a South African girlfriend who'd been living in England for six months. Since then, the humble farmyard bird has become more accepted. KFC and Nando's are two chains specialized in spicy chicken while O'Hagans, Steers, and Wimpy are other chains offering formulaic hamburgers and steaks. Most small towns will also have a steak house or two, serving food of varying quality but often very good, although vegetarians in rural areas are best advised to self-cater.

Of course, the perfect accompaniment to a perfect meal is a glass or two of good wine, and here, once again, South Africa excels. Vineyards were established in the very first days of the Cape, and the earliest date back to 1659. The Cape's vineyards have a Mediterranean climate, but there is a huge variety of conditions in a country of this size, from the hot inland regions to cool coastal and mountain areas. This means that a wide selection of grapes can be cultivated over a long vintage period, starting with early-ripening Chardonnay, Riesling, Pinot Noir, and Sauvignon Blanc, which are generally picked by the end of January, and ending with Cabernet Sauvignon, which is still coming to maturity in April. The best-known South African red table wine is Pinotage, first developed in 1959, which crosses Pinot Noir and Cinsaut into a beefy, wonderful wine that is actually best kept for 10 years before drinking. It's in the wrong place for aging, as most South Africans will weigh into a wine as soon as it is made available for sale.

Initially anarchic, until 1973 wine-makers weren't even required to fill their bottles to match what they wrote on the label. A new system of regulations was then introduced: look for a "Wine of Origin" sticker on the neck of the bottle. If a bottle comes from a single farm the word "Estate" will be printed on the label. Even in good restaurants, prices of quality wines rarely exceed R120, with the wine list starting at R40, so you can drink well without breaking the bank. Of course, prices will be lower in retail outlets, or direct from the estate. The country's vineyards are increasingly seen as a tourist asset, banding together into Winelands in the fight to attract visitors, who sometimes but not always are

expected to pay a tasting fee and are often expected to buy a case or two. As the wineries don't usually discount from the price in the shops this is not as tempting an opportunity as it could be. The best of the Winelands are in striking distance of Cape Town, being Constantia, Stellenbosch, Paarl, and Franschhoek, but there are more, including Wellington and Worcester. Even remote Upington, marooned in the great northern deserts, maintains a little wine route of its own, irrigated on the banks of the Orange River.

Restaurant prices, by world standards, are extremely reasonable. In most of the major chains it is possible to eat well for less than R40, while prices creep up to almost double that in smarter restaurants. Often the smartest restaurant in town will be attached to the best hotel or guest house, with service and cuisine taken seriously: prices at these establishments can creep up to international standards.

Meanwhile traditional black South African fare remains mealie meal, a stiff maize porridge. Maize was, itself, imported by the colonizing powers, and is neither nutritional nor especially tasty. Boiled into a porridge, ground maize is bland and trace flavors of vegetables or sometimes, meat, do little to improve a dish that does little more than stop you feeling hungry. Mealie meal is only served in restaurants as a slightly arch experiment. The best chance of trying it is if you are invited into a local home but usually your hosts will make great efforts to find something better — probably meat — to serve in your honor.

OPPOSITE: Showing off the evening's spread in Durban. ABOVE: Paarl's Grand Roche is one of South Africa's smartest hotels, with ingredients fresh from surrounding farms.

Special Interests

As the most developed country in Africa, South Africa combines a wealth of natural attractions all backed by sophisticated, first-world infrastructures that provide all the facilities to indulge the full range of special-interest holidays.

In a land of such scenic beauty and animal diversity the special interests best catered to are those of a natural kind. Ornithologists, entomologists, etymologists and botanists will all find there are specialist tour operators running guided expeditions with their own special interests as their focus: see TAKING A TOUR, page 56, for operators, or contact your local SATOUR representative.

There are also plenty of opportunities for cultural interests to be followed, with explorations of both the Afrikaner, colored, and black communities being arranged by local operators with special contacts and interests. These are generally small organizations operating on a local level, which are either listed in the relevant sections of the touring chapters or can be contacted through the regional tourism offices, who will be up-to-date with the current situation. Often they are less tours and more places of pilgrimage: an example is the Owl House, shrine to madcap mid-veld creativity in the heart of the Karoo.

The long history of conflict that shrouds South Africa's past is a magnet for those interested in the battles and conflicts of time gone by. Battlefield tourism was born around the town of Dundee and the great battlefields of the Anglo-Zulu War, and this is still the most advanced area in terms of skilled guides and informative tours. However the rest of the tourist industry is learning fast, and there are also tours from Eshowe into the cultural heartland of the Zulu Nation and further specialists concentrating on the battles of the Anglo-Boer wars.

Musical tours is one area where visitors might find it a struggle to find local artists. Traveling through conventional hotels and even backpacker lodges the music is hopelessly derivative, and even most music shops are stocked with artists from Europe and the United States. Often the local newspapers and listing magazines will not be very much help either, and the tourist bureaus worse than useless. It may not be much help to say this here, but apart from a few headline venues in the major cities, always listed in the touring chapters where appropriate, the only way of finding the live music performances will be to ask locally.

The most popular form of music among the local communities is Gospel, often seen at its best in churches. The classical European choral traditions are loosened and inspired in the mainstream churches, while the Pentecostal denominations spice their performances with American influences. The search for cultural roots has developed styles of neo-traditional music, including Iscathamiya, made famous by Ladysmith Black Mambazo (see SING OUT VAUDEVILLE, page 13 in TOP SPOTS). To get an idea of the contemporary traditional artists and styles tune in to SABC 1's Thursday night television program *Ezodumo*, where many of the best performances are showcased. South African ethnopop is, thanks to the country's recording and distribution skills, found all over the African continent, both in the older style of "Bubblegum" and its newer, more rap-like evolution of *kwaito*, but a greater diversity of traditional sounds will be found in nearby Madagascar or Zimbabwe. The most common form of music that most visitors will experience is South African jazz, with sounds evolved from Western hits of the 1920s to the 1950s still tirelessly exposed by a number of talented artists. Finally, if drinking out in an Afrikaner *dorp*, you might well come across *Boermusiek*, a blend of Dutch, French and hillbilly influences which is easy, if undemanding listening, that can on occasion rise to lyrical heights.

ABOVE: Restored steam locomotives still ride the extensive rail network in South Africa. RIGHT: A traditional Zulu "beehive" hut.

Taking a Tour

There is a mature and well-developed tour industry in South Africa, whose buying power will often mean that they can arrange your accommodation and transfers more cheaply than independent travelers making their own way around the country would. The only problem with this way of traveling is that the commission structure means those looking to the international market will invariably try to upgrade your experience in the hope of increased commissions. South Africans travel too, and are far less easily taken for a ride: to tour inexpensively, best to go for a local firm that caters to the local market as well as to overseas visitors. There are far too many operators to embark on a comprehensive list here, so the following is just a sample selection.

A good all-round nationwide operator is **Rennies Travel (** (011) 407 2800 FAX (011) 403 3698 WEB SITE www.renniestravel.co.za, Box 9395, Johannesburg 2000. Tour operators heading into the Kruger tend to operate from Johannesburg or Nelspruit. These include **Spurwing (** (011) 673 6197 FAX (011) 673 6197 E-MAIL spurwing@iafrica.com WEB SITE www.spurwing.co.za, Box 917, Melville, Johannesburg 2109, who offer tours throughout the country. Another operator is **Kwa'Nyathi (** (011) 465 6848 FAX (011) 465 2431 E-MAIL kwanyati@mweb.co.za WEB SITE www.globaltradecentre.co/kwanyati, Box 67373, Bryanston, Gauteng 2021, who offer a range of safaris in South Africa as well as bordering countries as well as day-trips from Durban, Cape Town, and Johannesburg. For accompanied self-drive safaris, **Africa Unlimited (/**FAX (011) 976 3486

Trichardt 0920, with cultural links with the Venda people as well as a range of more conventional tours.

To travel around Cape Town, **I&F Elegant Country Tours** ((021) 862 2665 FAX (021) 862 3412 E-MAIL ifkay@mweb.co.za WEB SITE members.rediff.com/boland, 29 La Moderne Street, Mount View, Paarl 7646, offer a huge range of tours in the Cape, Winelands and Overberg areas, with prices from R150 and travel in smart minivans. Specialists in the Garden Route and the inland areas of the Karoo are **Pembury Tours** ((041) 581 2581 FAX (041) 581 2332 E-MAIL info@pemburytours.com WEB SITE www.pemburytours.com, Box 13482, Humewood, Port Elizabeth 6013, who can arrange malaria-free Big Five viewing as well as scenic tours of the Little Karoo landscapes.

Further to the east and the Wild Coast is one of the few corners of the country that is hardly explored — a four-wheel-drive vehicle is needed to reach many little-known regions. Specialists in this area, based in East London, are **African Coastal Adventures** (/FAX (043) 748 4550 E-MAIL aca@imaginet.co.za WEB SITE www.africoast.co.za, who run four-wheel-drive tours between East London and Port St. Johns, though South Africa's least-disturbed environment.

Durban is a good base to explore KwaZulu-Natal, itself one of the most fascinating areas of the country. **Strelitza Tours** ((031) 266 9480 FAX (031) 266 9404 E-MAIL strelitz@iafrica.com, Box 1462, Westville 3630, are intimately familiar with the Durban area and run quick and painless tours to places in the area that otherwise might be hard to find.

Feel like shooting something? **Lew Harris Safaris** ((058) 622 2924 FAX (058) 623 1210 E-MAIL harris@dorea.co.za, Box 514, Harrismith 9880, offers big-game hunting from US$600 per day and plains game for US$300 per day, with a professional ranger on hand and guns available for rent. They suggest a 375 H&H Mag for big game and who am I to argue.

From whitewater rafting to canoeing, routes across Africa have been marked out by **Aquatrails** ((021) 762 7916 E-MAIL inbound.africa@ct.lia.net, who explore in two-man inflatable or Indian canoes, with camping adventures starting at R980 per person for two-day expeditions. Although you'll see plenty of birds from the water, true birders will want a professional specialist outlet. One of the best is **Lawson' Birdwatching and**

E-MAIL meijer@africansafaris.co.za WEB SITE www.africansafaris.co.za, Box 2712, Kempton Park 1620, offers a guiding service in rented Britz vehicles, which open up new and remote areas of the country. To combine game-viewing with a cultural experience you can't do much better than contact **Imbizo Tours** ((011) 838 2667 FAX (011) 781 1564 E-MAIL imbizo@iafrica.com WEB SITE www.backpackafrica.com, Box 25031, Ferreirasdorp 2048, with a wide range of tours in Johannesburg and Pretoria, including informative Soweto tours by day and hugely enjoyable *shebeen* crawls by night, with longer trips taking in the Kruger and the Diamond Fields around Kimberley. To explore the remote northern regions around Louis Trichardt the best local operator is **Face Africa Tours** (/FAX (015) 516 2076 or (015) 516 1037 E-MAIL facaf@mweb.co.za, Box 245, Louis

Mountain passes near George on the Garden Route.

Photographic ((013) 755 2147 FAX (013) 755
1793 E-MAIL lawsons@cis.co.za, Box 507,
Nelspruit 1200.

SELF-DRIVE TOURS

Many of the car-rental companies have put
scenic itineraries and selected hotels together
in an ideal combination of pre-planned travel
with a healthy level of independence, with
travelers being met at the airport with route
maps and travel plans. These can often work
out to be cheaper than DIY travel and take
advantage of a local's careful planning.
Whydah Tours ((011) 781 2093 FAX (011) 781
2096 E-MAIL whydah@pixie.co.za, Box 987,
Pinegowrie 2123, offer a well-planned choice
of itineraries starting in Cape Town, Durban,
or Johannesburg, with their Kruger Park
option taking in several of the best private
reserves. **YOUnique Options** ((011) 404 2440
FAX (011) 402 7299 E-MAIL tourlink@cis.co.za
WEB SITE www.tourlink.co.za, Box 169, Cresta
2118, with a particularly detailed view-by-
view travel planner. **Reservations Africa**
((011) 883 4832 FAX (011) 883 4302 E-MAIL
resaf@global.co.za, includes a mobile phone as
part of the standard package.

MOTORCYCLE RENTALS

Good roads make South Africa a natural place
to tour by motorcycle, and there are a number
of operators who offer guided tours of the
country. These include **Motor Bavaria** ((011)
463 4549 FAX (011) 463 5468 E-MAIL
info@motobavaria.co.za, at the corner of
William Nichol and Grosvenor roads,
Bryanston, who rent out BMWs from
Johannesburg and Cape Town; **Cape
Harleyday Tours** ((021) 882 2558 E-MAIL
anttract@iafrica.com WEB SITE
www.harleyday.co.za, Box 141, Koelenhof
7605, explore the Cape area by Harley-
Davidson. Tours on a 1.5-liter Honda are
offered by **1500 Wing Tours** (/FAX (013) 744
0018 E-MAIL gold@global.co.za, Box 12638,
Nelspruit 1200.

SPECIALIST OVERSEAS
OPERATORS

Literally hundreds of specialist tour operators
arrange travel to South Africa, far too many to
aim for any full listing here.

Operators from the United States include
African Travel Inc. ((818) 507-7893 TOLL-
FREE (800) 421-8907 FAX (818) 507-5802
E-MAIL ati@africantravelinc.com WEB SITE
www.africantravelinc.com, The Safari
Building, 1100 East Broadway, Glendale,
California 91205, on the west coast and **Park
East Inc.** ((212) 765-4870 TOLL-FREE (800) 223

6078 FAX (212) 265 8952 E-MAIL
infosales@parkeast.com WEB SITE
www.parkeast.com, 1841 Broadway, New
York, New York 10023, in the east.

From the United Kingdom the largest is
Thomas Cook Holidays (01733 417000
FAX 01733 417784 E-MAIL tch@thomascook.com
WEB SITE www.tcholidays.com, PO Box 5,
12 Coningsby Road, Peterborough PE3 8XP.
Specialist operators include **Travel 2** (0207 561
2244 FAX 0207 561 2456 E-MAIL web@travel2.com,
Fifth Floor, Hamlyn House, Highgate Hill,
London N19 5PR; **Union Castle Travel** (020 7229
1411 FAX 020 7229 1511 E-MAIL u-ct@u-ct.co.uk,
86-87 Campden Street, Kensington, London
W8 7EN; **Carrier International** (01625 582006
FAX 01625 586818 E-MAIL aspects@carrier.co.uk
WEB SITE www.carrier.co.uk, 31 London Road,
Alderley Edge, Cheshire SK9 7JT; and
Abercrombie & Kent (020 7730 9600 FAX 020
7730 9376 E-MAIL info@abercrombiekent.co.uk
WEB SITE www.abercrombiekent.co.uk, Sloane
Square House, Holbein Place, London
SW1W 8NS.

For a specialist in wildlife safaris, one of
the most knowledgeable is **Safari Consultants**
(01787 228 494 FAX 01787 228 096 E-MAIL bill@
safcon@pop3.hiway.co.uk, Orchard House,
Upper Road, Little Cornard, Suffolk CO10 0NZ.

OPPOSITE: Boulders and beaches as the summer
sun brings out bathers at Cape Town's Clifton.
ABOVE: A pilot with with his helicopter in
Wonder Valley, Central Drakensberg.

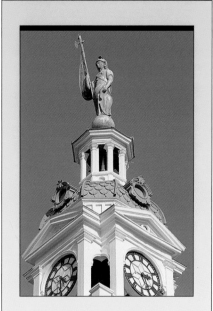

Welcome to South Africa

"A WORLD IN ONE COUNTRY" is the slogan of the new South African tourist board. And they have a point. Larger than France and Spain combined, South Africa stretches from the temperate Cape to the subtropical north, reaching up to border with Zimbabwe and Mozambique. In its boundaries are some of the world's most beautiful landscapes: clear canyons, wilderness areas scattered with game, cliffs dropping sheer into the ocean, and sheltering white-sand, deserted beaches.

It is also a country that is deeply confused. Clearly within Africa, it is a developed country with good roads and infrastructure, a lively theatre scene, and orchestras specializing in productions of the great European classical masterpieces. Stately whitewashed gabled wineries stand amidst stretching vineyards, aching with atmosphere and stripped-floor, antique-furnished charm.

Scratch the surface though and there's more. Within a few kilometers of smart townhouses,

fenced off with walls topped with razor-wire and guarded by large dogs, are some of the world's most invidious slums, townships where there are few schools struggling with limited resources to educate a generation with hope but no real prospects. Off to the side are midland suburbs, colored estates where aspiring communities strive to fit into an ill-defined role.

At first sight, then, a divided society. Look closer and the divisions don't blend: they get worse. The obvious divisions are stratified. The white community splits strictly into Afrikaner and British communities, with the memory of the Boer Wars still fresh. Colored communities come largely from the Cape Malay community but also include a range of genes from South Africa's history, with Indian immigrants on the eastern coast forming a separate group. Even the black population, though fragmented by repression, hang onto tribal groupings that retain traces of the 11 official languages

and countless dialects that mark out a whole spectrum of different — and not necessarily compatible — groupings.

It was in the face of this bewildering and little-understood diversity that the ancient, fumbling regime tried to establish the system of apartheid to make simplified sense of their society. This extreme experiment in social engineering ended badly, with political disenfranchisement enforced by brutal killings and covered by oppressive layers of violence and repression. And this left scars. Even today South Africa is clearly a traumatized country. Amidst some of the world's most spectacular scenery the old social patterns live on, with white landowners supported by a vast and underprivileged black population.

Despite their long and turbulent history, there is something superb happening in this most fascinating country. In the face of obvious and deep divisions, South Africa is coming together to build a new world at the tip of this troubled continent. It already has the largest economy in southern Africa, with mature industries and developed communications and computer skills. It has the most diverse landscapes and the greatest heritage of great cities, built proudly in stone by generations. After the early years of shoot-and-eat development it has learned from its mistakes and pioneered nature conservation, bringing the black rhino back from the edge of extinction. Even now it is leading the way in tearing down borders to establish new, transnational parks.

Dynamic and positive, the spirit of South Africa is gathering to build a new country. Troubled, it threatened the entire region; now, in a spirit of reconciliation, this is the country that gives hope to the continent.

Cape Town's Central Business District fills the City Bowl on the lower slopes of Table Mountain.

The Country and Its People

IT IS QUITE LIKELY THAT SOUTH AFRICA was one of the first places in which man came down from the trees, with fossil finds including transition species between ape and *Homo sapiens*. Known as *Australopithecus africanus*, these early people lived about three million years ago, and several separate finds confirm their widespread distribution around the highveld. More recently, they evolved into — or were replaced by — *Homo erectus*, developing into *Homo sapiens* about 100,000 years ago. Specimens 50,000 years old have been identified from the Klasies River in the Eastern Cape.

These people lived in small, nomadic units of 20 or 30 members, sleeping in tents or caves and using stone tools to kill and eat animals. The shells of ostrich eggs saved them developing the technology of pottery. This leaves archaeologists floundering to find evidence of their existence, a dearth of information that made it very easy for the settlers, and later the apartheid regime, to deny the numbers and races of the residents that predated the European invasion.

Clues to their numbers exist, however, in the numerous paintings that adorn many of the country's caves, created using natural dyes by the San people and portraying animals that have long become extinct, as well as trance paintings of religious significance. Although some of the images are obviously recent — men with guns are a complete giveaway — others date back as far as 30,000 years. Some paintings portray livestock, not necessarily the animals introduced by the settlers, but fat-tailed sheep traded with eastern African Sudanic tribes as long as 20,000 years ago. While the San people lived a sustainable existence inland, the Khoikhoi people had, long before the first European settlers landed on the Cape, established herds of domestic cattle and sophisticated systems of land ownership in the coastal areas of what is now South Africa. How long ago this happened is open to argument: some say this transformation occurred at around the time of Christ, while others suggest a far earlier date, up to 20,000 years ago. Between these two main ethnic groups were a number of distinct groups with their own languages and cultures — almost certainly far more than the nine black racial groups identified by the apartheid administrators many centuries later.

THE FIRST STEPS OF SETTLEMENT

Although countless indigenous dugouts had certainly blown past the bays of the Cape before the arrival of the European imperialists, the first European navigator to "discover" the Cape of Good Hope was Bartolomeu Dias. However he sailed past at speed in the teeth of a storm in 1488, and he didn't approach the coast until he was far to the east off Mossel Bay. Eleven years later

Vasco da Gama passed by, again being blown past Table Bay, landing instead at Mossel Bay. The first European to arrive in Table Bay arrived there by accident: Antonio de Saldanha sailed in with his squadron, and stayed long enough to climb Table Mountain. However, like all European visitors he experienced hostility from the indigenous people and didn't push his luck by staying too long.

For the next 10 years Portuguese sailors would occasionally land here, but generally found that their schedules were better suited by using their harbors in St. Helena, an island off the west coast, or Mozambique to the east. This preference was encouraged when, in 1510, a brush with the Khoikhoi cost 65 Portuguese lives. The British and Dutch however, without safe anchorage of their own, quickly learned to use Table Bay as a staging post on their way to British East India and the Dutch East Indies. The arrangement between British and Dutch sailors was amicable: ships would leave mail under stones to be picked up by following compatriots. The first step towards colonizing the Cape happened by chance. The *Nieuw Haerlem* became stranded and a group of 60 sailors were left to guard its cargo. After nearly a year spent living on African soil they reported back to Amsterdam that it should be occupied as a port of call. In 1652 Jan van Riebeeck was sent out with three colonizing ships and laid the foundation of the city that is now Cape Town.

EUROPEANS TAKE ROOT

The colony was, at first, modest. The local Khoikhoi represented a constant threat and at one point the idea of blowing a channel from Table Bay to False Bay was considered, which would have effectively turned the Cape into a huge, defensible island. In the end this rather silly idea proved impracticable. They found it difficult enough to build a fort, and even that had to be followed by six redoubts along the exposed eastern borders to make it at all defensible. Van Riebeeck was expected — indeed required — to provide meat and vegetables for passing ships and so gardens were dug and orchards planted. Initially he filled the meat requirements by trading with local tribes but soon there were 25 or 30 ships passing every year, far more than could be fed by local traders. In 1655 the decision was taken to use slave labor to help produce more food, and by 1657 there were nine Dutch and German farmers established in the Liesbeeck valley. Slaves were brought in from various areas. Those from Madagascar and East India proved to be most satisfactory, while those from Angola ran off into the bush and joined up with local Khoikhoi. Only extensive military action managed to get them back again and no more slaves were brought from West Africa.

Despite a rearguard action by the indigenous people, the colony thrived. In 1679 a new settlement was founded inland, in Stellenbosch, and a few years later these were joined by a group of French Huguenot refugees who set up camp at Franschhoek. A succession of Dutch governors all left their subtle marks. Simon van der Stel shared his knowledge of viticulture, forming the foundations for a successful wine industry, while Ryk Tulbagh established extensive botanical gardens and a library of 4,000 books. He also established a new set of rules governing the treatment of slaves, allowing them, among other rights, to work for money with the eventual aim of buying their freedom.

AFRICANS OFF BALANCE

This arrangement did not immediately benefit the indigenous Africans, whose collective name, according to the settlers, was not crowd or group, but "horde." The settler reaction was to keep the hordes at bay by force. Concerted military actions tried to drive the local people back across the Fish River and to seal the leaky eastern border beyond Grahamstown.

In one of the most significant developments it was decided to relieve Britain's domestic unemployment after the Napoleonic Wars by promoting a program of emigration from Britain.

Events in Europe, however, were about to make themselves felt. In 1795 revolutionary France overran the Netherlands, and the Prince of Orange fled to England. Faced with the horrific possibility that the French could take control of the Cape, and thus the main shipping lanes to its Indian Territories, a substantial British fleet was promptly dispatched under Admiral Elphinstone. The Dutch settlers were not convinced that following the authority of their deposed king was a good idea and resisted British occupation — in vain. From 1795 the Cape passed under British rule. The English really only wanted the colony to stop the French from getting it. In 1803 they gave it back to the Dutch kingdom of Batavia and only later claimed full ownership of the Cape, along with Ceylon and British Guyana, in a complicated cash deal with Holland's King William.

In 1820 the first wave of British settlers arrived to take up land offered by the British government. The idea was that these settlers would farm the wild colonial hinterlands and act as a buffer against tribal "hordes" of Khoikhoi and San people. Unfortunately British farmers were not, at the time, liable to be unemployed, and the settlers were generally tradesmen who knew nothing of the land. After their first season being marauded by tribes and watching crops fail, many quickly moved back to the nearest towns where they followed their own trades. Others held out in the countryside, blending their own influence with the Dutch farmers into the cocktail that now makes South Africa. Meanwhile, many Afrikaner settlers, infuriated in part by the British decision to outlaw slavery in 1833, set off

A dwelling in Zululand.

into the interior on the "Great Trek," opening up vast new tracts of land to the European colonists.

At the time that these settler movements were taking place the indigenous population was distracted by problems of their own. Then, as now, the Zulus made up the second-largest racial group in the country, and from their stronghold in northern KwaZulu-Natal launched a number of wars against their neighboring tribes. Displaced, these in turn had to travel to fight another war to lay claim to alternative land. Thus a chain of wars engulfed the indigenous population in a period of conflict known as the *difaqane* that would see a large proportion of South Africa's people displaced. Generations were dispossessed and wandering around the countryside, traveling as far north as Zimbabwe in the search for safe territory, at just the point when the settler forces were consolidating their hold on some of the best bits of land. In 1879 the British, having allowed the Zulus to comprehensively destabilize the black population, launched the Anglo-Zulu War and smashed the Zulu military machine.

WEALTH — AND THEREFORE POLITICS

With the Zulus neutralized things might have muddled on, with continual conflict between isolated farmers and individual indigenous groups, had the colony remained agrarian and unprofitable. But diamonds in Kimberley and gold at Witwatersrand (now Gauteng) changed everything. Suddenly South Africa was important to the British and they started to annex every bit of land they could map. The First Boer War — known to the Boers as the "War of Independence" — crushed the British at Majuba Hill in 1881. But there was another Boer War to follow, which started in 1899 and would prove to be longer, bloodier, and herald a different result. The war dragged on for three years, with support for the Boers coming from Europe. Growing criticism of the scorched-earth British policy sapped morale, and when the British were finally victorious in 1902 they handed over, in victory, most of the powers they had been contesting at war.

However the Boer fighters coming back from their commando life in the bush found a society fundamentally changed. The language in the cities was now English and the British oppressors had proclaimed the end of slavery. From this point on the Afrikaans language was to become a central symbol to the Boer settlers of their rights and achievements. The Union of South Africa, however, which took place in 1910, did not recognize this hybrid language and dictated English and Dutch as the official languages. A barrage of dis-

criminatory laws followed: black people were banned from many trades and their movements were curtailed. In 1913 the "Native's Land Act" set aside seven and a half percent of the country's land for 70% of its population. The blacks had lost out again. By this time fully 80% of black men were working away from home as migrant labor, forced by a system of taxation that demanded to be paid in coin to live in a hostile society.

The country's powerbrokers were then distracted by World War I. However it was far from clear which side the strategically vital and newly independent country would support. Under Prime Minister General L. Botha, Interior Minister General Smuts supported Britain and agreed to attack German West Africa (now Namibia). Despite considerable unrest in South Africa, the country continued to support Britain and was

rewarded with the gift of German South Africa
after the war finished in 1918. Soon afterwards
Smuts became Prime Minister. There was a political price to pay, however. As Europe drifted towards World War II, there was an upsurge of
Afrikaner nationalism. South Africa moved closer
to Hitler's position under a coalition of pro-British
Smuts and an Afrikaner leader called Hertzog
who favored neutrality. Rather to the surprise of
many of its people, South Africa came into the
war on the side of Britain and the Allies, fighting
with distinction in many of the most important
battles. Back home, the war-led demand for wool
and meat caused something of a boom and South
Africa emerged from the conflict wealthier than
it had been since the mineral booms at the end of
the nineteenth century.

South Africa, however, was a troubled place.
Resistance to white rule had already started, with

the ANC (African National Congress) coming
into existence as the South African Native National Congress in 1912, although their early aims
were confined to enfranchising the black population. The record was not encouraging: the black
population of the Cape, which had enjoyed
qualified franchise according to education and
property ownership, lost even that in 1930. It
wasn't until 1944, when Nelson Mandela, Oliver
Tambo and Walter Sisulu formed the ANC youth
league, that the new politicization following the
defeat of Fascism in Europe started to appear in
the African political scene. However, this was
to stampede the white population into a disastrous vote that brought the word "apartheid"
to the world.

The age of Queen Victoria is set in stone in
Pietermaritzburg, KwaZulu-Natal.

THE APARTHEID YEARS

The 1948 elections were the first to be fought with the policies of apartheid as a central issue. The National Party, led by Dr. D.F. Malan, gained 40% of the vote and with the help of the Afrikaner Party made sweeping changes. Mixed marriages and interracial sex were made illegal. A race and classification board was established and every citizen was slotted into the nearest racial category. The "Group Area's Act" specified the physical separation of residential areas and the "Separate Amenities Act" divided beaches, toilets, schools, and park benches.

This attempt to instill order on the country was doomed to failure. There were an unlimited number of spark-points. In 1958 the Pan Africanist Congress (PAC) split away from the ANC. Two years later at Sharpeville they demonstrated against the Pass Laws, which restricted the movement of black citizens. The police opened fire, injuring 200 and killing 69 demonstrators, many with bullets in their backs. Many white South African politicians had already decided apartheid was unsustainable, but when the United Nations called on South Africa to ban apartheid the National Government reacted by banning membership to the ANC and the PAC. The prime minister, Hendrik Verwoerd, was shot twice in the head by a white farmer, but hopes that apartheid would die with him were dashed when he survived and enforced even more draconian rules. Among these were plans for independent homelands, whereby the rich, established areas would be part of South Africa, ready for international acceptance, while useless tracts of desert were classified as "homelands," ideal for dumping displaced black populations. The idea was that an all-white Afrikaner republic would result. South Africa was thrown out of the Commonwealth.

Balthazar John Vorster took over as Prime Minister after Verwoerd was fatally stabbed by a messenger, and he increasingly used the police force as an instrument of repression. An important watershed followed the decision, in 1976, to make the Afrikaans language equal to English, to be used equally throughout the state education system. This was calculated to annoy and seen as an attempt to sabotage the prospects of the black population. It is hard to conceive of any alternative explanation. The black population saw Afrikaans as the language of the oppressor, more practically it was a much less useful language than English. Although most Afrikaner speakers are also fluent in English, the reverse is not true, and in the cities Afrikaans was spoken neither by students nor, often, by teachers. Despite major riots in Soweto this was retained as law, thus consigning a generation of black South Africans into a linguistic hinterland — now that the official language has reverted to English those educated in Afrikaans struggle to make their voices heard. During the first riot following the decision, 13-year-old Hans Peterson was fatally injured, and his picture made headlines throughout the world. With far less publicity at least 575 people died in a year of rolling violence that was to follow. In 1978 P.W. Botha took over, pouring troops into the township and destabilizing neighboring states such as Angola and Mozambique.

CRISIS POINT

Through the 1980s, detentions and executions increased. Australia and the United States severed air links with South Africa and many companies started to disinvest. In 1989 Botha was replaced by F.W. de Klerk, who released Nelson Mandela but presided over a descent to the brink of anarchy while the "third force," apparently renegade elements of the security forces, worked to destabilize the country by promoting and participating in violence between the ANC forces and Inkatha, the Zulu Nationalist party led by Mangosuthu Buthelezi. The assassination of Chris Hani, the most popular ANC leader after Nelson Mandela, in 1993, threatened to plunge the country into civil war. For three nights in a row Nelson Mandela appeared live on national television appealing for calm while the world held its breath. In 1994 the first fair election in South Africa's history swept the ANC to power with Nelson Mandela at its head.

Power, but also problems. Of the country's 39 million people, barely half had access to electricity, and destitution and unemployment were widespread. The rand had sunk to a new low and the economy was in no state to fund the investments necessary to build a more equal society. Even the crimes of the old regime were not to face justice, as amnesties were granted to persuade former security officials to give evidence in front of the Truth and Reconciliation Commission (TRC), set up to investigate the atrocities committed under apartheid. Under the chairmanship of Archbishop Desmond Tutu this commission interviewed a number of the leading figures of the old regime, including Botha and de Klerk, but their cooperation was widely thought to be less than wholehearted and some of the major accusations were met with bland and unconvincing denials. The TRC finally released its report in 1998, all 3,500 pages of it, but for many its sheer detail and length has buried some of the headline crimes.

THE RAINBOW NATION

Looking at his people through the bars of his prison cell, Nelson Mandela described his people as a "Rainbow Nation." South Africa's ethnic diversity is at once a cultural asset and a potentially divisive threat to the future of the country. About 75% of the population are black, with the Xhosas being the largest ethnic group, and the Zulus coming second. Three further groups have given their names to neighboring countries: the Tswana (towards Botswana), the Sotho (around Lesotho), and the Swazi (near and in Swaziland). The Shangana, Venda, Ndebele, and the Northern Sotho are

1996 a radical new constitution was approved, and in the 1999 elections power smoothly transferred from Nelson Mandela to his successor, Thabo Mbeki. The National Party is no longer an effective political party and the ANC still enjoys the support of most of the population. Thabo Mbeki has long been a champion of the ill-defined "African Renaissance" and much to the dismay of the white sector a policy of affirmative action, whereby black candidates are given priority for many jobs, has been put in place. The black population, which put up with most of the atrocities of the apartheid years and still suffer most of the privations of poverty, have shown remarkable powers of forgiveness. It remains to be seen, however, for how

further tribes identified by the apartheid regime, each with their own language and customs. The white population comprise 13% of the population, and are divided between English and Afrikaans linguistic groups. Just 3% of the population are described as Indian, with their origins in indentured laborers brought over from South Asia. Finally, there is the colored population, which is the hardest for most visitors to classify. Although they make up 9% of the country they are linked more by their culture than race. Some are descended from original Khoikhoi and San intermarriages with settlers, while others are pure Malay, brought in to the Cape to work on the farms. A full 80% of the colored population speak Afrikaans as their mother tongue, helping to make it the most widely-spoken language in the country.

There is hope that the future will see the Rainbow Nation steadily forge a united path ahead. In

long they will be prepared to put up with systematic discrimination that continues despite the removal of apartheid. In 1999 a black woman was jailed for six months for letting her goat graze on a white landowner's land, while a white farmer who shot and killed a black woman "because she was talking too loudly" was given a provisional sentence. Where the haves and the have-nots live side-by-side in a society still flushed with the weapons left over after years of living violently, crime is becoming an increasing problem. The future for South Africa looks, at the very least, interesting. But then South Africa, through its long history, has always been interesting.

This children's choir sings "Freedom".

Cape
Town
and the
Western
Cape

"THE FAIREST CAPE WE SAW in the whole circumference of the earth" was the reaction of Francis Drake when, in 1580, he sailed the *Golden Hind* into Cape Town's harbor. Since that time plenty more beautiful parts of the world have been discovered, but none that quite match the scale and grandeur of the Cape. To the northwest it is a rugged, wild landscape, blanketed in flowers every spring with caves adorned with the delicate shapes of San rock art. The heart of the Cape itself, the flat-topped Table Mountain, more often than not covered with the slipping blanket of cloud known as the "Tablecloth," is skirted by a chain of white-sand beaches. South, and the Twelve Apostles gaze evenly over the Atlantic Ocean. To the east a dramatic, surf-swept coastline runs towards the Garden Route: cliffs, ravines and gorges coated with *fynbos* (Afrikaans for "fine bush") — dense meadows of otherworldly plant life, strangely adapted to suit the environment.

CAPE TOWN

The first major European settlement in Southern Africa, Cape Town started life as a provisioning center for ships heading out to the British colonies in India and the Dutch possessions in the Spice Islands. More than in any other city in South Africa, its long history is still on display, in the stacked houses that slot neatly onto the foothills of Table Mountain, and the restored buildings of the Victoria and Alfred Waterfront. A welcome sight in the early days for its promise of fresh vegetables, clean water, and meat, as well as offering land-based entertainment for travel-weary sailors, it has continued its tradition of hospitality to the present day.

BACKGROUND

When European settlers first arrived there was a thin scattering of San and Khoi people, but, according to the settler's own account, no permanent structures on the Cape. The first to land was Antonio de Saldanha in 1501, traveling with three ships. Even though he was tired and lost he climbed Table Mountain and surveyed the area, but his crew got into a fight with the local Africans. This situation was to repeat itself nine years later, when the retiring Portuguese viceroy of India was among 75 Portuguese who died. This deterred the Portuguese settlers, who had the option of landing in the safer and more established possessions of St. Helena in the Atlantic and Mozambique to the west. From then on they sailed well clear of the Cape.

The Dutch and British started to land at the Cape at the end of the sixteenth century and quickly discovered that a few fragments of scrap metal could be exchanged for enough food to provision

a whole ship. In 1652 three ships belonging to the Dutch East India Company landed and offloaded building materials. The first construction was a wooden fort known as the "Goede Hoop." Soon there were so many British and Dutch ships landing here that the local value of scrap collapsed and it was clear the scrap-rich indigenous people were unable — or unwilling — to satisfy the demand for fresh food. Thus a policy of settling European farmers was adopted, with European plants being brought over to establish a local food supply. In 1679 the city was expanded greatly by Simon van der Stel, an energetic governor whose ambition was to build a new Holland in Southern Africa. It was he who established viticulture in the fertile valleys inland, founding Stellenbosch first and then settling a group of Huguenots displaced by the French revolution in Franschhoek.

The French Revolution was the spur that applied British energies to Cape Town. Although

previously the English had been at war with Holland the two monarchies made common cause against the new French republic and were determined that so valuable a strategic waterway should be kept away from the fervent guillotining Gauls. Liberty, Fraternity, and Equality were not qualities desired at home or abroad, and as the Dutch East India Company was, by this stage, a royal bankrolled bankrupt, the British took power at the Battle of Muizenberg in 1795.

This brought the Cape within the huge industrialized British economy. The scrap standard of exchange had long perished and the food the Cape was producing, from farms run by Boers, was expensive. The British solution was to import slaves from Madagascar and East India. Production increased but the Boers were not impressed, heading off into the interior in search of land that was free of intrusive British Governance.

One factor limiting development was the weather: every winter, storms would roll into the natural harbor, sinking ships and killing sailors. In 1745 a breakwater was half-built, and in 1831 two stone piers were constructed. None were proof against the powerful northwest winds that hurtled up from the polar ice cap and battered the shallow natural harbor. Plans were drawn up for an enclosed haven in 1856 but the British dithered about the cost. The final encouragement needed came in 1857 when a storm blew into Table Bay, destroying 16 major ships and many boats. Lloyds of London refused to insure ships moored in the Cape and in 1860 Prince Alfred, Queen Victoria's 16-year-old son, tipped the first rocks into the ocean. Ten years later the harbor, one of the great civil engineering achievements of the Victorian Era, was completed.

Sheltered by the brooding bulk of Table Mountain, Cape Town's City Hall.

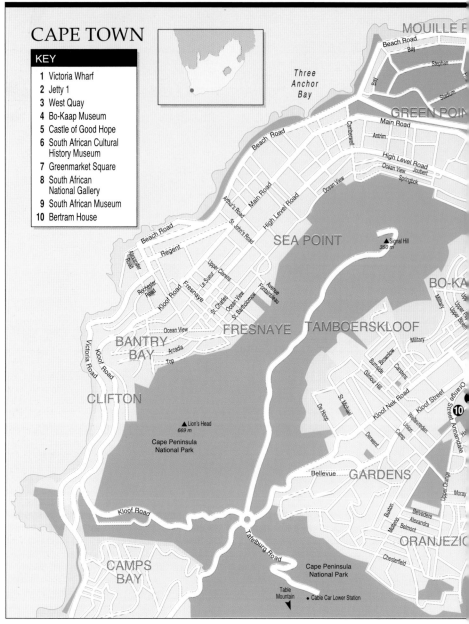

CAPE TOWN

KEY

1 Victoria Wharf
2 Jetty 1
3 West Quay
4 Bo-Kaap Museum
5 Castle of Good Hope
6 South African Cultural History Museum
7 Greenmarket Square
8 South African National Gallery
9 South African Museum
10 Bertram House

At about the same time diamonds and gold were discovered inland, changing Cape Town from a minor port of strategic importance into a world-class trading center, and the port grew to accommodate the increase in traffic. Ambitious schemes of land reclamation were to follow, and it was only in 1945 that the port arrived at its current shape. Reclaimed land has allowed the city to expand over the sea, which explains why many of the oldest parts of Cape Town are no longer near the waterfront.

That's not the only change the city has seen. The apartheid years also left scars. Most famously the District Six area of low-rent housing around the City Bowl was cleared, with the inhabitants forcibly moved out to the windswept and featureless Cape Flats to the east of town, to join the densely-populated shacks of Africans from elsewhere in the country.

Today Cape Town is one of the most cosmopolitan of all South Africa's cities. Black Africans, however, do not form the majority. The largest

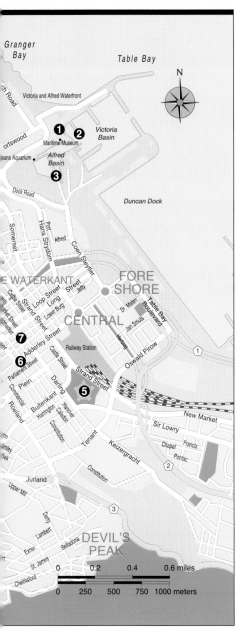

France, but the reality is wetter, windier, and far more dramatic, changing fast with four seasons passing in a single day.

GENERAL INFORMATION

The city is dominated by the bulk of Table Mountain, flanked by the Devil's Peak and trailing off into the serried ranks of the Twelve Apostles. These land features are the most reliable landmarks for easy orientation. Unlike most other coastal cities, the sea in Cape Town is apt to confuse as it rolls into inlets and bays, a plethora of beaches and cliffs to the east and west of the city itself. Downtown — the Central Business District (CBD) — is small and compact, and through the day is safe enough to explore on foot, while the cable car up Table Mountain and the restored shops and restaurants of the Victoria and Alfred Waterfront are short rides southwest and northeast respectively, by taxi or by city bus.

For orientation information, an initially confusing range of organizations can help, frequently and unhelpfully rebranded with new names and titles. The best for information about central Cape Town is **Cape Metropolitan Tourism** ((021) 426 4260 FAX (021) 487 2977 E-MAIL cmt@cmc.gov.za, Ninth Floor, Tarquin House, at the corner of Shortmarket and Loop streets, in the CBD, Box 16548, Vlaeberg 8018. It is open 8 AM to 4:45 PM daily. Note that the old offices in Adderley Street are now closed. There is also a new information center for **Cape Town Tourism** ((021) 426 4260 FAX (021) 426 4266 E-MAIL captour@iafrica.com, at the corner of Castle and Burg streets, Box 1403, Cape Town 8000, offering perhaps the most up-to-date service.

There are also peripheral information offices which are often more convenient for visitors. One of the best is the **Victoria and Alfred Waterfront Information Center** ((021) 418 2369 FAX (021) 425 2165 E-MAIL info@waterfront.co.za WEB SITE www .waterfront.co.za, Box 50001, Waterfront 8002, who have a central office in the Waterfront's Union Castle Building open from 9 AM to 6 PM daily and a further kiosk in the Victoria Wharf that stays open until 9 PM. There is also an office at the airport, which is helpful if arriving by plane.

For information about the Western Cape overall, the place to ask is the provincial **Western Cape Tourism Board** ((021) 914 4613 FAX (021) 914 4610 E-MAIL webcape@iafrica.com WEB SITE www .waterfront.co.za, Box 3878, Tyger Valley 7536, office hours only.

The **D. F. Malan International Airport** ((021) 937 1200 is 22 km (14 miles) from the city center along a fast road. Outside rush hour it takes little more than 20 minutes from the town center. Several of the major car rental companies have offices at the airport. Although a rental car is not abso-

ethnic grouping is of colored people, consisting largely of Cape Malay, a distinctive racial group descended from slaves brought over by the British, but including a whole rainbow that has evolved through 500 years of settlement and change.

Constant interaction with Europe has given the city a Mediterranean atmosphere, something that is accentuated by its climate, which is, unlike most of the country, temperate. The tourist board will tell visitors it's the climate of Mediterranean

lutely essential for Cape Town, which has a reasonable train and bus network, it certainly makes life easier, and a drive around the Cape is one of the "must-do" activities. There is a **Magic Shuttle bus** ((021) 934 5455 FAX (021) 934 5448, which travels to any hotel in the Cape peninsula, as does the **Intercape Shuttle** ((021) 386 4444 FAX (021) 943 0702. To take in the highlight sights the 15-seat **Waterfront Shuttle** ((021) 418 2369 does the circuit between the airport, the waterfront, and Table Mountain Aerial Cableway. **Airport taxis** are specially licensed and are required by law to use their meters. Expect to pay about R150 to the center of town and more for the suburbs.

Once in the town center, **Rikkis** ((021) 423 4888 are tourist-orientated, eight-seat minibuses that cruise around the city center or can be called to order. Fares are between R7 and R15. Metered taxis don't cruise the streets, although they can often be found around the major attractions; it's safest to call in to be picked up. Reliable taxi companies **Unicab** ((021) 448 1720, **Marine Taxi Hire** ((021) 434 0434, and **Sea Point Taxis** ((021) 434 4444.

If you're unfortunate enough to need a hospital, the largest is **Groote Schuur** ((021) 404 9111, Hospital Drive, Observatory, while the **Somerset Hospital** ((021) 402 6911, Beach Road, Mouille Point is nearer to the CBD and City Bowl. As long as your insurance is up to it, best go for **Western Cape Paramedics** ((021) 551 6823 TOLL-FREE 0800 225 599, with 24-hour land and air response. While Cape Town is one of the safer cities in South Africa, it is still possible to run into trouble here, especially after dark: the **Flying Squad** (1011 is backed by a **Tourist Assistance Unit** ((021) 418 2853.

WHAT TO SEE AND DO

There is more to see here than in any other South African city. The historic heart of the city is the Central Business District (CBD). There are many further activities and attractions in the southern suburbs and out towards the Winelands, all of which will be presented by region later. The top attraction, in terms of visitor numbers, is undoubtedly the Victoria and Alfred Waterfront. With a selection of hotels for all budgets adjoining or inside the development, many visitors never see Cape Town beyond the Waterfront.

The Waterfront

The **Victoria and Alfred Waterfront** ((021) 418 2369 has a collection of 240 shops, 42 restaurants, eight pubs, seven hotels and 11 cinemas, as well as an extensive crafts market and countless street entertainers. "That's what we call a working harbor" is their sales line and it has certainly worked as a tourist attraction: it attracts more visitors than any other part of South Africa. After 30 years of

neglect and stagnation the area was redeveloped and finally opened to the world in 1990. Orientation is easy and the Waterfront has one of the city's best views of Table Mountain.

Much of the development is little more than a scatter of huge neo-Victorian shopping malls. The quality of the goods on sale here is high but then so are the prices: retailers need to recoup some of the highest shop rents in the continent. Goods on sale here are very likely to be imported; although indigenous South African products are represented, there are plenty of European and American imports too. There are some goods imported from elsewhere in Africa, almost always of far higher quality than those laid out on plastic sheets at, for example, Sunday's Sea Point Market, and for visitors there is the significant advantage that there is little chance here of being robbed or mugged. The Victoria and Alfred Waterfront is firmly policed and two bombs in 1999 did little to dispel the atmosphere of security. In the unlikely event of any serious occurrence the gates of the complex would be shut until the problem was solved. The disadvantage is that goods here are twice the price.

But step out of the shopping malls and you'll find that the distinctive South African welcome has managed to establish itself in other parts of the Waterfront development. There are friendly bars where locals mix easily with foreign tourists. In this melting pot city this is not just a tourist ghetto. The rebuilt colonial buildings, colored pastel against the flat protected waters of the harbor, are undoubtedly beautiful.

There are a few significant attractions here that aren't purely retail. One is the **Two Oceans Aquarium** ((021) 418 3823 FAX (021) 418 2064 E-MAIL aquarium@twoocean.co.za WEB SITE www .aquarium.co.za, Dock Road. Among the extensive exhibits of fish in their natural habitats there is also a full skeleton of a whale and a huge tank that recreates ancient kelp forest, patrolled by a number of fully grown, ragged-tooth sharks and a huge stingray. Walking around this exhibit is impressive enough, and qualified divers can share the experience. In all more than 3,000 live organisms are on view. For children there's a touch pool where they can touch some of the deep-sea animals, though not the jellyfish, suspended strikingly in freestanding tanks lit by ultraviolet light.

One headline experience that cannot be repeated elsewhere is a **Robben Island Cruise** ((021) 419 2875 FAX (021) 419 2876 E-MAIL embark@ RobbenIsland.org.za WEB SITE www.robbenisland .co.za, terminal on Jetty 1 and the Clocktower, adjacent to Bertie's Landing. These cruises leave on the hour throughout the day from 9 AM to 3 PM and take about three and a half hours. The cost is R100 per person, although during the off season of June and July the first cruise of the day, at 9 AM, is half price. Many companies offer Robben Island tours on the waterfront, but this is the only operator licensed to actually land. After making the 25-minute crossing on board a comfortable catamaran, ex-prisoners are your guide to the island with a history dating back 400 years.

The island has been used as a whaling station, a hospital, and a mental asylum. It has housed banished slaves from Angola and West Africa, lepers, South African chiefs, and princes from the East. More recently it was used as a prison that housed a number of South Africa's political prisoners, including, for many years, Nelson Mandela.

.co.za WEBSITE www.robbenisland.co.za, who offer a range of cruises from R35 per person.

Other attractions that are less dependent on the weather include the **Imax Cinema** ((021) 419 7364, Dock Road, R30, with a five-story screen, and **Cyberworld** ((021) 419 0098, Alfred Wharf, open 9 AM to 11:30 PM, R40, where four-seat pods hurtle (virtually) through a range of fast-moving adventures. The emphasis is again on the hi-tech in the **Telkom Exploratorium** ((021) 419 5957, Union Castle Building, Market Square, open Tuesday to Sunday from 9 AM to 6 PM, R10, which explores the magic of telecommunications with hands-on exhibits and a laser show. Glancing back to the past the **South African Maritime Museum**

In 1996 it changed from prison to museum, and also serves as a sanctuary for a number of bird and seal species. The history of the island, recorded in photographs and memories, is vividly brought to life. This is also one of the easiest ways to get away from the city bustle, washed by the ocean waters.

Take the first ferry opportunity available to you though: if the weather forecast is bad — not unusual in Cape Town — sailings are cancelled, and many visitors who miss their first chance to experience Robben Island don't get another. While none of the other cruise boats are allowed to land on Robben Island some are still worthwhile, just for the chance to sail around and admire the spectacular coastline that shelters Table Bay. One of the best is aboard the 18-m (58-ft) Gaff rigged Schooner the *Spirit of Victoria* ((021) 418 5806 FAX (021) 418 5821 E-MAIL adventures@dockside

((021) 419 2505, Dock Road, open daily from 10 AM to 5 PM, R5, is appropriately set in one of the world's most strategically important harbors. There are restored boats, a period shipwright's workshop and displays covering some of the most notable shipwrecks that strew the waters off the often stormy Cape.

Table Mountain

Landmark, beauty spot and Cape Town playground, Table Mountain is always there. To visit the city without going up Table Mountain is almost unthinkable, with the various options for getting up being explored more fully elsewhere (see CLIMB TABLE MOUNTAIN, page 14 in TOP SPOTS). This is another Cape Town activity that should be done

As night falls, the Victoria and Alfred Waterfront lights up as the country's favorite tourist destination.

at the earliest opportunity: when the weather is good, go. Too often the top is clouded with the "Tablecloth," a blanket of cloud slipping off the summit and obscuring the view, and when the wind gets up the Aerial Cableway suspends service without much notice. If it's calm and sunny on the first day of your stay, don't delay.

The **Aerial Cableway** ((021) 424 8181, Tafelberg Road (open November 8 AM to 9:30 PM, December through January from 7 AM to 10:30 PM, February through April 8 AM to 9:30 PM, and May to October 8:30 AM to 3:30 PM), operates two cable cars, each carrying 65 people up the mountain. The cost of tickets is R45 to R65 round trip, depending on the season.

want to commit yourself in advance, but for most people the trip up the sheer upper slopes by the Cableway is a pretty effective deterrent.

The City Bowl

Cradled by the gentle lower slopes of Table Mountain, the inner suburbs and the Central Business District are known as the City Bowl. It is here that you'll find most of the stately buildings dating back to the city's early years, gently set in the original **Company Gardens**, established to grow the first European produce to provision passing ships. Now the gardens are a pleasant inner-city park, still with some recognizably imported plants. Starting from the top of Kloof Street and the land-

Another popular alternative is to take a **helicopter** flip around the mountain. Two companies offering this are **Civair** ((021) 419 5182 FAX (021) 419 5183 E-MAIL civair@mweb .co.za, and **Court Helicopters** ((021) 425 2966 FAX (021) 425 1941 WEB SITE www.court-helicopters.co.za. Prices for both are R1,800 for a four-seat and R2,400 for a six-seat chopper taking a half-hour tour.

If the urge strikes, it is possible to see Table Mountain from the inside. **Adventure Village** ((021) 424 1580 FAX (021) 424 1590 E-MAIL info @adventure-village.co.za WEB SITE www .adventure-village.com are the people to show you where the caves are. For the ultimate buzz, **Abseil Africa** ((021) 425 4332 E-MAIL abseil@iafrica.com WEB SITE www.adventurevillage.co.za, 229 Long Street, offers the opportunity to abseil from the top of Table Mountain. There are usually representatives on the top of the mountain if you don't

mark Mount Nelson Hotel there's an easy downhill stroll that takes in many of the best of the City Bowl sights. **Bertram House** ((021) 424 9381, at the corner of Orange Street and Government Lane, open Tuesday to Saturday 9:30 AM to 4:30 PM, R3, was the property of a wealthy British lawyer called John Barker and vividly evokes the privileged lives of South Africa's early wealthy professionals, with a collection of period silver and furniture. As a gesture to the New South Africa one room has been turned over to some rather average Zulu beadwork.

Just down the hill from here is the oldest museum in Sub-Saharan Africa, the **South African Museum and Planetarium** ((021) 424 3330 FAX (021) 424 6716, 25 Queen Victoria Street, founded in 1925 and open daily from 10 AM to 5 PM, R7. This is one of the country's finest museums of natural history, with displays including the only preserved specimen of the extinct quagga (a southern African zebra) and huge, free-floating skeletons of whales in a four-story "Whale Well," echoing with plaintive recorded sounds. Attached to the museum is a planetarium, with shows daily at 1 PM and on Tuesday evenings at 8 PM, introducing the very different constellations of the southern hemisphere. More controversially, the museum also includes a very thorough collection of tribal artifacts, examples of San rock art hewn from the Cederberg and Drakensberg Mountains and a set of displays relating to South Africa's indigenous people. Many South Africans are now unsure these belong in what is primarily a museum of natural history.

Across Government Avenue is the **South African National Gallery** ((021) 424 3330 FAX (021) 424 6716, Botanical Gardens, open Monday to Sunday 10 AM to 5 PM, R5, once known for paintings by the great European masters, although sanctions and the collapse of the rand have forced it to change direction. For the visitor this is a good thing: it now houses important collections by indigenous artists and hosts traveling shows. Call to see what's currently on display. Drop down the hill some more to South Africa's **Houses of Parliament** ((021) 403 2460, at the corner of Parliament Street and Government Lane, which offers tours Monday to Friday at 11 AM, with afternoon tours at 2:30 PM Monday to Thursday; admission is free. When parliament is in session from January to June it is possible to sit in on sessions; you'll need your passport to be admitted. If there are any foreign dignitaries around, the guest seats are usually filled with officials so you won't get in. It's pretty gloomy anyway.

The long, low building down from here is the **South African Cultural History Museum** ((021) 461 8280, 49 Adderley Street, open Monday to Saturday 9:30 AM to 4:30 PM, R5. Once a house for slaves working in the Company Gardens, it now has two displays, one with a collection of archaeological artifacts from around the world and the other celebrating black and white cultures in South Africa. To the east is the **Castle of Good Hope** ((021) 469 1249, Bultenkant, the oldest building in South Africa now restored with antiques and collections of militaria and maritime artifacts. Guided tours occur at 11 AM, noon, and 2 PM; admission is R12. At noon the changing of the guard is a bit of a spectacle.

Cross back over Government Lane, which this far downtown has now become Adderley Street, once *the* place to shop, but now somewhat decayed. The next landmark is **St. George's Cathedral** in Wale Street, open daylight hours, which looks from the outside like an oversized Welsh church but has some fine modern stained-glass by Gabriel Loire and, of course, the long history befitting the seat of Archbishop Desmond Tutu. Climbing now,

towards Signal Hill, and the **Old Town House** ((021) 424 6367, Greenmarket Square, open Monday to Friday from 10 AM to 5 PM and Saturday from 10 AM to 4 PM, free, was once a base for the eighteenth century volunteer police force, but is now a gallery with some important Dutch and Flemish art works.

If you've followed this tour you'll be artworked to exhaustion, but continue up towards Signal Hill and take a walk through **Bo-Kaap**, the city's Malay quarter, where the small, brightly-painted cubic houses comprise one of the only nonwhite areas of the city center. It is possible to be guided on a walking tour — contact **Tana Baru Tours** ((021) 424 0719 FAX (021) 423 2279, 3 Morris Street — or

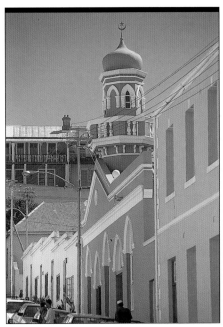

just stroll around on your own. For some background information the **Bo-Kaap Museum** ((021) 424 3846, 71 Wale Street, open Monday to Saturday 9:30 AM to 4:30 PM, R3, recreates the house of a nineteenth-century South African Muslim. At noon the suburb echoes with the sound of the **Noon Sun Gun** that fires from Signal Hill, overhead.

Around Cape Town: Table Mountain's Eastern Slopes

The N2 moves out from the city center around the lower slopes of Table Mountain and then the M63 curves up on the mountain's inland flank. Ten kilometers (six miles) from the city center are the **Kirstenbosch National Botanical Gardens** ((021) 762 9120 or (021) 762 1166 (for

OPPOSITE: The magic of mountains helps make Cape Town one of the world's most beautiful cities. ABOVE: Pastel buildings in the Malay quarter.

guided walks) FAX (021) 792 3229, Rhodes Drive, Newlands, open daily April to August 8 AM to 6 PM, September to March 8 AM to 7 PM; admission R10. Not only are these a good jumping-off point for climbs up Table Mountain (see CLIMB TABLE MOUNTAIN, page 14 in TOP SPOTS), they are also a must for anyone interested in South Africa's natural world. Six thousand of South Africa's 22,000 plant species are grown in the gardens, with 900 more spreading up the unfenced shoulder of Table Mountain. There are 36 hectares (nearly 90 acres) of cultivated gardens, marked out in informative trails including fragrance trails and even a Braille trail for the blind. Guided walks set out from the information center at 11 AM on Tuesdays and Saturday to introduce the nearer plants of interest, but the estate spreads out over 530 hectares (1,300 acres) in all, an invaluable treasure-trove of natural plant life. There's history too: the original almond hedge planted in 1660 to deter Khoikhoi rustlers, the only living evidence of Jan van Riebeeck's first landing, is still there. In summer months classical concerts are held in the gardens on Sundays, and the restaurant, once charming-but-basic, offering fish and chips to botanists in all-weather jackets, has been revamped into two restaurants: the Proted for self-service and Silver Leaves ((021) 762 9585 for à la carte dining.

Further south along the eastern slopes of Table Mountain are some of the oldest of the farms and vineyards in the country, established in the early years of settlement and still offering refined restaurants and sophisticated wine tasting just a few minutes from the city center. Perhaps the best is **Groot Constantia Museum** ((021) 794 5067 FAX (021) 794 7697, Constantia Main Road (M41), open 10 AM to 5 PM, admission R5, founded in 1685 by Governor Simon van der Stel, who planted the first vines. Time has not treated the estate gently: In 1860 phylloxera ruined the vines and in 1925 the Manor house burned to the ground. Both, however, are on the way back. The vineyards are once again producing desert wines and the elegant Cape Dutch House has been rebuilt and carefully restored to its former glory in dark, eighteenth-century style. There is also a museum of wine and cellars, with guided tours, and a restaurant in the old stables.

East of here the **Cape Flats** extend over featureless flatlands. Covered in shanties, these are not safe for unescorted tourists. If you want to experience this, very different, Cape Town, it is best to use an established tour operator such as **One City Tours** ((021) 426 4644 FAX (021) 423 5417, 1 Church Street, Cape Town 8000, which offers a range of tours including a Gospel Tour departing from the Grand Parade in front of City Hall — bookings are essential.

SPORTS AND OUTDOOR ACTIVITIES

Leisure is very important to Capetonians and there are full facilities for every sort of sport, on sea and on land. Spectator sports include **cricket**, with the main ground being at Newlands Cricket Ground ((021) 644146, 61 Campground Road, Newlands. If there are any important matches happening here *not* hearing about it will be your problem. **Rugby** takes place in the same area at Western Province Rugby Union Football Union ((021) 689 4921, Boundary Road, Newlands. **Horseracing** takes place most weekends at the Kenilworth Racecourse ((021) 797 5140 FAX (021) 762 1919, Rosemead Avenue, Kenilworth.

There is a huge range of participation sports available. For **diving**, a wetsuit is almost enough, though a dry-suit is better for exploring the kelp forests and shipwrecks of the area. Contact Two Ocean Divers (/FAX (021) 438 9317 E-MAIL campsbay@intekom.co.za WEB SITE www.two-ocean.co.za, 1 Central Parade, Victoria Road, Camps Bay 8001, or Table Bay Diving ((021) 419 8822 FAX (021) 418 5821 E-MAIL condor@iafrica.com, Box 50667, Waterfront 8002. For **surf skiing**, **kayaking**, and **sea canoeing** contact Coastal Kayak Trails ((021) 439 1134.

Mountain biking is a good, if strenuous, way to explore the area; one operator renting out bikes and providing maps and, if required, guides, is Rent 'n' Ride ((021) 434 1122, 1 Park Road, Mouille Point.

The best-placed **golf** course is the Milnerton Course ((021) 562 1097, Bridge Road, Milnerton, with great views of Table Mountain, while others include the Rondebosch Golf Club ((021) 689 4176, Klipfontein Road, Rondebosch, and the Royal Cape Golf Club ((021) 761 6551 FAX (021) 797 5246, Ottery Road, Wynberg, is the major venue for international events but does not rent equipment. Expect to pay about R100 in green fees. Perhaps the best starting point is the Action Golf Center ((021) 419 6767 on the Waterfront, which offers information about your many options.

Fishing is strictly controlled and getting through the bureaucracy daunting for a visitor. It is best to go through a charter operator such as African Fishing Safaris ((021) 438 5201 or Bluefin Charters ((021) 783 1756 in Hout Bay. For an overall range of adventure options contact the **South Africa Adventure Center** ((021) 419 1704, 48A Strand Street, with a number of operators representing their services. **Surfing** in Cape Town is largely a do-it-yourself experience, but at least surf reports are provided for the Atlantic Seaboard ((021) 557 4783 and for False Bay ((021) 788 1350.

Kirstenbosch Botanical Gardens contain 6,000 of South Africa's 22,000 plant species: the sixth floral kingdom.

SHOPPING

By far the greatest concentration of shops is in the Victoria and Alfred Waterfront, and although all tend to be expensive some offer quality goods that you won't find anywhere else. My personal favorite is **Fellowes Interiors** ((021) 419 5555, Shop 6115, with a range of crafts from South Africa, including a charming set of fat sunbathing blondes made from plaster, and crafts from elsewhere in Africa. The cast of Tintin characters from the Côte d'Ivoire are irresistibly collectable. **Vaughan Johnson's Wineshop** ((021) 419 2121, Pierhead, Dock Road, offers a good selection of

Cape wines, especially useful if you are leaving on Sunday and find the Winelands closed. Although it is irritating that an establishment that so blatantly caters to the tourist market stops visitors taking photographs of its racked displays of bottles, at least this is one place which is open seven days a week. For jewelry **Charles Greig Jewelers** ((021) 418 4515, Waterfront, has a sophisticated selection at a price, while the **Everard Read Art Gallery** ((021) 418 4527, Victoria Wharf, is a good place to buy South African art. You'll find a full set of smaller, cheaper goods at the Waterfront's **Red Shed** craft market.

Although the CBD is not the shopping center it once was, Long and Church Streets are still the place to look for antiques, while Cavendish Street is known for its interior design shops. Although the Waterfront dwarfs the other shopping malls, two of the best are Cavendish Square,

in Claremont, and the Gardens Center in the Company Gardens. On Sundays **Green Point Market** collects traders from all over Africa in a strolling flea market where a huge range of goods, from discarded household junk to rare sculptures from Zaire, are sold. Watch out for pickpockets here.

WHERE TO STAY

Waterfront and City Bowl

For travelers who like the safe, contained environment of the Victoria and Alfred Waterfront, there is a range of hotels in all budgets that are actually part of the development. At the top end

is the **Cape Grace Hotel** ((021) 410 7100 FAX (021) 419 7622 E-MAIL reservations@capegrace.com WEB SITE www.grace.co.za, West Quay, R2,400, one of the country's smartest hotels with every facility you can think of and a few more. It's consistently winning awards and overlooks the waterfront marina, a few minute's walk from the main malls and markets. At the heart of the development is the **Victoria and Alfred Hotel** ((021) 406 1911. The **Table Bay Sun International Hotel** ((021) 406 5000 FAX (021) 406 5050 adjoins the Victoria Wharf shopping center and the Hard Rock Café. On the far side of the Waterfront craft market is the mid-range **Portswood Hotel** ((021) 421 5264 FAX (021) 419 7570, while a few minutes further on is the budget option: the **Breakwater Lodge** ((021) 406 1911 TOLL-FREE (0800) 233 255 FAX (021) 406 1070 E-MAIL brkwater@fortesking-hotels.co.za, Portswood Road, Sea Point, R215 with shared facilities, R360 en-suite. Once a city-center prison, this now offers lodgings that might still have a touch of the institutional along the long corridors lined with small rooms (with baths), but certainly still offers exceptional value.

Grand *doyen* towards the top of the City Bowl is the **Mount Nelson Hotel** ((021) 423 1050 FAX (021) 424 7472, 76 Orange Street, Gardens, R2,000 room only, perfectly placed for the CBD's attractions in daytime but at night inhabited by small bands of marauding boys — who can mug, although they are relatively easily scared. The same caveat applies to the few remaining city center hotels, and several have closed or moved out. The **Cape Sun Inter-Continental** ((021) 488 5100

for up to three sharing, but it's a shame to stay in such a formulaic environment in this vibey city.

There's also much to be said for staying in the quieter suburbs overlooking the CBD and Waterfront, where there are a number of really outstanding small hotels. In a city where the views are so important room rates vary not just with the season: the views also make a big difference. The **Table Mountain Lodge** ((021) 423 0042 FAX (021) 423 4983 E-MAIL tml@iafrica.com, 10A Tamboerskloof Road, Tamboerskloof, R410, has a welcoming atmosphere, a friendly and informal bar and the rate includes a huge breakfast. **Mayville House** ((021) 461 9400 FAX (021) 461 9419 E-MAIL mayville@iafrica.com WEB SITE www

FAX (021) 423 8875, Strand Street, is a huge and modern eyesore sited on what used to be Cape Town's waterfront before land reclamation early in the 1900s. The institutional but central **Holiday Inn Garden Court Greenmarket Square** ((021) 423 2040 FAX (021) 423 6141, 10 Greenmarket Square, R600, has been converted from the old Shell headquarters. More character is found at the **Tudor House** ((021) 424 1335 FAX (021) 423 1198, Greenmarket Square, R500, which is small, warm and homely. **Rosedene Guest House** ((021) 424 3290 FAX (021) 424 3481 E-MAIL Deborah@rosedene .co.za WEB SITE www.rosedene.co.za, 28 Upper Kloof Street, Higgovale, R1,160 to 1,440 for bed and breakfast, is considerably smarter than most guest houses, with Balinese interior touches and great views. Emergency accommodation is available at the **Formule 1** ((021) 418 4664, Jan Smuts Avenue behind the Nico Malan Theatre, Waterfront, R145

.mayville.co.za, 21 Belvedere Avenue, Oranjezicht, R740 to R990, is an Edwardian mansion registered as a national monument, with white-painted gingerbread verandas overlooking Table Bay and the mountain. Of a similar standard is **Villa Belmonte** ((021) 462 1576 FAX (021) 462 1579 E-MAIL villabel @iafrica.com WEB SITE www.sih.ch, 33 Belmont Avenue, Oranjezicht, R830 to R1,250, is another restored mansion with a very good reputation for its restaurant.

To take a step down is not always easy. Bed-and-breakfasts are usually banned from advertising their accommodation with boards — the theory is it would make Cape Town look scrappy.

OPPOSITE LEFT: Upmarket mall means shopping in safety at the Victoria and Alfred Waterfront. RIGHT: Sidewalk vendors are more modestly priced. ABOVE: Built to impress, Parliament buildings in Cape Town.

Two in the smart suburbs in the City Bowl are **Parker Cottage B&B** (/FAX (021) 424 6445 E-MAIL pakerco@mweb.co.za WEB SITE www.bbnet.co.za/ parker_cottage, 3 Carstens Street, Tamboerskloof, R390, within walking distance of the Company Gardens, and **Villa Zeezicht** ((021) 424 2486 FAX (021) 423 7826 E-MAIL croux@mweb.co.za, 54 Buxton Avenue, Gardens, R350.

A far better option is to stay high above the Waterfront and also close to the city center adjoining the Bo-Kaap area in De Waterkant area, which is a safe area to walk around, even after dark. And it's one area where there are plenty of nightclubs and bars to walk to. Lavish bed-and-breakfast accommodation is available in

VICTORIA RI
·1837–1901·

De Waterkant Lodge (/FAX (021) 419 1097 or (083) 440 4040 E-MAIL waterknt@iafrica.com WEB SITE www.dewaterkant.co.za, 20 Loader Street, De Waterkant, where doubles cost R600 in season and much less in the austral winter. Better still, the manager here also operates 13 private cottages within this highly fashionable and characterful enclave. They can be rented by the night at a similar price, which can be negotiated downwards for longer stays or out of season. The cottages offer totally private bases to explore the city at your own pace. More cottages in the area are rented out by **Harbor View Cottages** ((021) 418 6031 FAX (021) 418 6082, Loader Street, De Waterkant. Perhaps because their office is more visible these are slightly more expensive, starting at R980 for at two-person, one-bed cottage.

A few backpacker hotels hang on in the CBD, including **Bob's Backpack & Bistro** ((021) 424 3584 FAX (021) 424 8223, 187 Long Street, above a

licensed bar, R50 for dormitory accommodation, and **Overseas Visitors Club** ((021) 423 4477 FAX (021) 423 4870 E-MAIL hross@ovc.co.za, 236 Long Street, which is small (18 beds), friendly and located over an Indian restaurant. **Long Street Backpackers** ((021) 423 0615, 209 Long Street, R40 for dormitory accommodation, is one of the original backpacker lodges.

The Seaside Strip

The city continues south of the Victoria and Albert Waterfront down the Atlantic seaboard with the districts of Green Point, which seethes with prostitutes and petty crime after dark; Sea Point, where you'll find many of the city's best restaurants; and Bantry Bay, which offers gentrified hotels. This strip is significantly cheaper than the City Bowl or Waterfront, with some relaxed and interesting accommodation. Frequent buses and minibuses link these areas with the city center, and they are not too far for Rikki's to travel either. Just outside Rikki range are the smarter suburbs of Clifton and Camps Bay.

There are several good options at the upper end of the market. In Sea Point the **Clarendon** ((021) 439 3224 FAX (012) 434 6855 E-MAIL clarendon@dockside.co.za, 67 Kloof Road, R600 to R1,200, is a bed-and-breakfast with seven en-suite guest rooms in elegant, chic surroundings. The **Movenpick Arthur's Seat** ((021) 434 3344 FAX (021) 434 0557 E-MAIL arthurs.seat@ movenpick.co.za, Arthur's Road, Sea Point, R900, is between Lion's Head and Table Mountain. At the top of the scale in Bantry Bay is the out-and-out luxury of **Ellerman House** ((021) 439 9182 FAX (021) 434 7257, 180 Kloof Road, Bantry Bay, R2,000 upwards, where guests are surrounded by flunkies all desperate to pander to every whim. If the personal touch is the last thing you feel like for a stay in the city — and sometimes the relentless hospitality of small establishments can become a bit suffocating — the **Bantry Bay** ((021) 434 8448 FAX (021) 434 8212 E-MAIL bbrelais@satis.co.za WEB SITE www.relais .co.za, 8 Alexander Road, Bantry Bay, R500, provides luxurious self-contained apartments, somewhat battered by the ocean breeze when the wind gets up, set in a mixed area of character where local communities struggle on underneath increasing developments cashing in on the tourist industry.

There are plenty of alternatives. The **Villa Rosa** ((021) 434 2768 or (082) 785 3238 FAX (021) 434 3526, 277 High Level Road, Sea Point, R300 to R500, is friendly and convenient, and the **Casablanca Guest House** ((021) 434 1385 FAX (021) 439 5296 E-MAIL info@casablanca.co.za WEB SITE www.casablanca.co.za, 7 Avenue Fontainbleau, Fresnaye, R400 to R500, has just four bedrooms and a classic blend of Oriental and African decor. Alternatively the **Villa Sunshine** ((021) 439 8224 FAX (021) 439 8219 E-MAIL sunshine@kingsley.co.za, 1 Rochester Road, Bantry Bay, R400, has seven bedrooms, most with patios or balconies. For a larger establishment the **Winchester Mansions Hotel** ((021) 434 2351 FAX (021) 434 0215 E-MAIL winman@mweb.co.za, 221 Beach Road, Sea Point, has elegant rooms right on the waterfront. Prices range from R440, depending on view, and they also offer live jazz music on Sundays.

There are a number of backpacker options in the area. **St. John's Waterfront Lodge** ((021) 439 1404 FAX (021) 439 1424 E-MAIL fedgeof@mweb .co.za, 4/6 Braemar Road, Green Point, R35 for

Constantia 7848, R800 to R2,200, with sheltered chalets set in the manor's own vineyards, a cricket pitch, and a choice of two truly excellent restaurants serving Provençal cuisine. My cousin, on the other hand, prefers the **Cellars Hohenhort** ((021) 794 2137 FAX (021) 794 2149 E-MAIL cellars@ct.lia.net WEB SITE www.cellars-hohenhort.com, Box 270, Constantia 7848, R2,400 to R5,000, but then he's a banker, which you need to be to stay in this luxury establishment. It also boasts of its Gary Player-designed one-hole golf course, which frankly doesn't have me reaching for my checkbook. Close runner-up is the **Alphen** ((021) 794 5011 FAX (021) 794 5010 E-MAIL reservations@alphen.co.za, Box 35,

dormitory accommodation, is one. Though it is not on the waterfront it has a good atmosphere and a friendly bar. **Birds Eye View** ((021) 434 4143, 55 High Level Road, Green Point, offers dormitory accommodation in a large family house from R35 per person.

Constantia

On the western, Kirstenbosch side of Table Mountain the exclusive Constantia Valley has some of the finest small and exclusive hotels. You won't find any backpacker lodges or public transportation out here but there's plenty of choice at the top of the market for travelers with a rental car. There's hot competition and regular guests get fanatical about their favorites. Mine is the **Constantia Uitsig Country Hotel** ((021) 794 6500 FAX (021) 794 7605 E-MAIL res@ilink.co.za WEB SITE www.constantiauitsig.co.za, Box 32,

Constantia 7800, which glows with the patina of ancient woods and is priced more reasonably at R800 to R1,200.

In the same area but more modest are the **Constantia Manor** ((021) 794 5417 FAX (021) 794 7371 E-MAIL conmanor@intekom.co.za, 10 Croft Road, off Klein Constantia Road, Constantia 7806, R600; or **Arderne Lodge** ((021) 794 1672 FAX (021) 794 4504 E-MAIL hohenhort@mweb.co.za, 9 Spilhaus Avenue, Constantia 7806, R700 to R900. Meanwhile, to the east of one of the smartest and most exclusive semi-rural suburbs of the country are the endless shanties of the Cape Flats, where inner-city blacks were banished during the apartheid years: poor, windswept, and squalid this is not a place to stray without a guide.

OPPOSITE: Queen Victoria looks down over her long-lost empire. ABOVE: Cape Town has a great variety of restaurants to appeal to all tastes.

WHERE TO EAT

Capetonians make much of the distinctive influence of Malay spices in their cuisine, but the truth is they look more to Europe for their inspiration, and some of the finest restaurants reflect the traditions of Italy and France. This is not to say the cuisine isn't very good: there's a discerning clientele, a tradition of fine wines and, perhaps most importantly, easy access to the freshest ingredients from the temperate farmlands that surround the city and seafood so radiantly fresh it practically jumps from the plate.

((021) 423 0850, on the corner of Wale and Pentz Streets, but it takes itself a little seriously and alcohol isn't permitted. In the town center, **Kaapse Tafel** ((021) 423 1651, 90 Queen Victoria Street, serves the staples of Cape cuisine: *waterblommetjie bredie*, *smoorsnoek*, and *bobotie* (traditional vegetable, fish, and meat dishes, respectively) served in a plain, rustic decor. Closed Sunday.

For those who can put up with rude service, there's some good Italian food, especially fresh from the sea, at **Nino's Restaurant** ((021) 424 7246, 52 Shortmarket Street. In a country famous for its steaks perhaps the best are served at **Hatfield's Restaurant** ((021) 465 7387, 129 Hatfield Street, which also serves seafood and pizzas at very good

The City Bowl is long on atmosphere and is a good nightlife center, but some of the best restaurants have joined the great South African rush to the suburbs. The highest standards are still maintained in the refined dining rooms of the **Mount Nelson Hotel** (see WHERE TO STAY, page 85), but the streets running down to the city center set a more casual, quicker standard. A great stop, better known for its live music drawn from all over Africa than its menu, drawn from every country from Morocco south, is **Mama Africa** ((021) 424 8634, 178 Long Street. Above the bar a chandelier made from 500 Coca Cola bottles sets the tone, and it's a fun evening venue, open from 7 PM until late. For an even funkier West African experience, try the **Africa Café** ((021) 447 9553, Lower Main Road, Observatory. Waiters greet guests in traditional *kente* garb to the background of a thudding bass line. For Cape cuisine, with its spicy Malay tang, the established restaurant is **Biesmillah**

rates. **Mario's** ((021) 439 6644, 89 Main Road, Green Point, is an exceptional restaurant, run by the same family for 29 years, and is the perfect place for a leisurely Italian meal with a bottle of wine, well placed for escapees from the Waterfront heading south. In the CBD, southern Italian food is well served by the **Osteria Antico Dolo** ((021) 424 6334, 84 Long Street, lightly served with the minimum of cream and fresh, scarcely-cooked, fare subtly crated with imported pasta.

For more Gallic cuisine, there are few choices better than **Rozenhof** ((021) 424 1968, 18 Kloof Street, which is set in an elegant Georgian House off the beaten track. For a change, the trend of the year in Cape Town is currently Kurdish cuisine: give it a try at **Mesopotamia** ((021) 424 4664, on Long Street. It has *kilims* from Russia and Turkey with copper trays doubling as tables. For a light meal defying categorization try the **Café Erté** ((021) 434 6624, 265A Main Road, Sea Point.

The Victoria and Alfred Waterfront

The restaurants of the Victoria and Alfred Waterfront deserve a section to themselves. They're always popular through the day and easy and safe parking (without the need to pay a "guard" not to break into your car) keep them full long after the shops have rolled up their shutters and closed for the night. One of the best is the **Hildebrand Restaurant** ((021) 425 3385, Pierhead, serving fine Italian cuisine and fresh seafood on the water's edge. For fresh seafood cross the footbridge and try **Berties** ((021) 419 2727, while **Morton's** ((021) 418 3633 is currently packing them in. Most of the restaurants are of a similar standard, geared largely to an overseas market, and

browsing around until an aroma catches your fancy is as good a way as any to find the restaurant that suits your mood.

NIGHTLIFE

The Waterfront is a good place to start a night out in Cape Town. **Quay Four Bar**, on, unsurprisingly, Quay Four, often has live music on Wednesdays, Fridays and Saturdays, while across Market Square the **Ferrymans** often put on a show to match: usually these are cover versions of Western bands but fun for all that. The **Green Dolphin Jazz Restaurant**, Pierhead, puts on a jazzier show. Classical music can be seen at the **Nico Malan Theatre** ((021) 410 9800, DF Malan Street, Foreshore, and the **Baxter Theatre** ((021) 685 7880, Main Road, Rondebosch, but the best classical music is seasonal: played outdoors at the **Kirstenbosch Botanical Gardens** ((021) 762 9120, Rhodes Drive,

Newlands, and **Josephine Mill** ((021) 686 4939, Boundary Road, Newlands, on the Liesbeeck River, perfect summer venues for concerts al fresco. Theatre, such as it is, usually takes place in the Nico Theatre or the Baxter Theatre, but is sporadic. Check in a listings magazine such as the *Cape Review* (R7) for up-to-date programs.

Later on and the smartly dressed crowds gather around Kloof Street and Long Street in the CBD, with a number of late-opening clubs. Some of the best include **169 on Long**, 169 Long Street, the **Lounge**, 194 Long Street, with dark colors in an open and airy Victorian Building and **Mannenburg's Jazz Café**, Second Floor, Dumbarton House, Adderley and Church Streets, for township jazz. **Mama Africa** on Long Street serves African specialty food against a background of live African music, usually imported from further north, and **Café Camisa**, 80 Kloof Street, has a cool, chilled atmosphere with live music on Wednesdays and Sundays and good food. **Café Bordeli** on Kloof Street is the place to spot models, while late on Wednesdays, **Alien Safari**, 19 Dorp Street, attracts an artier crowd when electronic music is switched off and the venue is taken over by the sound of drums.

HOW TO GET THERE

Most visitors to Cape Town arrive by air at D.F. Malan International Airport (for travel details see GETTING THERE, page 250 in TRAVELERS' TIPS). For overland travel the train network offers links for short journeys up to the Winelands of Stellenbosch and Paarl as well as long overland voyages to the other cities in South Africa, which even if they're not that far, at a stately 40 kph (25 mph) they will start to feel it. The saving feature is that you can rent sleepers. First- and second-class tickets must be booked in advance. The railway station is on Strand Street in the heart of the CBD. For mainline reservations call ((021) 449 3871 (Spoornet/Mainline) or ((021) 403 9080 (Suburban/Metro).

Coaches are rather faster and leave from a terminal adjacent to the railway station. The main bus companies are **Greyhound** ((021) 418 4310; **Intercape** ((021) 386 4400, reservations a minimum of 72 hours in advance; **Translux** ((021) 449 3333, all with offices around 1 Adderley Street. It's not such a good area though: watch out for pickpockets.

As elsewhere in South Africa, however, car rental is the best way to go: without a car you'll miss some of Cape Town's finest experiences, such as driving the Southern Cape, the Winelands, and the Garden Route.

OPPOSITE: The Jewish Museum in Cape Town.
ABOVE: In South Africa, classical musicians travel to their audiences: here playing at the V&A Waterfront.

THE SOUTHERN CAPE

If the city of Cape Town is beautiful, it is nothing compared to the coastline that heads south past the white beaches of Clifton and Camps Bay and on to Queen Victoria Drive, a dramatic road skirting the lower slopes of the Twelve Apostles and dropping down to the long white swathe of sand at Hout Bay, then hugging the sheer cliffs in Chapman's Peak Drive. This is one of the most exhilarating self-drives in the country. The road is narrow and the tarmac surface is beginning to wear, but don't be put off, the views are spectacular. And if you're driving from Hout Bay heading south it's the other drivers who have to steer close to the sheer drop on the seaward side.

Chapman's Peak Drive continues to the small artistic suburb of Noordhoek and across the Cape to Simon's Town and south to the Cape of Good Hope Nature Reserve and Cape Point.

HOUT BAY

The beach at Hout Bay is one of the most fashionable, crowded with small catamarans, paddleskiers, and surfers in summer although it's a bit cold — and fishy — for swimming. The village itself, sheltered by milkwood trees, is also well worth a wander. Fish are the main draw here. The offshore waters are known for their yellowfin and longfin tuna, broadbill swordfish, and marlin. Those who prefer fish on a plate are also well catered to. On the waterfront **Mariner's Wharf** ((021) 790 1100 is a retail homage to fresh fish, with the day's catch temptingly displayed in reconstructed fishing boats set around a stained-wood emporium. If you want to learn more the **South African Fisheries Museum** ((021) 790 7268, open Tuesday to Sunday 10 AM to 4 PM, R2, is a fascinating collection of fishing memorabilia and information about the long tradition of harvesting the oceans. To see birds up close the largest bird park in Africa is nearby. The **World of Birds** ((021) 790 2730, Valley Road, Hout Bay, open daily 9 AM to 5 PM, R25, has walk-through aviaries containing 3,000 birds of 320 species in natural surroundings.

The Hout Bay **Tourist Information Office** ((021) 790 1264 FAX (021) 790 0456, Andrews Road, Box 27091, Hout Bay 7872, is open Monday to Friday 9 AM to 5 PM and weekends 10 AM to 1 PM. Hout Bay is 20 km (12.5 miles) from Cape Town, easy to drive to with your own car, and it can also be reached using local buses that leave from the terminal at Adderley Street in the CBD.

Where to Stay

The best place to stay here is the welcoming **Chapman's Peak Hotel** ((021) 790 1036, Main

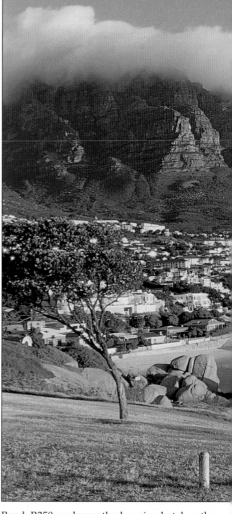

Road, R250, a pleasantly decaying hotel on the road out of Hout Bay at the start of Chapman's Peak Drive, with a large terrace overlooking the bay. If you don't mind self-catering the **Riverside Cottages** ((021) 790 7475 FAX (021) 790 8175 E-MAIL Riverside@Global.co.za, Welbevind Road, are a set of wooden chalets located in the Hout Bay Valley, sheltered by trees and flitted with birds. Cottage prices range from R300 to R1,500 per night. Overlooking the yacht marina is **Marlinspike Lodge** ((021) 790 7757 FAX (021) 790 7756 E-MAIL reservations@ marlinspike.com WEB SITE www.marlinspike.com, Marlin Crescent, R400 to R800. The backpacker option is **Whale House Rock Backpackers** ((021) 790 5849 FAX (021) 790 4087 E-MAIL pstaub@netactive.co.za, 9 York Close, but don't expect to see too many whales; there are more across the peninsula in False Bay.

NOORDHOEK

From Hout Bay the road (M6) climbs to a height of 600 m (nearly 2,000 ft) above the ocean and starts on the narrow but spectacular Chapman's Peak Drive road, snaking 10 km (just over six miles) along the shoulder of Chapman's Peak and the Silvermine Forest Reserve.

If it's been raining, "Road Closed Ahead" signs appear at regular intervals, obscuring but not blocking the road. Rain can dislodge boulders that fall on the road and, sometimes, drivers. The last driver this happened to sued the city authorities, hence the cautionary signs. The road is never finally, decisively, closed though, and if you're willing to take the risk this is actually a great time to do the drive as there's far less traffic. On a sunny day the road is a slightly tense mix of visitors traveling slowly and local BMWs testing their speed

and handling. There are plenty of blind corners and I'd rather risk the odd falling rock than impatient drivers.

Finally the road comes out at Noordhoek, a village at the heart of an agricultural region called "Sun Valley" now rapidly acquiring a reputation for its local artistic community as well as being one of the nearest areas to the city center where horseback riding is easy and rural. The best place to pick up local information is the **Noordhoek Farm Village**, just off the main road to the left, where among a scatter of craft shops you'll find a pleasantly chaotic **Tourist Information Office** ((021) 789 2812, open 9:30 AM to 5:30 PM daily. There's a restaurant, teashop and pub among the hanging batiks and wooden sculptures and it's a good place to break your journey.

The Twelve Apostles overlook Camps Bay.

Where to Stay

To stay longer, accommodation overlooking the village is available at **Logie Lodge** ((021) 785 3983 FAX (021) 785 4118 E-MAIL bydie@fast.co.za, 4 Yataghan Lane, Box 799, Sun Valley 7985, R300 to R700 (formerly Yataghan Lodge); **Afton Grove** ((021) 785 2992 FAX (021) 785 3456 E-MAIL afton@iafrica.com WEB SITE www.afton.co.za, Chapman's Peak Drive, Box 15, Noordhoek 7985, R400, which can arrange horse riding and bird watching excursions. On a budget **Montrose Cottages** (/FAX (021) 785 3730, 15 Chapman's Peak Drive, from R80 per person self-catering, also arrange rides on horses and camels.

ON TO FALSE BAY

The Cape Peninsula's mountainous spine lowers, and the road crosses here across to False Bay, so called because ships hauling home from the Indies frequently mistook this bay for Table Bay. There's no real point visiting the industrial town of Fish Hoek. Instead better turn south to Simon's Town, best known as home to the South African Navy.

SIMON'S TOWN

Simon's Town was founded in 1687 as a winter anchorage for the Dutch East India Company, but spent most of its life as a British possession. It was only handed back to South Africa in 1957. Its high street is Court Road, overlooking the ocean. Lined with the graceful gingerbread verandas of historic buildings it is best seen washed by the evening sun. Your first stop should be the **Tourist Information Office** ((021) 786 2436, Courts Road, open Monday to Friday 9 AM to 5:30 PM, Saturday 9 AM to 1 PM. The **Simon's Town Museum** ((021) 786 3046, Court Road, open Monday to Friday 9 AM to 4 PM, Saturday 10 AM to 4 PM, Sunday 11 AM to 4 PM, is located in the 1772 residence of the Dutch East India's governor, though it's since seen service as slave quarters and a brothel. Now it's rather tamer, with a collection of maritime material, much salvaged from shipwrecks and a fair display relating to whales, which can often be seen offshore. Next door the **Naval Museum** displays the inside of a submarine and various homages to the South African navy, though I emerged, blinking, still unsure as to what their great achievements had been to date.

Simon's Town's greatest draw is undoubtedly two kilometers (just over a mile) to the south: the unique **Boulders**. Stretching along the shoreline are a protected colony of jackass penguins, one of only two colonies on the African mainland, who frolic around the boulders and beaches while the humans get to watch from raised wooden walkways. Gates Four and Five overlook the largest colonies, while Gate Two leads down to a small beach where it's possible to swim with the penguins. The water in False Bay is a few degrees warmer than that on the Atlantic side of the peninsula, but even so this is a bracing activity only suited for warm days in the summer months. The views of False Bay and Table Mountain are spectacular, the penguins shuffling about their nesting business charming, and the whole experience tranquil and unforced. Admission to the park is R10, and a bargain.

Where to Stay and Eat

The best choice, for atmosphere rather than comfort or price, is the **British Hotel Apartments** (/FAX (021) 790 4930 or (082) 558 5689, 90 St. George Street, where three-bedroom apartments with sea-facing verandas in a restored Victorian building are let out with breakfast available on request. Rates are about R600 a night and it's well worth chasing for a reservation. Also overlooking the ocean are the well-equipped and spacious rooms of the **Quayside Lodge** ((021) 786 3838 FAX (021) 786 2241 WEB SITE www.quayside.co.za, St. George Street, R550, while below it **Bertha's Restaurant and Coffeehouse** ((021) 786 2138, 1 Wharf Road, serves delicious seafood and the town's finest coffee, on a terrace when the weather permits. Just up the road, the **Lord Nelson Inn** ((021) 786 1386 FAX (021) 786 1009, St. George Street, from R290, is the smallest three-star hotel in South Africa, according to its Scottish owner.

The best place to eat is five kilometers (three miles) south of town. The **Black Marlin Restaurant** ((021) 786 1621, Miller's Point, is an award-winning restaurant specializing in Cape rock lobster, linefish, and oysters. Unfortunately it's not a well-kept secret and attracts busloads of tourists. There's accommodation with the penguins in the **Boulders Beach Guesthouse** ((021)

786 1758 FAX (021) 786 1825 E-MAIL stumble@iafrica
.com, 4 Boulders Place, R300, with a restaurant,
called **Penguin Point**.

How to Get There

Simon's Town is about 40 km (25 miles) from Cape
Town via the southern suburbs and more like
60 km (37 miles) by the much more spectacular
coastal route described above. It is also at the end
of the Metro train line from Cape Town Railway
Station, an hour's journey, mostly along the coast.
Some trains terminate at Fish Hoek. For timetable
information call ((021) 507 2586. An alternative is
to take a round trip on **Biggsy's Restaurant Carriage & Wine Bar** ((021) 440 3870, which makes

it is a wild, windswept moor, ringed by cliffs
and ocean waters that have scuppered many a
ship in their long history. It's worth getting out
of your car, as the scrubby vegetation is actually nothing like as dull as it looks. This park
alone contains as many species as the British
isles and is a sort of dwarf *fynbos* found nowhere else in the world. There is also a great
number of endangered animal species, including the Cape mountain zebra, eland, bontebok,
hartebeest, striped mouse, and Cape gray mongoose. There are waymarked trails through the
park. For more details, and a timetable of
guided walks, contact the **Senior Nature Conservation Officer's Office** ((021) 780 1100

five return trips a day from Tuesday to Sunday,
serving drinks and meals. Demand often exceeds
supply despite an R3 booking surcharge, so do
book in advance.

CAPE OF GOOD HOPE

The road continues south from Simon's Town to
the **Cape of Good Hope Nature Reserve**, open
7 AM to 6 PM, and the Cape of Good Hope itself.
Many visitors make the 60-km (37-mile) drive from
Cape Town believing this is the southern tip of
Africa. It isn't. The southernmost point is Cape
Agulhas, which is where the Indian and Atlantic
Oceans meet.

Of the two capes, however, the Cape of Good
Hope is the more spectacular, and because of
its protected status is also uncluttered by Cape
Agulhas' endless bed-and-breakfasts. Instead

during office hours. An alternative source of
information about the area is from **Peninsula
Tourism** ((021) 788 6193 FAX (021) 788 6208
E-MAIL peninsulatourism@yebo.co.za, Box 302,
Muizenberg 7950.

Everyone gets out of their cars where the roads
end at the lighthouse on the Cape. The last couple
of kilometers can be scrambled on hands and
knees — it's steep. There's a funicular, which will
save you the trouble. It costs R21 round trip, R13
one way.

There is no public transportation to the nature
reserve. However it's well worth renting a car for
the drive alone, and a number of tour operators
run daily trips, stopping off at sites of interest en
route.

OPPOSITE: Fish fresh from the ocean at Hout Bay.
ABOVE: Sunset over the Cape of Good Hope.

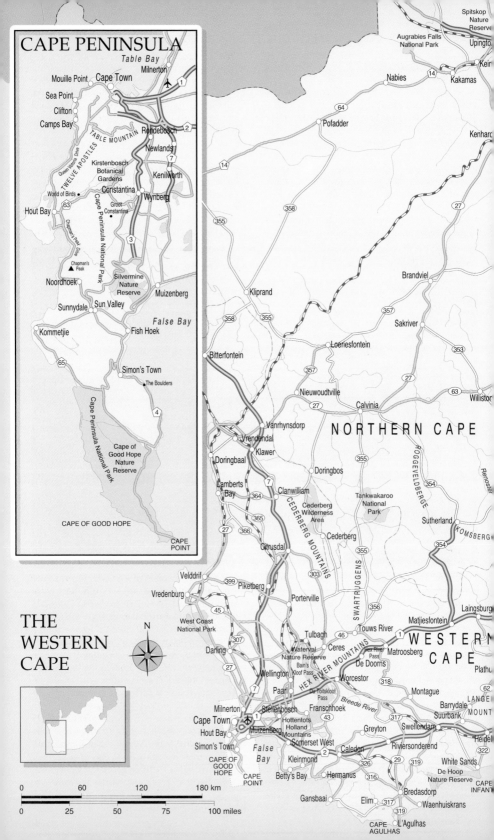

THE WINELANDS

Inland from Cape Town, the Boland's (or upland's) fertile valleys are gently coated in serried rows of grapevines — South Africa's Winelands, famed for their rich red wines and cool whites. Although there are wineries as far north as Upington, around the country town of Worcester, and as far east as port-producing Calitzdorp, it is the wine estates of Franschhoek, Paarl, Stellenbosch, and Wellington, all within 45 minutes of Cape Town by car, that are generally understood to be South Africa's Winelands. Majestic mountains shelter vine-covered valleys, quaint villages and cosmopolitan towns, with locally produced wines smoothing rural but sophisticated cuisine, arts, and music. It's a year-round destination — summers warm and sunny but not hot, autumns tinted with the rich colors of falling leaves, and stormy winters where snowcapped peaks are best viewed from your window as roaring log fires heat cozy sitting rooms, perfect for reading and relaxing. Spring is best of all: bright fields of flowers carpet the mountains' upper slopes while new shoots burst green from the neatly-tended vines.

The first grapes in South Africa were sown by Jan van Riebeeck in the Company Gardens. In a 1659 entry he praised the Lord for the first taste of locally-produced wine, but the enthusiastic consumption by sailors on shore leave was no doubt less spiritual. These valleys were among the first to be settled, and the countryside is dotted with the gracious, white-gabled farmsteads and leafy towns. Initially wines were produced by cottage industries, with most homesteads growing a vine or two in their garden, but a few estates produced wines that even became popular in France. The industry really took off with the introduction of new grape varieties, and currently about 100 different varieties are grown. The most successful are the Merlot, Pinotage, Sauvignon, Shiraz, Muscadel, and Muscat.

Although based in Cape Town there are tours of the Winelands that might go to the best-established wineries, their very nature devalues the experience, herding in groups of minivans and, worse still, coaches. The railways reach out to Paarl and Stellenbosch, but the vineyards are spread out and not designed for pedestrians. Without doubt the best way to experience these very special parts of the country is by car. Generally it is wise to choose one wine area at a time to explore, but one alternative is to follow "the Brandy Route" which takes in Stellenbosch, Paarl, and Franschhoek. One further consideration is that many vineyards, surprisingly in view of the importance of the Capetonian weekend market, close on Saturday afternoons, and almost all are closed on Sundays. It is best to time your wineland travels during the week.

STELLENBOSCH

Perhaps South Africa's most famous label, the Stellenbosch area is home to many of the finest vineyards. In 1679 the then governor, Simon van der Stel, realized the potential of this area of the Eerst River, ordered oak trees to be planted and founded South Africa's second-oldest city. In 1859 a theological seminary was founded, setting the town's reputation for educational excellence, and it now is home to one of the country's leading universities and a number of other educational establishments. Now it effortlessly combines its academic achievements with wine production: there

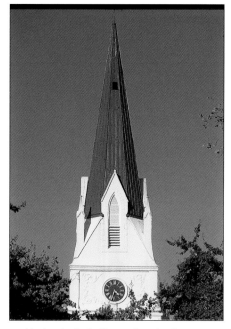

are 41 wineries, including my favorite, Overgaauw. Almost all offer tastings, at least, and many offer cellar tours, so a good first stop is the **Stellenbosch Tourism and Information Bureau** ((021) 883 3584 FAX (021) 883 8017 E-MAIL eikestad@iafrica.com, 36 Market Street, open Monday to Friday 8 AM to 6 PM, Saturday 9 AM to 5 PM, Sunday 9:30 AM to 4:30 PM September to May; Monday to Friday 9 AM to 5 PM, Saturday 9:30 AM to 4:30 PM, Sunday 10 AM to 4 PM June to August. The staff is exceptionally helpful, a cheap and quick cybercafé is attached and there is a collection of toys and miniatures, all set in a restored Rhenish complex. Local taxi companies include **Deon Taxis** ((082) 478 9889 and **Solomon Taxis** ((021) 881 3497. The tourist office, however, makes great efforts to send visitors off on foot. Perhaps because it is a university town

A Stellenbosch steeple overlooks all.

Stellenbosch is more pedestrian-friendly than most, and the city center has enough attractions within walking distance to make this feasible. There is a leaflet-guided walking trail in a range of languages, with guided walks leaving each day.

What to See and Do

The oak-lined town center blends Cape Dutch, Regency, and Victorian architectural styles. They're not so much old as painstakingly restored—regular fires have gutted the town and little remains of the first settlements. The **Village Museum (** (021) 887 2902, 18 Ryneveld Street, open Monday to Saturday 10 AM to 5 PM, Sunday 2 PM to 5 PM, R10, is the single most rewarding attraction. Four houses

spread over two blocks have been lovingly restored to reflect individual phases in the town's past, where even the gardens reflect the interests of each period. To reflect what was commonly available in shops in times gone by **Oom Samie Se Winkel (** (021) 887 0797, 82/84 Dorp Street, has been frozen in time. It is somewhere between a typical rural shop and retail therapy for less discriminating tourists, though the fish biltong is quite unusual. Appropriately enough there's a **Wine Museum (** (021) 888 3588, Strand Street, open Monday to Friday 9 AM to 12:45 PM and 2 PM to 5 PM, Saturday 10 AM to 1 PM and 2 PM to 5 PM, R10, and guided tours of the **Van Ryn Brandy Cellar (** (021) 881 3875, Van Ryn Road, depart Monday to Friday at 10 AM, 11:30 AM, 3 PM and Saturday at 10 AM and 11:30 AM, R6.

If this has left you feeling peckish, the **D'Ouwe Werf** is probably the oldest tavern in the country, dating back to 1802, and serves traditional Cape cuisine in a shady courtyard setting. The best place to walk this off is the **Stellenbosch Botanical Gardens (** (021) 808 3054, Neethling Street, open Monday to Friday from 8 AM to 5 PM, Saturday from 8 AM to 11 AM. It is a part of the university and has marked trails.

There's plenty to do in the surrounding countryside, including a visit to the **Heen & Weer**

Ostrich Farm ((021) 875 5393, N1 exit 47, Klapmuts, which is open daily 9 AM to 6 PM, R15. Balloon flights over the vineyards with **Wineland Ballooning (** (021) 863 3192 leave, weather permitting, at 5 AM at R1,100 per person for four to five hours including a champagne breakfast. There is the chance to see cheetah at the **Wiesenhof Game Park (** (021) 875 5181, 12 km (seven and a half miles) north of the city on the R44, open Tuesday to Sunday from 9:30 AM to 6 PM, R16.

If you've got energy to spare there are a number of **hiking trails** starting at the Oude Libertas Amphitheater. Some climb to the peak of Papegaai Mountain before meandering through the vineyards. Or let a horse take the strain. **Amoi Horse Trails (** (021) 887 1623 or (082) 681 4285 and **Spier Horse Trail Rides (** (021) 809 1100 offer country rides and wine tasting on horseback. Prices are in the region of R60 per hour, with a four-hour ride including wine tasting and snacks costing R250.

Tasting is all part of the Stellenbosch experience. Best to line your stomach with a cheese or two from the **Simonsberg Cheese Factory (** (021) 883 8640, 9 Stoffel Smith Street, not least because it is free. Choosing the vineyards to visit is very much a matter of your personal priorities. Several back their wine-tasting facilities with some of the best restaurants you'll find in the country. If you head out of Stellenbosch on the R44 Paarl Road for just under four kilometers (two and a half miles), **Morgenhof (** (021) 889 5510 FAX (021) 889 5266 WEB SITE www.morgenhof.com, R10 tasting fee, is a French-owned château serving light food al fresco. Tasting costs R10 and cellar tours take place at 11:30 AM and 3 PM by appointment. The family has been growing wine since 1210. Four kilometers (two and a half miles) further on and **Simonsig (** (021) 882 4900 FAX (021) 882 2545, tasting fee R15, is two kilometers (just over a mile) down the Kromme Rhee Road. There's no food here but the view is superb and there are cellar tours at 10 AM and 3 PM Monday to Saturday.

Four kilometers (two and a half miles) from the city center on the Strand Road (R44) towards Somerset West, **Blaauwklippen (** (021) 880 0133 FAX (021) 880 0136 is one of the original estates granted by Simon van der Stel, an H-shaped Cape homestead, which offers light lunches and horse-drawn coach rides when the weather is fine. Wine tasting costs R10 but cellar tours are free. **Spier Cellars (** (021) 881 3321 FAX (021) 881 3351 E-MAIL longridg@iafrica.com WEB SITE www.spier.co.za is a slick operation with cellar tours from Monday to Friday at 10 AM, noon, and 3 PM at R17.50 for the cellar tour and a tasting, R12 for the cellar tour only. They also have a choice of restaurants serving light meals to accompany the winery's award-winning wines. On the weekends they get very busy so book ahead.

My personal favorite, and not just because of the superb wine, is **Overgaauw** ((021) 881 3815 FAX (021) 881 3436, Vlottenburg. Cellar tours run Wednesdays at 3:30 PM, more often if you smile. There's no food, but the tastings are held in a polished-wood Victorian dining room, and the port is second to none.

Where to Stay

Accommodation options are plentiful. The top place to stay is **Le Quartier Français** ((021) 876 2248, 16 Huguenot Road, R900 to R2,400, which has an excellent restaurant and large rooms with fireplaces, set around a leafy courtyard. For a taste of traditional decor backed by modern facilities the **D'Ouwe Werf** ((021) 887 4608 FAX (021) 887 4626 E-MAIL ouwewer@iafrica.com, 30 Church Street, R660 offers 25 mellow antique-furnished rooms and a restaurant specializing in traditional fare in the heart of town. On the outskirts of town **Summerwood** ((021) 887 4112 FAX (021) 887 4239 E-MAIL summerwood@mweb.co.za WEB SITE www.winelands.co.za/summerwood, 28 Jonkershoek Road, R650, offers all the charm of the 1900s and a stately, rural atmosphere but near some of the town's best restaurants for your evening meal. **Power House** ((021) 887 9980 FAX (021) 887 9987 E-MAIL phlodge@mweb.co.za WEB SITE www.wineland.co.za/powerhouse, 34 Merriman Avenue, R400 to R700, is converted from an old electrical generating station in the historical town core offering character accommodation with its own licensed à la carte restaurant.

Out-of-town there are further options. **Papyrus** ((021) 842 3606 FAX (021) 842 3607 E-MAIL info @papyruslodge.co.za, Firgrove Road off R44 to Somerset West, Helderberg, offers Cape colonial-style cottages built on stilts above a lake. Great for fishermen, they are fully equipped for self-catering, but supply breakfasts and are within walking distance of two restaurants. Rates run R600 to R800 with off-season discounts. **Lanzerac Manor & Winery** ((021) 887 1132 FAX (021) 887 2310 E-MAIL info@lanzerac.co.za, Lanzerac Road, is a luxurious working wine estate with antique decor and period furniture from the Cape Dutch heyday. There is a choice of three restaurants, overseen by an executive chef, and a cognac and cigar bar, with rooms from R1,200. Backpackers can dream of this as they pile into the **Overseas Visitors Club** ((021) 886 6672, Van Riebeeck Street, or the **Stumble Inn Backpackers Lodge** ((021) 887 4049, 12 Market Street near the town center. Both charge about R35 for dormitory beds.

Where to Eat

I'd always recommend having lunch at one of the wineries. However there are a number of highly sophisticated restaurants vying for business, often making the most of their restored building settings, and these are a good choice for dinner. **96 Winery Road** ((021) 842 2020, for example, is a thatched house with rough brick floors and an open fireplace. Average price is about R70 for cuisine that is Cape nouvelle, with fresh seafood and fresh cannelloni. The **Auberge Rozendal** ((021) 883 8737, Jonkershoek Valley, specializes in French cuisine, served on yellowwood tables, with crystal glassware and period painting. The **Lord Neethling Restaurant** ((021) 883 8966, Vlottenburg Road, focuses on German, Austrian, and Swiss cooking styles, applied to ingredients at once fresh and exotic.

How to Get There

Stellenbosch is 47 km (30 miles) from Cape Town. Follow the R2 past the airport, between the sprawling townships of Mitchells Plain and the Cape Flats (stay on the main road) then, after 22 km (13.75 miles), turn left onto the R310: Stellenbosch is 16 km (10 miles). Alternatively, take the N1 Johannesburg road from Cape Town, turning right at Junction 39 onto the R304. By train it is one hour from Cape Town, by a regular service from platform 1. For train times call ((021) 808 1111.

PAARL

Researchers at the University of Cape Town decided that the three ingredients of a successful tourist attraction were: scenic beauty, historical buildings, and the wine routes. The academics, therefore, decided Paarl was perfect for tourism. Not all visitors agree, however — it's a bit big and rather spread out, factors the university didn't take into account.

While it might lack the student glamour of Stellenbosch, Paarl is in many ways a more important wine center. It is home to the huge KWV company, the largest exporter in South Africa whose Cathedral Cellars hold the five largest wine vats in the world, as well as Nederburg, the second best known winery. It is the second-largest conurbation in the Cape but still retains a provincial, almost rural feel. The valley was discovered in 1657, just five years after the establishment of Cape Town as a victualling center, by traders looking for Khoikhoi markets and the mythical gold of Monomotapa. Thirty years later Simon van der Stel granted the first farmlands to settlers, and it also became an important service stop for wagons on trading expeditions inland. It's an important center for Afrikaners, as it was here, in 1875, that their language movement was born, and the Afrikaans language museum is still situated in Paarl.

Wineland luxury at the Lanzerac Hotel.

The town's most interesting buildings are strung along Main Street at the foot of the huge granite dome of Paarl Mountain, but that doesn't mean it's compact: Main Street is 12 km (seven and a half miles) long and a car is needed to link spread-out sights. The very helpful **Paarl Tourism Bureau** ((021) 872 3829 FAX (021) 872 9376 E-MAIL paarl@cis.co.za WEB SITE www.wcapetourism.co.za, at the corner of Main and Auret Streets, open Monday to Friday 9 AM to 5 PM, Saturday 9 AM to 1 PM and Sunday 10 AM to 1 PM, spare no efforts in making visitors feel at home. A local taxi service is **Paarl Radio Taxis** ((021) 872 5671, and in case of medical emergency the **Mediclinic** ((021) 871 1330 is on Berlyn Street, while if your insurance has lapsed better try **Paarl Hospital** ((021) 872 1711, on Hospital Street.

What to See and Do

The **Paarl Museum** ((021) 872 2651, 303 Main Street, open Monday to Friday 10 AM to 5 PM, closed on Saturdays, R3 admission, has a unique collection of books and literature relating to the region. My favorite part though is the 1787 building, in which a collection of Victorian furniture and bric-a-brac is housed. One of South Africa's oldest **Dutch Reformed churches**, dating back to 1805, is also in Main Street. Paarl's Afrikaans residents claim that the town is the home of the Afrikaans language, especially in its development as a written and printed medium. To find out more visit the **Afrikaans Taalmuseum** ((021) 872 3411 FAX (021) 872 3642, 11 Pastorie Avenue, open Monday to Friday 9 AM to 5 PM, closed on Saturdays, admission R2, which is dedicated to the history and evolution of the Afrikaans language. This is more interesting than might be expected, with replica wallpaper from the 1860s, early printing presses, and some 1810 paintings by the mother of the original owner of the house. The **Afrikaans Language Monument** on the top of Paarl Mountain is also more affecting than I, for one, expected — the views are superb and the monument itself, organic with clean lines, complements the scene beautifully.

Most visitors go straight for Paarl's headline attraction: wine. **KWV** ((021) 807 3008 FAX (021) 863 1942, Kohler Street, a key wine-producing cooperative since 1918, has more than 100 different wines and brandies in copper and oak vats. Tours of the cellars are offered in a range of languages; in English at 10 AM, 10:30 AM and 2:15 PM daily, by reservation only on Sundays. The other big producer is **Nederburg** ((021) 862 3104, on the R303 towards Wellington, open Monday to Friday 10 AM to 5 PM, Saturday 9 AM to 1 PM. They produce 650,000 cases a year. German technology has much to do with the vineyard's success and cellar tours are conducted at 10:30 AM and 2:30 PM

in English with other languages offered if required and there's a lunchtime restaurant.

Simonsvlei ((021) 863 2486 FAX (021) 863 1240 E-MAIL simonsvlei@adept.co.za WEB SITE www.simonsvlei.co.za, tempts passersby with a huge bottle by the side of the road, and then presents visitors with an irresistible menu at their restaurant. My personal favorite uses a goat-tower to advertise its cheese as well as its wines: **Fairview** ((021) 863 2450 FAX (021) 863 2591 E-MAIL fairback @iafrica.com WEB SITE www.fairview.co.za, open 8:30 AM to 5 PM Monday to Friday and Saturday to 1 PM. They don't only produce wine, but also farm angora goats, milked in the afternoon, who live in traditional towers reached by spiral wooden slats. There is no restaurant but the cheese is good and the wine tasting free.

Paarl is quite a good place to escape outdoors. A four-kilometer (two-and-a-half-mile) stroll along the Berg River passes through the **Arboretum**, with 700 species of tree represented among 4,000 plants. To take a longer stroll, Klipkershout Walking Trails offer anything from two-and-a-half-kilometer (one-and-a-half-mile) to 10-km (six-mile) walks in Paarl Mountain nature reserve, for which no permit is needed. It is easy to climb Paarl Mountain, which on a clear day provides distant views of False Bay and the Cape. Alternatively Miaspoort, Donkerkloof and Limietberg are marked trails that go further afield, with limited numbers of permits issued to ensure you have the place to yourself. To book a trail call the **Boland District Office** ((021) 552 3688 or ask at the tourist office (details above).

Fishing is possible at three dams on Paarl Mountain. For **fishing permits** phone Paarl Tourism ((021) 872 3829 or Paarl Municipality ((021) 807 4500. There are 140 species of birds in the area from Cape sugarbirds to black eagles, and a **bird sanctuary** ((021) 872 4972 hides in Drommedaris Street. Alternatively join the birds in a **Winelands Hot Air Ballooning** ((021) 863 3192.

Where to Stay and Eat

If money's no problem, you can stay in one of two very refined eighteenth-century manor houses in Paarl. **Roggeland Country House** ((021) 868 2501 FAX (021) 868 2113, Roggeland Road, Dal Josaphat Valley, is a family-run hotel which manages to combine great food and service without too much formality (R940 to R1,100 for dinner, bed, and breakfast). The more expensive **Grande Roche** ((021) 863 2727 FAX (021) 863 2220 E-MAIL reserve@ granderoche.co.za WEB SITE www.granderoche.co.za, a member of Relais & Châteaux, is one of the most sophisticated of all South Africa's hotels, with luxury accommodation sited in the former stables and slave quarters of an imposing plantation house just out of town. Also in Paarl is **Mooikelder** ((021) 863 8491 FAX (021) 863 8361

E-MAIL mooikel@mweb.co.za WEB SITE www.isaa .com/mooikelder, R225 per person, once the home of British colonial statesman Cecil John Rhodes, with a dining room paneled with the oak from ancient wine barrels and simply furnished, comfortable rooms. Just outside town is **Mountain Shadows** ((021) 862 3192 FAX (021) 862 6796 E-MAIL mshadows@icon.co.za, a thatched manor house in the Dal Josephat Valley, where dinner, bed, and breakfast costs R800. In the heart of town — but surrounded by vineyards — **Goedemoed Country Inn** ((021) 863 1102 FAX (021) 863 1104 E-MAIL wsteenkamp@icon.co.za WEB SITE www.infoguide .co.za/goedemoed, Cecilia Street, R350 to R500, has nine bedrooms and period furnishings.

Country House being one of the most imaginative, while a range of local eateries have all the diversity you would expect from a busy commercial town. One of the best is **Saucy Maria's** ((021) 863 2285, 127 Main Road, set in a national monument building, which serves Italian cuisine indoors and out, while Provençal spices are on the menu at the **Country Elephant** ((021) 874 1355, Simondium Road.

How to Get There

Paarl is 65 km (41 miles) from Cape Town, just off the N1 Johannesburg road. There are two railway stations in town: Paarl Station is in the south (near the Berg River campsite) while Huguenot Station

At the time of writing there's no official backpacker lodge in Paarl, though **Amberg** (/FAX (021) 862 0982 E-MAIL amberg@mweb.co.za, Du Toits Kloof Pass/Langenhoven Road, Klein Drakenstein, and **Manyano Methodist Center** ((021) 872 5074 FAX (021) 872 3580, Zanddrift Street, take in young people seeking basic accommodation for a couple of nights. The self-catering chalets offered at the **Berg River Holiday Resort** ((021) 863 1650 FAX (021) 863 2583, run at R240 for a twin, with even cheaper camping in the grounds. They are located five kilometers (just over three miles) out of town towards Franschhoek (R45), well placed by the river but rather rundown and crowded, in season, with families.

Eating in Paarl divides into restaurants specially developed to complement wineries, with the Grand Roche, for example, being one of the most expensive in the country, and Roggeland

is the one used by long-distance trains and the one you want for the town center. Metro trains come from Cape Town every hour, while most of Cape Town's intercity trains to Pretoria and Durban also stop here. Translux and Greyhound stop in Paarl but the cost is very high thanks to a pricing structure designed for long-haul travel.

FRANSCHHOEK

In 1688, Huguenots from France and Belgium, suffering religious persecution, flooded out of Europe. Two hundred were offered passage to South Africa and established themselves in frontier land at Franschhoek, using their skills in viticulture on land already cleared of the indigenous Khoikhoi. For a long time a very rural *dorp*

Colonial comforts at the Grande Roche in Paarl.

(small town), it has recently surged in popularity, partly because of its beautiful setting and partly because it is not linked to the city by any bus or rail service, keeping urban problems at bay. Now a number of city dwellers have swelled the population, setting up antique shops, art galleries and restaurants, adding a further tier to the wineries that underpin the local economy. French as a language died out within a generation — governor Simon van der Stel forbade its use in church or public — but now is making a bit of comeback, already dominating local menus, to the bemusement of most villagers. But it's a manageably small and very attractive village with a number of world-class wines, and perhaps the best place of all to enjoy the wineland experience. It's certainly the best place to eat.

The helpful and accommodating **Tourist Information** ((021) 876 3603 FAX (021) 876 2768 E-MAIL info@franschhoek.org.za, Main Street, is open in winter from 9 AM to 5 PM Monday to Friday, Saturday from 9:30 AM to 1:30 PM, and Sunday 10 AM to 1:30 PM; their summer hours are 9 AM to 6 PM Monday to Friday, 9 AM to 5 PM Saturday, and 10 AM to 5 PM Sunday. Perhaps most useful, given what a gastronomic center the village has become, is a display of all the town's restaurant menus, a facility that deserves encouragement. There is no local taxi service and no public transportation, so almost all visitors will have arrived in their own cars anyway, but in any case the vineyards are near enough to explore on a mountain bike, on horseback (see EXPLORE THE WINE ROUTES, page 24 in TOP SPOTS), or even on foot.

What to See and Do

The most important museum in Franschhoek is the **Huguenot Memorial Museum and Monument** ((021) 876 2532 FAX (021) 876 3649, Lambrecht Street, open Monday to Saturday 9 AM to 5 PM, Sunday 2 PM to 5 PM, R5 admission, almost a site of pilgrimage for French visitors. Inside is a thorough register of the genealogy of French families in South Africa over the past 250 years, and a collection of old furniture and household effects. Opposite the museum the monument, designed by architect J.C. Jongens, is set in a rose garden with the Franschhoek mountains forming a dramatic backdrop. Across the road is the embryonic **Village Museum**, open Monday to Friday 10 AM to 5 PM, Saturday 10 AM to 1 PM, a collection of memorabilia, including a number of original period dresses, devoted to the village in general. They don't say the non-French part of the village but it's tempting to think that they might, one day, come out and admit it.

The main action here is in the wineries. A number have achieved worldwide recognition but haven't yet been spoiled by success. Almost

invariably small, most are well off the coach-trip circuit and welcome anyone with an informed interest or genuine enthusiasm. For further information contact the **Vignerons de Franschhoek** ((021) 876 3062 FAX (021) 876 2964 E-MAIL franschhoek@wine.co.za.

An exception to the small-and-friendly rule is **Boschendal** ((021) 874 1034, open Monday to Saturday 8:30 AM to 5 PM, Sunday 10 AM to 12:30 PM, tasting fee R10, an award-winning vineyard with a particular reputation for it's white wine tinted with the skin of black grapes. It retains the best of neither, but their sparkling white is good. It counts itself in Franschhoek because it was originally granted to a Huguenot settler but in fact it is midway between Franschhoek and Stellenbosch, at the junction of the R45 and the R310. Now owned by an Anglo-American corporation Boschendal is a beautiful winery, housed in a number of stately buildings, some of which are restored with period furniture into a richer recreation than many of South Africa's museums can manage, with a collection of VOC glassware and Ming porcelain as a bonus. The whole property is expansively set in tree-lined avenues. The restaurant has a good reputation, open for (expensive) buffet lunches even when the *taphuis* (pub), where the tasting is done, is shut, and Le Café serves light meals and snacks throughout the year. It's quite hard for me to justify not liking it, in fact. But I didn't. Maybe I should have come in on one of the coaches shuffling parties with prepaid tickets, who were better welcomed. Don't take my word for it: see for yourself. The Boschendal restaurant can be reached at ((021) 870 4274.

Back to Franschhoek village and things improve remarkably. One of the best-positioned, and friendliest, wineries is the **Mont Rochelle** ((021) 876 3000 FAX (021) 876 2362 E-MAIL montrochelle@wine.co.za, Daniel Hugo Road, open Monday to Saturday 11 AM to 4 PM and Sundays to 1 PM. These are civilized hours: who wants to start wine-tasting any earlier than 11 AM? The vineyard, set on the valley's shoulder and overlooking the village, is owned by eighth generation descendants of one of the original Huguenot settlers, though it has to be said they haven't lived in the village continuously since then. But the tasting environment is second to none, with plates of cheese made available if requested, with notable vintages including the 1996 Cabernet Sauvignon and a limited supply of un-oaked Chardonnay. The winery is also a starting point for a horseback tour of the area (see EXPLORE THE WINE ROUTES, page 24 in TOP SPOTS). You know you're in the right place when coffee-table books left out in the Victorian tasting room include a field guide to South African ducks.

Follow the Franschhoek River along Daniel Hugo Road and find the **Haute Provence** ((021)

876 3195, Daniel Hugo Road, open daily 9 AM to 4 PM, now owned by an Italian Count, it is best known for its Angel's Tears blend of Chenin Blanc and Muscat d'Alexandrie grapes. Best, the tasting is in a traditional room with armchairs and good South African art. To keep things authentic, the ceiling is made by the local technique of cane and mud, but the wine is more sophisticated. Other vineyards worth exploring are **La Motte** ((021) 876 3119, open Monday to Friday 9 AM to 4:30 PM, and to noon on Saturday, with cellar tours by appointment. The tasting here is sadly no longer in the old cellars, built in 1752, which were a cool and atmospheric setting for a quaff, but are now in a new tasting center, L'Omarains ((021) 874 1026.

There's more to Franschhoek than just wine. Main Street, which turns into Huguenot Road, is lined with antique shops and art galleries. **L'Afrique** has traditional local crafts, the **Three Streams**, out of town but with a stall at the Farm Stall, is known for its smoked salmon and trout, and **Bordeaux** has a selection of antique Cape china and furniture. The **Hottentots Holland Nature Reserve** borders the town. Because of its proximity to Cape Town it is popular hiking country and permits are required for even the shorter hikes, with rangers wandering round the mountains checking. There are several shorter trails, but the main trail in the reserve is the **Boland Trail**, 50 km (31 miles) long, which takes three days, overnighting in Park Board huts. Permits for this cannot be obtained locally and must be obtained from the Hottentots Holland Nature Reserve ((021) 886 5858 FAX (021) 886 6575. There are other hiking trails including the Mont Rochelle, Cats Path, Safcol-La Motte plantations, and other areas controlled by the Department of Nature Conservation. Permits are required for all, and most can be arranged through the Franschhoek Tourist Information.

Where to Stay and Eat

The smartest place to stay — and, traditionally, to eat — is **Le Quartier Français** ((021) 876 2151 FAX (021) 876 3105, at the corner of Berg and Wilhelmina streets, where 15 rooms and suites are arranged around herb gardens in the center of the village. It is perhaps worth the R445 to R1,200 rates for a splurge. An upstart establishment, overlooking the village on a small mound, is currently giving the Quartier a run for its money: **La Couronne** ((021) 876 2770 FAX (021) 876 3788 E-MAIL enquiries @lacouronne.co.za WEB SITE www.lacouronne .co.za, Robertsvlei Road, R800 for bed and breakfast, with a particularly adventurous menu. Just down the hill, set among the vineyards, is the **Auberge Clermont** ((021) 876 3700 FAX (021) 876 3701 E-MAIL clermont@mweb.co.za, Robertsvlei Road, at R700 for bed and breakfast, with a fantastic

honeymoon suite. The other rooms are also good but you'll need to drive for an evening meal. Just off the Main Road, the **Auberge Bligny** ((021) 876 3767 FAX (021) 876 3483 E-MAIL bligny@mweb .co.za, 28 Van Wijkstreet, R400 to R500 for bed and breakfast, is in the heart of the village. It is antique, floral and draped. **Auberge la Dauphine** (/FAX (021) 876 2606 E-MAIL moates@ct.lia.net WEB SITE www.franschhoek.co.za, costs R450 including breakfast.

There are a number of bed-and-breakfast establishments, for example **La Gileppe** ((021) 876 2146 E-MAIL info@cyberads.co.za WEB SITE www .cyberads.co.za, 47 Huguenot Road, at R300. For backpackers the cheapest place to stay is four kilo-

meters (two and a half miles) out of the village at the **Sunflower Cottage** ((021) 876 2573 or (082) 650 1500, Happy Valley Road, off Paarl Road, at R120 for two sharing with breakfast.

While many of the wineries offer lunch, the village has some excellent restaurant options for dinner. For Le Quartier and La Couronne see above, while **Polfyntjies Restaurant** ((021) 876 3217, Main Road, offers traditional Cape country cooking; closed Mondays.

How to Get There

There is no public transportation to Franschhoek. The village is 71 km (44 miles) from Cape Town, reached either off the N1 Johannesburg road, turning right on the R303, or through Stellenbosch over Helshoogte.

The past, polished at Boschendal's Wineland mansion.

WELLINGTON

Often overlooked and generally overshadowed by its better-known neighbors, the farming town of Wellington was, by early settlers, thought to be the very edge of the "civilized" world. However the distant diamond fields of Kimberley spurred a growth in demand for wagons, and the construction, in 1847, of Bain's Kloof Pass put Wellington firmly on the route to the interior. The town established an early reputation for its religious seats of learning, and now has several well-respected wineries, five of which have joined to form a short wine route.

Tourist Information ((021) 873 4604 FAX (021) 873 4607 E-MAIL welltour@cis.co.za, 104 Main Road, Box 695, Wellington 7654, open Monday to Friday 9 AM to 4:30 PM and Saturday 10 AM to noon, is sited in the old market building and is especially informative about the hiking trails through the area's mountains. The **Museum** ((021) 873 1410, Kerk Street, is largely devoted to the area's history, from the Stone Age onwards, but strangely also contains the country's largest collection of Egyptian relics. The vineyards aren't open on Sunday — nor, noticeably, is the town — but it is an alternative wineland town through the week, so far uncluttered by tour buses.

The few visitors tend to drive over from Paarl but Wellington's guest farms and bed-and-breakfasts usually offer better value. **Diemersfontein** ((021) 873 2671 FAX (021) 864 2095, two kilometers (just over a mile) from Wellington on the Paarl Road (R303), R310, is one of the best, a graceful colonial building with 16 guestrooms. To stay on a wine estate, try the **Oude Wellington Guest Farm** ((021) 873 2262 FAX (021) 873 4639 E-MAIL rrs@cls .co.za WEB SITE members.rediff.com/wellington, Bain's Kloof Pass Road, R420. Of the restaurants, the liveliest is the **Farmhouse Kitchen** ((021) 868 2808, off Diemersfontein Road, or the **Overwacht Restaurant** ((021) 864 2552, Addy Street, with dinner dances on Fridays; closed Mondays.

The great reason for passing through Wellington is to drive along Bain's Kloof Pass, built in 1847 by Andrew Geddes Bain, the inspector of roads who pioneered many of the routes still used by South Africans and visitors today. This was the golden age of road building, using convict labor to blast and chip routes through towering mountains and endless plains. Even now the achievements of the road builders cannot fail to inspire awe. A total of 1,608 working days were needed to complete this pass, with dry-stone culverts, aqueducts and drains. At the time it was regarded as one of the country's great achievements: two days and 57 km (36 miles) of grueling mountain tracks were shaved off the wagon journey to Worcester, and it did much to open up Africa's interior.

THE BREEDE RIVER VALLEY

Another good reason for taking Bain's Kloof Pass is to leave the Winelands and enter the wilder, drier world of the Breede River Valley and its capital Worcester, a flat, spread-out farming town just off the N1 Cape Town to Johannesburg road. Most drivers, intent on speeding between the cities, ignore Worcester and the valley, skimming across with little more than a glance at the vineyards that carpet the wide valley floor, interested only in making the best time over a short stretch of straight roads between Du Toitskloof Pass and the Hex River Pass. This is a pity. The Breede River Valley, though intensively farmed, is one of the most beautiful areas of the country.

WORCESTER

Although it was a late boarder on the Winelands tourist gravy-train, the Worcester area produces a fifth of the country's wines and is the largest wine-producing area in South Africa. Generally grapes are grown in cooperatives and the wine bottled as easy-drinking plonk for the local market, but this lack of pretension can be refreshing if you've come from some of the stuffier wineries. It has long been a center for community care, with the two oldest institutes specializing in disabilities; the Institute for the Blind was founded in 1881 and the Institute for the Deaf opened a few years later. Both now sell handicrafts.

A first port of call is the **Tourist Information Center** ((023) 347 1408 FAX (023) 347 4678, Stofberg House, 23 Baring Street, Worcester 6850, open 8 AM to 5 PM and Saturday 8:30 AM to 12:30 PM, who are nicely modest about their town's attractions. Local taxi services include **Stanley Shuttle Service** ((082) 557 8058 and **Winston Shuttle Service** ((083) 303 3700, but the town is quite spread out and the meter will clock up quickly — it's a good place to have your own car. The city hospital is the **Eben Dönges Hospital** ((023) 348 1100 off Durban Street, while the **Mediclinic** ((023) 348 1500 on Fairbairn Street is the private hospital. To get to either call the **Ambulance** (10177.

The town center is flat and spread out, but contains some fine examples of Cape Victorian architecture, shady whitewashed buildings laid out on a grid pattern that is easy to navigate. The **Worcester Museum**, open Monday to Saturday 9 AM to 1 PM and 2 PM to 5 PM, is spread over three buildings on the corners of Baring and Church streets; R5 gains access to all. **Beck House** is one of the country's best preserved town houses, dating from 1841, while **Stofberg House**, 23 Baring Street, was the residence of a dentist practicing in the 1920s. The fertile Breede Valley is the last strip of life-sustaining farming land before the countryside

crosses the Hex River Mountains and flattens out to the near-desert Karoo. The town's finest attraction celebrates this new climatic zone just out of town, across the N1, in the **Karoo National Botanical Garden** ((023) 170 785 E-MAIL karroid@ intekom.co.za, off Roux Road, open 8 AM to 6 PM. Admission to "half the country in one garden" is R8 from August to October and on weekends, otherwise free. This is an excellent introduction to the dry Karoo lands that spread from here north. Ten hectares (25 acres) of landscaped gardens are packed with the exotic plants of this near-desert environment, with a further 144 hectares (356 acres) of indigenous semidesert parkland. There's also a hugely informative information center, where your questions will be answered against a background of botanists carrying pots in and out, while guided tours can be arranged on request. If there's been rain, August to October are great times to visit, as the exotic flowers burst into bloom.

In town, the big draw is the **Kleinplasie Living Open Air Museum** ((023) 342 2225 FAX (023) 347 4134, Robertson Road (R60), open Monday to Saturday 9 AM to 1:30 PM, Sunday 10 AM to 4:30 PM, R10, which recreates early settler life in one of the most complete and authentic exhibits in the country. In large grounds traditional houses have been constructed with period utensils. The focus is on settlers rather than indigenous people — the Khoikhoi hut that was once in the collection has now been dismantled — but the shepherd's huts, working stills, bucket pumps, and dipping kraals give a good idea of life in South Africa's early years. Various characters in costume wander around plaiting tobacco and stoking up kilns. There's also an indoor museum with candle-machines and restored kitchens, and to keep visitors lubricated there's a *witblitz* stall, serving six different fla-

The Hex River Valley marks the start of the Karoo.

vors of the powerful local spirit that fuelled the early settlers after a day on the fields. The portions are generous and can unravel morning visits. Fortunately there's a very good museum restaurant ((023) 347 5118 serving local dishes à la carte through the week and traditional buffets on Sundays — their *bobotie* (spicy minced meat) was among the best I've tasted. There is a separate **Reptile World** (/FAX (023) 342 6480, open daily 9 AM to 5 PM, R10, with a collection of more than 30 snake species and a reptile pit, and accommodation in self-catering **Chalets** (/FAX (023) 347 0091 or (083) 258 7087, R200 weekdays, R360 weekends.

On the wine front there are 27 cellars open to the public. There's nothing too old here; the wine

warned: in addition to a swimming pool the hotel also has a fountain, which either soothes or irritates at night. The **Cumberland Hotel** ((023) 347 2641 FAX (023) 347 3613 E-MAIL cumberland@xpoint.co.za, 2 Stokenström Street, R500, is a business-class hotel with spa, tennis and squash courts among other facilities. There's nowhere for backpackers at time of writing, although if finances are getting thin the **Nerina Hotel** ((023) 347 0486, Van Huyssteenlaan Street in suburban Worcester, offers cheap accommodation from R150.

Most of the town's best restaurants are linked to these hotels: Table Talk for Church Street Lodge and Barlinka in the Cumberland Hotel, while the restaurant at the Open Air Museum is good for

industry only took root in this irrigated valley in 1946, and nor has the tradition of establishing good restaurants as part of the experience got far yet. Best to get in touch with the **Worcester Winelands Association** ((023) 342 8710 for detailed information. If wine is beginning to pall, the **KWV Brandy Cellar** ((023) 342 0255, Church Street, has the largest brandy cellar under a single roof in the world, with tours (R7) in Afrikaans, English, and German threading through 120 vats of spirit and the heady aromas of distillation.

Where to Stay and Eat

The best place to stay in Worcester is in the heart of the town, in **Church Street Lodge** ((023) 342 5194 FAX (023) 342 8859, 36 Church Street, R340 to R380 with breakfast, which serves light meals at its attached café, Table Talk, but is within easy walking distance of the area's restaurants. Be

lunch. For seafood the best restaurant is the **San Geran** ((023) 342 2800, Church Street, while **Burchells** ((023) 342 5388, De Breede Estate, specializes in innovative Cape cuisine and also offers wine tasting, sales, and horseback tours from a 200-year-old thatched homestead; booking essential. Failing that you're now in Steak House country, with the national chains such as O'Hagen's and the San Diego Spur serving sides of cow.

How to Get There

Worcester is 112 km (70 miles) from Cape Town on the N1 Johannesburg road. This is an easy drive in your own car, and the R60 also heads across through Robertson and Swellendam to link in with the N2 leading from Cape Town to the Garden Route. Although the intercity Translux and Greyhound buses stop here, their price is high to focus on their long-haul markets. Train, on the other hand, is not a bad way to get to Worcester — most of the intercity services between Cape Town and Johannesburg stop here, and it is also linked in with the Southern Cross, which heads down the Breede Valley once a week to Port Elizabeth.

MATJIESFONTEIN

One hundred and thirty kilometers (80 miles) from Worcester along the N1 towards Johannesburg is the tiny town of Matjiesfontein, pronounced "Mikiesfontein" a historic village centered round a single hotel, redolent with the great British names that have shaped South Africa's history.

Matjiesfontein was founded in 1884 by a Scot called Jimmy Logan, who bought a farm in the arid southern Karoo and proceeded to turned the disadvantage of being in a desert into an asset, lauding its dryness and proclaiming his hotel, the Lord Milner, as South Africa's premier health resort. His marketing worked: Cecil John Rhodes, Sir Randolph Churchill, and the Sultan of Zanzibar were regular guests, with author Olive Shreiner moving to the area permanently. Perhaps because many of the top brass knew where it was, it became the headquarters of the Cape Command in the 1899–1902 Boer War. When the main road bypassed the village, the hotel might have faded into obscurity, but was bought by hotelier David Rawdon and has been awarded the status of a National Monument.

The town is little more than two dusty streets, redolent with Victoriana, with tin roofs, turrets, and verandas. At its center — and key to its popularity — is still the **Lord Milner Hotel** ((023) 551 3011 FAX (023) 551 3020, Logan Road, Matjiesfontein 6901, rather expensive at R600. The lounges are filled with antique furnishings and accommodation is either in the period rooms of the hotel itself or in the other buildings nearby. In the brass-fitted dining room the food recreates the not-so-golden colonial era.

Tourist trains will stop in Matjiesfontein, at least for a meal and often staying the night, on their journey between Cape Town and Pretoria. Alternatively, it is three hours — and 300 km (188 miles) — from Cape Town along the N1, passing the spectacular Hex River Pass.

TULBAGH

The Breede River heartland, to the north of Worcester, is best explored from Tulbagh. The R43 follows the river from Worcester to Tulbagh and then on towards the river's source. This town is best known for its historic Church Street, which owes its current pristine state to a devastating earthquake that flattened the village in 1969. At the time the Victorian houses were in poor repair, but in South Africa's largest restoration project a row of

32 were rebuilt to the original specifications. This street alone contains more national monuments than any other in the country, with several operating as museums, restaurants, and hotels. The town itself is now, rather self-consciously, trying to reinvent itself as an artistic community, but the setting and mountain landscapes are magnificent. And if it needs a claim to fame, the Tulbagh area produces 70% of the nation's prunes.

The main road going through the town is Van der Stel Street, a scrappy agglomeration of bottle shops and supermarkets with white farmers double-parking to buy provisions, and crowds of black partially employed agricultural workers hanging around, drinking and waiting for something to happen. Just one block away, the restored Church Street runs parallel, a white-painted row of façades, preserved in aspic in a genteel recreation of life long gone. This is where you'll find the **Tourist Information Office** (/FAX (023) 230 1348, 14 Church Street, 9 AM to 4:30 PM, Saturday 10 AM to 4 PM, Sunday 11 AM to 4 PM. Although the whole street serves as a bit of a museum the **Oude Kerk Volksmuseum**, 2 Church Street, is the best. It is open Monday to Friday 8 AM to 1 PM and 2 PM to 5 PM, Saturday 10 AM to 1 PM and 2 PM to 4 PM, only opening at 11 AM on Sunday. Light and airy, it is crammed with Victoriana. The **Town Museum** is spread over numbers 4, 14, and 22 Church Street, all within easy walking distance of each other, and contains period furnishings and lifestyle exhibits as well as some dramatic pictures of the earthquake damage. A single R5 ticket gains access to all the above.

On the other side of the main street in the village suburbs is a strange little museum, dedicated to doll houses. The **Miniature Houses Museum** ((023) 230 0651, 4 Witzenberg Street, is open 9:30 AM to 12:30 PM and 2:30 PM to 4:30 PM Monday to Saturday, open mornings only on Sundays, R5. Four kilometers (two and a half miles) out of town east along Van der Stel Street, the **Old Drostdy** ((023) 230 0203, open Monday to Saturday 10 AM to 12:50 PM and 2 PM to 4:50 PM, Sunday afternoons only, R3, has a collection of sherry vats and Victorian furniture in a house designed by Louis Thibault as the court house and governor's dwelling. Next door the **Drostdy-Hof** ((023) 230 1086 FAX (023) 230 0510, hosts cellar tours Monday to Friday at 11 AM and 3 PM. There are also plenty of outdoor options in the area: hiking, mountain biking and fishing are all popular.

Where to Stay and Eat

To make the most of the period experience, choose to stay in Church Street. Best are the three guest rooms of **D'Oude Herberg** (/FAX (023) 230 0260, 8 Church Street, R300, run by a couple of Johannes-

Time is told to stand still in the restored village of Matjiesfontein.

burg refugees who "keep a good kitchen" as the locals say, but not on Mondays as the restaurant is closed. This is a quiet place where the evening meals specialize in local Cape cuisine. The other options are out of town and include the **Waterval Bush Camp** and the **Waterval Country Lodge** ((023) 230 0807 FAX (023) 230 0757, off the R46, with rates at R400 (lodge) R300 (camp). It is a consistent award-winning establishment where accommodation is in either the eighteenth-century lodge or safari-style tents, in a pine plantation bordering directly on the *fynbos*-rich Waterval Nature Reserve. **Rijk's Ridge** ((023) 230 1006 FAX (023) 230 1125 E-MAIL neville@rijksridge.co.za WEB SITE www.rijksridge.co.za, two kilometers (just over a mile) along the R44, R500 to R700, is a far slicker operation, a new out-of-town resort hotel with views of the Witzenberg and Winterhoek Mountains.

The village's smartest restaurant is the **Paddagang Restaurant** ((023) 230 0242, Church Street, housed in ancient slave quarters and specializing in traditional Cape cuisine. It is closed Sundays.

How to Get There

There is no public transportation to Tulbagh. It's easy to get there from Worcester by car, just take the R46 for 27 km (17 miles). From Cape Town take the N1 towards Paarl, then turn left onto the Klapmuts/Wellington R44. Before Wellington turn left again on the R44, signposted Hermon/Ceres. Continue through the Nuwekloof Pass and take the Tulbagh turn on the left.

TOWARDS THE DESERT

The Atlantic Ocean washes Africa's western coast, cold and unforgiving, spreading mists over an area of fishing villages and farms scarcely discovered by the world. Further north and Clanwilliam, queen of the Cederberg, is a good base to explore these dry and beautiful mountains, always a fascinating open-air museum of ancient San rock art, bursting with bright meadows of flowers in spring. North of here South Africa flattens out: drylands stretching up to Namibia, remote, with sudden bursts of wild beauty and the frontier town of Upington.

CLANWILLIAM

The town of Clanwilliam slumbered peacefully at the foot of the Cederberg mountains until the N7 highway heading from Cape Town north to Namibia was constructed in the 1960s, passing within a few hundred meters of the rural, farming settlement. Clanwilliam is, however, one of the 10 oldest towns in South Africa. It was first settled by Jan Dissels in 1726, at a time when rhino,

elephant and hippo were his friendly neighbors, and Khoikhoi cattle rustlers the not-so-friendly ones. In 1808 a British garrison was established here, and settlers were brought over to occupy a buffer between the settlers to the south and the "native hordes" (as they were known) to the north. The dry land was hard to farm and most of the buffer farmers moved on to the more peaceful Eastern Cape region.

Still, the town survived and is now an important leisure center for Capetonians, who drive here and charge up and down the artificial lake just south of town on jet-skis. Foreign visitors tend to head east, into a beautiful arid mountainscape littered with examples of San rock art, and north, across the flat desert lands that explode, after rain, into color with the blooming meadows of flowers, generally at their best from August through September. Seeing the flowers themselves is not quite as simple as it appears (see CALVINIA, FLOWER COUNTRY, page 110 for further details). The Cederberg mountains are not a good destination in Cape Town's peak season, however, as January and February are hot hot hot.

The single high street is a genuine time warp, not prettied up for the tourist industry but far from your average "dorp." It's a friendly place where orientation is quick and easy and the views of the Cederberg Wilderness Area, just across the valley, offer a constantly changing but always dramatic backdrop.

General Information

In the old jail building the **Tourist Information Center** ((027) 482 2024 FAX (027) 482 2361, Main Street, open 8:30 AM to 5 PM Monday to Friday and to 12:30 PM Saturdays, shares the building, open hours and telephone with the small town museum. The tourist office is an energetically run and very helpful, though personally I think that in Clanwilliam they're pushing against an open door — on every level the town, and the area should be an easy sell. There is no local taxi shuttle service though, which is a bit of a drawback if traveling with public transportation, as the Intercape buses from Cape Town stop two kilometers (just over a mile) out of town above the Clanwilliam Dam. There is, at least, a **Hospital** ((027) 482 2167, Old Cape Road.

What to See and Do

Without doubt the best activity here is out of town, driving through the craggy and beautiful Cederberg mountains and taking a hike to discover the open-air gallery of San rock art. The tourist board can help with a range of booklets written and illustrated by Peter Slingsby which include trail maps and detailed descriptions of what you should

White paint signifies San rock art in the Cederbergs.

be seeing if you're not lost (see HIKE THE WORLD'S LARGEST ART GALLERY, page 31 in TOP SPOTS). One of the few trails you can hike on your own is the Sevilla Trail, for which permission is needed from local farmer Haffie Strauss, who runs the **Travelers Rest** (/FAX (027) 482 1824, Box 209, Clanwilliam 8135, and a copy of *Rock Art of the Western Cape*, Book 1, "The Sevilla Trail and Travelers Rest," which costs R25 from the Tourist Office in Clanwilliam. The Sevilla Trail — and Travelers Rest — are 36 km (22 miles) out of Clanwilliam on the Augsburg Road, dirt all the way.

If your budget is up to it, a private game reserve nearby has 125 sites of recorded rock art: to help preserve this fragile piece of the nation's heritage they don't let visitors wander round unsupervised but operate an expert guiding service. Unfortunately they will only share their rock art treasures with guests at their lodge, and as rates are between R1,300 and R1,590 full board this prices a tour beyond most guests' reach. For further details, contact **Bushman's Kloof** ((027) 482 2627 FAX (027) 482 1011 or for reservations ((021) 797 0990 FAX (021) 761 5551 E-MAIL santrack@ ilink.co.za WEB SITE www.bushmanskloof.co.za, Box 53405, Kenilworth, Cape Town 7745. Alternatively, you can find plenty of rock art of your own hiking in the **Cederberg Wilderness Area**, which stretches south and east of the town. For **trekking permits** contact ((027) 482 2812 FAX (027) 482 2406 Bag XI, Citrusdal 7340.

Art apart, there are a couple of outstanding retail opportunities in town. The **Veld Shoe Factory** ((027) 482 2140 FAX (027) 482 1812, open Monday to Friday 8:30 AM to 6 PM, Saturday 9 AM to 1 PM, on Main Street above the tourist office, is a nationally-famous shoe factory, founded in 1834 in nearby Wuppertal and now operating out of Clanwilliam. Known in South Africa as *velskoene* or "vellies" this comfortable, handmade and tough footwear is perfectly designed for this rugged environment, with custom designs produced overnight on overtime rates. Prices start at R200. Once you have a pair you'll find total strangers lifting their own feet onto tables and chairs to compare their shoes with yours, and offer congratulations on a wise and lasting purchase.

Further up Main Street is another national institution, the **Rooibos Tea Factory** ((027) 482 2155 FAX (027) 482 1844, with guided tours Monday to Friday at 10 AM, 11:30 AM, 2 PM, and 3:30 PM. The spiny Rooibos bush was used to brew tea by the San people, who would hack off the branches with axes and bruise them before leaving them to ferment in heaps then drying them in the sun. The resulting brew is an aromatic, heady tea. It's more than a beverage: for South Africans it's an important symbol of their country. Enthusiasts credit it with the ability to cure a range of health problems, including insomnia, stomach cramps, and con-

stipation, as well as hayfever and asthma. But they'll quickly go further, suggesting it for nappy rash, treating acne, and any disease you mention, backing its effectiveness against cancer and old age by quoting experiments from Japan. The most interesting thing about the Rooibos bush, however, is that it steadfastly refuses to grow anywhere except the Cederbergs around Clanwilliam. This is the only place in the world you'll get a fresh cup. And when you've finished your factory tour, boxes of Rooibos Tea and packets of beauty products are, of course, on sale at reception.

Where to Stay and Eat

The best place to stay in Clanwilliam is the **Rectory** ((027) 482 1629 FAX (027) 482 1179, 35 Main Street, R400, a period building on the high street that has been transformed into a private villa, perfect for parties or individuals. The rooms are individually furnished around an open courtyard,

lime-washed colors and delicate murals bringing a taste of Tuscany to the Cederbergs. Sadly, there are only four bedrooms, so on occasion the Rectory will be full. A good alternative is the **Saint du Barry's Country Lodge** (/FAX (027) 482 1537, 13 Augsburg Street, R320 to R480, antique-furnished thatched chalets on the edge of town towards the Cederberg Wilderness Area. The town center is dominated by the **Strassberger's Hotel Clanwilliam** ((027) 482 1101, High Street, R290, with a lively bar and friendly atmosphere.

Out of town, **Travelers Rest** (/FAX (027) 482 1824, charges R140 for rustic but well-located self-catering chalets, converted from farm workers' buildings, 36 km (23 miles) out of Clanwilliam on the Augsburg Road. If your budget is up to it, the upmarket option is the lavish **Bushman's Kloof** ((027) 482 2627 FAX (027) 482 1011 or for reservations ((021) 797 0990 FAX (021) 797 5551 E-MAIL santrack@ilink.co.za WEB SITE www.bushmans

kloof.co.za, Box 53405, Kenilworth, Cape Town 7745, is three kilometers (just under two miles) further on — but followed by a seven-kilometer (four-and-a-half-mile) driveway. There's nothing in town for backpackers — yet.

The smartest place to eat in Clanwilliam is certainly **Reinholds** ((027) 482 1101, 4 Main Street, a restored Victorian house opposite — and owned by — Strassberger's Hotel, which is open from Wednesday to Saturday, evenings only. Strassberger's own hotel dining room, open every day, is rather cheaper and serves huge portions.

How to Get There
Clanwilliam is 240 km (149 miles) from Cape Town, on the N7 highway to Namibia. Intercape buses stop two kilometers (just over a mile) from the town, above the dam.

Fields pattern beauty onto an Overberg landscape.

CALVINIA, FLOWER COUNTRY

North of Clanwilliam the countryside flattens out into a huge, dry expanse, and the N7 road flies on towards the Namibian border. To the west is the cold Atlantic coast, washing small settlements with a cold morning mist, home to a motley selection of gemstone prospectors and fishermen, hanging on to a tenuous existence far from the comforts of the modern world. To the east the Hantam Karoo, an arid country broken by flat-topped mountains, erupts into glorious flowers after the annual rains, usually at their best through August and September. At all times of year the Hantam Karoo is a hauntingly beautiful landscape, with horizons that seem to reach forever, scarcely touched by the process of colonization or development.

The largest city in the Hantam Karoo, Calvinia comes to life for the **flower season**, when it is deluged with tourists from Cape Town and botanists from all over the world. If you're coming to see the flowers, it is worth taking the trouble to plan your tour carefully, down to the details such as making sure you drive with the sun at your shoulder, to make sure the flowers are turned towards you. There is a **Flower Hotline** ((021) 418 3705, which gives information about where the best flowers are, with 1,400 different species blooming around Calvinia, Nieuwoudtville, and Loeriesfontein, all dependent on vital and erratic winter rain and then far-from-certain sunshine. There is no point getting up at dawn to see the flowers — they need sunlight to open, and even if the weather is good the flowers will not open until 10:30 AM or so. To add to the confusion there are 23 evening species, which need a full day's sun before lighting up the sunset. And although it is tempting to imagine the sight will still be rewarding when the flowers are closed, the proteas hide their brilliance well in dull weather and if conditions aren't right the display is bound to disappoint.

Calvinia celebrates the middle of the flower season with the **Hantam Meat Festival** ((027) 341 1794, The Secretary, Box 111, Calvinia 8190, usually held in the last weekend of August, when the larger members of the rural community gather to eat hugely and their slimmer counterparts lurch out into folkloric dancing and singing. The town was first settled by Dutch, German and French settlers, and although Jewish and British communities established themselves in the area in 1880 they soon drifted away for a livelier life in the cities. Perhaps the climate was too much; summers here are hot and through the winter most nights are frosty. Now the atmosphere is deeply Afrikaans, rural Africa at its most unspoiled.

What to See and Do

The **Tourist Office** ((027) 341 1712 FAX (027) 341 2750, 44 Church Street, 8 AM to 1 PM and 2 PM to 5 PM, closing at noon on Saturday and open Sunday afternoon by appointments only, shares a 1920s synagogue with the **Town Museum**, R1. Settler life, once again, forms the centerpiece of most exhibits, but there are gems: there's a Merino sheep with a fleece measuring 38 cm (15 in) which causes particular excitement in these parts, a traditional black wedding dress and, strangely, six pianos.

The early days are preserved in the village center in the **Hantam House**, the oldest building in the village, which dates back to 1853. The builder must have been pleased the next year, when Daniel Halladay invented the wind pump that brought life to the desert. There's a quirky collection of antiques here, including the meals, which are highly traditional. The restaurant — and building — is open through the day but closed in the evenings outside the flower season. There's also a huge grain silo painted red to resemble a postbox; letters posted here get a special stamp. This might sound tacky but in a dusty one-horse *dorp* it's actually a bit of a highlight.

To fully experience the Karoo it is necessary to get out of your car and explore on foot. Four kilometers (two and a half miles) north of Calvinia the Akkerendam Nature Reserve has two walking trails: a two-kilometer (just over a mile) easy walk and a strenuous 12-km (seven-and-a-half-mile) hike. For permits call ((027) 341 1712, and remember to carry your own water. The summer sun, especially, is unforgiving.

Where to Stay and Eat

A selection of restored village-center houses are rented out on a self-catering basis by the **Hantam House** (/FAX (027) 341 1606, Hoop Street, with rates from R120. Alternatively **Home Sweet Home** ((027) 341 1560, 10 Hantam Street, rents out a bedroom for R120 with breakfast, or try **Pionierslot** (/FAX (027) 341 1263, 35 Water Street. The **Commercial** ((027) 341 1020 FAX (027) 341 2835, Water Street, R200 with breakfast, has 20 rooms and a bar enlivened by a collection of 2,000 neckties. Many are donated by visitors passing through, who realize they won't be needing such formality here. For eating, Afrikaner food is the norm here, with Die Blou Nartjie, in the Pionierslot guest house, and a restaurant in the Hantam House to choose from.

How to Get There

Surprisingly, Calvinia is on the main Intercape bus service running from Upington to Cape Town, which stops at Trokkies service station, but timetables mean they do so in the middle of the night. There's no local taxi shuttle service.

With a rental vehicle Calvinia is midway between Cape Town and Upington, six hours from each.

UPINGTON

The last significant town before Namibia, the small town of Upington was established to bring law to one of the last areas to be brought under central control, in 1879, and it grew around a police station built to protect a drift across the river. Thanks to the year-round water of the Orange River it became a prosperous farming center when, after the Boer Wars, irrigation channels were dug. It is still very much frontier country, and mainly visited as jump-off point for the national parks of the far north, the Kalahari Gemsbok and Augrabies Falls national parks. These days its isolation remains extreme, and a seemingly irreversible drift is sucking its population to the towns.

The town itself runs along the riverbank, with the **Upington Tourist Information Bureau** ((054) 332 6911 FAX (054) 332 7064, the Library Building, Mutual Street, open Monday to Friday 9 AM to 6 PM and Saturday to noon, and very helpful. There are no taxi companies in the town but there are two hospitals, the best of which is **Upington Private Hospital** ((054) 332 3011.

The town's attractions are few but rewarding. The **town museum**, Schroder Street, open 8 AM to 12:30 PM and 1:30 PM to 5 PM, includes an unusually complete restored manse house where Reverend Schroeder first settled in the area in the 1870s, bringing Christianity to this patch of desert, with a compendium of Victorian games for distraction.

Most visitors here are using the town as a base to stock up for the **Kalahari Gemsbok National Park**, 338 km (211 miles) to the north. Combined with Botswana's Gemsbok National Park it covers a protected land area of more than 3.6 million hectares (8.8 million acres), one of the largest parks in the world. There is superb game-viewing but take care: in the austral summer it gets very hot and 10 liters (about three gallons) of drinking water, at least, should be carried at all times. The sparse scrub clinging to the red dunes mean that the wildlife is easy to spot, and it is one of the finest places to see game, as predators and prey alike scour the countryside for sources of water. Entry to the park is R36 per person. By the time you've traveled that far it would be madness to drive straight back. There are three rest camps all with a range of chalets and camping facilities, and charges from R105 for a hut sleeping up to three people to R400 for a chalet sleeping up to six. In peak season the limited facilities are likely to be fully booked, and it is worth reserving your bed in good time through the **Park Authorities** ((012) 343 1991 FAX (012) 343 0905 E-MAIL reservations @parks-sa.co.za.

The other national park that can be visited from Upington is the arid but spectacularly beautiful sandstone vistas of **Augrabies Falls National Park**, 88 km (55 miles) east along the N14 and then right for 28 km (17.5 miles) on a dirt road. It can be a hostile environment and is closed from October to March because of the searing heat, but it has all the colors of the desert landscapes, and a surprisingly diverse wildlife population. There is one small camp with chalets and cottages with prices from R270 for a three-bedded bungalow. Book, once again, through Park Authorities ((012) 343 1991 FAX (012) 343 0905 E-MAIL reservations@parks-sa.co.za during office hours, or the local park office ((054) 451 0050 FAX (054) 451 0053. Entry to the park is free. It helps to have a four-wheel drive vehicle, otherwise it is best to use a local operator to take you into the park. The **Augrabies Rush** ((054) 451 0177 arrange river-rafting trips in the park for R145 per person.

On a totally different budget, Upington is also the nearest town — a mere three hours drive — northwest to **Tswalu** ((053) 781 9311 FAX (053) 781 9216 E-MAIL tswalures@kimberley.co.za WEB SITE www.tswalu.co.za, Box 420, Kathu 8446, a private reserve on the Botswana border, although this can also be reached by a daily charter flight leaving from Johannesburg Airport. At 60,000 hectares (nearly 150,000 acres) it is one of the largest private reserves in the world. It is also one of the most remote. If distance alone is not enough to guarantee exclusivity, it only accommodates 22 people, and to ensure it never gets overcrowded it charges R5,000 per couple, including all game-drives and meals.

Where to Stay

Upington has an adequate range of accommodation. **Le Must Restaurant and Guest Manor** ((054) 332 3971 FAX (054) 332 5779 E-MAIL lemusttravel @gem.co.za, is a very sophisticated restaurant with guestrooms at R300 including breakfast. The **Oasis Protea** ((054) 331 1125 FAX (054) 332 1232, 26 Schroeder Street, R300, is a good hotel though a touch businesslike. Try to get a room overlooking the river. Backpackers can go for the **Halfway House** ((054) 332 1852, Schroeder Street, R45 per person in dormitory.

How to Get There

The easiest way to get to Upington is by air. **SA Airlink** operate a daily service to Cape Town and Johannesburg. The **airport** ((054) 331 1364 is seven kilometers (just over four miles) north of town. The railway service no longer serves the town, but **City to City** ((054) 328 2203 or (021) 405 3333 runs to Cape Town while **Intercape** ((054) 332 7091 or (021) 386 4400 travels also to Johannesburg. By road Upington is 894 km (559 miles) from Cape Town and 804 km (503 miles) from Johannesburg.

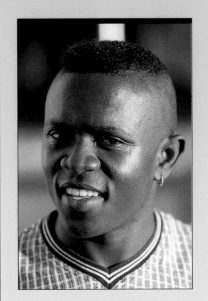

The Southern Coast

EAST OF CAPE TOWN the N2 flies for 400 km (250 miles) to the start of the Garden Route, traveling inland passing through the Overberg area, an ill-defined region south of the Langeberg mountains but east of the Hottentot Holland Mountains. These were the natural obstacle that for many years blocked development of the area, sending settlers spreading instead inland, over flatter country to the Winelands. The highway passes close to the northern mountains through towns such as Caledon and the historic streetscapes of Swellendam. If time is of the essence this is the fastest way to the Garden Route, but it misses out many areas of interest, especially on the southern coast, now known as the Whale Coast. Pockets of unspoiled *fynbos*, high views over whale-filled waters, and the opportunity to dive with sharks are among the many good reasons to take the minor roads that cross the bird-filled farmlands to the south. While the smarter hotels are generally further east, the Whale Coast is surprisingly undeveloped, with agricultural communities living in a beautiful landscape, reaching south to the southernmost point of Africa, where the oceans meet.

The Garden Route itself starts around Mossel Bay, continuing through Knysna to Tsitsikamma Forest, but it is well worth taking one of the spectacular mountain routes that head inland to the Klein Karoo to the north. Many Garden Route drivers stop at Port Elizabeth, perhaps making a short outing to the Addo Elephant Park and Shamwari, but there is plenty to justify traveling further. Inland is the striking desert city of Graaff-Reinet while further east the colonial city of Grahamstown and the homeland cultures of East London are natural extensions to a Garden Route tour.

EAST OF CAPE TOWN

The central **Cape Overberg Tourism Association** ((028) 214 1466 FAX (028) 212 1380 E-MAIL cota@ cyberhost.co.za, Box 250, Caledon 7230, is very helpful and keen to promote the whole Overberg area. This takes in the historic towns of Swellendam and Caledon, as well as the unspoiled agrarian peninsula reaching down to Africa's southern tip, Cape Agulhas.

CALEDON

Most travelers pass straight past Caledon on the N2 on their way to the Garden Route. At 110 km (69 miles) from Cape Town it might have been time for a break in the days of wagon-trains, but in the age of the car it's too early for a stop, too soon for a small detour, and its attractions don't really justify a day-trip. Now that the Overberger Hotel has been rebuilt this might change. However, Caledon is the administrative capital of the Overberg region and a good base for exploring the area. It owes

its existence to six hot springs that pump 800,000 liters (over 210,000 gallons) a day of carbonated water from the foot of the Swartberg mountains, originally used by the indigenous Khoi people, who would wallow around in mud springs. The water's amazing healing properties saw it boom in popularity at the end of the eighteenth century. Advances in medical science eclipsed its appeal, and when the sanatorium and baths burned down in 1946 they weren't rebuilt until 1990. The town is now, more prosaically, an agricultural center. The **Caledon Tourism Bureau** ((028) 212 1511 FAX (028) 214 1427, 22 Plein Street, Box 258, Caledon 7230, open Monday to Friday 8 AM to 1 PM and 2 PM to 5 PM, Saturday 9 AM to 1 PM, has information about the region.

What to See and Do

The best thing to do in town is to take a hot bath in the mineral springs in the reconstructed

Victorian Bathhouse ((028) 214 1271, Nerina Avenue, 8 AM to 8 PM daily, R10, in the grounds of the Overberger Hotel. There's a **Town Museum** ((028) 212 1511, 16 Constitution Street, R3, with a collection of domestic paraphernalia. Out of town the **Caledon Nature Reserve**, which includes the **Victoria Wild Flower Garden**, open 7 AM to 5 PM daily, R5, has 200 of the 630 known species of *erica*, best seen on a self-guided trail that takes about five hours to complete.

Where to Stay and Eat

The best place in town to stay is the **Overberger Country Hotel and Spa** ((028) 214 1271 FAX (028) 214 1270, Nerina Avenue, which has three spa pools, a beauty clinic, an 18-hole golf course, and all the trimmings for R420 including breakfast.

Less expensive, the **Alexandra Hotel** ((028) 212 3052 FAX (028) 214 1102, Market Square, charges R280, while the Caledon Tourism Bureau has

information about bed-and-breakfast establishments and about guest houses. If your budget won't stretch to dining at the Overberger Country Hotel and Spa's two restaurants, the Alexandra Hotel has the **Dahlia Restaurant** attached, with good meals also available at the **Venster Restaurant**, Hoop Street, overlooking the *fynbos* of the Victoria Wildflower Garden. Caledon is just a few kilometers off the N2, 110 km (69 miles) west of Cape Town.

SWELLENDAM

South Africa's third oldest settlement, Swellendam is a quaint village of whitewashed Dutch homesteads lined with oaks, many of which were unfortunately flattened in a 1974 road-widening scheme, but enough have now been rebuilt to

Knysna's salt-water lagoon feeds to the ocean through the narrow opening of the Knysna Heads.

regain the village's charm. The **Swellendam Tourism Bureau** (/FAX (028) 514 2770 E-MAIL infoswd @sdm.dorea.co.za, Oefeningshuis, 36 Voortrek Street, Box 369, Swellendam 6740, is open Monday to Friday 8 AM to 1 PM and 2 PM to 5 PM, Saturday 9 AM to 12:30 PM.

What to See and Do

The greatest sight in Swellendam is the **Drostdy Museum** ((028) 514 1138, Swellengrebel Street, open Monday to Friday 9 AM to 4:45 PM, Saturday and Sunday 10 AM to 4 PM, R5, one of the country's architectural treasures, much of it preserved as the original 1747 *landross* (magistrate). The rest of the town is best explored on foot, to see the his-

toric **Oefeningshuis**, which now houses the tourist office, and a number of period properties in the center. Out of town the **Bontebok National Park** protects valuable swathes of indigenous vegetation as well as valuable herds of the endangered bontebok themselves.

Where to Stay and Eat

The best place to stay here is just outside town, in the restored family home of past presidents Steyn and Reitz, the **Klippe Rivier** ((028) 514 3341 FAX (028) 514 3337, Klippe Rivier, R800 to R1,100 including breakfast. Back in town a bland but central base is the **Swellengrebel Hotel** ((028) 514 1144 FAX (028) 514 2453, 91 Voortrek Street, R480. Alternatively, in a rural setting the **Old Mill Guest Cottage** (/FAX (028) 514 2790, 241 and 243 Voortrek Street, is not too far from town and offers al fresco dining by the stream or in the Mill Restaurant. Rates run R260 including breakfast. Otherwise, it's bed-and-breakfast country: there are more than 20 in the town, all regulated by the town council. For backpackers, **Swellendam Backpackers** ((028) 514 2648 FAX (028) 514 1249, 5 Liechtenstein Street, offers dormitory accommodation for R40 and free pickups from the town center, a distance of two kilometers (just over a mile).

How to Get There

Swellendam is 240 km (150 miles) from Cape Town and 225 km (141 miles) from George on the N2. **Greyhound**, **Intercape** and **Translux** all stop here.

THE WHALE COAST

From Cape Town the N2 climbs through the Hottentot Holland Mountains, using a pass carved through the rock by Sir Lowry Cole, first used in July 1830, through the industrial town of Strand and past Somerset West. While the N2 continues inland the R44 turns right to stay on the coast, passing along the eastern shores of False Bay, skirting the crashing waves and passing Cape Town's weekend resorts of Betty's Bay and Kleinmond before looping back towards the N2. The Overberg's Whale Coast starts at the town of Rooiels, continues through all these resort towns and carries on to include Hermanus, Gansbaai, L'Agulhas, and De Hoop Nature Reserve, extending as far as the mouth of the Breede River. To stay on the coast from the N2, turn right on the R43 for the town of Hermanus.

HERMANUS

The Hermanus area started life as a vacation resort. Farmers from the interior would bring their families here during the summer and indulge in a bit of fishing while their herds grazed nearby. Gradually the fishing industry built up and it started to make a living from fishing. Later it acquired a reputation for good health with referrals coming from as far away as London's Harley Street, prescribing the area's "champagne air." The Windsor Hotel was built as a sanatorium and a harbor was added.

Currently booming, the town trumpets its status as the best place for land-based whale viewing. Trumpets, literally — through the whale season from June to November the council employs the world's only whale crier, who takes sightings on a mobile phone and toots a megaphone made of dried kelp when a whale is spotted offshore. It has to be said that during my visit the crier was being trained at the tourist office, and although the town-center car parking lots were filled with people gazing hopefully through binoculars, there were no whales to be seen. The best months to spot whales are from July to November, when southern right whales flip into Walker Bay to calve. In fact, they can be seen from viewpoints all along the coast, but Hermanus is certainly one of the best places to spot them. Although of course they don't appear to order, sightings are daily from September through October, and the whale crier has a sandwich board, which maps out the day's sightings. From the lower rocks of the town-center cliffs it has often been known for whales to come within 10 m (32 ft) of their watchers: an unforgettable experience.

General Information

The **Hermanus Tourism Bureau** ((028) 312 2629
FAX (028) 313 0305 E-MAIL infoburo@ilink.nis.za,
105 Main Street, Box 117, Hermanus 7200, open
9 AM to 5 PM Monday to Saturday, is large and organized. A local taxi company is **Grab-a-Cab** ((028)
212 1388, 17 Long Street. The **Hospital** ((028) 312
1166 has a good reputation—patients often don't
want to leave.

What to See and Do

Whale watching is the main game in town. The
World Wildlife Fund lists Hermanus as one of the
12 best places to spot the mammals. Up to 120
southern right whales have been seen in Walker

but storms have scuttled so many the feature had
been abandoned on my last visit. Even so, there
are recordings of a whole range of whale species
that can be heard while standing by a wide picture window overlooking the sea, and a telescope
to zoom in on patches of water disturbed by wind
or whales. Outside there is a small collection of
restored fishing boats, with the earliest dating back
to 1855.

In the open air there's a cliff path, stretching
12 km (seven and a half miles) from the new harbor all the way round Walker Bay to Grotto Beach,
with benches along the way. It's a level walk and
perfect for picnics, while Grotto Beach is the best
for swimming. Hermanus is actually enclosed by

Bay; not bad out of a world population of no
more than 6,000. They got their name because
they were the "right" whales to hunt. They float
when dead, and their 80-ton weight produced
a good supply of oil and baleen. Perhaps unsurprisingly the northern right whale, which used
to frequent the waters of the northern hemisphere,
is almost extinct. The sea shelves deeply down
from Hermanus' cliffs, and the town is set high,
allowing a good view through the usually clear
water. There's a **Whale Hotline** (083) 910 1028 or
(083) 910 1074, to inquire about recent sightings
and a special number to record any **strandings**
((021) 402 3911; alternatively, call the Tourism
Bureau. One good place to look is from the **Old
Harbor Museum** ((028) 312 1475, on Marine
Drive, with detailed exhibits on fishing as well
as, of course, whales. There used to be a sonar
buoy broadcasting whale song live from the sea,

nature reserves. There's the **Marine Reserve** offshore while inland the **Fernkloof Nature Reserve**
protects valuable areas of *fynbos* on the surrounding mountains. There are three color-coded trails
and it is possible to go hiking, staying in a fourperson overnight hut; for permission and reservations call ((028) 312 1122.

There are a number of wreck dives in the area
as well as cold water coral reefs. Contact **Scuba
Africa** ((083) 310 2303 or **Aquadyne** ((028) 312
2212. There is horseback riding available from
Cilla's Stables ((028) 312 3679. Although fishing
is strictly regulated there are no shortage of game
fish in the sea. Contact **Lagoon Charters** ((028)
312 1596.

OPPOSITE: Freelance scarecrows keep the birds
away from a Swellendam strawberry farm.
ABOVE: If you don't spot whales off the
coast near Hermanus, look for birds.

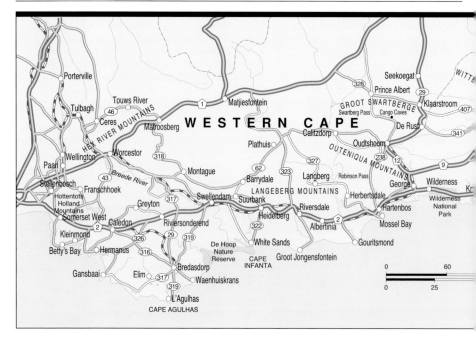

Where to Stay and Eat

In its boom years as a health spa Hermanus had 16 hotels. There are fewer now, and at peak times — through the whale season, during school holidays, and particularly at Christmas — it can be hard to find a bed. Book ahead. The town's main hotel is the **Marine** ((028) 313 1000 FAX (028) 313 0160 E-MAIL marine@hermanus.co.za, Marine Drive, from R800 to R2,500 room only. This 47-room five-star hotel is one of the town's originals, dating back to 1902, but has recently been refurbished and retains its setting overlooking the ocean. A member of Relais & Châteaux, the Marine has two of the best restaurants in town and steps lead down to a tidal swimming pool. Another good place to stay, **Auberge Burgundy** ((028) 313 1201 FAX (028) 313 1204, 16 Harbor Road, somewhat surprisingly is not burgundy in color but painted light tan instead. This central hotel has a mix of double rooms and suites set in shady gardens from R580 including breakfast.

The **Windsor** ((028) 312 3727 FAX (028) 312 2181 E-MAIL windsor@hermanus.co.za WEB SITE www .hermanus.co.za/accom/windsor, 49 Marine Drive, R400 to R450 including breakfast, is another grand old lady in the center of town, with a covered veranda overlooking the sea and many rooms with whale-watching balconies. Mountain-view rooms are cheaper at R350. **Sandbaai Country House** ((028) 316 3603 FAX (028) 316 3078 E-MAIL sandbaai@satis.co.za WEB SITE www.satis.co.za/ sandbaai, 70 Beach Road/Marine Drive, Sandbaai, is not in the country but in the Sandbaai coastal suburb. Only by looking at their brochure or keeping your eyes fixed firmly out to sea can you imagine it is in fact a country house. Large picture windows and custom-made furniture help make the most of this relatively modern guesthouse, whose rates run R400 to R700.

Back near the town center in Westcliff the **Whale Rock Lodge** ((028) 313 0014 FAX (028) 312 2932, 26 Springfield Avenue, R300, is a friendly bed-and-breakfast with 10 rooms. Since the Travelers Lodge closed, backpackers tend to stay at the **Zoete Inval** (/FAX (028) 312 1242 E-MAIL zoetein @hermanus.co.za, 23 Main Street, which has prices from R40 per person sharing.

A popular restaurant in town is **Bientang's Cave** ((028) 312 3454. This actually is in a cave, so it's best to call ahead for directions. They are generally busy so reservations are, in any case, essential. Fresh seafood is cooked and served on rustic wooden tables in an undeniably exotic location; dress casual. The **Burgundy** ((028) 312 2280, on Marine Drive, is one of the area's top restaurants, in a restored Victorian cliff-top house. For Italian food, **Rossi's Restaurant** ((028) 312 2848, 10 High Street, is your best option. For seafood the **Fisherman's Cottage** ((028) 312 3642, Old Harbor, is known as the smaller pub in town and when the weather is good offers seafood al fresco in an unbeatable setting.

How to Get There

The mainstream bus companies don't run to Hermanus, but there is a share car service to and from Cape Town operated by **Hermanus Courier** ((028) 312 4019, 12 Dirkie Uys Street, Hermanus,

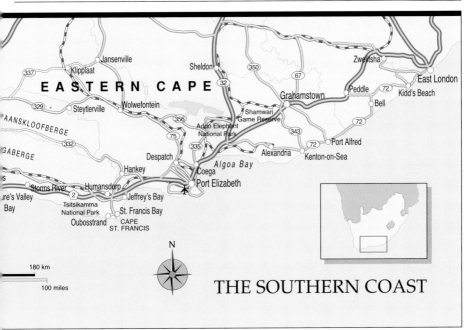

THE SOUTHERN COAST

which runs from Monday to Friday. By road, the quickest route is along the N2 and taking the R44 right at Botrivier and the R43 left to Hermanus. The distance of 120 km (75 miles) takes little more than an hour.

GROOTBOS PRIVATE NATURE RESERVE

From Hermanus the R326 curves inland past the Walker Bay Nature Reserve: a right turn takes the R43 back towards the coast and Gansbaai. Most of the activities here are nautical, but it would be a shame not to look inland. Some of the Cape's best-preserved areas of *fynbos* are found here, along with a private research station, and this is one of the best places to learn more about South Africa's "Sixth Floral Kingdom." Seven kilometers (just over four miles) before Gansbaai a turning on the right leads up to Grootbos Private Nature Reserve ((028) 384 0381 FAX (028) 384 0552 E-MAIL grootbos@ hermanus.co.za.

"Grootbos" means, in Afrikaans, "large forest," and takes its name from the milkwood trees that here form the largest forest in South Africa — and therefore the largest collection of milkwood trees in the world. It's a melancholy fact that there aren't that many of them — certainly not a fraction of the surrounding commercial forests. The milkwoods here are a sad remnant pocket of the forest that once clothed much of the Cape, and was shouldered aside by the agricultural settlers from Europe. Invading plants introduced from Europe disrupt the milkwood's propagation techniques, which rely on regular cool-burning fires

to germinate. The introduced plants, such as rooikrans and port jackson, burn at a far higher temperature and cause the milkwoods to die, rather than germinate.

The reserve also enclosed swathes of *fynbos*, including more than 500 catalogued plant species, many of which flower between August and October. Alongside a fully staffed research laboratory investigating the bird and plant life, there's a lodge that caters to a maximum of 26 guests, housed in sheltered luxury in chalets scattered about the reserve, with guided trails for four-wheel-drive vehicles, horseback, and walking. From the main lodge there's a superb view of Walker Bay, with Leica telescopes set up to bring any passing whales into sharp focus. A stay here isn't cheap — R1,800 per day, full board, with a minimum stay of two nights — but this includes all activities in the reserve including guided horseback rides, with boat excursions into the bay costing extra. The dynamism of owners Michael and Tertius Lutzeyer does much to make it worthwhile. The lodge is closed for a complete overhaul for a month between June and July, to maintain its very high standards.

GANSBAAI

Shark-infested waters surround Gansbaai, set on Danger Point, and there are plenty of sharks in the town itself too, feeding on the recent craze for cage diving with great white sharks. Fishing is still the main source of income here, with catches landing daily at the harbor and proceeding quickly to the canning factory, but visitors are more likely to come into contact with the shark-diving boats. These sail out to Dyer Island, an important seal colony, where great white sharks are attracted to the fast-swimming meals gamboling in the water. For more on shark diving see DIVE WITH A GREAT WHITE, page 17 in TOP SPOTS.

General Information

Gansbaai Tourism Bureau ((028) 384 1349 FAX (028) 384 0955, at the corner of Berg and Main streets, Box 399, Gansbaai 7220, open 9 AM to 4 PM Monday to Friday and 10 AM to noon Saturday, is moderately helpful, though perhaps wisely it won't step into the cutthroat waters of shark-dive operations. The bigger operators are trying to set up a licensing scheme for shark-dive boats, but signs are this will just end up with a cowboy cartel.

Sightings of sharks are not guaranteed, and baiting sharks is no guarantee they will either come to the boat, nor stay around for long enough for everyone on board to get a good sighting. The boat operators all have their favorite and jealously guarded techniques for attracting sharks but none are foolproof. Newspaper and magazine features invariably focus on the great approaching jaws and a flurry of bloodlust, but this does not accurately reflect the experience for many. Through December and January, especially, the shark have plenty of seal pups to keep their stomachs full and are unlikely to be drawn by fish entrails chummed from a powerboat, and bad weather will cause cancellation. Bear in mind also that all the operators in Gansbaai use free-floating cages and so you need a scuba license to play.

The established operators include **White Shark Diving** ((028) 384 0782 E-MAIL divemaster@cape-explorer.com; **White Shark Expeditions** ((028) 313 0156 FAX (028) 313 0129 E-MAIL bookings@sharklady.co.za WEB SITE www.sharklady.co.za; **White Shark Adventures** ((028) 381 1380 FAX (028) 381 1381 E-MAIL shardkiv@itec.co.za WEB SITE www.steerage.co.za/seafaris; and **South Coast Seafaris** ((028) 384 1380 FAX (028) 384 1381 E-MAIL seafaris@iafrica.com. Prices are kept in line by competition. From Gansbaai, they should be about R300 for a day-long expedition just viewing, with divers paying R450 to R700 including the rental of scuba equipment, some of which has definitely seen better days. Ask about their policy if no shark is sighted, as sometimes a higher fee includes a partial refund. The decision is up to you: it's a straight gamble.

Alternatively, **San-Doo Ecocruises** ((028) 384 1266 travels out to Dyer Island to look at the penguins, seals, and cormorants without getting bogged down in the endless hunt for shark sightings. Polarized sunglasses help to see all the animals, whether sharks or seals, as they frolic around beneath the water surface.

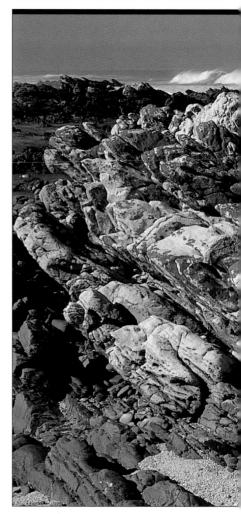

Where to Stay and Eat

De Kelders, the time-warp Victorian hotel overlooking the sea, has gone out of business, and now most accommodation is aimed at backpackers. For example, **Great White Backpackers** ((028) 384 1380 FAX (028) 384 1381, Main Street, is a pleasantly relaxed place spread out through two 1950s bungalows. On the high street **Tolbos** ((028) 384 1560, 34 Main Street, is a good place for light lunches and the **Barnhouse Grill** ((028) 384 1502, 33 Main Street, is a lively venue for steaks and seafood, with dancing when the mood strikes.

How to Get There

There is no form of public transportation to Gansbaai, but shuttle services feeding the shark boats with customers run daily from Cape Town. It is best to travel in a rental car; it is two hours drive from Cape Town.

CAPE AGULHAS: AFRICA'S SOUTHERN TIP

A visit to Cape Agulhas is irresistible: the chance to overlook the meeting of the Atlantic and Indian oceans at Africa's southern tip and the nearest point to Antarctica. Unfortunately the general consensus is that it is a disappointment. Certainly you get more of a feeling of space and occasion at Cape Point, even though this is far to the north. South Africa dribbles to the south in a wide empty road crossed by countless speed bumps and traffic-control cameras through a suburb of guesthouses, with their seasonal bloom of bed-and-breakfast signs. At the tip there's a red-banded lighthouse, two kilometers (just over a mile) shy of Cape Agulhas, where a sign and a plaque are set in the rocks, and… that's it. Driving back through the sprawling development there are occasional teashops and cafés but nothing irresistible.

After years of such piecemeal development the Agulhas Plain was finally declared a national park in 1999. The decision was taken because of the species and plant biodiversity. It contains 2,000 species of indigenous plants including 110 Red Data Book species internationally recognized as highly endangered. The wetlands are home to the endangered Cape platanna and the micro frog. Initially 100 hectares (nearly 250 acres) of land have been proclaimed park, with plans to expand over the sensitive lands to the west. It is hoped that the project works out.

Cape Agulhas can be reached from the west through a network of minor roads, but the easiest route is to turn off the N2 at Caledon and take the R316 to Bredasdorp, turning right onto the R319.

Forty kilometers (25 miles) to the north of Cape Agulhas is the Moravian settlement of **Elim**,

Cape Agulhas is the southernmost tip of South Africa, where the world's largest continent slides into the sea.

which is worth a drive through. The village is a national monument, with whitewashed thatched cottages home to church members only. It takes its name from the resting place where the Israelites settled after crossing the Red Sea, but I didn't realize they'd traveled so far before stopping: some 9,600 km (6,000 miles)! Even now, all residents have to be members of the church and make their living from the land. The town now makes its living drying indigenous plants for exports. **Elim Tourism Bureau** ((028) 482 1806 FAX (028) 482 1750, Churchyard, Box 33, Elim 7284, open Monday to Friday 8 AM to 1 PM and 2 PM to 4:30 PM, Saturday to noon, has guides available to interpret the settlement to villagers and there is a tearoom for lunch.

DE HOOP NATURE RESERVE

East of Cape Agulhas, the De Hoop Nature Reserve stretches some 50 km (31 miles) up the coast and five kilometers (three miles) out to sea. In a space of little over 36,000 hectares (nearly 89,000 acres), more than seven different ecosystems can be found, from the tidal pools on the shore through marshes and sand dunes, rising up to limestone hills and the Potberg Mountain. There are thought to be at least 1,500 plant species here and a range of animals, including Cape mountain zebra, and leopard, bontebok, along with other grazing animals. It's paradise for birdwatchers, with the black oystercatcher often being seen, and it is also the only breeding colony of the endangered Cape vulture. There are even more whales offshore than there are in Hermanus, but they're less easy to see as they stay out beyond the breakers. While the western section remains given over to hikers, the eastern side has been developed with mountain biking trails, but there's no bike rental so it appeals more to South Africans.

Numbers are limited. For (essential) reservations contact the **Manager** ((028) 542 1126 FAX (028) 542 1679, De Hoop Nature Reserve, P/Bag X16, Bredasdorp 7280. The park gates are open from 7 AM to 6 PM, but overnight visitors have to check in with the De Hoop office which is only open from 8 AM to 4 PM weekdays, 8 AM to 11 AM weekends. There is a fee of R4 per person. To use the mountain bike trails in the eastern sector of De Hoop you need to book the overnight hut (R100 for four people) and pay entry fees and bike charges. Once again, reservations are essential.

Although it is one of the most important wildlife areas in the Cape and well worth a detour for anyone interested in the natural world, it's not easy to get to and there's nowhere to stay, apart from a campsite and some rather ordinary self-catering cottages set well back from the sea. In the surrounding area some farmhouse bed-and-breakfasts and self-catering chalets are available,

with details best obtained from **Suidpunt Tourism Bureau** ((028) 414 2584 E-MAIL suidpunt@ brd.dorea.co.za, Dr. Jansen Street, Box 51, Bredasdorp 7280, open Monday to Friday 8 AM to 7 PM, Saturday 9 AM to 1 PM. De Hoop is reached from Bredasdorp along the R319. After 40 km (25 miles) Ouplaas is a good place to stock up as it is the nearest shop. The park boundary is 10 km (just over six miles) away, whether right to the western section or straight on to the eastern part. From the east, take the R322 from the N2 to White Sands, turning right onto dirt roads after 35 km (19 miles).

REINS NATURE RESERVE

Falling rather between the Overberg and the start of the Garden Route is an unusual and beneficial piece of fallout from South Africa's stop-go nuclear policy: Reins Coastal Nature Reserve. In 1980 a huge tract of land was ringed with security fencing and troops placed on patrol. Fishermen were turned away and overflying rights removed. Squat offices went up and a few choice administrators moved in. This area, it had been decided, would be the site of South Africa's second nuclear power station.

After the 1994 elections someone did their sums and realized nuclear power was prohibitively expensive. The project was abandoned, and when the site came on the market electronics manufacturer Gerhard Rein, who already owned a neighboring farm, bought the property with the specific aim of saving this unspoiled patch of *fynbos* and gently restock it with some of the animals that once roamed this part of Africa.

A condition of purchase was that no new buildings could be constructed. So the original civil service quarters have been renovated into very comfortable and practical accommodation. What was once a civil service canteen has reemerged into the new millennium as an à la carte restaurant, and the main building has become a huge reception and display area.

It's not the architecture that brings visitors here. The units still retain a faintly institutional feel despite huge displays of dried *fynbos* that permeate the rooms with their distinctive scent. Some are built in little estates while others are remote, marooned in the wilds. They're perfect bases to explore the reserve. The shore teems with birds, picking off fish from 4,000-year-old traps built out of boulders by Africa's earliest residents. Inland are bands of unspoiled *fynbos*, dotted with eland, bontebok and ostrich, framed by the sky and sea. It's the sort of place where you share your breakfast with academics down from Cape Town University and naturalists over from Europe — serious academics with an interest in South Africa's natural world, but budgets that preclude staying at more expensive establishments aimed at the tourist market. Days are filled with guided and unguided walks, bird watching, fly-fishing, and mountain biking. It's an oasis of the natural world, just to the west of the more commercialized Garden Route.

Reins Coastal Nature Reserve ((028) 735 3322 FAX (028) 735 3324 E-MAIL info@reinsouthafrica .com WEBSITE www.reinsouthafrica.com, Box 298, Albertinia 6695, charges R440 to R520 including breakfast. Take the right turn off the N2 onto the R325 towards Gouritsmond. After 18 km (11 miles) turn right towards Still Bay. After eight kilometers (five miles) the entrance to Reins Coastal Nature Reserve is on the left.

(19 miles) to the north across the rain-catching mountains, and is really a world of its own.

The N2 highway flies through the Garden Route, straight as an arrow and almost as fast. But stay on the main road and after two hours of seeing nothing you'll land up in Port Elizabeth and wonder why you bothered. The highway generally stays close to the mountains and doesn't clutter up the shoreline. To enjoy the Garden Route it's essential to stop off at least in the three towns that mark each of the Garden Route's three principal bays: Mossel Bay, Knysna and Plettenberg Bay. There are some of South Africa's finest hotels to tempt travelers off the main road, and plenty of hikes, walks and sights to enjoy over quieter

THE GARDEN ROUTE

Hemmed in by a continuous range of mountains, the lushly forested coastline strip of land between Mossel Bay to the west and the Tsitsikamma National Park to the east, an area of around 200 km (125 miles), is known as the "Garden Route." There's always some argument about where the Garden Route starts and stops. This is one of the most popular tourist destinations for overseas travelers as well as a favorite vacation spot for South Africans, and towns either end are always anxious to be included. But here the towns of Albertinia, though nice enough, and Port Elizabeth, which is coastal enough, are left out. On the ground, the Garden Route is unmistakable. With plentiful rain and a Mediterranean climate the Garden Route strip contrasts dramatically with the drylands of the Little Karoo, just 30 km

moments. Although there are subtler pleasures in other parts of South Africa, for first-time visitors to the country at least, the Garden Route is often the highlight of their stay.

The best way to experience this part of the country is to stop off at a few places along the route, establishing yourself for long enough to explore the minor roads and hikes through day-trips. To make the most of your time a rental vehicle is strongly recommended. And although the area's attractions are here divided up into their specific locations bear in mind that the whole Garden Route is only 200 km (125 miles) long. As driving in these surroundings is generally a pure pleasure this means most of the highlights are within day-tripping distance of a reasonably

There's no need for supermarkets as farmers set up shop by the side of the road near Bredasdorp.

central point. It would be easy to spend several weeks on the Garden Route; sadly few of us have that much time. For more information about the Garden Route as a whole, contact **Garden Route Tourism Marketing** ((044) 874 4040 FAX (044) 874 6626 E-MAIL gardenroute.tourism@pixie.co.za WEB SITE www.gardenroute.org.za, Box 1514, George 6530, or refer to the regional tourist offices listed below.

MOSSEL BAY

The first sight of Mossel Bay is not inspiring. Coming from Cape Town are a succession of ugly industrial factories, refineries, and silos. However

the Maritime Museum, and it is still possible to post letters here.

General Information

The **Tourism Bureau** ((044) 691 2202 FAX (044) 690 3077 E-MAIL info@mb.lia.net WEB SITE www .gardenroute.net/mby/, at the corner of Market and Church streets, Box 1556, Mossel Bay 6500, is open Monday to Friday 9 AM to 5 PM, Saturday to 1 PM. They will help find accommodation, which can be useful in the peak holiday seasons, especially at Christmas when the town is taken over by farmers. A travel company that will provide a taxi shuttle service is **Rendezvous Cape** ((044) 691 3781, and the local **hospital** is at ((044) 691 2011.

as you drop into the old city center, with its horseshoe working harbor and small pubs and restaurants, things rapidly improve.

This sheltered bay was where the first European ship landed in South Africa. Bartolomeu Dias was blown here in 1488 but his attempts to communicate with Khoikhoi herdsmen ended in a fight. Nine years later Vasco da Gama made better progress, discovering a freshwater spring that put it on the map for generations of sailors. It was more than 100 years before the bay got its name, from the mussels that were the only food found by another Dutch navigator, Paulus von Caerden. In 1500 it found a role as an important communication center: a sailor left a message in an old shoe, hung on an old milkwood tree, and over the following years this became an established postal system. Even today the tree, "probably" the same one, still stands just outside

What to See and Do

The undoubted highlight of any visit to Mossel Bay is found in the **Bartolomeu Dias Maritime Museum** ((044) 691 1067, at the corner of Short and Market streets, open Monday to Friday 9 AM to 4:45 PM and Saturday and Sunday 9 AM to 4 PM, R5. The museum is arranged around a full-size replica of the original caravel. The replica was built in Lisbon to celebrate the 500th anniversary of the first landing in South Africa, and was sailed over in 1987. That such a small craft could manage such a journey, even in the present day, is almost inconceivable. Further maritime exhibits are displayed within the complex in a selection of historic buildings, all within a short stroll of the tourist office. Two land-based museums include the **Culture Museum**, with a collection of Khoi artifacts and the **Granary Museum**, which concentrates on wagon trails, mountains, and *fynbos*.

If you're planning some beach combing, the **Shell Museum and Aquarium** ((044) 691 1067 has the largest shell collection on the Garden Route. All are open daily.

It's just a short walk to the **Model Shipyard** ((044) 691 1531 FAX (044) 691 1539, Shop 10, Ochre Barn, Market Street, where there's an impressive collection of hand-carved model ships, with more for sale.

Out of the city center there are plenty of other attractions. A short walk to the north is Santos Beach, the only beach in the country to face due north, and a real suntrap, with gentle surf. The town's bathers would prefer sharks, who prey on the seals from offshore **Seal Island**, to be kept clear,

but cage diving happens here, spreading trails of bait out across the bathing beaches (see DIVE WITH A GREAT WHITE, page 17 in TOP SPOTS). Run by **Infanté Great White Shark Experience** ((082) 455 2438 FAX (044) 691 3796 E-MAIL Infante@pixie.co.za, Box 2979, Mossel Bay, costs range from R300 for viewing only to R450 to cage dive with no guarantees of a sighting. Bravely, scuba divers share the waters, with operators including **Mossel Bay Divers** ((044) 691 1441, but sharks don't generally go for humans underwater. They prefer their humans on the surfaces. For **boardsailing** information contact Michelle Pitt ((044) 691 6488 and to learn more about **surfing** address yourself to "Friends" ((044) 961 1269.

On land there are a number of hiking trails, including **Cape St. Blaize**, a 15-km (94-mile) trail along the cliffs, and inland the **Koumashoek Circular Trail** up the Robinson Pass. Neither require

permits but for maps contact tourist information. Neither land nor sea is involved in bungee jumping — the Gouritz River Bridge is the (slightly) lower of two spots on the Garden Route. Contact **Wildthing Adventures** ((021) 461 1653 FAX (021) 461 9693 E-MAIL wildthing@icon.co.za WEB SITE www.wildthing.co.za for further details.

More conventional pleasures at the village of **Hartenbos**, seven kilometers (just over four miles) along the old coast road, where the **Great Trek Museum** ((044) 950 1111, open Monday to Friday 9 AM to 4 PM, Saturday 10 AM to 12:30 PM, goes into great detail about the Voortrekkers route north, covering wagon-building techniques and the characters involved.

Where to Stay and Eat

Both for location and comfort the best place to stay here is the **Old Post Office Tree Manor** ((044) 691 3738 FAX (044) 691 3104 E-MAIL posttree@mb.lia.net, Market Street, R550 to R660, in the Museum Complex. Using one of the town's oldest buildings, this hotel is centrally located and very comfortable. Its restaurant, the Gannet, is one of the best in town for seafood. Another good and central lodge is **Allemans Dorpshuis** ((044) 690 3621, 94 Montagu Street, three blocks above the tourist bureau in a Victorian house, R350 including breakfast. Close by, near the beach, is the **Santos Beach Protea Hotel** ((044) 690 7103 FAX (044) 691 1945 E-MAIL santos@mb.lia.net, Santos Road, R450, with rather more comfort and rather less character. By Mossel Bay's famous lighthouse a smart option is the **Point Hotel** ((044) 691 3512 FAX (044) 691 3513 E-MAIL thepoint@pointhotel.co.za, R495, with a huge tidal pool for safe bathing, surf nearby, and a walking trail along the coast.

If the beach isn't too much of a draw a very good place to stay near here is 35 km (22 miles) north along the R328. The **Eight Bells Mountain Inn** ((044) 631 0000 FAX (044) 631 0004 E-MAIL 8bells@mb.lia.net, R360 to R460, on the Robinson Pass between the Garden Route and the Little Karoo. This delightful hotel has a range of chalets set high in the mountains. It is a peaceful base to explore the area, with gentle, well-trained horses to take the strain.

Back in town and perhaps the best location goes to backpackers in the **Santos Express** ((044) 691 1995, a stationary train on Santos Beach with compartments available for R100, suitable for up to three people. Once the novelty of the beachfront train hotel has worn off backpackers tend to move to **Mossel Bay Backpackers** ((044) 691 3182, 1 Marsh Street, where shared rooms are available from R50 per person.

Train carriages have been converted into backpack accommodation at Santos Beach on the Garden Route.

Such a busy fishing port can hardly help a reputation for seafood. The best restaurant in town is the **Gannet** in the Old Post Office Tree Manor, but **De Bakke (** (044) 691 1321, George Street, also performs marvels with a good catch. The **Pavilion** on Santos Beach is a very good place for a sundowner, which you can sip on its wooden deck overlooking the water; it also does good food. Another pub in a good setting is **Tidals**, Point St. Blaize, which overlooks the oceans and cliffs west towards Boggomsbaai.

How to Get There

By road, Mossel Bay is 365 km (228 miles) from Cape Town and 116 km (72.5 miles) from Knysna along the N2 highway which comes within seven kilometers (just over four miles) of the town. Inland it is 80 km (50 miles) from Oudtshoorn. It is well served by buses: the Baz Bus runs daily from Cape Town to Port Elizabeth and stops here;

Intercape links Mossel Bay with Cape Town; and Greyhound also serves Johannesburg and Durban. The above travel from the railway station. Translux stops only at the Voorbaai Shell Station, seven kilometers (just over four miles) out of town on the N2. Trains run from Cape Town via Worcester and Swellendam once a week and on to Port Elizabeth but don't stop in Mossel Bay. The nearest station is Hartenbos, a small coastal village to the east.

OUDTSHOORN

This history of this otherwise unremarkable town in the Little Karoo has long been inextricably linked with Africa's tall, flightless bird, the ostrich. The town is generally dated from the first church, inaugurated in 1838, but early farmers found the land too dry. Water was brought to the town in barrels in the early days, though the settlers quickly

9 AM to 1 PM and 2 PM to 5 PM Monday to Saturday, is manned by a knowledgeable and enthusiastic crew who will help with accommodation and finding your way around. A local taxi service is **Protea Enterprises (** (083) 337 5122 and for hospital treatment **Outdshoorn Provincial Hospital** is at **(** (044) 222 8921 while the **Cango Klein Karoo** is at **(** (044) 272 0111.

What to See and Do

Half a block from the Tourism Association is the **CP Nel Museum (** (044) 272 7306, Baron van Rheede Street, 8 AM to 1 PM and 2 PM to 5 PM Monday to Friday, 9 AM to 4 PM Saturday, R3. The museum is set in a sandstone boy's school, now devoted to a full and fascinating history of the ostrich industry. It also contains a reconstructed trading store, synagogue, and chemist. Within strolling distance are two further restored buildings, not, sadly, including any of the Ostrich Palaces, which are all in private hands.

Top on most visitors' list is to visit an ostrich farm. As the value of feather dusters and ostrich steaks declined, several farms opened up to visitors (see SADDLE UP A LEGGY BIRD, page 20 in TOP SPOTS). Here you can watch young chicks, meet the adults, play with the eggs, and eat the steak. If you're under 80 kg (175 lbs) in weight, you can even ride the animals, though most people are happy just to watch professional ostrich jockeys stage a small race. The original show farm is **Highgate Ostrich Show Farm (** (044) 272 7115 FAX (044) 272 7111 E-MAIL highgate1@pixie.co.za, off the R328 to Mossel Bay, whose tours cost R20 and last about an hour. Highgate opened to the public in 1937 but the other farmers in the area have quickly caught up. One of the rival operators is the **Cango Ostrich Farm (** (044) 272 4623 FAX (044) 272 8241, on the road to the Cango Caves.

The **Cango Caves** are the other main attraction. "Nature's Underground Gallery," a spectacular network of caves extending under the Swartberg foothills, these were first explored in 1780 and are definitely one of South Africa's most beautiful sights. For much of the early years the greatest expert on the caves was "Oubaas Johnnie," who started as a guide in 1880 and explored by the flickering light of magnesium lamps for the next 48 years, to depths of 26 km (16 miles). After his death electricity was installed.

The caves have been much changed since: the floors have been leveled and walkways installed; electric lights, first installed in 1929, illuminate the stalactites and stalagmites; and a visitor's complex has been built, offering a restaurant, museum, kennels and, of course, a curio shop. There are a range of tours offered. The easiest is the 30-minute tour, which explores the two largest and most

mastered the secrets of irrigation, making the most of the sudden seasonal rains.

It was the catwalks and salons of Europe, however, that sparked off the town's success. Two booms in the fashion for wearing ostrich feathers, from 1865 to 1870 and 1900 to 1914, raised the value of ostrich feathers to more than the price of gold. Fortunes were made in a few short years, and the wealthy and successful traders built massive Edwardian mansions in town, still known as "ostrich palaces." By the 1880s, Oudtshoorn was the most important town east of Cape Town. Although the craze for wearing feathers has long gone, ostrich farming is still an important aspect of the local economy. There are 250,000 of the leggy birds in the area, and only 40,000 human residents.

General Information

Oudtshoorn Tourism Association ((044) 279 2532 FAX (044) 279 8226, Baron van Rheede Street, open

The world's ostrich capital is at Oudtshoorn: 250,000 big birds outnumber 40,000 human residents.

spectacular halls. Standard Tours last for 60 minutes, going further into the "African Drum Chamber," with several steep stairways. The Adventure Tour lasts for a full hour and a half, including a certain amount of crawling and the "Devil's Chimney," a narrow vertical shaft (down to 45 cm, or 18 in, wide) that rises three and a half meters (nearly 12 ft). Well-built people get stuck here. By the end of your tour you'll have covered more than a kilometer (half a mile) and trodden over 400 stairs. In season, especially, it is worth getting to the caves early in the morning as crowds can build up, and booking is strongly advisable, especially for the adventure tour. For inquiries and bookings contact the Cango Caves ((044) 272 7410

FAX (044) 272 8001, 40 km (25 miles) north of Oudtshoorn. Entrance is R10, R20, or R40, depending on the length of tour chosen.

After visiting Cango Caves the temptation is irresistible to drive over the **Swartberg Pass**, one of the most spectacular in the country, 55 km (just over 34 miles) to the small village of **Prince Albert**, ideally returning through Meiringspoort. Don't resist the temptation! If you decide to stop off for a night, the **Prince Albert Tourism Association** (/FAX (023) 541 1366, 42 Kerk Street, Box 109, Prince Albert 6930. To get a taste of the pass, there's one company with the excellent idea of taking you to the top and letting you come down by mountain bike. Contact **Joyrides** ((044) 279 1163 for further details.

Alternatively, visitors to the caves will already have passed a number of Oudtshoorn attractions that have set up on the road out to Cango, fluttering their advertising hoardings at the many drivers who pass this way. The **Cango Wildlife Ranch** ((044) 272 5593 FAX (044) 272 4167 has some rather lethargic crocodiles but some other more lively animals. Children, especially, love to stroke the tame cheetahs, who purr contentedly, though the sound is more like a small motorcycle than that made by a domestic tabby. Entrance R50.

Where to Stay and Eat

Probably the best place to stay is the **Rosenhof Country Lodge** ((044) 272 2232 FAX (044) 272 3021, 264 Baron van Rheede Street, R590 with breakfast, a restored Victorian house with period furniture and yellowwood beams. The home-cooked meals are especially good. Good alternatives include **Adley House** (/FAX (044) 272 4533 E-MAIL adley@pixie.co.za, 209 Jan van Riebeeck Road, R300, built in the feather boom and set in tranquil gardens, and **Hlangana Lodge** ((044) 272 2299 FAX (044) 279 1271 E-MAIL hla@pixie.co.za WEB SITE www.hlangana.co.za, 51 North Street, R420, with facilities including a saltwater pool and fitness center. Twelve kilometers (seven and a half miles) out of town on the Cango Caves Road is **De Opstal** ((044) 279 2954 FAX (044) 272 0736 E-MAIL deopstal @mweb.co.za, R328, R300 to R460. Converted from an 1830s farm, it has stables and milking parlor, complete with terracotta floors and heavy wooden shutters. Travelers on a budget can save by staying at **Oudtshoorn Backpackers Oasis** ((044) 279 1163, 3 Church Street, from R30. For meals, often the hotels offer the best, while all flavors of ostrich are prepared in the restaurants attached to the show farms.

How to Get There

The town is a latterly spectacular 510 km (319 miles) drive from Cape Town, but more generally reached by the R328 from Mossel Bay (93 km or 58 miles) or the N12 from George (60 km or 37.5 miles). It is well served by public transportation. **SM Greef** ((044) 279 2088 domestic airport is less than one kilometer (three quarters of a mile) from the town center, with flights from Cape Town and Johannesburg, although awkwardly the Avis Car Rental desk at the airport has closed. The **train station** ((044) 223 2203 is south of the town center, and trains from Cape Town and Port Elizabeth stop here. Greyhound buses leave from the airport to George but not directly to Cape Town. Intercape departs from the Pic'n'Pay terminal in the town center, the Baz Bus stops four times a week at the Backpackers Oasis, and Translux services destinations as far — and unlikely — as Bloemfontein, Kimberley, and Johannesburg.

ABOVE: A lion at the Cango Wildlife Ranch.
RIGHT: Dramatic beauty over the Swartberg Pass.

GEORGE

Novelist Anthony Trollope described George as "the prettiest village on the face of the earth," but that was a long time ago and things have changed. Trollope probably wasn't a swimmer, so didn't mind that it wasn't on the sea, and nor did he probably appreciate the downside of its role as a logging center, masterminding much of the deforestation wreaked on the Garden Route area. It is known as the gateway to the Garden Route, however, because it has a domestic airport 10 km (just over six miles) east of town. Many visitors fly in here and pick up their rental cars before driving off somewhere nicer. Wilderness, for example, is just 15 km (just over nine miles) to the east of George airport and makes a much better stop for visitors. George remains an administrative center for the district, an important junction between the N2 coastal highway and the N12, which heads into the Karoo through the Outeniqua Pass, and a key stop for trains. It comes as rather a surprise to find it's a city instead of a town. In 1850 St. Mark's Cathedral was consecrated, thus technically giving George city status. It's one of the smallest cathedrals in the world.

General Information

The **Tourism Association** ((044) 801 9295 FAX (044) 873 5228, 124 York Street, Box 1109, George 1109, open Monday to Friday 8 AM to 4:30 PM and 9 AM to noon Saturday, will help with accommodation and transportation queries. Useful telephone numbers include a local **Taxi Service** ((044) 874 6707 and the **George Hospital** ((044) 874 5122.

What to See and Do

The main attraction in George is a bit of a fraud. The tree outside the tourist office is known as the "Slave Tree" because of a chain embedded in the wood. The truth is more prosaic. The chain was slung around the tree in the days when the municipal tennis courts were sited in the town center so the roller could be chained up.

The **Drostdy Museum** ((044) 873 5343, on Courtenay Street, open Monday to Friday 9 AM to 4:30 PM and to 12:30 PM, donation, is one of the least politically correct in the country, dividing its attention between the achievements of the early logging industry and those of the city's most famous son, P.W. Botha, last of the hardline apartheid prime ministers. Apart from this George's main attractions are in getting away. The N2 streaking over towards Knysna is the obvious, but far from the nicest route. Much better to drive along the original "Seven Passes" road, which twists and turns through the landscape. Alter-

natively, take the N9 through the Outeniqua Pass and drop down the final 35 km (22 miles) to Oudtshoorn and its ostrich farms (see SADDLE UP A LEGGY BIRD, page 20 in TOP SPOTS, and OUDTSHOORN, page 126).

Better still, leave vehicle rental to another day and take the **Outeniqua Choo-Tjoe** ((044) 801 8288 FAX (044) 801 8286, R50 round trip, South Africa's last scheduled mixed steam train service which winds through some of the country's most picturesque scenery. Since 1928 the restored carriages of this historic train have curved through fern-covered hills, forest, cuttings and tunnels, and crossed lakes, streams, and the final denouement of the Knysna Lagoon. The trip takes two and a half hours each way, leaving twice every day from Monday to Saturday except Christmas day and also carries freight in the low season.

Where to Stay and Eat

The smartest place to stay is, sensibly, outside town. **Fancourt** ((044) 870 8282 FAX (044) 870 7605 E-MAIL hotel@fancourt.co.za WEB SITE www.fancourt .co.za, seven kilometers (just over four miles) north along the N9 in Blanco, R900 to R3,000, is built around two Gary Player-designed 18-hole golf course with the nineteenth hole offering four restaurants, three swimming pools, and manor house accommodation. You can save a lot by staying immediately opposite Fancourt in **Angels Lodge** (/FAX (044) 870 8668 E-MAIL marionw@pixie.co.za, who offer self-catering flats for R250.

In George itself the **King George Protea** ((044) 874 7659 FAX (044) 874 7664, King George Drive, R500, is housed in a graceful Victorian building. The **Oakhurst Manor House Hotel** ((044) 874 7130 FAX (044) 874 7131 E-MAIL oakhurst@forteskinghotels.co.za, at the corner of Cathedral and Meade streets, R500, is in a thatched, gabled Cape Dutch Manor House, and the **Loerie Guest House** ((044) 874 4740 FAX (044) 874 4704, 91 Davidson Road, R350 including breakfast, is centrally located and comfortable. Backpackers have no real choice but **George Backpackers** ((044) 874 7807, 29 York Street, R40 in dormitories, a huge place that also takes long-term residents and so misses the classic backpacker atmosphere.

For traditional South African food try **De Oude Werf** ((044) 873 5892, 53 York Street, and pizzas and pasta are available up the road at **Panarotti's** ((044) 874 7084, 126 York Street. For an evening meal try the **Rill and Rustic** ((044) 884 0707, 79 Davidson Street, for meat and seafood but of a very high standard, backed by a good wine list.

How to Get There

George is 420 km (263 miles) from Cape Town and 320 km (200 miles) to Port Elizabeth along the N2. Inland the N12 heads up 60 km (38 miles) to

Snaking along the Garden Route, the Outeniqua
Choo-Tjoe uses rails laid by South Africa's pioneers.

Oudtshoorn and the N9 leads northeast across
semidesert to Graaff-Reinet.

By air, George Airport is served by **SAA** and
SA Express ((044) 873 8434 and **SA Airlink** ((011)
973 2941, with daily flights to Johannesburg, Cape
Town, Port Elizabeth, and Durban and East
London through the week. Johannesburg flights
are also offered by **Sabena Nationwide** ((011) 390
1660. At the airport Avis, Budget and Imperial all
have desks. The airport is 10 km (just over six
miles) from the city and there is no regular public
transportation.

The **Railway Station** ((044) 873 8202 is in the
center of the town, and sees the weekly "Southern Cross" service that runs between Cape Town
and Port Elizabeth, as well as the Outeniqua Choo-
Tjoe twice a day. Intercape, Translux, and Greyhound leave daily from St. Mark's Square while
the Baz Bus picks up from backpacker lodges; seats
must be reserved in advance.

VICTORIA BAY AND WILDERNESS

Nine kilometers (five and a half miles) east of
George, the N2 passes over the Serpentine Channel. Before the bridge a turning to the right leads
off to Victoria Bay, a small sandy beach sheltered
by high cliffs, a "spot so special even the dolphins visit twice a day" according to the locals.
Six meters (about 20 ft) from the high-water mark
is a small lodge, the **Land's End Guest House**
((044) 871 3168 FAX (044) 871 0024 WEB SITE
www.meditnet.com/~iclub/landsend, R320,
which offers self-catering studio apartments and
bed-and-breakfast accommodation. Higher up
the mountain **Hilltop Country Lodge** ((044) 889
0142 FAX (044) 889 0151 E-MAIL hilltop@cyberhost
.co.za WEB SITE www.hilltopcountrylodge.co.za,
Victoria Bay Heights, R400 to R700, is set in a

private *fynbos* reserve with high views over the mountains and ocean.

Pass over the bridge and the N2 scoops down to scrape the beach at Wilderness, a low-key resort spread around the foothills of the Outeniqua Mountains and tucked behind high sand dunes along the Touws River estuary. Rumor has it the beach was bought at a blind auction in 1830 by a young man and it was named by his fiancée when they cut their way through the forest to see what they'd bought. The center of the village clusters round the gas station, with the post office, a supermarket, a few restaurants, and **Tourist Information** (/FAX (044) 877 0045, Box 188, Wilderness 6560, which is open Monday to Friday 8:30 AM to 5:30 PM, Saturday 9 AM to 2 PM, and Sunday 9 AM to 1 PM.

Most of the activities here are of an outdoor nature, using it as a base to explore the rest of the Garden Route, to canoe on the Touws River or to hike in the surrounding Wilderness National Park.

Where to Stay and Eat
Out of peak season it is usually easy to find accommodation to suit your taste and budget. The smartest hotel is the **Karos Wilderness** ((044) 877 1110 FAX (044) 877 0600, R570. There are several good family-run hotels that offer a slightly more intimate welcome, however. The **Villa Sentosa** ((044) 877 0378 FAX (044) 877 0747 E-MAIL villa@intekom.co.za WEB SITE www.gardenroute.co.za/wilder/villa/, R500, is a modern palace with huge picture windows overlooking the Serpentine Bay and the national park — an elegant place to stay set in 58 hectares (143 acres) of indigenous bush.

To stay nearer the beach the **Palms Wilderness** ((044) 877 1420 FAX (044) 877 1422 E-MAIL palms@pixie.co.za WEB SITE www.palms-wilderness.com, R580, is just a two-minute walk from beach and lagoon, with a well-respected restaurant. Also near the beach is **Wilderness Manor** ((044) 877 0264 FAX (044) 877 0163 E-MAIL wildman@george.lia.net WEB SITE www.gardenroute.co.za/wilderness/manor, 37 Waterside Road, R400 to R600, with afro-colonial decor, billiard room, etc. If your tastes are for the inexpensive the best backpacking option is **Faerie Knowe Backpackers** ((044) 880 9589 FAX (044) 877 1403, Waterside Road, a small establishment set in a Victorian beach villa on the banks of the Touws River. Backpackers always seem to ferret out the most beautiful places to stay and it is a sign of Wilderness' success that there are two more backpacking options, called **Wilderness Backpackers** and **Wilderness International Backpackers**. If they can't be more original with their names I can't be bothered to insert their telephone numbers.

A good alternative for self-caterers is to stay in **Wilderness National Park** ((012) 343 1991

FAX (012) 343 0905 E-MAIL reservations@parks-sa.co.za, Box 787 Pretoria 0001. There are a range of restcamps and bungalows, huts and campsites, especially reasonably priced for groups of four or more. For an example, two-bedroom huts at Ebb and Flow Restcamp cost R180. There are canoes and pedal-boats available for rent to explore the coastal waterways. It's not a very wild park, being too close at all times to the highway, but does contain some beautiful patches of coastal forest, rivers, lakes, and 250 bird species.

How to Get There
The Outeniqua Choo-Tjoe stops at Wilderness if you ask the driver, and the Baz Bus will drop off passengers for the backpacker hotels. Wilderness is 450 km (281 miles) from Cape Town and 18 km (just over 11 miles) from George—but only 15 km (just over nine miles) from George's domestic airport.

KNYSNA

Don't pronounce the "K" of Knysna, it's pronounced as little as the "k" in know. Once you know how to ask directions for this beautiful place do so immediately. It is very much a high spot of the Garden Route and one of the most beautiful places in Africa. The town itself is probably best approached on the Outeniqua Choo-Tjoe, which chugs across the flat glassy waters of Knysna Lagoon.

The town itself is on the southern shores. The name Knysna itself, in Khoi, means "hard to reach," and for much of the town's existence this was true. It was brought to life by an English colonial administrator George Rex, rumored variously to have been an illegitimate child of George III and to have a reputation for picking up colored mistresses on his colonial postings. This colorful personality spent his final days here establishing a timber

industry, chopping down the Knysna Forest. By 1880 it was facing destruction, but a farsighted conservation program saved a few shreds of one of South Africa's most important wilderness area. The area is a key biosphere resource: the forest was hoped to be the last refuge in the south of the country for wild elephant and the lagoon itself, which fills and drains every day with tidal water from the ocean, is a haven for endangered aquatic life including Knysna seahorses, as well as millions of birds. A gold rush briefly boomed and then bust, and the town itself drifted quietly through the twentieth century, emerging sleepy and blinking into the 1960s as a major center for crafts and hippies. The natural beauty of the area and the fast N2 highways mean it has since exploded into a popular resort and the hub of the Garden Route.

Knysna's last remaining elephants find refuge at the Knysna Elephant Park.

General Information

The helpful **Knysna Tourism Bureau** ((044) 382 5510 FAX (044) 382 1646 E-MAIL knysna.tourism @pixie.co.za WEB SITE www.knysna-info.co.za, 40 Main Street, Box 87, Knysna 6570, is open 9 AM to 5 PM Monday to Friday and noon to 5 PM Saturday. Busy and efficient, they will help with adventure bookings as well as accommodation. They share offices with the Knysna **Booking Service** ((044) 382 6960 FAX (044) 382 1609 who perform much the same functions, privately, and sometimes stay open for longer. Over Christmas the town gets booked out completely, and even getting an evening meal becomes a problem. Book ahead. For medical attention the starting point is the **International Medical Service** ((044) 382 6272, after hours ((044) 382 6366, Gray Street. A local taxi shuttle service is **Rikkis** ((044) 382 6540.

What to See and Do

Most of Knysna's attractions are found outdoors. However, if it's raining it is worth visiting the **Knysna Museum** ((044) 382 1638, Queen Street, open Monday to Friday 9:30 AM to 4:30 PM and Saturday to 1 PM, newly opened in the Old Jail. This was the first public building constructed by the colonial powers, and used to house prisoners on their way to building mountain passes. Fishing is a major activity here and the museum concentrates on angling — nets and tackle. The centerpiece exhibit is a stuffed coelacanth, the four-legged deep-sea fish thought to be an early relative of man.

There is a **Gold Mining Museum** ((044) 382 5066, at the corner of Pitt and Green streets, open Monday to Friday 9:30 AM to 4:30 PM and Sunday to 12:30 PM, donation, to commemorate the nearby overgrown ghost town of Millwood, with a collection of Victoriana relating to the town's history.

An interesting outing is to see the **Knysna oyster beds** ((044) 382 6941, at the southern end of Long Street on Thesen's Island, where tours of the oyster beds are followed by a tasting session. Open Monday to Friday 8 AM to 5 PM, weekends 9 AM to 3 PM, free. **Knysna Heads** are some way out of town. Without your own vehicle or boat a taxi will be needed. The leading attraction here is the **Aquarium** (no telephone), open daily from sunrise to sunset, admission free/donation, with a few of Knysna's famous seahorses.

More actively, this is the location for **abseiling** ((044) 382 6299 or (083) 654 8755 E-MAIL seals@mweb.co.za, and **wreck diving** ((044) 384 0831 FAX (044) 382 2938 or (082) 465 5317, Waterfront Divers, Knysna Heads. The currents are strong, especially at the heads themselves as water floods in to fill the 13-sq-km (five-sq-mile) lagoon, and reports indicate diving here can be a bit of a panic, but there are ragged-tooth sharks and huge rays as lures. Staying above water there are a

number of operators running boat charter expeditions to explore the waterways. **Knysna Blue Dolphin Charters and Adventures** ((082) 773 8071 operate diving and fishing trips, **Knysna Eco-Ventures** ((044) 382 5920 run guided canoe-based bird-watching tours, and **John Benn** ((044) 382 1693 runs pleasure cruises on covered "rivercats" that reach the **Featherbed Nature Reserve** on the western of Knysna's heads.

The few remaining hardwoods of Knysna Forest are also well worth exploring, but don't expect to see elephant. Whether there are any left in the area is open to doubt, apart from three who are kept in **Knysna Elephant Park** ((044) 532 7732, on the N2 east of Knysna towards George. Various reintroduction programs have been attempted but with mixed success; it seems the patches of remaining forest are too fragmented to support a viable elephant population. The remaining patches go under a variety of names: Diepwalle Forest, 20 km (12.5 miles) northeast of Knysna, Ysternek Reserve 25 km (15.6 miles) north with mountain *fynbos* and wet mountain forest, and Goudveld State Forest, 25 km (15.6 miles) northwest of the town. All have marked trails exploring the forests and some particularly old trees are separately fenced off with signs. For further information contact the **Forestry Department** ((044) 382 5466.

It is the last of these forests that is most interesting, because it contains the remains of **Millwood**, a gold rush town that in 1889 had six hotels, three newspapers, and a music hall. In 1890 boom turned to bust and the town was left to rot. There's only one of the original buildings still standing, but some of the mine reduction works can still be seen and it's a relaxing place to reflect on man's passing influence as the natural world reclaims its own. From Knysna take the N2 towards George and cross the Knysna River, then turn right onto the Reheenendal Road for 25 km (15.6 miles) following signposts for Goudveld.

A good way to see the forests is on horseback. **Forest Horse Rides** ((044) 382 4764 arrange horses and guides for R60 per person per hour.

Many visitors to Knysna just want to know one thing: Where is the beach? The short answer is that there isn't one — although it is possible to swim and even dive in the lagoon, this is not ideal. There are plenty of beaches within easy reach with your own vehicle. On the eastern end of town at Leisure Island is Bollard Bay, a family beach with safe waters, though look out for the deeper channel where currents and powerboats constitute significant hazards. There is another beach at Knysna Heads. West of Knysna a turning heads out to Buffalo Bay, and a sandy beach which extends all the way to Brenton on Sea — safe swimming and good surfing here. **Noetzie Beach**, overlooked by castles, is 15 km (just over nine miles) by road, with a little lagoon and a river which are safe for swimming. The sea, just here, isn't: it shelves steeply and there are currents.

Where to Stay

There are a number of excellent hotels and guesthouses in Knysna. Several are set around the edge of Knysna Lagoon. These include the **St. James of Knysna (** (044) 382 6750 FAX (044) 382 6756 E-MAIL STJAMES.KNYSNA@pixie.co.za WEB SITE www.stjames.co.za The Point, Main Road, R500 to R3,000; the self-catering **Knysna River Club (** (044) 382 6483 FAX (044) 382 6484 E-MAIL knysna.riverclub@pixie.co.za WEB SITE os2.iafrica.com/krc, Sun Valley Drive, from R290 for a twin chalet; and the **Leisure Isle Lodge (** (044) 384 0462 FAX (044) 384 1027 E-MAIL lilodge@mweb.co.za WEB SITE www.lodgeview@mweb.co.za, 87 Bayswater Drive, Leisure Island.

Others are elevated over the town. The oldest is **Belvidere Manor (** (044) 387 1055 FAX (044) 387 1059 E-MAIL manager@belividere.co.za, Duthie Drive, Belvidere Estate, R760 to R1,500, with detached chalets spreading down to the waterfront from a restored 1834 manor house. The 1899 **Falcons View Manor (** (044) 382 6767 FAX (044) 382 6430 E-MAIL falcons@pixie.co.za, R600 to R1,000, has an à la carte restaurant open through the high season only. Another elegant option is **Parkes Manor (** (044) 382 5100 FAX (044) 382 5124 E-MAIL parkes@gardenroute.co.za WEB SITE www .gardenroute.co.za/parkes, Azalea Street, R700 including breakfast, nine en-suite bedrooms with wide verandas overlooking the banks of the lagoon in a restored national monument building. The newest hotel in the town center, and claiming to be the largest wooden structure in the southern hemisphere, the **Log Inn (** (044) 382 5835 FAX (044) 382 5830 16 Gray Street, R500, has huge beams and acres of open glass — a truly impressive modern piece of design that is good as long as there aren't any conferences on. On a budget, another central option is **Mike's Guest House (** (044) 382 1728 or (082) 784 4599 FAX (044) 382 1728, 67 Main Street, R250.

There are also some good options out of town. For the ultimate getaway the Forestry Department have built a hi-tech tree-house in the heart of the forest: **TreeTop Forest Chalet (** (044) 382 5466 FAX (044) 382 5461 P/Bag X12, Knysna 6570. Just to the east of town the little inlet settlement of Noetzie has a scatter of castles, built early this century but complete with crenellations and parapets, which take guests, either bed-and-breakfast or self-catering. Contact **Knysna Castles (**/FAX (044) 375 0095 or (044) 375 0100 E-MAIL kynsna castles@mweb.co.za, R500 to R900 depending on season. These offer one of the best places to stay, being set on a sandy bay with a swimmable lagoon and adjoining the Sinclair Nature Reserve.

Backpackers can stay at the **Backpack (**/FAX (044) 382 4362 E-MAIL backpack@gem.co.za WEB SITE www.backpackers.co.za, 17 Tide Street, R45 for shared accommodation.

Where to Eat and Nightlife

There are plenty of restaurants in Knysna; the problem is that they can often fill to capacity, especially in the summer season. Best is **La Loerie (** (044) 382 1616, 57 Main Street, which specializes in fresh lagoon oysters and other seafood. The **Knysna Oyster Company (** (044) 382 2168, Long Street, Thesen's Island, is a tasting tavern for one of the largest oyster farms in the world, perfect for lunch but closed in the evenings. The **Pink**

Umbrella ((044) 382 2409, 14 Kingsway, Leisure Island, is an al fresco dining place, colored a bright pink, for seafood and vegetarian cuisine; booking essential.

A young meeting place that also serves food is **Cranzgots** at Knysna Heads, while the late-nights are best spent at the **Tin Roof Blues** at the corner of St. George's and Main streets, where music is played live every night. In season, Knysna wakes up to become one of the liveliest and most cosmopolitan of all the Garden Route's towns, with live music thumping out from **Crabs Creek** in Belvidere Village, **Jetty Tapas** on Long Street at Thesen's Island, and the **Main Street Café**.

How to Get There

With your own vehicle Knysna is hard to miss. The N2 funnels down 500 km (312.5 miles) east of Cape Town and 244 km (152.5 miles) west of Port Elizabeth to use the Main Street. Plans for a bypass have been blocked by the importance of the remaining forest. Intercape, Translux, and the Baz Bus all stop here, as does the **Outeniqua Choo-Tjoe Railway line (** (044) 382 1361.

A step up from your usual bed and breakfast, accommodation at Noetzie Bay near Knysna is in castles.

PLETTENBERG BAY

"Plett" is one of South Africa's favorite vacation destinations, filled in a flood by Johannesburgers through vacation season who make the most of Plettenberg's own domestic airport. It has a beautiful setting, a chain of beautiful beaches and some of the country's finest restaurants, but to the foreign eye the scatter of modern vacation developments that make up the town are less captivating than some of the older towns and communities of the Garden Route. Its saving grace is in the coastline: a broad swathe of sand, fringed by temperate jungle, washed by surf speckled with the dark shapes of dolphin and the lighter crests of wetsuited surfers. In season, calving southern right whales also come into the bay, clearly seen from hotels and restaurants elevated on the hills.

The bay was first visited by a Portuguese ship, the *San Gonzales*, which ran aground 20 years before the Cape was settled, and sank. For eight months the sailors used the wreckage to cobble together another boat, and finally sailed on to reach the safety of Mozambique. The town was used as a timber port but Knysna was safer, and from then on was used as a whaling station. There are still a few old buildings which remain, including the remains of the old Timber Store, but most of Plett is much more recent, hothoused by a domestic tourist industry bottled up by sanctions.

General Information

The **Plettenberg Bay Tourism Association** ((044) 533 4065 FAX (044) 533 4066 E-MAIL plett.tourism @pixie.co.za WEB SITE www.plettenbergbay.co.za, Victoria Cottage, Kloof Street, Box 894, Plettenberg Bay 660, open Monday to Friday 8 AM to 5 PM and Saturday 9 AM to 1 PM, will help with accommodation problems, which can be serious in peak season. Conversely, out of season it is often possible to negotiate some real bargain rates as places lie empty. A local taxi shuttle company is **Muvu Wood Transfers** ((044) 533 3680, while for hospital treatment call ((044) 533 4421.

What to See and Do

Likely to be uppermost in most visitor's minds is where to find the best beach. They start southeast of the town center with **Robberg Beach** and **Central Beach**, where sheltered waters are ideal for families. East and **Lookout Rocks** attract surfers who ride the breaks into **Lookout Beach**, which is also good for general swimming, while the more easterly **Hobie Beach** is more for surfers and bodyboarders. The sand stretches 10 km (just over six miles) down the coast to **Keurbooms** and **Keurbooms Lagoon**.

There's more to do here than lie on the beach. One of the best activities is to go out to sea and spot some of the aquatic life of the area. The original pioneer of boat-based ecotourism is **Ocean Adventures** (/FAX (044) 533 5083 or (083) 701 3583 E-MAIL info@oceanadventures.co.za WEB SITE www .plettbay.co.za/oceanadventures, run by the hugely knowledgeable Dave Rissik. Boat trips from two to three hours cost R200 to R270 per person depending on season, with space for up to 12 passengers and longer expeditions arranged on request. What you see depends on luck. There are usually plenty of bottlenose dolphins around and sometimes the rare Indo-Pacific humpback dolphin. There are resident Bryde's whales, seasonal southern right and humpback whales, and occasional sightings of minke and pygmy sperm whales. Seals and sea lions flip around the Robberg Peninsula and any number of seabirds can be spotted. Take polarized sunglasses for seeing through the water surface.

A surer way of spotting whales is to take to the air: from a height the waters are more transparent and huge distances can be surveyed. **African Ramble** ((044) 533 9006 or (083) 375 6514 FAX (044) 533 9012 E-MAIL aframble@cis.co.za WEB SITE www.aframble.co.za, from R280 for a 30-minute flight, price per person with a minimum of two, operates high-wing aircraft perfect for scenic flights.

In the area there are five designated trails. Of these **Milkwood** is a three- or five-kilometer (about two- to three-mile) trail through the center of town passing what historical monuments there are. Much more rewarding is a loop through the **Robberg Nature Reserve** which includes trails from two to nine kilometers (just over one to about five and a half miles), passing seal colonies and with the chance of spotting dolphin and whales offshore. Permits are available at the entrance gate, R15. More information is available from the Tourist Office. Horse trails are an easier way to explore, and **Equitrails** ((044) 533 0599 offer two-hour trail rides for R70, with longer rides a possibility.

An unmissable tour is up the Keurbooms River Estuary into the heart of some unspoiled forest. **Keurbooms River Ferries** ((044) 532 7876 FAX (044) 532 7823 E-MAIL ferries@visit.co.za WEB SITE www .visit.co.za, have scheduled departures daily at 11 AM, 2 PM and sundown, with a five-kilometer (three-mile) cruise and 30-minute walk through indigenous forest lasting two and a half hours, R20 per person. To get closer to nature — and the water — overnight canoe safaris with a night in a mountain hut are offered by **Nature Conservation** ((044) 533 2125.

Divers have plenty of choice here. A number of operators offer diving and snorkeling equipment, including **Beyond the Beach** ((044) 533 1158 and **Diving International** ((044) 533 0381. Soft coral and two wrecks are offshore, and these are also the nearest scuba operators to the Tsitsikamma

National Park, which has two designated diving and snorkeling trails.

A final excursion from Plettenberg Bay is 16 km (10 miles) east along the N2 at **Monkeyland** ((044) 534 8906 FAX (044) 534 8907 E-MAIL monkeys @global.co.za WEB SITE www.monkeyland.co.za. This private nature reserve has netted off a patch of forest where indigenous primates, more from South America and their more vocal relatives from Madagascar, have been reintroduced. There's a central bar and restaurant while tan-clad young rangers take guests off for hour-long tours to meet the monkeys, many of which are tame, and tour the rehabilitation cages where new residents are quarantined. Rates, including the services of a

area's finest cuisine in a friendly, unpretentious atmosphere. Even smaller is the nearby **Mallard River Lodge** ((044) 553 2982 FAX (044) 533 9336 E-MAIL mallard@pixie.co.za, Rietvlei Road, R780, where five rooms are set on the high south bank of the Bitou River, overlooking the wetlands; perfect for birdwatchers.

An ostrich farm and horse stud are part of **Forest Hall** ((044) 534 8869 FAX (044) 534 8883 E-MAIL foresthall@pixie.co.za WEB SITE www .foresthall.co.za, The Crags, R630 to R1,520, an 1864 National Monument furnished with antiques and with a private beach. Ten kilometers (just over six miles) the other side of Plett towards Knysna is the considerably more formal **Hunters Coun-**

safari guide, are from R36 to R54 depending on season, and are well worthwhile.

Where to Stay

With more than 160 accommodation options in and near town this will not be a comprehensive guide, instead just the best in each category are listed.

When it comes to accommodation, there's a lot to be said for staying out of town. There are a number of out-of-town hotels set in the countryside, particularly in the far less commercial "Crags" area to the east of Plett. By far the best place to stay is **Hog Hollow** (/FAX (044) 534 8879 E-MAIL hoghollow@global.co.za WEB SITE www.hoghollow .co.za, Askop Road, R750 to R1,130 with breakfast. With an absolute maximum of 24 guests, this small lodge is set in a private reserve 18 km (11.2 miles) east of Plett and serves some of the

try House ((044) 532 7818 FAX (044) 532 7878 E-MAIL hunters@pixie.co.za, R1,180 to R2,780, in a lavish country manor, previous hotel of the year and a member of Relais & Châteaux. Both these hotels close in June.

Back in town the **Plettenberg** ((044) 533 2030 FAX (044) 533 2074 E-MAIL plettenberg@pixie.co.za WEB SITE www.plettenberg.com, 40 Church Street, Look Out Rocks, from R1,300 bed only, is the grand old dame of Plettenberg with spectacular views over both swimming beaches and the ocean beyond. Confusingly similar in name, the **Plettenberg Bay** ((044) 533 9067 FAX (044) 533 9092, Robberg Road, R2,400 full board including local beverages and laundry, is, if anything, even more luxurious.

Dutch architecture at this Huguenot guest house brings character accommodation to Plettenberg.

Mid-market accommodation options in town include two family-run guest houses. **Periwinkle Lodge** (/FAX (044) 533 1345 or (083) 447 1033, 75 Beachy Head Drive, R550 to R800, is an unassuming little place where dinner is on request but breakfast is magnificent. A few paces away the **Lodge on the Bay** ((044) 533 4724 FAX (044) 533 2681 E-MAIL info@thelodge.co.za WEB SITE www .thelodge.co.za, 77 Beachy Head Drive, R450 to R850, adds a private day spa and massage service to the conventional guesthouse formula.

Backpackers have two main options, both charging R45 per person in season for dormitory accommodation, private rooms costing R95 and up. The **Albergo** (/FAX (044) 533 4434 E-MAIL absolut @mweb.co.za WEB SITE www.abso.co.za, Church Street, and the **Weldon Kaya** ((044) 533 2437 FAX (044) 533 4364 E-MAIL info@weldonkaya .co.za WEB SITE www.weldonkaya.co.za, rather out of town but busy with travel arrangements and with a free shuttle to beaches and town. Perhaps better to stay out of town, in the Crags, at **Garden Route Backpackers** (/FAX (044) 534 8837, Askop Road, R45 for dormitory rooms, who rent one of their bicycles — or their microlight — to get around.

Where to Eat and Nightlife

When it comes to eating, Plett offers a fair selection, with the focus often on produce fresh from the sea. Many of the best hotels take their cuisine very seriously and take reservations from non-residents, with Hog Hollow, the Plettenberg, and the Hunters Country Lodge standing out. **Cornuti's** ((044) 533 1277, at the corner of Odland and Perestrella streets, experiments with pizza toppings with varying degrees of success. The **Islander** ((044) 532 7776, eight kilometers (five miles) from Plett towards Knysna off the N2, produces one of the area's finest seafood buffets; booking essential. In town the **Med Seafood Bistro** ((044) 533 3102, Main Street, Village Square, is another seafood specialist, as is **Moby Dick's** ((044) 533 3682, Central Beach.

For nightlife, the **Flashbacks**, Main Street, is a good place to start, a rough and ready drinking haunt for locals. The **Lookout** on Lookout Beach provides great views and serves light meals, while Weldon Kaya (see above) has live music, pool tables, and great views, often hosting the best party in town. Later on the **Cave** ((044) 533 2118, the Arches Hotel, Marine Drive, is the biggest rave venue on the Garden Route, where you'll find the western Cape's biggest population of e-bunnies gathering on weekends.

How to Get There

Plettenberg Bay is 525 km (328 miles) from Cape Town and 236 km (147.5 miles) from Port Elizabeth along the N2 highway. The Baz Bus is the most convenient form of overland public transportation, dropping passengers off at their hotels in town. Translux, Greyhound, and Intercape stop at the Shell Ultra City Service Station, two kilometers (just over a mile) outside of town. The domestic airport receives daily flights from Johannesburg and three a week from Durban via Port Elizabeth.

TSITSIKAMMA NATIONAL PARK

Midway between Plettenberg Bay and Port Elizabeth, Tsitsikamma National Park is very much a highlight of the Garden Route. The village of Storms River (see below) is the community center but the area's interest is more in the natural world. Although Tsitsikamma is one of South Africa's youngest national parks, being proclaimed only in 1962, it is the second most visited, after the Kruger (see THE KRUGER NATIONAL PARK, page 200). It stretches 80 km (nearly 50 miles) up the coast from Nature's Valley to Oubosstrand, generally extending only about 500 m (about a quarter of a mile) inland, but widening to three and a half kilometers (about two miles) at its western boundary. The park drops down from Tsitsikamma Mountain range, peaking between 900 to 1,600 m (2,950 to 5,250 ft), to a plateau at about 230 m (750 ft) riven by deep gorges before dropping down to the sea.

The forest is the last remnant of the high humid forest, comprising milkwood, Outeniqua yellowwood, stinkwood, Cape blackwood, forest elder, white pear and candlewood, festooned with creepers such as wild grape, red saffron, and milky rope. There are more than 220 bird species in the park and small mammals including caracal, genet, rock dassie, bushbuck, blue duiker, grysbok, bush pig, and the very rare Cape clawless otter. The sea offshore is protected to a distance of up to five and a half kilometers (just under three and a half miles), with boats and fishing prohibited. There is a snorkeling trail in the Storms River mouth but conditions here aren't ideal and it's quite unusual for people to complete the course.

Access is restricted through much of the park. The most popular way to experience it is via the five-day **Otter Trail** which follows the coastline west to De Vasselot, but you'll need to book ahead. In the 1970s huts were helicoptered in to give some basic accommodation. Trail permits and park chalets can be booked 13 months in advance, and spaces are often snapped up in days, so most overseas visitors will end up staying in private lodges and guest houses outside the park and find it practically impossible to find a place on the Otter Trail. For information about the hiking trails and accommodation at the rest camp contact the **Park Authorities** ((012) 343 1991 FAX (012) 343 0905.

Most trail permits book out up to a year in advance. Nearer to the time of your reservation confirm arrangements with the **Warden** ((042) 541 1607 FAX (042) 541 1629. It's also worth trying for cancellations as places do sometimes become available.

It is easier to get onto another trail running through the foothills of the mountains called the **Tsitsikamma Trail**, which also taking five days but staying in the rather better-built huts erected by the forestry department, for which they charge R20 per night. For the Tsitsikamma Trail contact the **South African Forestry Company Ltd.** **(SAFCOL)** ((042) 391 0393, Regional Forestry Manager, Downing and Atwood Building, Main

Street, P/Bag X537, Humansdorp. Reservations are only accepted six months before you propose to hike off, and places are generally far more available.

There are two reception areas in the park. The western one, which is reached from the R102 Nature's Valley Road, is the **De Vasselot Camp**, which is basically just a caravan park and camping site but with hot water, at least, laid on. The main one is the **Storms River Mouth Rest Camp**, reached by a turning off the N2 four kilometers (two and a half miles) before the village of Storms River, where you'll find a restaurant among other facilities for day visitors. For both reservations are through South African National Parks ((012) 343 1931 FAX (012) 343 0905 (Pretoria) or ((021) 422 2810 FAX (021) 424 6211 (Cape Town) E-MAIL reservations@parks-sa.co.za. Gates are open from 7 AM to 9 PM daily; fees are R14. The **reception**

center's restaurant ((042) 541 1607 is open from 7:45 AM to 8 PM, and it is necessary to book evening meals before 5 PM.

How to Get There

Tsitsikamma National Park is some 615 km (384 miles) from Cape Town, and 295 km (184 miles) from Port Elizabeth, along the N2. Car rental is available at Plettenberg Bay, which is also the nearest airport.

STORMS RIVER

It is generally easier to give the cumbersome and bureaucratic Parks Board a wide berth and make your own arrangements for accommodation near, rather than in the Tsitsikamma National Park. The base for shops and accommodation is Storms River, reached by a short surfaced road from the N2, 60 km (37.5 miles) east from Plettenberg Bay, two kilometers (just over a mile) past the turning for the Storms River Mouth Rest Camp.

General Information

Storms River is in fact the first town in the Eastern Cape. There's no need to leave the N2 to pick up information, as the **Total Village Petroport**, once a humble gas station over the Storms River, has expanded to include curio shops, a museum, and a restaurant as well as a helpful **Tourist Information Bureau** ((042) 750 3910 FAX (042) 750 3954, open daily 9 AM to 5 PM unless unexpectedly closed. There is no taxi shuttle service. The **Kareedouw Hospital** ((042) 228 0210 can cope with most emergencies, but it is 55 km (34 miles) away so try not to break anything vital.

What to See and Do

Activity is the key here. The headline attraction is the daredevil leap from Bloukrans Bridge, the highest bungee jump in the world — the bridge is 216 m (709 ft) high. With a 100% safety record over 6,500 jumps this is only likely to shave a few minutes off your life. Step over the edge for a five second free-fall and two seconds of cord stretch. It costs R500 including a video of the experience, a glass of cider and a certificate, though it is free for pensioners (over 60). Contact **Face Adrenalin** ((042) 281 1458 to book your jump.

Blackwater tubing in the Storms River is another popular activity that will leave the unfit limping for weeks (see *KLOOF* SOUTH AFRICA'S RIVERS, page 26 in TOP SPOTS), run by **Stormsriver Adventures** ((042) 541 1836 FAX (042) 541 1609 E-MAIL adventure@gardenroute.co.za WEB SITE WWW

The world's highest bungee jump is from the Bloukranz River Bridge: prepare to plummet.

.stormsriver.co.za, Adventure Center, Darnel Street, Storms River, who also run trails through the woods, abseiling expeditions, and boat cruises. To explore the area on horseback **Shadowland Horse Trails** ((042) 750 3601 arranges mounts and guides, with rates from R50 an hour. If seeing the beautiful Protea flowers has awakened your desire to send some home, **Flowerland Protea Farm** ((042) 750 3718 prepares plants for export, and for local crafts the **Khoisan Village Market** ((042) 281 1450, by the N2 Bloukrans Bridge, has a wide selection of wool and mohair woven products.

Where to Stay and Eat

The best place to stay is the **Tsitsikamma Lodge** ((042) 750 3802 FAX (042) 750 3702 E-MAIL tsitsilodge@pixie.co.za, N2, R450 to R530 for luxurious log cabins, all with whirlpool baths which are about what you need after a day clambering around the rocks, and their home-cooked buffet suppers are also the sort of substantial fare inspired by the activities here. It regularly wins awards. Alternatively the **Old Village Inn** ((042) 541 1711 FAX (042) 541 1669 E-MAIL the_inn@global.co.za, Darnell Street, R500 to R700, a village of cottages reconstructed to reflect the different aspects of life in the area. There's a fisherman's cottage, for example, and an austere magistrate's Cape Dutch dwelling. All bedrooms have under-floor heating and there's a good restaurant. The backpacking option is the spacious and friendly, but smelling somewhat of cat, **Stormsriver Rainbow Lodge** (/FAX (042) 541 1530, Darnell Street, Storms River, R45 for dormitory, R110 for double room.

How to Get There

The Baz Bus drops off at Storms River when requested, while the main Translux and Greyhound buses will stop at the Petroport at Storms River Bridge. By car, the village is 62 km (38.7 miles) east of Plettenberg Bay, which has the nearest domestic airport.

BEYOND THE GARDEN ROUTE

Although the Garden Route technically ends at Storms River, there are plenty of very good reasons to keep heading east. On the coast, there's the surfing Mecca of Jeffrey's Bay and the transportation hub of Port Elizabeth. Inland, there is Addo Elephant Park, home to herds of grazing pachyderms, and Shamwari Game Reserve, where you can see the Big Five in a non-malarial area. Back from the animal world, Grahamstown is famous for its annual drama festival that provides a cultural focus for South African drama every July. In the arid hinterland the Karoo towns of Graaff-Reinet and Cradock retain the atmosphere of Afrikaner life on the frontline, perfectly preserved under the desert sun.

JEFFREY'S BAY

Immortalized in the film *Endless Summer*, Jeffrey's Bay is a key place of pilgrimage for the world's surfing community. The reality is somewhat disappointing, with a scatter of boxy modern buildings disfiguring the coastline and the pleasures of water stay generally far out to sea. It does have other attractions — dolphin and whale-watching, hiking and angling and a number of nature reserves in the area, but the town only really wakes up for the surfing season, reversing the normal pattern of tourism for the south coast by getting the best waves during the austral winter.

General Information

Jeffrey's Bay Tourism ((042) 293 2588 FAX (042) 293 2227 E-MAIL jbay@ilink.nis.za, Shell Museum Complex, Da Gama Road, Box 460, Jeffrey's Bay 6330, is open Monday to Friday 9 AM to 5 PM, Saturdays to 1 PM. A local taxi service is **Sunshine Express** ((042) 293 2221.

What to See and Do

Most visitors head straight for the surfing beaches. Six different surf breaks each have their own characters, and keen surfers will want to try them all. Near Main Beach **Kitchen Windows** is a good place to learn how to surf. **Magna Tubes** is a powerful and classic wave, while **Super Tubes** is fast, hollow and very long — an ultimate test of surfing skill and only for the experienced. **Tubes** is a short but perfect hollow wave, while **Point** and **Albatross** are uncrowded and varied. For surfing tuition, contact the **East Coast Surf School** ((082) 933 8015. For non-surfers there are a number of good bathing beaches, particularly **Main Beach** by the center of town and **Aston Bay**, **Paradise Beach**, and the **Kabeljous River Estuary** a short drive away.

Before heading for the beach, however, it is worth exploring the town's obsession with the sea at the **Shell Museum** ((042) 293 1111, based on the collection started by an eccentric shell collecting spinster, Charlotte Kritzinger, who began beach combing in 1945. She devoted the last 20 years of her life to picking up sea shells and marine skeletons, brought here by the intermingling Benguela and Agulhas Ocean currents. On her death her collection, which, stored in boxes, practically filled her house, was bought by the local council and established as the Shell Museum on Diaz Road, sharing a building with the Tourist Information office.

There are a number of hikes in the area, exploring the little-visited nature reserves of Seekoei, set around Aston Bay with a penguin sanctuary at its heart; Kabeljous, one of the last unspoiled river estuaries, rich in waterfowl; and Noorekloof, stretching up a valley with a trail following the river's course. For further information contact **Cape Conservation** ((042) 292 0339. Surf fishing catches kob, leerfish, grunter, and white steenbras as well as the occasional shark or ray. For most of the fishing beaches a four-wheel-drive vehicle will be needed. Rather than kill the fish, better to join them. There's good diving offshore, with plenty of soft corals and invertebrates. There is, however, no place to rent equipment here.

Where to Stay and Eat

Much of the accommodation here is aimed at surfers, who invariably prefer backpacker accommodation, almost never have much money, and

(/FAX (042) 293 1625, 10 Dageraad Street, R25 to R45 again.

For dining, most of the national steak and hamburger chains are represented. **Breakers** ((042) 293 1975, Ferreira Street, has a reputation for its seafood, as does **Walskipper** ((042) 292 0005, Marina Martinique Harbor, while **Luigi's** ((042) 293 2440, Sovereign Center, 26 Da Gama Road, offers Italian and Chinese cuisine. **O'Hagans** bar has the surliest staff of any branch of this national chain of mock-Irish pubs.

How to Get There

Jeffrey's Bay is 206 km (129 miles) from Knysna and 74 km (46 miles) from Port Elizabeth just off

don't much care what they eat. An award-winning self-catering hotel is **Diaz 15** (/FAX (042) 293 1779 E-MAIL info@diaz15.co.za WEB SITE www.diaz15 .co.za, 15 Diaz Road, R400 to R570 apartment only, with luxury self-catering apartments within walking distance of beach and shops. More conventional hotels include the **Savoy Hotel** ((042) 293 1106 FAX (042) 293 2445, 16 Da Gama Road, R360 to R400, and the **Seashells Beach Hotel** (/FAX (042) 293 1104, 25 Da Gama Road, R260 to R300 with breakfast. Out of town **Sandals Beach House** ((042) 294 0551 FAX (042) 294 0748 E-MAIL donnelly @agnet.co.za WEB SITE www.stfrancisbay.co.za, 4 Napier Road, St. Francis Bay, R570 to R780 is 14 km (8.7 miles) south.

Otherwise it's back to backpackerland at the **J-Bay Backpackers** ((042) 293 1379 FAX (042) 296 1763, 12 Jeffreys Street, R25 to R45 per person in a dormitory, or **Island Vibe Backpackers**

the N2 highway. Greyhound and Translux only serve Humansdorp, 20 km (12.5 miles) to the west, but the Baz Bus goes right into town and stops at the backpacker lodges. Intercape stops in Jeffrey's Bay but the fare structure makes this expensive. **Sunshine Express** ((042) 293 2221 or (041) 581 3790 (after hours) runs a local service to Port Elizabeth.

PORT ELIZABETH

For many years rather an ugly-duckling, industrial city, Port Elizabeth, known to everybody as "P.E.," has started to enjoy something of a renaissance. This is partly to do with visitors "falling off" the end of the Garden Route and using Port Elizabeth as their departure airport. However more and more people are finding the attractions

Port Elizabeth's sunny beaches mean many visitors stay longer than planned.

of the Eastern Cape enough reason to linger awhile in its major city.

Port Elizabeth is capital of the Eastern Cape, a disparate province that was home to both Khoikhoi tribes to the west and Xhosa to the east, with the inland areas harsh and unforgiving desert. During the early years of white settlement it was frontier country and saw some of the largest battles of the colonial wars. At the same time, it also was the scene of frenzied missionary activity, laying the foundations for a good education, and many of the country's future leaders, including Nelson Mandela, Walter Sisulu, and Steve Biko spent their formative years in this state.

The first British settlers landed in 1820 and founded the city of Port Elizabeth, which grew as a trading center and port for the agricultural areas inland. Gradually the indigenous herds of game were shot out and scared off, and the city expanded as a manufacturing center in the 1920s and was the site of the first automobile assembly factory. Around the original nucleus a sprawl of suburbs and factories grew up, ringed by extensive shanty towns, and the center was split off from the waterfront by a huge, ugly, and unnecessary highway. Only recently has any attention been turned to the warm waters of Algoa Bay, with 10 excellent bathing beaches and the small but charming Victorian center.

General Information

The city as a whole covers a huge area, and it is even more important than usual to first visit **Port Elizabeth Tourism** ((041) 585 8884 or (041) 586 0773 (voice mail) FAX (041) 585 2564 E-MAIL pepa @iafrica.com WEB SITE www.pecc.gov.za, Lighthouse Building, Donkin Reserve, off Belmont Terrace, Box 357, Port Elizabeth 6001, open Monday to Friday 8 AM to 4:30 PM and weekends 9 AM to 3 PM, for a map and some orientation information. There's little public transportation but reliable taxi companies include **Amies** ((041) 487 3798 and **Anchor** ((041) 484 4798. For hospital treatment there are **Provincial Hospital** ((041) 392 3911 and **St. George's Hospital** ((041) 392 7921.

What to See and Do

Forty-seven of the city's most significant buildings and sights are linked on a five-kilometer (three-mile) **heritage trail**, promoted by PE Tourism from their base in Donkin Reserve, a preservation area in the heart of the town. The trail includes the City Hall, the Campanile (with the largest carillon of bells in the country), and a number of statues including Queen Victoria and Prester John. More rewarding perhaps are some few remaining unspoiled streets: the Regency buildings that line Cora Terrace and the Victorian mansions of Donkin Street. The Museum Complex, one of the largest in the country, is on the beachfront

Marine Drive and is divided into various sections. Most popular among children is the **Oceanarium** ((041) 586 1051, Beach Road, Summerstrand, open Monday to Sunday 9 AM to 5 PM, with dolphin displays daily at 11 AM and 3 PM; entry R15. The **Main Museum** ((041) 586 1051 includes dinosaur models and fully rigged models of early sailing ships, while the **Snake Park** has reptiles in cages — and charges a healthy fee to see them.

Elsewhere in the city the **Castle Hill Historical Museum** ((041) 582 2515, 7 Castle Hill, Tuesday to Saturday 10 AM to 1 PM and 2 PM to 5 PM, closing at 4:30 PM Sunday and Monday, R3, is the oldest house in PE, with a good collection of colonial art and some old clothes and furniture.

For many locals and visitors alike the main attraction is nearer the ocean. PE hosted the 1995 world windsurfing championships and there is also plenty of surf, with good swimming beaches stretching 40 km (25 miles) down Algoa Bay. The

beaches are south of the center. Kings Beach and Humewood beach, south of the harbor, are sheltered, while there's more wind at Hobie Beach, five kilometers (just over three miles) to the south. Surfing and water sports equipment can be rented from the **Beachbreak Adventure Center** ((041) 585 4384, 109 Russell Road. Nearer the town center is a tidal swimming pool at MacArthur Baths on King's Beach Promenade. There are several wrecks offshore and a marine reserve around the **St. Croix Islands** that is well worth a visit or more, with diving operators including **Ocean Divers** ((041) 585 6536 and **African Coastal Adventures** ((041) 686 2259.

Where to Stay and Eat

A sudden boom in guest houses and hotels in Port Elizabeth have rather outstripped the supply of visitors, which keeps rates reasonable. The city also prides itself on being South Africa's friendliest city (as does Bloemfontein) and makes a creditable effort to keep the corners up on the edges of its welcome smile.

If your budget allows it, the best place to stay is **Hacklewood Hill Country House** ((041) 581 1300 FAX (041) 581 4155 E-MAIL pehotels@ mweb.co.za WEB SITE www.pehotels.co.za, 152 Prospect Road, Walmer, R1,100 with breakfast. Set in the leafy and wealthy suburb of Walmer, this is a restored Victorian mansion with antique furnishings in eight guest rooms and an excellent restaurant. It sometimes seems a bit strange to have this much comfort so close to the Walmer Township, a very different environment to Walmer suburb although only separated by a strip of waste ground, but that's just one of the things you have to get used to in travel in South Africa. Nearby and rather cheaper is **Oak Tree Cottage** ((041) 581

King's Beach hosts some of Port Elizabeth's most keenly contested sailing races.

3611 FAX (041) 581 6392 E-MAIL duff@global.co.za WEB SITE www.time2travel.com/pe/oak, 112 Church Road, Walmer 6070, R250.

Your nearest neighbors are fish if you choose the **Beach Hotel** (/FAX (041) 583 2161 E-MAIL pehotels@mweb.co.za WEB SITE www.pehotels .co.za, Marine Drive, Summerstrand, a 58-bedroom resort hotel on Hobie Beach with a choice of restaurants and waterfront comforts, but still retaining something of an unspoiled 1930s feel, at R440. Nearby **Brighton Lodge** ((041) 583 4576 FAX (041) 583 4104 E-MAIL brightonlg@hotmail .com, 21 Brighton Drive, corner of Fifth Avenue, Port Elizabeth, R280, is near but not on the beach and close to several restaurants. It has comfort-

The best food is generally in your chosen hotels, but there are many restaurants in the city, specializing, perhaps unsurprisingly, in seafood. **Santorini** ((041) 365 4776, Mall on Fourth Avenue, Alma Street, Newton Park, is an irrepressibly cheerful Greek restaurant with specialties including mussels in white wine on linguine and butterfish, as well as occasionally reviving the Greek restaurant tradition of breaking plates. For seafood, **De Kelder Restaurant** ((041) 583 2750 in the Marine Hotel, Marine Drive, Summerstrand, offers some of the best in town.

For nightlife, the best night in PE is, for some reason, Wednesdays. Fridays and Saturdays run a close second. There are a couple of centers that

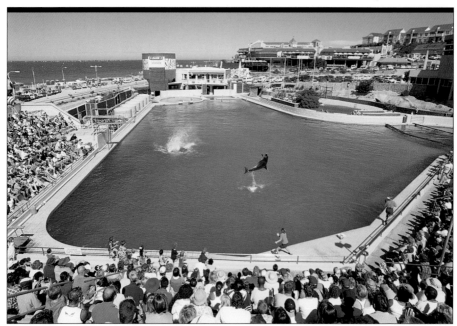

able rooms in a variety of styles with breakfast served in the room; for dining, walk. For those who prefer to stay in the city center the **Edward Hotel** (/FAX (041) 586 2056, Belmont Terrace, Central Port Elizabeth, R250, is a graceful 1903 building that is within walking distance of the Opera House, Campanile, and Fort Frederic. There's also a **Formule 1** ((041) 585 6380 FAX (041) 585 6383, corner La Roche Drive and Beach Road, Humewood, near the beach with its simple formula of R145 for up to three, room only. Backpackers can choose between the town center, and **Jikeleza Lodge** (/FAX (041) 586 3712, 44 Cuyler Street, R50 in twin or three-bed rooms, or on the beachfront where the best is **Kings Beach Backpacker Hostel** ((041) 585 8113, 41 Windermere Road, Humewood, with camping and weekly rates knocking off the headline rate of R35. Recommended.

set the scene in the early evenings. The **Broadwalk** on Marine Pier, over Shark Rock Pier, contains a selection of bars and restaurants, and the **Brooke's Pavilion Entertainment Complex** on the corner of Brookes Hill Drive and Beach Road in Summerstrand has a number of bars and restaurants overlooking the Indian Ocean. From these two centers the evening splits into a number of strands, with **Thew Blinkingf Owl**, 306 Cape Road, Newton Park, and **Cadillac Jack's**, Hobie Beach, and the **Sundowners Pub'n'grub & Palm Beach Roadhouse**, Marine Drive, Summerstrand, being a selection of good starting points.

How to Get There

With your own vehicle, Port Elizabeth is 763 km (477 miles) from Cape Town along the N2 Highway, which continues on to East London (310 km/194 miles) and, eventually Durban

(984 km/615 miles). It is 72 km (45 miles) from Addo Elephant Park and 74 km (46.2 miles) to Shamwari Game Reserve. Port Elizabeth is a key hub of the South African transportation system, with air links from the airport four kilometers (two and a half miles) from the city center. The **Airport** ((041) 507 7301 will provide information about air links that reach Johannesburg, Bloemfontein, East London, George, Cape Town and Durban using SAA, Comair, and SA Airlink. Hotels provide transportation from the airport but public transportation doesn't. The Algoa Express and the Southern Cross serve the railway station at the center of town and Greyhound, Intercape, and Translux buses serve the city, but stop at the Greenacres shopping center, eight kilometers (five miles) out of town. The Baz Bus, meanwhile, drops off at city center backpacking lodges.

AROUND PORT ELIZABETH

Visitors to South Africa generally hope to see a full range of Africa's animals, and the heavily-populated southern coastal area is not the best place to do this. But in the area around Port Elizabeth are a number of small national parks and private reserves, which are the best places in the non-malarial south to come close to the safari experience.

Addo Elephant Park

In the Sundays River region of the Eastern Cape Province, 72 km (45 miles) from Port Elizabeth along tarred roads, the Addo Elephant Park is one of the best places in Africa to see elephant and is also good for a number of other wildlife species. In 1931, when the park was proclaimed, there were only eleven elephants surviving from the huge herds that once roamed the area. Now there are between 200 and 300 elephants as well as less populous Cape buffalo, a range of antelope species, and some rarely-seen black rhino. It is also one of the only places in the world you'll find the rare flightless dung beetle. If you look.

The elephant are the main draw. It's worth asking at the gate where they have been recently sighted, but both times I visited I started to hear trumpeting almost as soon as I drove into the reserve, and it doesn't usually take too long to track one down. One of the stranger conditions of entry, alongside the routine bans on firearms and pets, is a ban on citrus fruits. This is a legacy of an early conservation experiment: in an attempt to stop the ellies straying into the surrounding farmlands they were fed oranges in the park. Unfortunately they liked this diet too well and the elephants would fight each other to increase their share. Feeding oranges was stopped in 1978 but elephants have famously long memories, and if some of the older, and therefore larger,

elephants smell an orange in the trunk of your car they might just flip it open to indulge in a half-forgotten treat.

There is a park office and a restaurant in the heart of the reserve, along with a shop selling everything from elephant dung to beer. There are also some very well-finished and equipped self-catering chalets (sleeping two: R220) overlooking a dusty dam that is often thronged with elephants, especially in the mornings and evenings. These can be booked through **South African National Parks** ((031) 304 4934 or (012) 343 9770 E-MAIL reservations@parks-sa.co.za; more than 72 hours in advance call ((042) 233 0556 and ((042) 233 0557 less than 72 hours ahead. Caravanners and camp-

ers can stop off in remote campsites in the park, and there is a range of forest huts. The park management also organizes game drives for groups of four or more; two hours cost R60. The park is open daily 7 AM to 5 PM.

Should the park accommodation be full—and it often is in season—or if you want a touch more comfort the **Zuurberg Mountain Inn** ((042) 233 0583 FAX (042) 233 0070 E-MAIL zuurberg@ilink .co.za WEBSITE www.addo.co.za, R600 with breakfast, is a restored 1861 staging post on the R33 near the park entrance. There is no public transportation to the park so backpackers will have to take an organized tour from Port Elizabeth; lodges are only too keen to make the arrangements.

OPPOSITE: Dolphins on display at Port Elizabeth's Oceanarium. RIGHT: Safari style at the Zuurberg Mountain Inn, near Addo Elephant Park.

EARLY INLAND SETTLEMENTS

One of the oldest towns in the country, and certainly the oldest in the Eastern Cape province, Graaff-Reinet was founded in 1786 in an attempt by the very distant authorities to bring order to a lawless area. The first settlers who came here found huge numbers of game, herds of springbok that took three days to pass. In between shooting everything that moved the early settlers also took issue with the indigenous people, regarding it as routine to interrupt their daily bloodbath to raid Khoi cattle and attack San tribes, killing the men and taking the women and children as servants or, more realistically, as slaves. Nine years later the magistrate was expelled from the town at gunpoint for enforcing the law and Graaff-Reinet declared the "First Boer Republic." It took the colonial authorities five years to amass a force large enough to restore the rule of law. Sheep farming gradually spread an agricultural base around the town, and the 1850s boom in wool price brought prosperity, finally bringing an upright respectability. It didn't stop the rape of the environment. In 1896 one trader alone sold a million springbok skins. Most of the ancient buildings built at this time still line the atmospheric high street, and Graaff-Reinet has the distinction of having more national monuments than any other town in South Africa: 200 buildings are accorded monument status, and several recreate period values in a new life as hotels and guest houses.

But it's not just the upright, whitewashed settler architecture that brings visitors flooding into the town. It is surrounded by the Karoo Nature Reserve, an arid wilderness of outstanding, haunting beauty. The Valley of Desolation, in particular, is one of the great views of South Africa, and the desert floor is littered with fossils. Paleontologists call Graaff-Reinet the "Fossil Capital of the World." Add to this the weird appeal of nearby Nieu Bethesda and the owl house and it is easy to see why this is more than just a popular stop between Johannesburg and Port Elizabeth — there are enough attractions here to justify making a special trip into the desert heartlands.

GRAAFF-REINET

From any direction long, straight desert roads across the flatlands known as the Camdeboo are the prelude to entering the town's gabled, whitewashed Church Street stretching down from the graceful Dutch Reformed church, designed after Britain's Salisbury Cathedral but, sensibly, built smaller. If you need medical attention the major **Clinic(** (049) 892 2231 is at 41 North Street and if that doesn't help the **Undertaker(** (049) 892 2755 is on Murray Street. The **Tourist Information (**/FAX (049) 892

4248 E-MAIL graaffreinet@elink.co.za WEB SITE WWW .graaffreinet.co.za, Old Library Museum, Church Street, Box 153, Graaff-Reinet 6280, open Monday to Friday 9 AM to 12:30 PM and 2 PM to 5 PM, Saturdays to noon, is part of a good introductory display of fossils, San rock art, and period costumes. Across the street the animated period costumes of staff bustling to and from the Drostdy Hotel are a more vital sign of time gone by.

What to See and Do

Although you can walk around most of the town center attractions, a vehicle and driver are needed to get up to the Valley of Desolation. A good local guide is **Karoo Connections Adventure Tours (** (049) 892 3978 FAX (049) 892 1061 E-MAIL karooconnections@intekom.co.za, Box 538, Graaff-Reinet 6280. Many of the town center's attractions are close by, with Cradock Street alone, running parallel to Church Street, containing more

than 50 historic houses. Of a selection of houses restored into museums, the best are the **Reinet House**, Parsonie Street, open Monday to Friday 9 AM to 12:30 PM and 2 PM to 5 PM, Saturday to noon, Sunday 10 AM to noon, R5, containing six rooms packed with desirable relics and antiques, and the **Old Pharmacy**, Caledon Street, with the same hours except closed on Sunday. South Africa has plenty of restored pharmacies, but this one is the most complete.

The town center is small enough to explore on foot, dropping into shops and museums as the fancy takes you. There are so many however that I emerged blinking from the last with the feeling that my wallet had already been adequately chipped, three, five and ten rand at a time. After all, I'd just wanted to visit, not buy the furniture. Although I could have, at **Reinet Antiques** at 15 Church Street or **Toentertyd Antiques** at 20 Church Street.

At least both the **Karoo Nature Reserve** and the **Valley of Desolation** are free. To reach either take the Murraysburg Road for five kilometers (just over three miles) to the turning to the valley and eight kilometers (five miles) more to the entry to the reserve. The Valley of Desolation is a dolerite intrusion into the Camdeboo plain, exposed by years of erosion and now towering over the flat landscape. There's a marked 45-minute trail which is best explored at nightfall as the light paints ochres and reds on the rock and if you're lucky the resident black eagle will circle lazily in thermals before returning to its nest. There's also a hut — which gets very cold — that can be booked through **Nature Conservation** ((049) 892 4535, Bourke Street. The Karoo Nature Reserve has a 19-km (12-mile) game drive circling the dusty pan of the town's irrigation dam — about once every

The Valley of Desolation in the heart of the Karoo.

10 years it fills with water and the town's boat club springs into life. Even when the dam is dry there are good chances of seeing mountain zebra, Cape buffalo, kudu, and springbok.

Where to Stay and Eat

Amidst so much restoriana, choosing an atmospheric place to stay might be difficult. It isn't, however, because the **Drostdy Hotel** ((049) 892 2161 FAX (049) 892 4582, 30 Church Street, is so clearly the best in town. Designed in 1804 to strike, if not awe at least a little respect into the unruly local population, this building was the seat of government, as still reflected in its imposing façade and large restaurant, lobby, and courtyard. Guests sleep in the extensive slave quarters around the back, which were home to workers until the Group Areas Act in the 1950s declared the area white. These days the small houses have been revamped into comfortable cottages with en-suites. Room only from R280, with suites at R550 represents very good value.

Also good is the **Kingfisher Lodge** (/FAX (049) 892 2657 E-MAIL kingfisher-lodge@intekom.co.za, 33 Cypress Grove, R200 to R400, in a quiet suburb. Moving down the scale two historic bed-and-breakfasts are **Impangele** ((049) 892 5266, 96 Cradock Street, R150, and **Buitenverwachting** ((049) 892 4504, 58 Bourke Street, R200. Even backpackers go historic at **Le Jardin** ((049) 892 3326, 50 Somerset Street, R50.

The best place to eat is **De Camdeboo** ((049) 892 2161, a private restaurant in the grounds of the Drostdy Hotel, for candlelit dining on yellowwood tables; reservations required. The area's specialty is Karoo lamb, which shares a menu with ostrich and smoked springbok at the **Stockman's Restaurant** ((049) 892 0142, 3 Church Street, housed in the Graaff-Reinet Men's Club, which, thanks to a very recent change in their club rules, now accepts women. **Andries Stockenstroom** ((049) 892 4575, 100 Cradock Street, also serves bush meat in a small, intimate setting; book early as it fills fast.

How to Get There

Graaff-Reinet is 250 km (156 miles) north of Port Elizabeth on the R75, 670 km (419 miles) from Cape Town along the N1 highway, turning right onto the R61, and 420 km (262.5 miles) from Bloemfontein on the N9 and N1. Intercape leaves from outside the Drostdy Hotel, while Translux stop outside the Kudu garage.

NIEU BETHESDA

Either as a day-trip from Graaff-Reinet or as a destination in its own right Nieu Bethesda is worth the drive. This is a classic farming village in the fertile valley of the Neeuberg mountains, so remote that many of the streets were until recently used to grow potatoes and lucerne. Once an important agricultural center, it fell into decline through the 1930s and 1940s, as other towns in the Great Karoo were linked by road and grew in importance. Neglected and hard to find, it has retained the atmosphere of these middle-of-nowhere frontier towns, to such an extent that now it is beginning to be a cult residence for artists and writers. What has put it on the map is one eccentric and striking local building: Helen Martin's Owl House. More than any other single building in South Africa this, for me, sums up the isolation, idiosyncrasy, and creativity of the life on the world's frontier communities, salted in this case with a deep and passionate bitterness.

The Owl House

Born in Nieu Bethesda in 1897 as the youngest of six children, Helen Martin was a bright girl who studied, got married (it lasted a day), and traveled before returning in 1930 to look after her ailing parents. Unfortunately her mother, who she'd liked, died in 1941 and her father, who she didn't, lived on. He was sent to live in an outhouse to fend for himself, dying in 1945. She was left, alone and with few prospects, isolated in the heart of the Karoo, and turned her energies into transforming her bungalow into a blaze of color. There's nothing gentle about the way she did it. Using her coffee-grinder she crushed colored glass and embedded it in paint, creating vivid patterns that turned every surface into an unforgiving, encrusted plane of luminous color. The windows were all replaced with intricate stained glass, sunfaces and owls predominant images. Once she finished the house — making it almost uninhabitable in the process — she turned her energies to the garden, casting cement sculptures. At this point she employed an itinerant sheepshearer, Koos Malgas, and with his help constructed more than 500 sculptures that are still crammed into her tiny garden. In her later life she became increasingly shy of her appearance and took great pains to avoid being seen. In 1976 she took her own life by drinking caustic soda.

Critics are divided on her talent as a sculptor. I found it very moving and playwright Athol Fugard, who has a house in the village, used her as a basis for his play The Road to Mecca. But one thing is sure: you don't visit the Owl House and forget it. A local concrete company, appropriately enough, sponsors it as a museum and on my visit Koos Malpas, though now retired, was busy in the garden fixing an angel's broken finger. The Owl House (/FAX (049) 841 1605, Poste Restante, Nieu Bethesda 6286, 9 AM to 5 PM, R10.

ABOVE: Art at the Owl House, Nieu Bethesda. RIGHT: Restoriana in the Karoo town of Graaf-Reinet.

Where to Stay and Eat

Elsewhere in the village the **Ibis Gallery** ((049) 841 1682 has a good selection of art, often by local artists, and offers accommodation (preferably to artists). The **Village Inn** (no phone) provides light meals and teas with home-baked scones. The best known of many farmstay bed-and-breakfasts in the area is **Wellwood** ((049) 891 0517, Nieu Bethesda Road, R200, a merino stud farm with a notable collection of fossils. Perhaps unsurprisingly in a village that claims to be the UFO capital of the world, there's even a village backpackers: **Owl House Backpackers** ((049) 841 3667 E-MAIL pepbakpak@global.co.za, Martin Street.

How to Get There

There is no public transportation to Nieu Bethesda, but transportation can be arranged by Port Elizabeth Backpackers ((041) 586 0697, 7 Prospect Hill, Port Elizabeth. By car it is 23 km (14.4 miles) off the N9 between Graaff-Reinet and Middelburg on a dirt road. They don't still grow vegetables in the high street but expect a quiet time.

ACROSS THE EASTERN CAPE

For those traveling round the Cape but who don't want to go north into malarial districts for the Kruger Park and adjoining reserves, the only chance to see the Big Five is at the private game reserve of Shamwari, 72 km (45 miles) from Port Elizabeth on the Grahamstown (N2) highway.

SHAMWARI

Either on day trips or more expensively with an overnight stay Shamwari is one place where it is usually easy to see elephant, rhino, buffalo, leopard and lion, even though many of these can scarcely be described as free-ranging, being kept, virtually, in pens. There is also a traditional African village, Khaya Lendaba, where a traditional lunch is served and traditional fabrics are made. Am I saying traditional too much? That's because it's sanitized out of sight.

The wildlife experience is not bad. The reserve is 14,000 hectares (nearly 35,000 acres), so there's space to pretend the animals are wild but there's little suspense about whether you'll find the animals or not. South Africans on a game drive complain if they don't get the Big Five and are not above asking for their money back.

There's a choice of accommodation at Shamwari. The main hotel is Shamwari Lodge, a five-star lodge offering every comfort. Long Lee Manor is a restored 1910 mansion, is the flagship of the reserve with period furniture, under-floor heating in winter and air-conditioning in summer, and is also highly luxurious. Three lodges, Carn Ingly, Highfield and Bushman's River Lodge are

converted from 1820 settler cottages, furnished with antiques and equipped with all the facilities of the modern age — all, for example, have swimming pool — and has its own game ranger, chef and service staff. You can't just drop in to Shamwari. Booking is essential. And the wildlife experience does not come cheap in these luxurious surroundings. The day tour of the African Village, starting at 11 AM, followed by an afternoon game drive costs R295, while to stay rates are, depending on season, R2,000 to R4,000, full board. Contact **Shamwari** ((042) 203 1111 FAX (042) 235 1224 E-MAIL shamwaribooking@global.co.za WEB SITE www.shamwari.com, Box 91, Patterson 6130.

If this is too steep — and it was for me — it's best to bite the bullet and pay for the day-trip, tick the animals off your wish-list, and then stay four kilometers (two and a half miles) up the road at the far more characterful **Leeuwenbosch Country House** ((042) 235 1252 E-MAIL fowldsg@iafrica.com, Box 20, Paterson 6130, R450 for dinner, bed, and breakfast. This is a superb old farmhouse, cool through the summer thanks to 45 cm (18 in) of sawdust in the roof, with period furnishings imparting huge character. It is a bit unfortunate that the beds are period too, rather than comfortable, but there's no denying that it's a good place to stay, with a small cellar pub where the conversation ranges far and wide, often coming back to guns. The owners also operate a small wooden lodge, stilted, overlooking a panoramic view, which can be rented if required.

How to Get There

Shamwari is 70 km (44 miles) along the N2 from Port Elizabeth, on the left; Leeuwenbosch is four kilometers (two and a half miles) further on, on the right. There is no public transportation, but many tour operators, grateful for the commission, will happily arrange for you to visit Shamwari.

GRAHAMSTOWN

Located 127 km (about 80 miles) east of Port Elizabeth, Grahamstown is a quintessentially English, civilized town with a pleasantly faded, period atmosphere. Sedately pretty, it started life as a garrison for the British colonial forces between the Fish and Bushman's rivers. It played a key role in the military conquest of South Africa in a series of frontier wars, as well as being at the heart of the 1820 campaign to use settlers to form a human barrier against Xhosa tribesmen.

This didn't work as well as hoped. With the advent of so many English neighbors the resident Boers packed up and trekked off north. Meanwhile the new immigrants from England were bribed with free farms, but it soon became clear that the land wasn't always suitable for farming. More importantly the settlers themselves weren't always suitable farmers; quite apart from the threat of hostile natives they didn't know how to make plants grow. They quickly abandoned their land and headed back to the cities, to make a more secure living by exercising their own trades. Many of them gravitated back to Grahamstown, helping to create some elegant stone buildings that still ring Church Square. By 1853 underemployed stonemasons had already built the cathedral that makes Grahamstown a city. It was later joined by a well-respected university, a number of private schools, and no fewer than 40 churches.

In the apartheid years, the Fish River marked the beginning of the independent homeland of Ciskei, an artificially created ethnic statelet where

the local hospital is the **Settlers Hospital** ((046) 622 2215, Milner Street.

What to See and Do

The **Albany Museum Complex**, five museums within strolling distance, is the second oldest in the country. The **Natural Science Museum** ((046) 622 2312, Somerset Street, Monday to Friday 9 AM to 1 PM and 2 PM to 5 PM, weekends afternoons only, R5, is the oldest component of the museum. Notable items include a portion of the Gibeaon meteorite, a working Foucault pendulum, and a reconstruction of Africa's first dinosaur. The **History Museum** ((046) 622 2312, Somerset Street, same hours, R5, focuses on the 1820 British

the black population was resettled by the South African government. Grahamstown, naturally, was not in it. Even now, the view over the river from the prosperous farms on one side is of scattered, tin-roofed dwellings. It's a pleasant, relaxing city that wakes up in July for its annual theatrical festival, the Standard Bank National Arts Festival, which attracts all South Africa's artists and most of their audiences.

General Information

The **Grahamstown Tourism Office** ((046) 622 3241 FAX (046) 622 3266 E-MAIL tourgtn@imaginet.co.za WEBSITE www.grahamstown.co.za, 63 High Street, Grahamstown 6139, open Monday to Thursday 8:30 AM to 1 PM and 2 PM to 5 PM, Friday to 4 PM, Saturday 9 AM to 11 AM, is a good place to start exploring. A reputable local taxi service is **Beeline Taxi** ((082) 651 5646 or (082) 652 0798, while

settlers as well as a small ethnographic collection relating to the southern Nguni peoples. Strangely, it includes an Egyptian mummy. The **Observatory Museum** ((046) 622 3212, 10 Bathurst Street, same weekday hours and Saturday 9 AM to 1 PM, R8, originally a nineteenth-century jewelry shop, is linked with the discovery in 1867 of South Africa's first big diamond, the Eureka. It now houses the only Victorian Camera Obscura in the southern hemisphere, a subject of considerable pride, and also some well-restored period rooms and a herb garden.

More interesting, for its atmospheric pathos, is **Fort Selwyn** ((046) 622 2312, Gunfire Hill, an 1836 Fort built as a telegraph system which never worked, and cunningly designed to fight off foes who never attacked. The orderly room has been

Period shops in downtown Grahamstown have barely changed since the years of settlement.

restored to 1840 standards and there's a fascinating collection of weapons. Best of all, it's only open by appointment (call) and entrance is free. A final site of interest is the **JLB Smith Institute of Ichthyology** ((046) 636 1002, Somerset Street, a leading center for the study of fish. Surprisingly located a 45-minute drive from the ocean, it houses the largest collection of dead fish in the southern hemisphere and one of the biggest in the world. Open Monday to Friday 8 AM to 1 PM and 2 PM to 5 PM, admission free.

If all this settler focus becomes wearing **Umthathi Township Tours** ((046) 622 5051, High Street, Box 6010, Grahamstown 6010, works with local people to introduce Xhosa ceremonies and customs.

Where to Stay and Eat

The best place to stay in Grahamstown is not the most expensive. It is the **Settlers Hill Cottages** ((046) 622 9720 E-MAIL hadeda@imaginet.co.za, a collection of period cottages dating back to 1823 scattered between Cross and Donkin streets, beautifully restored and costing from R250 with breakfast. The **Graham Protea Hotel** ((046) 622 2324 FAX (046) 622 2424, 123 High Street, R359 with breakfast, is well-featured and has a good reputation for its restaurant but is dull. The **Cock House** ((046) 636 1295 FAX (046) 636 1287, 10 Market Street, R440 with breakfast, is a beautifully restored veranda'd building with a good à la carte restaurant attached. Backpackers should head to the **Old Jail Backpackers** ((046) 636 1001, Somerset Street.

For an evening meal, a good option is the Cock House, with a warmly sociable pub and garden setting. Nelson Mandela ate here once — with all his years in prison not many restaurants can make this claim — and it was home in the 1970s to famous writer André Brink, who restored the building. Meanwhile **Die Tap Huijs** ((046) 622 3243, Cawood Street, provides live music on weekends and a huge selection of estate wines, but is closed from Sunday to Tuesday.

How to Get There

Grahamstown is 130 km (81.2 miles) from Port Elizabeth and 170 km (106 miles) from East London on the N2. Port Alfred is 58 km (36 miles) to the south. By public transportation, Greyhound and Translux buses stop in Grahamstown's Market Square.

PORT ALFRED

Due south of Grahamstown, Port Alfred is nicknamed "Kowie" after the river, navigable for 29 km (18 miles), that joins the ocean here. At first sight it is a rather depressing collection of vacation homes set on rolling dunes overlooking the Indian Ocean. The beach is frequented by wet-suited

surfers and celebrating students from Grahamstown. **Tourism Port Alfred** ((046) 624 1235 FAX (046) 624 3739, the Causeway, Box 63, Port Alfred 6170, will help with accommodation queries though the first question I felt like asking was how to leave. The best things to do here are to head off on the **Kowie Hiking Trail**, three kilometers (nearly two miles) from the town, within the **Kowie Nature Reserve** (no telephone number), with walkways and a mixture of coastal and grassland animals. If you happen to have a canoe, take the 21-km (13-mile) **Kowie Canoe Trail** ((046) 624 2230, booking essential, entailing a night on the **Horseshoe Bend Nature Reserve**.

For accommodation, better hold back from the coast altogether here. The **Kariega Game Reserve** ((046) 636 7904 FAX (046) 636 2288 E-MAIL kariega @yebo.co.za WEB SITE www.kariega.co.za, Kenton-on-Sea, R500 with breakfast, sets log-built chalets in beautiful surroundings. In town the smart option is **Halyards** ((046) 624 2410 FAX (046) 624 2466, Albany Road, overlooking the Royal Alfred Marina, R450 room only. A step cheaper is **Big Tree Guest House** (/FAX (046) 624 2049, 58 Southwell Road, R200 with breakfast. Backpackers can rely on **Port Alfred Backpackers** ((046) 624 4011, 29 Sports Road, near town, R40 sharing.

Port Alfred is 58 km (36.2 miles) due south of Grahamstown.

EAST LONDON

Most visitors arrive in East London by mistake. It has a major domestic airport, a train station, and buses stop here, but apart from a lively and unexpected surfing crowd it does not have any obvious appeal. Even so, people do arrive here, by mistake or otherwise, and stay to enjoy one of South Africa's most unlikely cities.

East London doesn't have an ancient tradition; it has only recently risen as an industrial center. Motor assembly, textiles, and electronics dominate the local economy. South Africans flock to the seaside attractions of miniature trains, waterslides, go-carting, and arcade games. As the South African "AA" guides say "it is a super place for a holiday." Visitors flock to the airport and bus stations.

Stay a while, however, and East London can work its magic. It's at the heart of the "Sunshine Coast," with good surf and golden beaches.

General Information

Tourism East London ((043) 722 6015 FAX (043) 743 5091 or 24-hour Information Service ((043) 722 6034, Old Library Building, 35 Argyle Street (behind City Hall), 8:30 AM to 4:30 PM and Saturday to 11 AM, is very helpful and will help you make the best of their town. For information about the wider area visit **Eastern Cape Tourism Board** ((043) 743 9511 FAX (043) 743 9513, Lock Street Jail, Fleet Street. For hospital services the **East London Private Hospital** ((043) 722 3128 is one of several, while a local taxi shuttle service is **Border Taxi** ((043) 722 1884 or **Smith's Taxi** ((043) 743 9918.

What to See and Do

The **East London Museum** ((043) 743 0686, open Monday to Friday 9:30 AM to 5 PM, Saturday to noon, and Sunday 11 AM to 4 PM, R2, has the only known dodo egg along with a number of maritime exhibits including some bits of sunken ships and the first-discovered, stuffed, coelacanth. The **Lock Street Jail**, constructed in 1880 to house women prisoners, has now been converted to a shopping center, and still retains the well-used gallows. Meanwhile **Latimer's Landing** is East London's answer to the Victoria and Alfred Waterfront, on the banks of the Buffalo River overlooking a small marina.

Out of town the more active can call **Three Sisters Horse Trails** ((046) 675 2619 who arrange horseback trails. Most visitors find the beach more of a draw. The town's best swimming, in the rapidly warming waters of the Indian Ocean is at **Orient Beach**, best accessed through Currie Street.

Places to Stay and Eat

Those who are determined to stay here can choose from the waterfront **Halyards Hotel** ((046) 624 2410 FAX (046) 624 2466, Albany Road, R800 upwards, or rather less expensively at the **Kowie Grand Hotel** ((046) 624 1150 FAX (046) 624 3769, 1 Kowie West, R200 with breakfast. Backpackers with their own vehicles, or Baz Bus tickets, should certainly make their way to Cintsa, 35 km (22 miles) to the east, where one of the country's best backpackers is **Cintsa Backpackers** ((043) 734 3590 E-MAIL moonshine_sa@hotmail.com, Moonshine Bay, Cintsa.

How to Get There

The domestic **airport** ((043) 736 0211 is connected to the city by a **shuttle service** ((082) 569 3599. Trains arrive, weekly, at the town's commercial center, with Spoornet passenger information ((043) 700 1729, as does the Intercape ((043) 722 5508 and Translux ((043) 700 1999 bus service. Greyhound, however, drops off at the seafront. Motorists find East London 300 km (187.5 miles) east of Port Elizabeth and 667 km (417 miles) west of Durban along the N2. It is also 582 km (364 miles) to Port St. Johns on the Wild Coast (see page 218.)

City Hall is the administrative heart of East London.

Gauteng and the Gold Fields

THE ECONOMIC POWERHOUSE and the governing legislature are 50 km (31 miles) apart in Gauteng province, the richest and most troubled of all South Africa's regions. There's huge, dynamic Johannesburg, where rising crime rates mar economic growth and a rapid loosening of the entrenched attitudes of apartheid. Pretoria, the staid, rather complacent seat of government, is a grand city center surrounded by townships where only the most superficial changes seem to have taken root. More than 45% of South Africa's white population live in these two cities, and out of the country's entire population of around 40 million people, six million live in this, the smallest province of all; of these, four million live in Soweto alone.

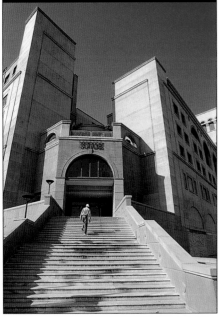

It is not the most beautiful area of South Africa. Pretoria's Nguni name meant "Salt Pan." And it is just as well that Johannesburg was never spectacular as the first thing the settlers did here was dig up the ground and leave it out in piles. Now the deepest mines tunnel 3.8 km (1.94 miles) underground, into 30% of the world's gold reserves. Occupying an area of land called the Highveld, the towns are at an average altitude of 1,500 m (about 4,900 ft) above sea level — hot in summer, and cold enough to suffer frosts in the heart of winter in June and July. But with mineral deposits like these there's no question of getting put off by anything so trivial as weather.

"Gauteng" is a relatively recent name for the province, meaning literally "place of Gold" in Sotho. Before it was known as "PWW" — Pretoria, Witwatersrand Vereeniging. Pretoria is the grand and imposing seat of government, a home to civil servants and a watering-hole for national politicians. Vereeniging is an industrial center, using labor commuting from the scandal-hit townships such as Sharpeville. The cities are separated by the Witwatersrand, the "Ridge of White Water," ground stiff with gold, uranium, diamonds, chrome, silver, and platinum. Johannesburg, with its skyscrapers and rush-hour traffic, is the place that makes it all happen. If the current growth continues, Gauteng will, in time, become one great city as the cities grow together; less than 40 km (25 miles) separate Johannesburg and Pretoria, and the suburbs expand continually.

JOHANNESBURG

E'goli — City of Gold. It was gold that built this city and even now money is the driving force which powers this, the largest and richest city in Southern Africa and the economic powerhouse of the entire continent. This is not to say you can't have fun in Johannesburg — it's the cultural center of the country and the residual racism and entrenched positions enforced by apartheid have faded fastest here. The society is by far the most cosmopolitan and, in a slightly driven way, friendly.

Most of the world's great cities are kicked into life by some resource or another. Usually there's a river involved, for drinking water, and sometimes a port. Johannesburg's *raison d'être* was far simpler: gold. So much that it deserves a capital letter: Gold. There's no mistaking its influence. Great man-made mountains of yellow dusty tailings form huge backdrops to shanty-towns and suburbs, adding geographical features to the flat plain. South Africa's capital city burst into life with the discovery of gold in 1886 and has been growing like crazy ever since. There's not nearly enough water. It has to be piped over from Lesotho. But none of that mattered with the wealth just waiting to be dug out of the ground, launching the fledgling republic of South Africa onto the world economic stage when, in 1886, Australian prospector George Harrison struck his spade into what turned out to be the world's richest goldfield. Immediately a tented city appeared. Within 10 years the city's population was 100,000, none remotely interested in the Boer/British politics, but all seriously concerned with getting rich, fast. The Boer Burgers regarded these new immigrants as a threat and refused to acknowledge their existence, denying them the vote. They also decreed that blacks and Indians should be moved to the outskirts. The British government, never slow to detect such an important natural resource, annexed the city and continued the trend of township development.

As the economic might of South Africa, it has always played a key role in shaping political change in the country. While the apartheid authorities played their power games in Pretoria, the seat of government, the increasingly unionized mine-workers of the Rand gold fields were flexing their political muscle. The Black Consciousness Movement was active here in the 1970s and regular states of emergency, especially in townships like Soweto, kept South Africa in the world headlines and were an important motive for the final dismantling of the repressive apartheid regime.

Few tourists stay long. Although 80% of visitors to the country fly in to the airport most fly straight on to their final destination. The big problem, for visitors, is crime.

would hardly be worth reporting unless the owner was shot in the process — actual, firsthand experiences of violent crime are thinner on the ground, and there are initiatives to try to reduce the problem. Although it's not something that should be reassuring, the people who seem to get shot most are policemen.

Faced with such a united barrage of negative publicity, most tourists avoid Johannesburg altogether. From JHB International Airport it takes just half an hour to drive to Pretoria, which has plenty of hotels, a number of museums and is altogether calmer. However it's also a lot duller: grasp the nettle and give South Africa's most dynamic city, called "the Big *Naartjie*" (tangerine) a chance.

SECURITY

The figures are, it is true, appalling. Every week car-jackings, muggings, and murders make many headlines. You might expect the white community to try to minimize the problem; in fact the reverse is true. They're not embarrassed about it. They're proud. Thousands of miles from their hometown you can recognize a Johannesburger because they are talking about crime. It sometimes seems to have replaced South African's shared obsession with sport. In Johannesburg it is crime that forms the common link that lubricates the social whirl.

In fact it is not that easy to gauge the real risk. Pry closer and most of the crime stories seem to refer to friends of friends, the house next door, the street along. Although it's hard to find meaningful statistics — a mobile phone theft, for instance,

There are no-go areas. The Hillbrow area, once smart and dominated by wealthy whites, now is anything but. It seems to be dominated by West Africans, especially Nigerians, and although no doubt they're not all involved in the drugs trade it sometimes seems like it. A lost tourist who enters here is lost indeed. Much of the city center is off-limits after dark, and the car-jacking figures add a further layer of paranoia. Most people feel strangely safe in their vehicles — but not here. However with a little common sense the risks can be minimized.

The first rule is to know where you are going. The smarter suburbs, impeccably cool Melville, pricey Sandton and super smart Rivonia, are reasonably safe, but stray from them and you can

OPPOSITE: Cathedral to Commerce: Sandton City Shopping Mall. ABOVE: Medicinal herbs are sold at *muthi* markets.

put yourself at risk. If you do get lost, the worst mistake you can make is stopping by the side of the road, switching on your interior light, and looking at your map; you might as well just put a target on the outside of your car and a flashing pink light. It is much safer to pull into a brightly-lit service station or hotel forecourt. Stopping to ask directions from strangers is also not advisable, not least because they rarely seem to have any clear idea about the area's geography. Keep your windows closed, even if it is hot, which is a powerful incentive to upgrade your car to an air-conditioned model. Even when you're driving along, keep the car clean inside. Any visible object tempts traffic-light thieves who use spark plugs to smash car

suffering a problem. Although visitors should take care during their visit, it would be a shame to miss out on what Johannesburg has to offer. There are 60 museums to choose from, for a start. Beyond these Johannesburg has always had a reputation for immorality, greed, and violence — and its refreshing to see a city that lives up to its image.

GENERAL INFORMATION

Most visitors' first impressions are formed at **JHB International Airport** ((011) 921 6359 (departure and arrival information), 20 km (12.5 miles) east of the city center. Here you'll find banks, an ATM machine for money, and a range of shops. The

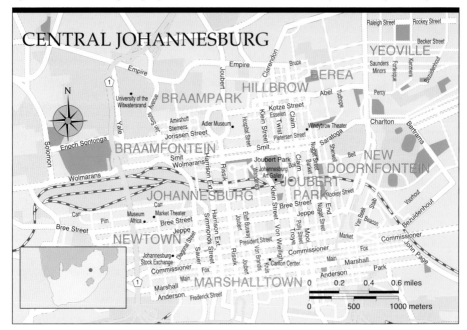

CENTRAL JOHANNESBURG

windows and grab what they can. Also car-jackers, who are usually stealing cars to order, prefer to steal cars with optional extras — like cameras or even clothes — that they won't have to declare to their employers. Mobile phones put you immediately at risk. They are valuable in South Africa and easy to hide. A person making a mobile phone call is not paying full attention to their surroundings, especially when they're driving as at the same time. This is one city where it's not advisable to lower your guard in this way.

If things do go wrong, the **national emergency telephone number** is (10111. Having said all that, driving is a lot safer than walking. Even smart areas are designed for people who can afford cars, and pedestrians in Johannesburg are never walking by choice.

Millions of the city's residents, however, successfully go through their daily lives without ever

Domestic Terminal adjoins the International Airport. The **Johannesburg Publicity Association** ((011) 970 1220, has an office in the International Arrivals hall, with opening hours Monday to Thursday 8 AM to 4:30 PM, Friday to 4 PM, and weekends to 1 PM. They will arrange bookings for car rental and more expensive hotels but are more useful for comprehensive leaflet collections for the city's attractions. *Go Gauteng* is among their best as it has comprehensive maps of Johannesburg's most visited suburbs, while the monthly *Hello Johannesburg* and *Time Out* magazines are great sources of what's-on and where-to-eat information.

Taxi drivers hustle for fares but make sure you choose one of the metered Johannesburg taxis, and that the driver knows your destination. There is an airport **Shuttle Bus** ((011) 805 2017 to Sandton and the town center, but don't board any that don't take you to the door. Most of the major hotels operate a shuttle service of their own. This is no place for visitors, jetlagged from an international flight, to blunder around laden with luggage on overstretched public transportation facilities.

If you're spending any time in Johannesburg it's worth renting a car. With over 2,750 km (1,709 miles) of road, distances in this city are huge, and reliance on taxis quickly gets expensive. Most of the rental companies have offices at the airport. Don't rent a BMW, they're a favorite with car-jackers.

Although 80% of visitors to South Africa first land in Johannesburg, the city doesn't make too much effort to make them stay. Tourism Johannesburg has temporarily lost its space at the air-

There are a number of taxi companies, but the distances involved in travel round Johannesburg will quickly make this an expensive business. **Maxi Taxis** ((011) 648 1212 are based in Yeoville while **Good Hope** ((011) 723 6431 and **Rose Taxis** ((011) 725 1111 are based in Hillbrow, heading out to the northern suburbs.

Getting around Johannesburg in your own vehicle is relatively simple, with fast motorway ring roads circling the town. These grind to a stand-still at rush hour, which starts early in the morn-ing, but at other times of day make it easy to arrow in to the destination of your choice. It would be a brave visitor who started to use the local mini-bus taxis. In any case, passengers have to indicate

port (though it is negotiating its way back) due to a refurbishment project. It still has two offices in town: one is in the Central Business District at the **Carlton Center** ((011) 331 2041 FAX (011) 331 2015, 46th Floor, Carlton Center, Johannesburg 2001, open from 8:30 AM to 5 PM Monday to Fri-day and 9 AM to noon Saturday, and a further kiosk on the ground floor. Their head office has joined the rush from the city center and is out in one of Sandton's plusher shopping malls: **Tourism Johannesburg** ((011) 784 1354 FAX (011) 883 4035 E-MAIL marketing@tourismjohannesburg.co.za WEBSITE www.tourismjohannesburg.co.za, Village Walk Shopping Center, corner Maude Street and Rivonia Road, 9 AM to 6 PM Monday to Friday and 9 AM to 1 PM Saturday. They are more of an ad-ministrative center although they do have an "infoshop." You almost need to be a local to find their office.

their destination by a complex system of hand signals so strangers are unlikely to get where they want to go.

Useful Telephone Numbers

As the capital of South Africa, this is where you'll find most of the airlines and national organiza-tions. Too many, in fact to list here: contact Tour-ism Johannesburg (see above) for the one you need. For central reservations for shows and also travel tickets, contact **Computicket** ((011) 445 8445, with kiosks across the city. The only thing you might need in a hurry — though it's hoped not — is a hospital. Best private clinic is the **Morningside Clinic** ((011) 783 8901 or (011) 282 5000, off Rivonia Road in Sandton. To call an **ambulance**, dial ((011) 403 4227.

Some visitors find a birds-eye view of Johannesburg's central district is quite close enough.

WHAT TO SEE AND DO

The Central Business District and Braamfontein

The Central Business District (CBD), unsafe at night, has been badly afflicted by South Africa's urban problems. The moneyed institutions move out of town to quieter, safer suburbs with better parking and once-grand buildings are subdivided into fast-food outlet and cheap shops. Safe enough during the day, it becomes less so as soon as the shops shut and night falls. Even so, the CBD still houses some of the city's top attractions and few remaining grand colonial buildings and shouldn't be overlooked. Overlooking, in fact, is one of the options here: the **Carlton Center**, at the corner of Commissioner and Von Wielgh Streets, is a 50-story building that used to be a hotel and is still topped by its **Observatory**, open daily 9 AM to 11:30 PM, free admission, which offers breathtaking views of the city, even though the hotel has closed and shopping center suffers a bit from urban blight. From here you can see the spreading suburbs and, closer, the CBD's principle attractions.

Southeast is the **Standard Bank Center and Gallery** ((011) 636 4231 WEB SITE www.sbgallery .co.za, Simmonds Street corner Frederick Street, open Monday to Friday 8 AM to 4:30 PM and Saturday 9 AM to 1 PM, free, where three exhibition halls play host to a constantly changing set of displays including photography and contemporary art. For more art the **Johannesburg Art Gallery** ((011) 725 3130, Klein Street, Joubert Park, has a collection of South African art as well as plenty from Europe. Changing exhibitions staged by contemporary artists are often the best bit.

From 50 stories up you can also see your route over to **Diagonal Street**, where the frenetic life on the street, teeming with vendors and long-established shops spreads out around the **Johannesburg Stock Exchange** ((011) 337 2200, where tours of the trading floor take place at 11 AM Monday to Friday with afternoon tours at 4 PM Tuesday to Thursday; booking required. Check before you visit the Stock Exchange: it is joining the rush to the suburbs and plans to move to Maude Street, Sandton. To bring you luck on the floor it might be worth consulting a *sangoma* or witchdoctor — there's a *muthi* **shop** on the corner of Diagonal and President streets that sells the full range of herbs and animal parts needed to bring about some helpful black magic.

From here it is an easy walk round to the Newtown district, a relatively recent attempt to bring life back into the center. In this area the **South African Breweries Centenary Center** ((011) 836 4900 FAX (011) 834 3836, 15 President Street, offers R10 tours of a museum of beer, with exhibits devoted to the first beers of ancient Egypt

and the sorghum beer of the African tribes. The tour includes a number of glasses to sample and as such represents the cheapest drink in town. At the heart of Newtown is the **Museum Africa** ((011) 833 5624, 121 Bree Street, which is a new museum focussing on the black experience in South Africa, an aspect which many travelers manage to miss. Starting with some examples of ancient rock art it goes on to illustrate both the struggle towards democracy and the realities of life in a township, with several squatter homes rebuilt inside the museum.

This museum is very close to the **Market Theatre** ((011) 832 1614, corner Bree and Becker streets, which is far more than just a theatre. Every day it

buzzes with activity, with a daily mineral market selling chunks of mineral rock and crystals, and a huge range of small shops, specializing in antiquarian goods and collectibles, interspersed with a scatter of street cafés. On Saturdays traders from all over Africa congregate in the area to sell their handicrafts. In the evenings security patrols keep criminal elements at bay, and theatrical and musical performances as well as several good restaurants attract Jo'burgers back into the city center (see NIGHTLIFE, page 165).

Just to the north of the CBD is the Braamfontein district which contains the Rotunda and Park stations. There are two other good reasons for going here, however. The **Gertrude Posel Gallery** ((011) 716 3632, Senate House, University of Witwatersrand, Jorissen Street, open Monday to Saturday 10 AM to 4 PM, free admission, has a collection of South African beadwork and art as well as a good selection of West African sculpture. More unexpected are the weirder treasures of the **Adler Museum of the History of Medicine (** (011) 489 9482 FAX (011) 489 9001, corner Hospital and Kotze streets, Hillbrow, also in the university complex, open Monday to Friday 9 AM to 4 PM, free admission. It has a traditional *muthi* shop recreated as well as a collection of early medical instruments, guaranteed to strike a chill into any hypochondriac.

The inner-city suburbs of Joubert Park, Berea, and Hillbrow are multicultural and exciting, but certainly not recommended for an evening stroll. Rather marooned in Hillbrow is the **Windybrow Theatre (** (011) 720 7094 FAX (011) 725 5006, corner

Nugget and Pietersen streets, which is a classic example of gold-rush architecture and still a good place to see a show on one of the three stages, though these days only frequented by community arts aficionados, apart from during its March theatre fiesta. A useful landmark is the needlelike point of the **Hillbrow Tower**, soaring high overhead and ending in a bulbous, onion shape that once served as a revolving restaurant. Whether on foot or in a car, if you have to crane your neck to see the top you are too close.

Johannesburg's Suburbs

As the city center approaches disintegration point the suburbs are increasingly where Johannesburg comes to life. The northern suburbs are where visitors are likely to spend most of their time. Just north of the CBD a ridge runs from east to west, containing some of the most interesting suburbs,

including **Claremont** and **Melville**, trendy by day and with a lively café scene at night. Further to the west **Yeoville** and **Observatory** are closest to approach the multiracial ideals of the Rainbow Nation, and nowhere more perhaps than the shops, wine bars and restaurants that line **Rockey Street**, a line of shops built in the 1920s and 1930s. Rockey Street still teems with students and artists day and night, but the parallel streets aren't safe, and unless Johannesburg's trend to crime abates even this street can't really be recommended. Asking advice on the current position will depend who you ask. Most crime-obsessed Johannesburgers wouldn't recommend going for an evening wander south of Pretoria.

Going towards Pretoria, follow the N1 north and pass first **Johannesburg Zoo (** (011) 646 2000, Jan Smuts Avenue, Parkview, open 8:30 AM to 5:30 PM, R15, where more than 3,000 species, many endangered, are housed. Especially recommended are the night tours, where it's possible to forget your urban setting in a torchlight quest for nocturnal animals. Scarcely less fortified are the houses of the increasingly wealthy, spread-out suburbs to the north. **Rosebank** is good for shopping, with a huge range of upmarket shops and boutiques while Sundays see one of the city's best markets: on the roof of the Rosebank Mall on 50 Bath Avenue.

By the time you've reached **Sandton** you're 24 km (15 miles) from the center of the city, and you're in classic new Johannesburg, with the most expensive shopping malls and plushest hotels. To the east of here the **Randburg Waterfront (** (011) 789 5052 WEB SITE www.rwaterfront.co.za, is the city's answer to Cape Town's harbor: an artificial lake is surrounded with bars, shops, and restaurants. In fact this works quite well; parking is secure and the area is very safe, with shop prices well below those charged in more fashionable Cape Town. In the evenings the lake waters are lit with colored fountains that surge to the stirring sound of Afrikaans music, blending a touch of Africa with oompah music to entertain the strolling shoppers. Another 10 km (six miles) north and you're out of the city itself, but it's worth the drive to Fourways to get to the **Lion Park (** (011) 460 1814, corner Hans Strydom and R55 Honeydew / Old Pretoria Road, open daily from 9 AM to 5 PM, R60 per vehicle, with more than 50 lions and herds of plains game facing a somewhat uncertain future. The highlight, however, are the small cubs which are well used to being cuddled.

South of the CBD are a couple of attractions. **Gold Reef City (** (011) 496 1600 FAX (011) 496 1135 WEB SITE www.goldreefcity.co.za, 18 km (11.2 miles) from the city center, blends Johannes-

Bicycle acrobats and Zulu dancers perform in daily shows at Gold Reef City.

burg's past with Disney's future, and is more or less a theme park with exhilarating rides ("Golden Loop" and "Thunder Mountain" are the best) and semi-educational tours and museums. Some are dedicated to representing Old Johannesburg; there is also a shallow gold mine you can descend 220 m (721 ft). If you don't have time to go to Kimberley (see DIG DEEP FOR DIAMONDS, page 22 in TOP SPOTS), this is a good way of getting underground. To see a working mine in operation there is a more authentic alternative: for those aged between 16 and 60 can take part in the full day mine tour organized by the **Chamber of Mines** ((011) 498 7100 — moderately strenuous but far more rewarding.

imbizo@iafrica.com WEBSITE www.backpackafrica .com, Box 25031, Ferreirasdorp 2048, with a wide range of tours including informative Soweto tours by day and hugely enjoyable *shebeen* crawls by night. Run by the irrepressible Mandy Makanzana, Imbizo can arrange for you to spend a night in Soweto, staying with rich or poor families, special tours exploring African jazz or music, as well as trips out of town to Lesedi Cultural Village, Ndebele villages and visits to Zulu, Xhosa, Sotho and other tribes (see TAKE ON A TOWNSHIP, page 25 in TOP SPOTS).

Pioneer of township tours **Jimmy's Face to Face** ((011) 331 6109 FAX 331 5388 E-MAIL face2face@ pixie.co.za, Second Floor, Budget House, 130 Main

One of the city's top sights of course is **Soweto**, the huge township that became a household word the world over through its key role in the breakdown of apartheid and the uprising of 1976. To take a tour of this township, whether by day or night, is one of the best things to do in Johannesburg and is described in more detail elsewhere (see TAKE ON A TOWNSHIP, page 25 in TOP SPOTS).

RENT-A-FRIEND

Given the hazards of traveling around Johannesburg, there's a lot to be said for using a local tour operator to show you where to go and where to avoid. There are a number of individuals and organizations that run a series of tours exploring various facets of this fascinating city. One operator is **Imbizo Tours** ((011) 838 2667 or (011) 787 0194 (after hours) FAX (011) 781 1564 E-MAIL

Street, Johannesburg, is run by Jimmy Ntintili who started taking friends to visit Soweto and now has the largest operation of its sort in the city. Alternatively, **Mindwalks** (/FAX (011) 837 2247 or (083) 348 8080 E-MAIL eabrink@global.co.za, 70 Hampton Avenue, Auckland Park 2092, offers a range of rather different and specialist tours. Run by two historians it explores precisely targeted aspects of the city, including day-trips focussing on the "Real and imagined world of mining magnates and miners" and "literary journeys through Johannesburg."

SPORTS AND OUTDOOR ACTIVITIES

Greater Johannesburg has many sporting venues of all kinds. Three of the major ones are situated three kilometers (two miles) east of the CBD. The largest is **Johannesburg Stadium** ((011) 402 2460,

Van Beek Street, New Doornfontein, host to the 1999 AllAfricaGames,whichcanseat37,500 spectators now, with plans to expand to 65,000 in due course. It's a multipurpose stadium and is one of the four best track and field venues in the world. The **Standard Bank Arena** ((011) 402 3510 is an indoor arena where tennis is the main event, flanked by 16 all-weather tennis courts, but it also plays host to a wide range of musical, ice and cultural shows and seats up to 5,000. Finally, **Ellis Park Rugby Stadium** seats 65,000 and is not used just for rugby, but has also been the venue for music concerts and stadium golf.

For soccer, the **FNB Stadium** ((011) 494 3640, also known as Football City, holds capacity crowds of 80,000 and is close to the M1 and N12 highways to the southeast of the city center. Johannesburg is at the heart of South Africa's football, with the most intense rivalry between the two main Soweto teams: the Kaiser Chiefs and the Orlando Pirates. For **horse racing**, there are three racecourses: Turffontein in Johannesburg, while Newmarket is in Alberton, and Gosforth Park is in Germiston.

The city's sunny climate makes it a natural Mecca for golfers, and there are 16 major **golf** courses in the area. Internationally renowned courses include the Royal Johannesburg, Huddle Park, Houghton Golf Club, Randpark Ridge, Wanderers, Parkview, and Glendower to name but a few. The Wanderers Golf Course ((011) 788 5010, 21 North Street, Illovo, is part of the Wanderers Club and is a regular PGA venue, whilst the Glendower Golf Course ((011) 453 1013, just outside Johannesburg on 20 Marais Road, Edenville, has consistently been ranked as one of the top five layouts in the country and is sited in a bird sanctuary where, presumably, the residents fly with care.

As one of Africa's leading cities there are also a whole range of activities and sports on offer. For example the art of **Spanish riding**, in which coordinated performances by the world's oldest human-bred horse, the Lipizzaner, reflect a riding tradition 400 years old. Sold out years in advance in its other venue, the European city of Vienna, Lipizzaner riding is easy to see here every Sunday at 11 AM; contact the Lipizzaner Center at Kyalami ((011) 702 2103.

SHOPPING

For antiques and collectibles, the search is half the fun. There's no substitute for hunting out bargains yourself on the shops and stalls along **Rockey Street** (see above). There are also a number of markets. The largest and the best for curios is the **Bruma Flea Market** that takes place on Ernest Openheimer Drive by the artificial Bruma Lake to the east of the city center every day from Tuesday to Sunday — there's a shopping center there

with stalls all week but the weekends are the best. The **Rosebank Mall** ((011) 788 5530, 50 Bath Avenue, Rosebank, three kilometers (two miles) from the city center along Oxford Road, has a good rooftop market on Sundays but on any day of the week offers the classic South African shopping experience: huge pedestrian malls with the large brand-name shops drawing in customers to a range of smaller, more specialist shops. The city's other best malls include **Sandton City** ((011) 783 7413, corner Rivonia Road and Fifth Avenue in the northern suburb of Sandton, and the **Village Walk** ((011) 783 4620, corner Maude Street and Rivonia Road, Sandton.

For last-minute bargains on the way to the airport the **Eastgate Shopping Mall** claims to be the largest in Africa and is conveniently located if you have a few minutes to spare before your flight. They say that what you can't find in Eastgate you won't find in Johannesburg. The malls have taken over to such an extent that of Johannesburg's once preeminent department stores only two are left in the CBD: Markhams, built in 1886, and Cuthberts, an upstart who opened as a shoe shop in 1904.

Johannesburg is also a world center for diamonds. While these are unlikely to be sold below their international value, the fact that visitors can reclaim their value-added tax at the airport (see SHOP TILL YOU DROP, page 49 in YOUR CHOICE) means there are some bargains to be had. Stick to a reputable dealer though. There are sharks in the diamond industry everywhere. Perhaps the best advice is to learn something about diamonds before you buy. A good way to do so is to take part in an educational tour of the **Erikson Diamond Center** ((011) 970 1355, 20 Monument Road, Kempton Park, which takes visitors through the cutting process, manufacture, design and setting, with a diamond museum attached and, of course, a jewelry shop.

WHERE TO STAY

Johannesburg has no shortage of good accommodation in all price-ranges, but rather fewer character properties. Most are geared more to the business, not the leisure, traveler, which means there are plenty of opportunities for ostentatious consumption, but stiff competition means most provide plenty of comforts per rand. Few still expect to tempt any wealthy visitor to stay in the CBD. The **Hilton Sandton** ((011) 322 1888 FAX (011) 322 1818, 138 Rivonia Road, Sandton, R1,495, is one of the city's top hotels in a smart area. A (short) South African chain is the Cullinan Group: their two Johannesburg hotels are the **Cullinan Inn Morningside** ((011) 884 1804 FAX (011) 884 6040,

Cool waters and classical sculpture help put visitors in the mood to splurge in Sandton City Shopping Mall.

1 Cullinan Close, corner Rivonia Road, Sandton, R900, while for travelers who want to stay close to the airport the **Cullinan Inn JHB International Airport** ((011) 823 1843 FAX (011) 823 2194, 100 North Rand Road, Bardene, Boksburg North, East Rand, R800, is a good option.

The **Park Hyatt** ((011) 280 1234 FAX (011) 280 1238, 191 Oxford Road, Rosebank, offers considerable luxury for R1,200 in the Rosebank area, while around the corner a small but unutterably elegant hotel in the is the **Grace at Rosebank** ((011) 280 7300 FAX (011) 280 7333 E-MAIL graceres@grace .co.za WEB SITE www.grace.co.za, 54 Bath Avenue, Rosebank, R1,000 to R2,000 room only, a member of the Small Luxury Hotels of the World. Although

Melrose, R500 to R975, reflects the history of the randlords and the gold mining era. Alternatively, if the Randburg Waterfront is a big enough draw, try the **Randburg Towers** ((011) 886 8432 FAX (011) 886 8577 E-MAIL randtower@webware.co.za, corner Republic Road and Main Avenue, Ferndale, Randburg, R256.

Many travelers in Johannesburg go into defensive mode, not in itself an irrational response to this challenging city. One option that offers safe parking and reliable, if not lavish accommodation is the **Formule 1** Hotel group. They have six branches in Johannesburg, of which the most convenient are the **Airport Formule 1** ((011) 392 1453, corner Herman and Kruin Street, Isando; the

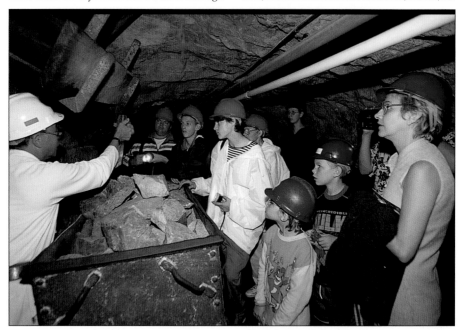

it's not immediately obvious why anyone would travel to South Africa for a Tuscan experience, that's what you get at the small and select **Room with a View** ((011) 482 5435 FAX (011) 726 8589 E-MAIL roomview@pixie.co.za WEB SITE www .guestnet.co.za, 1 Tolip Street, corner Fourth Avenue, Melville, R510 to R850, a haven of Italian style with seven individually decorated guest rooms in a Tuscan villa far from home, sited in the most fashionable and sociable part of the city, with great views from every room. Another small gem is set in tropical gardens in the northern suburbs: the **Thandidille Mountain Lodge** ((011) 476 1887 FAX (011) 678 0371, 5 Linda Place, Northcliffe, R440 to R600 with breakfast, is designed in ethnic style, reflecting the city's African heritage. For a touch of colonial luxury the **Vergelegen Guest House** ((011) 447 3434 FAX (011) 880 5366 E-MAIL vergelee@iafrica.com, 6 Tottenham Avenue,

Berea Formule 1 ((011) 484 5551, 1 Mitchell Street, Berea; and the **Wynberg Formule 1** ((011) 887 5555, 1 Maree Street Bramley Park, Wyneberg. All the above charge R145, room only, for up to three people sharing. More characterful mid-range hotels include the **Sans Souci Hotel** ((011) 726 8623 FAX (011) 480 5983, 10 Guild Road, Parktown West, with modern rooms set around a delightful old building in calming gardens with a swimming pool, bar and restaurant; R300 with breakfast. The **Linden Hotel** ((011) 782 4905, corner Seventh Street/Fourth Avenue, Linden, offers comfortable accommodation in a family-run hotel with à la carte restaurant for R290 with breakfast.

Backpackers can choose from a range of hostel-style accommodation. The following hostels all offer free airport pickups as well as a host of helpful advice for new arrivals. Don't be too overwhelmed with gratitude: they expect to make commission on selling tickets and tours, and even if the pickup is free they will generally charge to return travelers to the airport or wherever. For a vibrant nightlife, perhaps the best is **Rockey Street Backpackers** ((011) 648 8786 FAX (011) 648 8423 E-MAIL bacpacrs@icon.co.za WEB SITE www.icon .co.za, 24 Regent Street, Yeoville 2188, R45 per person in dormitory accommodation with twins at R105. Nearby and even cheaper is **Backpackers Underground** ((011) 648 6132, 20 Harley Street, Yeoville, R27. To stay in a much quieter setting in the northern suburbs, the **Backpacker's Ritz** ((011) 327 0029 FAX (011) 327 0233, 1A North Road, Dunkeld West off Jan Smuts Avenue, R35 in dormitories, is a friendly lodge popular with overlanders.

WHERE TO EAT

There are more than 200 restaurants in Johannesburg, offering a range of cuisine from all over the world, and fierce competition keeps prices low and standards of service high. Often choosing a restaurant is more a matter of selecting an area and then looking around what is available: the Randburg Waterfront, for example, has 35 restaurants bringing the tastes of the world to a small, secure setting. Some of the best restaurants are found in shopping malls, with the Carlton Center, Rosebank, and the Village well-known for restaurants as well as nightspots, but these struggle to match the buzz of those found in outdoor environments such as the suburb of Melville or Rockey Street in Yeoville.

Italian, French, and Chinese restaurants are found across the city, bringing the tastes of the world to South Africa with varying degrees of success, with Japanese and Thai restaurants rather thinner on the ground. And of course there are endless steak bars and all the restaurant chains, Steers, Nando's, Wimpy, etc. represented across the suburbs.

For something a little different it's worth heading to **Iyavaya Restaurant** ((011) 327 1411, 169 Oxford Road, Shop 14 Mutual Square, Rosebank. This restaurant has played host to Hugh Masakela, Mick Jagger, and Denzel Washington, although history does not relate whether they tasted the restaurant's specialty: mopane worms fried in chili butter. The decor is African and the cuisine an eclectic mix of African and totally original, and all for about R50 per head. Reservations are essential, closed Mondays, secure parking. Another fine restaurant is **Gramadoelas at the Market** ((011) 838 6960, Market Theatre, corner Bree and Wolhunter streets, Newtown, which specializes in traditional South African, African and Cape Malay cooking, with an exotic range of specialties. The average price is R40 lunch and R65 dinner, open daily, secure parking. Up your meat

intake at **Leopoldt's Restaurant** ((011) 804 4231, Pavilion Center, corner Rivonia & Kelvin Street, Morningside, where buffet-style dishes include bobotie, ostrich, *smoorsnoek* (literally, "smothered fish"), kudu, and buffalo. Buffet price is R90, plenty of parking, closed Saturday lunch and Sunday.

For a taste of Russia **Le Samovar Tea House** ((011) 788 3651, Hutton Square, Jan Smuts Avenue, Hyde Park, specializes in tastes of Eastern Europe, with starters including zakuski and borscht with main courses offering bulibiaka, caviar or baklazannaya; closed Sunday evening, R75 per person, approximately.

When it's not being too clever **Jaspers International** ((011) 442 4130, 108 Rosebank Mall, Cradock Avenue, Rosebank, has won a number of awards in its day and certainly defies convention. Dishes include black ink pasta, crêpes with smoked salmon and mesclun salad, and for dessert, Schlosserbuben — stuffed prunes with marzipan and whole almonds in beer batter, served with a mocha sauce. Closed Sunday evening; R70 per head approximately.

NIGHTLIFE

There are plenty of cultural options to fill the evening here. Theatrical venues include the **Civic Theatre** ((011) 403 3408 FAX (011) 403 3412 E-MAIL civic@theatrekom.co.za WEB SITE www .africanfocus.co.za / arts / civic.htm, Loveday Street, Braamfontein, which is the leading venue for theatre and opera. There are plenty more. The **Market Theatre** ((011) 832 1614, Newtown Cultural Precinct, has three stages and produces some of the country's most innovative performances. The **Alhambra** ((011) 402 6174, Sivewright Avenue, Doornfontein, has three stages and holds performances that can vary from musicals to stand-up comedians. For a full listing of what is on check out the local listings magazines, copies are found on stands around the city or — sporadically — at Tourism Johannesburg's offices. There are also regular performances of Classical Music by the **National Symphony Orchestra** ((011) 714 4501, who often play at the Linden Auditorium.

This is too cerebral for many of the city's residents. Jo'burgers work hard — and play hard. Much of the nightlife revolves around bars and music venues, which change with the fashions of the fickle party crowd, and most of the venues are far busier on weekends, being quiet or even shut early in the week. Most popular currently include **Kippies** ((011) 834 4714, at the Market Theatre complex, which is a small and intimate venue playing great jazz; arrive early to get a seat at cabaret-style tables. Also within the Market

In the city built on gold the Gold Reef City theme park shows visitors how to mine and smelt.

Theatre complex is the **Megamusic Warehouse** ((011) 832 2761, at the corner of Bree and Wolhunter streets, Newtown, which attracts a number of Johannesburg's finest bands; call for their current listings.

In Yeoville, the **Tandoor** ((011) 487 1569, 26 Rockey Street, specializes in bands from the townships and the Congo — good fun but a little seedy. In the area you'll also find plenty of soul, rock, disco, and African sounds. In the rather whiter northern suburbs the sounds tend towards rock. Two exceptions to this are the **Bassline** ((011) 482 6915, 7 Seventh Street, Melville, which hosts some of the city's finest jazz as well as African sounds, and in Sandton there are several alternatives. One of the best is the **Blue Room** ((011) 784 5527 WEB SITE www.bluesroom.co.za, Village Walk Shopping Plaza, while the current weekend favorite is the **Calabash**, at the corner of Grayston and Eleventh Avenue, which on week-

ends is a late-night disco that is very much in vogue. Through the week it's anything but, being a lap-dancing venue.

HOW TO GET THERE

As the economic capital of the country, Johannesburg has communication links to every corner. Rail travels slowly but surely to all the major towns: there are 32 trains a day running to Pretoria, one a day to Bloemfontein, Cape Town, Kimberley, and Nelspruit. Full details are available from **Transnet** ((011) 773 2944 or **Metro Passenger Services** ((011) 773 5878 FAX (011) 773 7475, Box 11579, Johannesburg 2000. There are buses every day that leave for a huge range of destinations and most of the transport companies have their head offices here as well. Companies include Translux, Greyhound, Intercape, and the Baz Bus (see GETTING AROUND, page 252 in TRAVELERS' TIPS).

Just 50 km (31 miles) from Johannesburg, Pretoria could hardly be more different. While the financial center tears down old buildings, Pretoria huddles round their buttresses. Johannesburg was fueled by a gold boom, but Pretoria, originally a farming *dorp* built on fertile land, was founded by a man who named it after his father and the first building to go up was a church. First declared the state capital in 1860, Pretoria was annexed by the British in 1877, but most of the practical power stayed with the Boer rulers. It was buoyed across the turn of the centuries on a wave of tax revenue from Johannesburg's gold and donated armaments from Europe, remaining however the unexciting administrative center for the new republic although it's far from obvious why. Nelson Mandela was inaugurated at the Union Buildings in 1994, but this was largely symbolic; the country's Parliament still takes place in Cape Town and it is hard to see that situation changing.

Pretoria does have some attractions. The prison is nice, though probably not if you're a resident, and has an interesting, though slightly weird, museum attached, while the city center is a compact grid of wide, busy streets. The almost completely useless SATOUR, the national tourist bureau ((012) 482 6200, has its head offices here; there are a couple of theatres in the city center as well as a range of museums and some nice zoological gardens. Most significantly, crime here is a fraction of that in rowdy, neighboring Johannesburg. For many visitors, this is enough reason to base their travels in Pretoria, fleeing to this small, model capital from the moment of their flight's arrival. They may live longer as a result but will certainly feel every long minute.

GENERAL INFORMATION

Johannesburg is the nearest international airport, 50 km (31 miles) to the south along a fast highway. Every hour **Pretoria Airport Shuttles** ((012) 323 0904 or (082) 566 7242 FAX (012) 325 3469 leave from the corner of Prinsloo and Vermeulen streets, although pickups can also be arranged.

The **Pretoria Tourist Rendezvous Center** ((012) 308 8909 FAX (012) 308 8891, Box 440, Pretoria 0001, in Sammy Marks Square at the corner of Vermeulen and Prinsloo streets, always seems about to close. More reliable information comes from the smarter **Bitts Center Tourist Information** ((012) 337 4337 WEB SITE www.pretoria.co.za, Old Nederlandsche Bank Building, Church Square West, conveniently in the heart of the city, and open from 7:30 AM to 3:45 PM Monday to Friday.

Reliable taxi companies include **Rixi Mini Cabs** ((012) 325 8072, **City Taxis** ((012) 321 5742,

PRETORIA

For the cautious, Pretoria, traditional seat of government and establishment heart of old South Africa, is a more sensible base for the first few nights in the country than the brasher, more dangerous Johannesburg.

There are plenty of factors in its favor. It has a small, relaxing city center, packed with buildings from the colonial era, perfect for exploring on foot, with a number of museums, some of them interesting, and a scattering of bars and restaurants. In the Hatfield area, east of Arcadia, it even has the basis of a nightlife ghetto. Crime is low. Unfortunately Pretoria is undeniably dull. It is still a very white, very privileged bastion of power and, from the fun levels that seem to result, welcome to it. There might be more boring towns in South Africa, but surely, no cities.

Pretoria's Strijdom Square commemorates the Prime Minister from 1954 to 1958, controversial because of his support for apartheid.

and **Baby Cabs (** (012) 324 6222. For hospital treatment, two choices offering 24-hour emergency facilities are the **Pretoria Academical Hospital (** (012) 329 1111, Dr. Savage Road, and the Pretoria West Hospital **(** (012) 386 5111, Transoranje Road.

What to See and Do

Pretoria does have some of South Africa's best museums and galleries — there are 35 of them in all. The **Pretoria Art Museum (** (012) 344 1807, Schoeman Street at the corner of Wessels Street, has an extensive collection of Dutch and Flemish paintings with touring exhibitions of international significance and guided tours available. Some of these exhibitions attract huge lines, especially on

park in the heart of the city center, which does feel a bit strange so close to so much wild African countryside. It is one of the best in the world, however, and sometimes arranges nocturnal tours for groups.

To the east, the imposing **Union Buildings** are in the Arcadia district. You can admire these buildings from a distance — these buildings seem to expect no less — but you need a good excuse to talk your way inside. The gardens are pleasant though and give panoramic views over the city.

Of particular interest to children are two science museums: the **Museum of Science and Technology (** (012) 322 6406, Didacta Building,

weekends. If, instead of buying tickets at the door you buy them through Computicket, who have nationwide offices including one at Pretoria's Tramshed Shopping Center, at the corner of Van der Walt and Schoeman streets, you go straight to the front of the line.

Church Street contains many of the significant buildings of South Africa's history. At 43 km (27 miles) long it's a bit long for a stroll, but the Old Raadsaal (parliament), the Palace of Justice, the South African Reserve Bank, the Transvaal Provincial Administration Buildings, and **Paul Kruger House (** (012) 326 9172, Church Street, open 8:30 AM to 4 PM Monday to Saturday, R5, are all on the its western end. North of here are the **National Zoological Gardens (** (012) 328 3265, at the corner of Paul Kruger and Boom streets, open every day from 8 AM to 5:30 PM, where 3,500 animals from Africa and beyond live in a 600-hectare (1,482-acre)

211 Skinner Street, open Monday to Friday 8 AM to 4 PM and Sunday 2 PM to 5 PM, R5, and the **Transvaal Museum of Natural History (** (012) 322 7632, Paul Kruger Street, open Monday to Saturday 9 AM to 5 PM and Sunday 11 AM to 5 PM, R5, with a huge collection of stuffed wildlife, geological samples, and fossil remains of early man.

Leave Pretoria to the south on the Johannesburg Road, and after passing UNISA, the largest university in the country, you pass the prison and the **Correctional Services Museum (** (012) 314 1766, open Monday to Friday 9 AM to 3 PM unless the curator goes walkabout (which she does), which houses a fascinating collection of homemade and ingenious weapons, forged keys, and bits of prison memorabilia. Sadly Pretoria's other law-and-order museum, the **Police Museum** on Pretorius Street, has closed its doors with no immediate plans to reopen. Continue south for the

Voortrekker Monument ((012) 326 6770, open daily 9 AM to 4:45 PM, commemorating the Great Trek of 1835. It is a 40-m (130-ft) block ringed by 64 granite ox-wagons. At the center is a granite cenotaph lit by a shaft of sunlight at noon on December 16 every year, the anniversary of Blood River. There is also a museum of Boer relics, a curio shop, and a family restaurant.

SHOPPING

The Tramshed is a city-center shopping center in an old building—small and all the better for it. Its record shop has a huge range of, often cheap, African CDs, as well as the more conventional

429 9300 E-MAIL sheraton@iafrica.com, 643 Church Street at the corner of Wessels Street, R1,035, with smartly dressed concierges and lavishly over-the-top construction. It's a lot of hotel for the money. Those who prefer to stay in smaller hotels where they don't have to dress up can stay at the **Rozenhof (** (012) 460 8075 FAX (012) 460 8085 E-MAIL rozenhof@smarnet.co.za, 525 Alexander Street, Brooklyn, R500 per person with breakfast, which is set in a graceful white mansion.

The best nightlife in Pretoria is in the Hatfield area, and within walking distance of the bars and shops is the **Mutsago Guest House (**/FAX (012) 437193 E-MAIL roberto@lantic.co.za, 327 Festival Street, R450. In the Embassy district is **48 Florence**

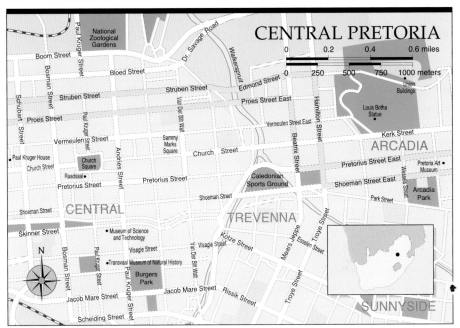

imported fare. The new waterfront development at Faerie Glen is Pretoria's answer to the successful equivalents in Johannesburg and, more especially, the Cape Town model; time will tell if this proves a successful draw. Otherwise, Pretoria's shopping opportunities are limited, with the central business district suffering from South Africa's endemic inner city rot and a few new malls failing to match their Johannesburg equivalents. The best new shops are around Hatfield Square, where there is also an cybercafé at shop 3/12 that is open 10 AM to midnight and licensed; WEB SITE www.netcafe.co.za.

WHERE TO STAY

There is no shortage of accommodation in Pretoria, with a selection to suit all budgets. The newest hotel is the **Sheraton (** (012) 429 9999 FAX (012)

Street ((012) 342 2109 FAX (012) 342 2175 E-MAIL florence@intekom.co.za, 48 Florence Street, Colbyn R480. To stay in the city center there is always the central and economical **Formule 1 (** (012) 323 8331, 81–85 Pretorius Street, R145 for up to three, or the **Protea Hotel Boulevard (** (012) 326 4806 FAX (012) 326 1366 E-MAIL bphotel@satis.co.za, 186 Struben Street, Pretoria, which offers good service for R450 including breakfast. For longer stays self-catering apartments offered by **Orange Court (** (012) 326 6346 FAX (012) 326 2492, at the corner of Vermeulen and Hamilton streets, Arcadia, R280 per night represent good value in a quiet but central setting.

Central for backpackers is **Pretoria Backpackers (** (012) 343 9754 E-MAIL PtaBack@hotmail.com,

---

The only safe elephant is a stuffed one, say the curators at the Transvaal Museum.

34 Bourke Street, Sunnyside, Pretoria, which is overpriced for what it is, at R120 for a double room, perhaps because it's recommended in so many guide books. On that budget you'd be better off staying over the road in the **Park Lodge ((**012) 320 8230 FAX (012) 320 8230 E-MAIL parklodg@ global.co.za, at the corner of Jacob Mare and Andries Street, where R130 goes much further. A better alternative with the backpacker social scene is **Word of Mouth Backpackers (** (012) 343 7499 FAX (012) 343 9351 E-MAIL wom@mweb.co.za WEB SITE www.travelinafrica.co.za, 450 Reitz Street at the corner of Vos Street, R40 for a dormitory bed, rooms available, with a West African Drum Bar — *djembes* supplied.

WHERE TO EAT AND NIGHTLIFE

There are plenty of restaurants in Pretoria but they lack the spirited competition of Johannesburg. In the city center they are often quite over overpriced, and the city center is very quiet at night, even on weekends. One of the best restaurants in the country is **La Madeleine Restaurant (** (012) 446076, 258 Esselen Street, Sunnyside, which specializes in French cuisine but influenced by Japanese techniques and tastes. Unfortunately the waiters think they're pretty good too. Expect to pay about R95 a head. Nearby **Bacini's (** (012) 341 0689, 216 Esselen Street, Sunnyside, offers much cheaper Italian specialties for about R30 each. For fine South African cuisine, head for the **Gerard Moerdyk**

((012) 344 4856, 752 Park Street, Arcadia, close to the Union Buildings. Dining here is in four elegant rooms, with glowing pink walls, flounces, and polished wooden floors. Food is classic South African, with *waterblommetjies* (spiced buds of the white water hawthorn, a spring Cape flower), liver-in-a-caul, and walnut mousse. The cost of all this is usually R95 per head. Another especially South African restaurant, but rather cheaper, is **Die Werf** (no phone) at Plot 66, Olympus East, where helpings are huge. The **Sirocco (** (012) 341 3785, 109 Gerard Moerdyk Street, Sunnyside, presents Mediterranean cuisine in a beautifully restored house; R60 per head. **Parkstreet Chagall's (** (012) 342 1200, 924 Park Street, Arcadia, tempts with dishes such as duck carpaccio and butternut soup. There's an extensive wine list, which might put the price per head over R90; closed Sunday.

There are a number of theaters. The main one is the **State Theatre (** (012) 322 1665, Church Street, while around is the corner the **Basement Theatre (** (012) 328 3173, below Café Riche, Church Square. Student productions can be seen at the **Breytenbach (** (012) 444834, Gerard Moerdyk Street, Sunnyside.

For nightlife, Pretoria is pretty quiet, despite having three tertiary education institutes; perhaps their students work in the evening. One place you can rely on finding a range of full bars, all within walking distance of each other, is around Hatfield Square and Hatfield Avenue. When I first visited Pretoria — far too long ago — the nightlife area was Sunnyside, and the Hatfield area had just a single takeout chicken outlet as its focus after dark. This nightlife focus kicked off the entire area, which just goes to show how boring Pretoria was then. Since then a host of bars and restaurants have opened up. The chicken takeout is still there, though not doing particularly well, but the area around it has been transformed. Meanwhile the more established nightlife area of Sunnyside struggles rather for business, despite having the **Café Galleria**, 60 Esselen Street, and **Up the Creek** ((082) 895 0238, Gerard Moerdyk Street, which put on regular live music performances. This is Pretoria though: any African sounds are generally banished to the townships.

HOW TO GET THERE

Pretoria's main claim to transportation fame is that it is at the heart of South Africa's railway network. There are 32 trains a day running to Johannesburg, one a day to Bloemfontein, Cape Town, Kimberley, and Nelspruit. Full details from **Transnet (** (012) 488 7111 FAX (012) 488 7125, Box 72501, Parkview 2122, or **Metro Passenger Services (** (011) 773 5878 FAX (011) 773 7475, Box 11579, Johannesburg 2000. There are buses every day all across the country and a shuttle bus leaves the Tourist Rendezvous

ABOVE: The Voortrekkers Monument commemorates the historic settler migration. RIGHT: The imposing façade of the Transvaal Museum, Pretoria.

Center every hour, on the hour, for Johannesburg International Airport. Although Pretoria is one town where you can survive quite adequately without a rental car, the easiest way to get there is to drive. It is on the N4 and the N1.

GREATER GAUTENG

There are undoubted attractions in the Greater Gauteng area, mainly to the west. The **Magaliesberg mountain range** (pronounced "*mohalisburg*") are a set of low, intensively farmed hills scattered with weekend resorts and conference centers which attract crowds of city-dwellers on weekends. Gauteng's oldest archaeological site is the **Sterkfontein Caves** ((011) 956 6342, open Tuesday to Sunday 9 AM to 4 PM, R40, 40 km (25 miles) west of Johannesburg (take the R28 Krugersdorp Highway, turn right onto R47, then left onto R563). They were home to prehuman primates in the dawn of humanity. The cave's most famous resident is "Mrs. Pless," a female hominid whose skull was discovered in 1947. She would now be about two million years old. Other finds here include an early man whose big toe was, like our thumbs, opposable, and the earliest remains date back three and a half million years. In 1998 the oldest complete human skeleton was discovered. Evacuations continue. Guided tours explain the significance of the discoveries here, though many important pieces of evidence were lost to the first visitors to the cave. More developed are the **Kromdrai Caves** ((011) 957 0241, open Tuesday to Sunday 9 AM to 4 PM, three kilometers (two miles) from Sterkfontein, illuminated by recessed lights but not by the same standard of informative tour.

The area isn't all farmed, and there are still some patches of thornveld, generally protected in many wildlife reserves, which include the **Rhino & Lion Nature Reserve** ((011) 957 0109, R28 Krugersdorp Highway, right onto Hendrik Potgeiter Drive; the **Rietvlei Nature Reserve** ((012) 345 2274, R21 to the airport, Rietvlei off-ramp; and the **Wonderboom Nature Reserve** ((012) 543 0918, Lavender Road, a park designed to protect a single (1,000-year-old) tree. There are also bird sanctuaries such as the **Austin Roberte Bird Sanctuary** ((012) 348 1265, Boshoff Street, Nieu Mucklenuck, and the **Makalani Bird Park** ((012) 253 0656, on the R27 to Hartbeestpoort.

Meanwhile 40 km (25 miles) to the north of Pretoria and the **Tswaing Crater Museum and Ndebele Village** ((012) 790 2302, M35 Soutpan Road, 9 AM to 4 PM daily, R50, is a huge water-filled meteorite crater surrounded by bushveld vegetation and with an Ndebele Village thrown in. Eastern Gauteng and most of the countryside is taken up by a sprawling industrial area that is not of obvious interest to visitors. However there are so many other beautiful parts of the country it is hard to see a good reason for putting up with the crowds and the development of this, South Africa's most urban province.

However rural Gauteng can be good a place to stay. This won't suit businessmen who need to get into town in the morning, as Johannesburg's rush hour is infamous, but travelers on a vacation schedule will have no problem zipping in and out of town in their rental car through the off-peak hours and it is certainly far removed from the bustle of the city center and suburbs. Out of town accommodation options include the fantastical **Hakunamatata** (/FAX (011) 794 2630 E-MAIL hakunamatata@gem.co.za WEB SITE www.southafrica.co.za/hakunamatata, Plot 171, Rocky Ridge Road, Muldersdrift, R690 with breakfast, 15 km (just over nine miles) west of the city near the Sterkfontein Caves. Here an African fantasy comes to life in two self-contained *kayas* (cottages), set against a lake in a lush garden setting. They're equipped for self-catering with meals available on request. The rolling hills of Magaliesberg, especially centered round the Hartbeestpoort Dam, attract crowds of Johannesburgers on weekends but in no way matches the beauty of many other parts of the country. At least the proximity to the city means it is well stocked with luxurious country house hotels, many of which will offer discounts through the week. Perhaps the best is **De Hoek** ((014) 577 1198 FAX (014) 577 4530 E-MAIL dehoek@iafrica.com WEB SITE www.webfeat .co.za/dehoek, Magaliesberg. Rates run from R880 in one of seven individually furnished rooms, with walks and hikes in the grounds the perfect prelude to à la carte cuisine prepared by the hotel's Swiss chef.

SOUTH OF GAUTENG: THE FREE STATE

Two main roads head south of Gauteng across the Vaal River into the Free State. The N3 heads off through an undulating plain of sparsely populated prairie towards Harrismith before climbing the Van Reenen Pass into KwaZulu-Natal and the battlefield area of Ladysmith (see THE BATTLEFIELDS, page 242). The N1 is the direct road route to Cape Town, flying southwest across first through scrappy industrial areas opening out into a huge, deserted countryside, fertile, temperate, flat, and monotonous. Past the uninspiring town of Kroonstad the road passes the bleak headgear of gold mines and dumps, with shallow saline pans left by the mining operations now acting as havens for flamingo, providing flashes of interest. There are a scatter of isolated villages; some are very black, others very white. In between, while the few inhabitants track the endless horizons tending their crops of maize, wheat, and sorghum in the shade of a scatter of creaking *windpomp*, the

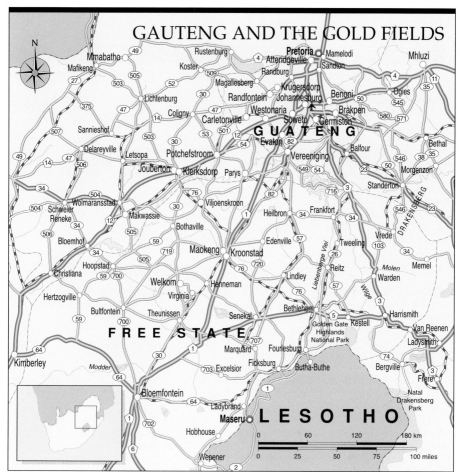

GAUTENG AND THE GOLD FIELDS

average visitor flies past with his foot on the gas to the provincial capital of the Free State, Bloemfontein, and the spectacular eastern highlands that border the mountain kingdom of Lesotho. If you'd like to find out more call the **Northern Free State Tourism Association** ((016) 976 0765 FAX (016) 973 3903. Nelson Mandela, for one, loved the feeling of space. "When I am here I feel that nothing can shut me in, that my thoughts can roam as far as the horizons." So do drivers — it is four hours at least from Johannesburg to Bloemfontein, and by the end it is hard to repress the thought that Nelson Mandela was being polite.

BLOEMFONTEIN

The fourth city and judicial capital of South Africa, the city of Bloemfontein is often overlooked by visitors as well as locals. Residents claim, rather defensively, that they are the "friendliest" city in the country, and this might well be true. Although not a place for an extended stay the city does have a character all of its own.

The first large Voortrekker encampment north of the river was established in the area in 1836. Four years later a Boer called Johannes Brits built a farm, which he called "Bloemfontein" after the flowers that bloomed around his spring. The British authorities bought his farm for £37, which must make it one of the world's cheapest towns, and built a garrison. By 1854 it was declared capital of the new Orange Free State. British writer Anthony Trollope, who visited the town in the 1870s, said "the town is so quiet... and removed from strife and want and disorder, that the beholder as he looks down upon it is tempted to think that the peace of such an abode is better than the excitement of Paris, London, or New York." It was not to stay quiet for long. The city has always been a Boer stronghold, and the area was the scene of some of the fiercest fighting in the Boer Wars, only the nature of the conflict — small commando actions in rural areas — keeping the fighting from the streets of the capital. After the British victory and the establishment of the South African Republic this provincial town was also the birthplace of the ANC, now the party of government. In 1912 members of the black population met here to found the South African Native National Congress, precursor of the modern political party.

The local priorities were all centered on the land, farming and raising cattle, and producing wool for the booming European market for uniforms. And while World War II raged the land was to repay their efforts with an unexpected bonus. Gold was discovered in the Welkom-Odendaalsrus-Virginia triangle in 1946 and these would prove to be among the richest gold fields in the world, rivaling those of Johannesburg and bringing even more prosperity to the area.

As a result, most of Bloemfontein now is modern, a light and airy city blooming with flowers and civic parks, but still somehow austere: even the buildings are restrained, flat-fronted, and faintly forbidding.

General Information

First stop should be the **Bloemfontein Publicity Association** ((051) 405 8490 or (051) 405 8489 FAX (051) 447 3859 E-MAIL transgariep@intekom .co.za WEB SITE www.places.co.za, 60 Park Road, Box 639 Willows 9300, open Monday to Friday 8 AM to 4:15 PM and Saturday to noon, located on what used to be the Market Square. The main shopping and business street is Maitland Street which runs west into President Brand Street, the R700, where many of the city's grandest public buildings, stately and imposing in sandstone, are found. There is almost no public transportation in the city, without even a bus from the airport, so travelers without their own vehicles will have to be ready for some long hot walks or rely on shuttle taxis — reputable firms include **President Taxis** ((051) 522 3399 and **Rosestad** ((051) 451 1022. For medical attention best avoid the state hospital, and try one of the private clinics such as **Hydromed** ((051) 404 6666, Kellner Street.

What to See and Do

As an Afrikaner Center, many of the attractions here hark back to the Voortrekker years. The **National Women's Memorial and War Museum** ((051) 447 3447 FAX (051) 447 1322, Monument Road, Box 704, open Monday to Saturday 9 AM to 4:30 PM and Sunday 2 PM to 5 PM, gives a dramatic but one-sided account of the Boer Wars, with endless pictures of calm, dignified Boers and evil British soldiers, less empire-builders than concentration-camp guards. British visitors might want a refund on their entrance fee of R5.

The city is also host to the **Afrikaans Literary Museum** ((051) 405 4711, at the corner of President Brand and Maitland streets, open Monday to Friday 8 AM to 12:15 PM and 1 PM to 4 PM and

Saturday 9 AM to noon, free, in the former government building. This houses some of the most important Afrikaans manuscripts and has a section devoted to the history of the Afrikaans theatre, while it also recreates theme offices around the characters and achievements of various writers. Little mention is made of the use of the Afrikaans language as a tool of oppression, nor the compulsory introduction of Afrikaans into education in 1976, which sparked off protests such as that which ended in the Sharpeville Massacre. Colored poet Adam Small perhaps best expressed the anguish of this era in one of the museum's displays: "I grew up with Afrikaans. Afrikaans is part of my culture. And when people said to you that Afrikaans was the language of the oppressor it pained you, because it was also the language you got from your parents, it was your mother tongue and it was beautiful and full of humanity."

More rewarding is the **National Museum** ((051) 447 9609 FAX (051) 447 6273, 36 Aliwal Street, Box 266, open Monday to Saturday 8 AM to 5 PM and Sunday noon to 6 PM, R5, which is the final resting place of the Florisbad skull, South Africa's first resident *Homo sapiens*. It also has a range of historic exhibits including a recreated nineteenth-century street with wonderful details in the shops. Perhaps the best museum of all is the **Oliewenhuis Art Gallery** ((051) 447 9609, Harry Smith Street, to the north of the city center. Open Monday to Friday 8 AM to 5 PM, Saturday 10 AM to 5 PM and Sunday 1 PM to 5 PM, free, this gallery has one of the country's finest collections of South African landscape art.

Where to Stay and Eat

It might not be that easy to find fine cuisine in Bloemfontein, but there is no shortage of accommodation, often priced very reasonably. The **Hobbit House** (/FAX (051) 447 0663 E-MAIL hobbit @intekom.co.za WEB SITE www.hobbit.co.za, 19 President Steyn Avenue, Westdene, R450 including breakfast, is a consistent award-winner, making much of the fact that JRR Tolkein, author of the *Hobbit*, was born here. At the age of four he was taken abroad, and in any case it is unlikely that the Calvinist flatlands around Bloemfontein inspired the mountains and monsters of his fantasy world, but this beautifully furnished hotel has four guest rooms, each individually furnished with antiques, and an excellent table. Hobbit-like accommodation on a budget is available at the **Formule 1** ((051) 444 3523, at the corner of Krige and Zastron streets by the university, R145 for up to three. For a bed-and-breakfast, the family-run **Die Rusplek** (The Resting Place) ((051) 522 5008 FAX (051) 522 4386, 50 Scholz Street, Universitas, from R120 including breakfast, represents even better value, with comfortable units with their own entrance. Backpackers are best heading for **Taffy's** ((051) 436 4533 E-MAIL taffys@global.co.za, 18 Louis Botha Street, Waverley, three kilometers (just under two miles) north of town, R30 for dormitory accommodation. It's not ideal for the city, but is very useful for information on Lesotho, with the possibility of getting a lift over the border with the owners. For dining, the **Acropolis** ((051) 447 0464, CR Stewart Building, Elizabeth Street, previously known as the Carousel, offers Greek cuisine and revolving views of the city, while **District Six** ((051) 430 4440, 24 West Burger Street, specializes in Cape Malay food. For an Afrikaner splurge, one of the country's finest Boer restaurants is the **Oude Kraal** ((051) 564 0636, 40 km (25 miles) south of town; booking is essential.

How to Get There

By road Bloemfontein is 415 km (260 miles) from Johannesburg and 1,000 km (625 miles) from Cape Town. It is an important transportation center and it is possible to travel to Namibia or cut across the top of Lesotho into KwaZulu-Natal. The **airport** ((051) 433 1482 is 10 km (just over six miles) east of the city center, off the N8, where it is possible to rent cars. Otherwise taxi is your only option for getting into town. SAA, in conjunction with SA Airlink and SA Express fly from here to Cape Town, Durban, East London, George, and Johannesburg. For other destinations it is best to fly to Johannesburg and change. Greyhound buses stop at the Tourist Center, Park Street, while Translux has a coach terminus at 164 Zastron Street, Westdene. Part of the original 1890 railway station still exists, watching the passing of three different long-distance train services every week. This means that you can travel from here to all of South Africa's major cities.

THE EASTERN HIGHLANDS

To the east, the Free State rears up into the sandstone outcrops and eroded river valleys of the frontier lands with the independent Kingdom of Lesotho, reached along the N8 highway. This is not a country with much public transportation, it's not good for hitchhiking, and there are not many hotels either. However it is a remote area that rewards travelers who have their own transportation.

The last city before the frontier is **Ladybrand**. This area was once part of the "Homeland" of Bophuthatswana and retains a wild edge. Now part of the Free State, it is still scattered with unspoiled San rock art sites, the local tribes whose empire predated any arbitrary borders marked on maps. Their art is still vivid, preserved in caves hidden in the mountains but you will need guidance to find them. There's a Christian cave too, 15 km (nine and a half miles)

north of Ladybrand, built in 1869 by an order of Augustine monks. The mountains can be blanketed in snow during the winter but in spring are spectacularly clad in cherry blossom. In town the best — indeed the only — hotel is **Cranberry Cottage** ((051) 924 2290 FAX (051) 924 1168 E-MAIL crancott@lesoff.co.za WEB SITE www.cranberry cottage.co.za, 37 Beeton Street, Ladybrand, R310 including breakfast. This is a turn-of-the-century sandstone home decorated in the colonial style.

Head north from Ladybrand and the R26 runs parallel with the frontier through the dramatic range of flat-topped mountains through Ficksburg and to **Fouriesburg**. There is sometimes the chance to ski here if the winter conditions are right — enter Lesotho at Butha-Buthe and head to the **New Oxbow Lodge** ((051) 933 2247 which rents out ski equipment and will update callers on the state of the snow. The slopes are nine kilometers (six miles) away at the Mahlasela Pass. Fifty kilometers (31 miles) west of here is the small but remote and beautiful **Golden Gate Highlands National Park** ((058) 255 0021, where self-catering chalets offer basic accommodation at R200. Otherwise, stay in South Africa and the R26 continues towards Bethlehem and links to the N3 highway heading back to Johannesburg or east across the Van Reenen Pass into KwaZulu-Natal.

Go south, on the other hand, to Hobhouse, Wepener, and then the N6 arrows south to Jamestown. Stay close to the mountains and the border of Lesotho and you'll find South Africa's only **ski resort**. There are snow machines and the area is usually skiable from June to August. **Tiffindell** ((011) 454 0660 E-MAIL tiffindell@global .co.za WEB SITE www.webpro.co.za/clients/ tiffindell/, will provide snow reports. Chalet accommodation is available on the slopes with packages including ski pass (for the one ski lift) meals and evening entertainment from R1,660 before the snow arrives to R5,000 at the peak of the season. The resort is 12 hours from Cape Town, and eight hours from Durban, though charter flights in season can cut the travel time. Alternatively, the Tiffindell slopes can be reached with a four-wheel-drive vehicle far more cheaply from the base station town of **Rhodes** in the Eastern Cape, staying at **Walkabout** ((04542), ask for 9203, signposted off the main road, R180, whose owner, Dave Walker, is a mine of information about the region and can arrange anything — especially fishing. This is arguably the finest fly-fishing area of South Africa; the mountain streams and rivers around Rhodes were last stocked in the 1920s, but the area is so remote even now the fish outnumber the fishermen.

Ladybrand is 15 km (nine and a half miles) from the main entry point into Lesotho and the capital, Maseru.

WEST OF GAUTENG

The great African plains spread out to the west of Gauteng, with great highways flying straight across flat, featureless landscapes of huge horizons, scattered with a thin fur of Kalahari grasslands. Starved of rain, the land only supports limited herds of cattle and small thinly spread numbers of sheep. A new campaign is promoting goats in the area — apparently they have more road sense. As the hours clock by on these roads, that is the sort of trivial information that circles endlessly in the mind.

The towns here were settled by a rough crowd, hunters cleaning out the final ivory from the bush, Voortrekkers at the end of their great trek, forced north by the British, and, of course, the British administrators in charge of patrolling what was then British Bechuanaland. It was of course all to end in tears. The area's small towns featured heavily in the news reports of the Boer Wars. Mafikeng, Rustenburg, and Potchefstroom were all scenes of fierce fighting and drawn-out military actions. These days, these towns are remote, farm-orientated *dorps:* flat, spread out and depending on agriculture and the beaten-up *bakkies* (pickup trucks) bouncing in to town to pick up provisions.

KIMBERLEY

One city sprang up to transcend its rural roots in a rush of spectacular growth, fed by a sparkling, glittering flow of diamonds. And that was the city of the "Big Hole," Kimberley. In 1866 a teenager found a pretty white pebble on the banks of the Orange River. Soon afterwards a local farmer traded all his possessions — horse, bath, saucepans and all — for an 83.5 carat diamond, "the Star of Africa," described by the British Colonial Governor as "the Rock on which the future of South Africa will be built." When, three years later, the first "chimneys" of volcanic, diamond-bearing rock were found in the ground, the diamond rush really took off, and the diamonds from Kimberley's Big Hole were indeed to form the basis of the South African economy. In the age of ox-cart travel it was impossibly remote — 979 km (612 miles) from Cape Town and 485 km (303 miles) from Johannesburg — but fed by the huge wealth of the diamond mines it flourished in the desert. By the end of the nineteenth century there were more millionaires meeting in the Kimberley Club than under any other roof in the world. The most famous residents, Barney Barnato and Cecil John Rhodes, left plenty of traces in their wood-paneled clubhouse, still open to overnight visitors a hundred years on.

Even now it is a little-visited oasis of colonial comforts, so far almost undiscovered by the tourist industry. The Big Hole, once a mountain and now a round canyon 500 m (550 yards) across and 1.1 km (0.69 miles) deep, dug by hand in the desert, must surely rate as one of the most impressive of South Africa's man-made sights. It is also possible here to go down a diamond mine. The initially chaotic diamond rush had settled down by the time the town was besieged by the Boers in 1899, but this siege — and its final relief — were key turning points in the war and it is one of the most significant Boer War battlefields. Even though it is right on the edge of the newly-redefined Northern Cape province it has been proclaimed provincial capital, which may do something to stop its slow decline in status since the heyday of the diamond mines.

General Information

These days Kimberley's days of great wealth do not show in the narrow (by South African standards) streets of the old city center. There is a singularly helpful and unusually organized **Tourist Information Center (** (053) 832 7298 FAX (053) 832 7211 WEB SITE www.kimberley-africa.com, Visitor's Center, 121 Bultfontein Road, Box 1976, Kimberley 8301, open Monday to Friday 8 AM to 5 PM, Saturday 8:30 AM to 11:30 AM. There's little or no public transportation, and so visitors without cars will be forced to use taxis. Two local firms are **AA Taxis (** (053) 861 4015 and **Ricki's Taxis (** (083) 342 2533. If you're forced to use a hospital as well, there's a **Medi-Clinic (** (053) 838 1111 FAX (053) 838 1199, 177 Du Toitspan Road.

What to See and Do

The main attractions are on the edge of town, with the most important — the Big Hole and the Kimberley Mine Museum — being reached by a restored **tramway** from Market Square. The **Big Hole** is an overwhelming sight, dwarfing the few highrise buildings of the city center. Fences and restrictions mean it can only be seen from the **Kimberley Mine Museum (** (053) 833 1557, Tucker Street, open daily 8 AM to 6 PM, R5. This has a collection of diamond rush-era shops and houses, railway carriages and mining equipment, relocated to this out-of-town site when demolition threatened. Most are fully furnished with their original fittings and it presents one of the most complete pictures of South Africa's early years that you'll find anywhere in the country, and there's a good, if expensive curio shop (see also DIG DEEP FOR DIAMONDS, page 22 in TOP SPOTS).

The **McGregor Museum**, 2 Egerton Road, open Monday to Friday 9 AM to 5 PM and Saturday to 1 PM, R5, is housed in a spa building built by statesman Cecil John Rhodes, which he used as a refuge through the siege. Later it became a luxury 1920s hotel, until the diamond wealth started to fade at which point it became a convent. Every trace of its history is preserved, along with a number of educational exhibits and period artifacts. One of the best excursions is to go down a diamond mine and tours are run by **Bultfontein Mine** ((053) 842 1321, Molyneux Road, by appointment Monday and Wednesday to Friday departing from reception at 8 AM, while Tuesday the tour starts at 9:30 AM; the cost is R60 per person. There are also surface tours Monday to Friday at 9 AM and 11 AM, at R10.

Where to Stay and Eat

By far the best place to stay, but not to eat, is the **Kimberley Club** ((053) 832 4224, 70-72 Du Toitspan Road, R300, a time-warped wood-paneled throwback to the diamond rush years: comfortable, great service, and still relatively cheap. The bar, lined with pictures of local celebrities, the mines in their heyday and plot-claim maps, still recaptures the spirit of a lost era, echoingly empty and on my last visit containing two members of the rotary club interviewing a third over crab sticks and beer. After they left I was alone with the ghosts of the past; perhaps their business will pick up when they allow ladies into the bar. The rooms' televisions don't always work but there's a free copy of the *Diamond Fields Advertiser* under the door in the morning.

There's more period charm at the **Savoy Hotel** ((053) 832 6211, De Beers Road, R279 including breakfast, but it's in a part of town that, once smart, is on the slide. There's a bit more elegance at **Egerton House** ((053) 831 1150 FAX (053) 831 1785 E-MAIL egerton@kimberley.co.za, 5 Egerton Road, R490 with breakfast, in the historic Belgravia suburb. Both the **Diamond Protea Lodge** ((053) 831 1281, 124 Du Toitspan Road, and the **Holiday Inn Garden Court** ((053) 833 1751, 120 Du Toitspan Road, charge R300 and, though comfortable enough and efficient, have rather a businesslike atmosphere. There is currently only one establishment aimed at the backpacker market, and although nice enough, with a pool and shady garden, it is about five kilometers (just over three miles) out of town: **Gum Tree Lodge** ((053) 832 8577 FAX (053) 831 5409, Bloemfontein Road, R120 with dormitories at R25.

The smartest restaurant in town is **Tiffany's** ((053) 832 6211, De Beers Road, which is part of the Savoy Hotel. Much less formal is **Mario's** ((053) 831 1738, 159 Du Toitspan Road, closed Saturday lunch and Sundays, where you can eat inside or out. The more usual pleasure in Kimberley is, however, drinking. The **Halfway House Pub**, on the corner of Du Toitspan and Egerton roads, is where Cecil John Rhodes used to drink, half way between the town's two main mines. Thankfully it hasn't been prettied up and is still a serious

drinking establishment. Kimberley's oldest pub is the **Star of the West**, on the corner of West and North circular roads, which does huge pub meals and is conveniently close to the Big Hole and the Kimberley Mine Museum.

How to Get There

Kimberley is a five-hour drive from Johannesburg and 10 from Cape Town along the N12 highway. The **airport** ((053) 851 1241 is 10 km (just over six miles) south of the town center, with two flights to Cape Town and five to Johannesburg every weekday, with fewer flights on the weekends. There is a collection of old steam trains in the Beaconsfield marshalling yard south of the city cen-

ter, while three mainline trains stop at Kimberley Station; for **information** call ((053) 288 2060. The local representative for Greyhound is the **Northern Cape Bus Service** ((053) 831 1062, 5 Elliot Street, while **Intercape** ((021) 386 4400 leaves from the Shell Ultra City, Transvaal Road. **Translux** leaves from the train station and Shell Ultra City. Alternatively, **Tickets for Africa** ((053) 832 6043 provide all sorts of travel tickets. With your own vehicle it is also possible to head west through Griquatown along the R64 or up on the R31 up to Kuruman and the Kalahari Gemsbok National Park (see under UPINGTON, page 111).

Kimberley's Big Hole, dug by hand by diamond miners.

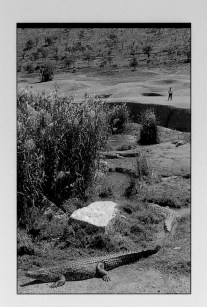

Sub-
tropical
South
Africa:
The North

NORTH OF GAUTENG SOUTH AFRICA STRETCHES up to border with Botswana, Zimbabwe, and Mozambique. From Gauteng, once you've passed the Magaliesberg Mountains you are in a little-visited region where not much English is spoken and the landscape is timeless and agrarian. The exception for this is the apartheid homeland of Bophuthatswana, which piles in the visitors to the Sun City Resort and the Pilansberg National Park. Leave this and travel west and you'll find the remote but rewarding Madikwe Game Reserve. Go north instead and you'll drive through the cattle country of the Waterberg Mountains, once a place of internal exile for troublesome politicians. As the value of farming land declines much is being turned back to conservation with a number of private initiatives restocking with Africa's endangered game. To the east there's no need to do any restocking: the mighty Kruger National Park runs down the border with Mozambique, southern Africa's premier wildlife destination, lined with private reserves offering lavish luxuries in a bush setting.

SUN CITY AND THE NORTHWEST PARKS

The area to the northeast of Johannesburg is one of the least visited in the country. Sun City, devised largely to exploit the regulations which banned gambling in South Africa with its location in the nominally independent homeland of Bophuthatswana, has rather lost its role in the new South Africa. It still features on many tour operator programs, and although it doesn't actually offer a particularly African experience it is a quite rewarding place to visit for a day or two, especially if traveling with children. Nearby, the Pilansberg National Park is the fourth biggest national park in the country with plenty of grazing animals. Further north the Waterberg Mountains are a remote but wonderfully wild landscape where the new reserve of the Lapalala Wilderness is pioneering conservation in an area where farming stalled in land better suited to game. In an area that sees so few tourists, this is one of the best places to explore the natural world on horseback and encounter sleepy *dorps* where Afrikaans is the only language if you're white, and many black people speak only Tswana.

SUN CITY

South Africa's Las Vegas, Sun City is a huge, extravagant monster of a resort, created from a patch of barren bush by the freewheeling visionary, Sol Kerzner. If that sounds like a eulogy, it's not, really, but it's impossible not to admire the imagination and ambition of his Sun City development.

Construction started in 1977, at a time when sanctions kept South African vacationers at home and tight gambling laws protected them from losing their shirts on the tables. In the newly proclaimed kingdom of Bophuthatswana, however, there was plenty of land doing nothing, and no gambling laws. Just a two-hour drive from Johannesburg it was perfect for soaking up the city's many spare rand. Initially there was a 340-room hotel, a casino, and a Gary Player golf course. Now there are four hotels and some timeshare units, two golf courses, an outdoor swimming pool with fake sand and ocean waves, a man-made rainforest topped by transplanted baobab trees, a 6,000-seater superbowl where Frank Sinatra, Rod Stewart, Shirley MacLaine and Elton John have all performed, and a theatre that stages extravaganzas every day. There are three cinemas, lakes, lagoons, canals and waterfalls, all fed with recycled water, and a huge children's

pool and playground with waterslides, rivers, mines, and mountains. The Hall of Treasures alone glows with 2,000 fluorescent wooden flowers flown in from Bali and the rainforest is supported by 9,000 overhead misters, 2,500 sprinklers and 10 fan-driven humidifiers. Every hour, on the hour, an imitation earthquake shakes the bridge of time and smoke trails up from the Temple of Creation in a mock volcanic eruption. There's a recreated Greek amphitheater, Roman baths and, of course, a palace, while through it all a stream of buses and shuttle minicabs drift around the tarmac roads, dropping guests off wherever they want to go. Michael Jackson has certainly bought into the fantasy: the singer is a regular guest and is said to have bought a chunk of the action. Sneer — and there are plenty who do — and someone will soon point out that an area of land scarcely big enough to support an elephant now provides employment to thousands

as well as funneling cash back into schools and hospitals over a wide area.

You don't arrive at Sun City floundering for information. From first contact it's a slick organization: **Sun City** ℂ (011) 780 7800 FAX (011) 780 7457 E-MAIL info@sunint.co.za, Box 784487, Sandton 2146. Guests first arrive at a Welcome Center where they're greeted by uniformed professionals with smiles that stay resolutely warm and friendly, anxious to explain what happens where.

Most people never stir from the resort, although the Pilansberg National Park is just 23 km (14.4 miles) away does at least allow guests the chance of seeing most of Africa's spectacular animals without seriously upsetting their leisure schedule, which can get busy. There are two championship golf courses that are widely thought to be among the best in the country — dotted with

The Palace of the Lost City, Sun City's luxury hotel.

birds who come for the water-hazards — one of which they share with 38 crocs — and easy pickings on the manicured greens. Punters line up against tiered gambling machines ("slots" as they are called in South Africa), there's a full casino with blackjack and roulette, and an arcade of games which range from the standard motorcycle racing machines to team camel races. Children are looked after in "Kamp Kwena," which works out juvenile energies in a range of team sports and games, seven days a week. Meanwhile adults can relax in the health club and spa. If that puts them in romantic mood they can follow this up by getting married in an African chapel with wind-chimes, not bells.

Where to Stay and Eat

The best place to stay here is at the **Palace of the Lost City**, which is truly built on a palatial scale and surrounded by a moat. Huge halls with marbled floors, crenellated turrets topped with green copper domes, and a selection of restaurants stretching South Africa's culinary tradition make this the flagship of the resort. It is also a member of the "Leading Hotels of the World" group. Guests pay for this, of course: rooms are R2,085. From there the resort drops down the hill and the quality threshold. The **Cascades** are built near the entertainment center, and although the rooms are comfortable, they're not stunning. The price reflects this, at R1,230. Further down again and the **Sun City Hotel** is set around a lobby dimly filled with trickling water and lush, tropical plants and has the resort's main disco, Harlequins. Rooms here, once again, are comfortable at R1,130. Further down are the **Cabanas**, aimed squarely at families, with easy access to Waterworld but far from the refinement and sophistication of the Palace at the top of the hill and significantly cheaper at R755, sharing access to all the resort's facilities. All booking is done through the main Sun City office.

Otherwise, the least expensive way to experience the resort is through day-trips — on entry the R50 fee is transferred into vouchers which can be used against a variety of meals and services within the resort. When it comes to dining There are two gourmet restaurants, the **Villa del Palazzo** up in the Palace of the Lost City and the **Peninsula** on the water's edge in the Cascades complex, which are smart, refined, and expensive. There are also any number of smaller establishments, bringing ersatz world cuisines cheerfully and quickly to a not-very critical market of fun-lovers.

How to Get There

You can fly to the small airport seven kilometers (just over four miles) from the resort with SA Airlink. Sun City buses leave daily from Johan-

nesburg and Pretoria: book through **Computicket** ((011) 331 9991. You can drive from Johannesburg, taking the R24 to Rustenburg and then turning right on the R565, which goes to Boshoek and Sun City. From Pretoria, drive west along the N4 and then take the R556 for the final 70 km (44 miles) to the resort. Shuttle buses within Sun City make having a car during your visit something of an irrelevance and for many the easiest answer is to arrange for a Sun City minibus to shuttle you direct from Johannesburg Airport; the cost is R200 per person.

THE PILANSBERG NATIONAL PARK

This is the fourth biggest national park in the country and the nearest park to Johannesburg that contains Africa's most spectacular animals. Opening hours are from 5:30 AM from September to April and 6 AM to 6:30 PM from May to August. The volcanic landscape was home to a thin scatter of Tswana tribesmen until Operation Genesis, organized by "Bop Parks," a bunch of parastatal eco-cowboys, cleared off the inhabitants and shipped in a range of animals in the 1970s in a project probably closely connected with the development Bophuthatswana as an internationally respected country, and of Sun City. The restocking was thorough. There are lion, buffalo, elephant, hippo, leopard, and giraffe. Recently they've installed a pack of 10 captive-bred wild dogs, the latest hot endangered carnivores of the wildlife industry's marketing departments. If you're based in Johannesburg and on limited time this is quite a good place to come and see Africa's wildlife.

For further details contact the **North West Parks & Tourism Board** ((018) 384 3040 FAX (018) 384 2524 E-MAIL nwptb@iafrica.com WEB SITE www.tourismnorthwest.co.za, Suite 101 Borekelong House, James Maroka Drive, Box 4488, Mmabatho 2735. At the park's Manyane Gate is **Pilansberg Community and Development Association** ((014) 555 5351 FAX (014) 555 5535, Box 1201, Mogwase 0314. In the Manyane Complex the park authorities run two-person self-catering chalets for R385 and there are camping facilities available. Of the private lodges, the best is possibly the **Tshukudu Game Lodge** ((014) 552 1861 FAX (014) 852 1621, with thatched cottages set high on a steep hillside, R1,500 for two including game activities.

Having said which, it's not one of my favorite national parks and I would strongly recommend traveling for an extra hour to the Waterbergs (see page 184). The five private lodges in the Pilansberg National Park tend to be expensive and bland, the roads crowded with large trucks packed with tourists, and park rangers jaded by many years of trying

Myths, magic, legends and antiquities are blended with an artificial beach at Sun City.

to clock up Big Five sightings for audiences with little interest in the natural world. In your own car the park entry fee is R20 per person and R10 per vehicle, while guided expeditions leaving from Sun City booked through Sun City's welcome desk cost R250 for four hours or so.

MADIKWE GAME RESERVE

At the border with Botswana, coming to within 35 km (22 miles) of the capital, Gaborone, Madikwe is an even younger game reserve than the Pilansberg, and came about thanks to the activity of "Bop Parks," by this time renamed "The North West Parks & Tourism Board." First they ripped out many alien plants and hundreds of miles of fencing, and ringed the reserve with 140 km (87.5 miles) of electric fence. Then, in 1991, they embarked upon a huge shopping spree, buying up wildlife from all over Africa. More than 10,000 animals of 28 species have so far been released, including elephant, white and black rhino, lion, cheetah, hyena, giraffe, and many antelope species. The happiest animals to witness this development were the leopard, which were already found in the reserve. Partnerships exist among local communities and private-sector lodgebuilders. Reintroduction was completed only in 1998 and it remains to be seen whether the reserve can settle down to escape a theme-park atmosphere.

For more information about the reserve contact the main office of the **North West Parks & Tourism Board** ((014) 565 5960 FAX (014) 565 5964, Box 4124, Rustenburg 0300. Day visitors are not allowed in the reserve. You have to stay in one of the participating lodges. Most upmarket — and expensive — of the lodges is **Tau** ((011) 775 0000 FAX (011) 784 7667 E-MAIL information@ccafrica .com WEB SITE www.ccafrica.com, P/Bag X27, Benmore 2010, R3,000 all-inclusive. Currently the least expensive of the lodges, but not the worst, is the simple **Mosetlha Bushcamp** (/FAX (011) 802 6222 E-MAIL bushwise@netactive.co.za, R1,300 operated by Honeyguide Trails, in the heart of the reserve and with good rangers and guides. Both of these include game drives and all meals in their rate, as is normal with private South African game lodges.

How to Get There

To reach Madikwe by road from Johannesburg or Pretoria, travel west to Rustenburg and then on the N4 through Swartruggens, Groot Marico and Zeerust, where you turn right onto the R47/505 towards Gaborone. The first Madikwe Game Reserve gate is 90 km (56.2 miles) further on. Alternatively, there is an airstrip taking charter flights from Johannesburg, Sun City, or Gaborone International Airport.

THE NORTHERN PROVINCE

North of Gauteng the Northern Province stretches up to the Zimbabwe border and the Limpopo River, a remote hot landscape of thornbush increasingly dotted with the characteristic shapes of baobab trees. West there are the undulating rocky landscapes of the Waterberg Mountains, north the traditional home of the Venda people, farming country where Voortrekker settler descendants still work the land. To the east the spectacular beauty of the Northern Drakensberg Mountains, and the unspoiled lands where wildlife still reigns supreme, in the huge expanses of the Kruger National Park.

THE WATERBERGS

Named by the early settlers who, struggling through the Waterbergs in the wet season through mud and streams bursting from the ground, thought they'd hit a land that would support their farms, this part of South Africa has spent the intervening period proving itself spectacularly misnamed. Farmers who stayed quickly discovered that regular droughts made agriculture difficult if not impossible, and for many years the land was thinly populated, one of the least-known and most secretive of all South Africa's mountain massifs. Straddling an area of some 15,000 sq km (nearly 5,800 sq miles), the Waterberg area was once home to early hominids, whose stone age implements can be found. They were displaced by iron age peoples 2,000 years ago, who were the only residents until 150 years ago, living quietly among plentiful wildlife.

In the 1800s, the advent of the muzzle-loading rifle destroyed the game population. An early hunter was Sir William Cornwallis Harris, who described the sight of "three hundred gigantic elephants, browsing in majestic tranquility among the wild magnificence of the African landscape, and a wide stretching plain, darkened, far as the eye can reach, with a moving phalanx of gnoos and quaggas whose numbers literally baffle computation." The same hunter went on to identify a new species of sable antelope, which he shot. The Swedish naturalist Wahlberg passed through in the winter of 1844, returning home with literally thousands of specimens, dead, of course. In a letter he complained that his shoulder was "black and blue and bloodshot" from shooting. He didn't let this interfere with his scientific research though, but shot left-handed until the pain had passed, bagging three elephant that, he noted, earned him double his salary as an engineer when he sold the tusks. In 1856 this canny naturalist was trampled to death by a bull elephant at Lake Ngami.

Amidst the decimation of the wildlife in the area, the quagga and bluebuck, which had for centuries survived the traps, pitfalls and spears of the Tswana people, were two of the species that were hunted to extinction. Apart from these hunters this area was a byword for remoteness — Paul Kruger is reported to have said of a troublesome citizen "give him a farm in the Waterbergs." In the end it was a quiet blend of serious-minded British and Afrikaner settlers who put down fragile roots in this area, one of the most famous being Eugène Marais, who qualified as a lawyer in London but returned to the Waterbergs to study baboons and termites, about all that was left by that time.

these will dead-end into small offices where you may or may not find someone to help with information, but are more likely to be steered to a private operator who wants to take you hunting. The one good place to get orientation information is the **Waterberg Center for Environmental Information** ℂ (014) 765 4041 FAX (014) 765 0116 E-MAIL chw@ref.org.za, Box 157, Vaalwater 0530, attached to a small **Rhino Museum**, 9 AM to 5 PM Monday to Friday and 9 AM to 1 PM Saturday, R5, devoted to the dramatic history of South Africa's rhino population. Attached is the **Walker's Wayside Restaurant** which do evening meals by arrangement but light lunches and drinks through the day.

Now it is home to some of the country's foremost conservation projects, especially the Lapalala Wilderness Area, least-heralded luxury lodges and uncrowded, atmospheric camps. Although it lacks some of the headline predators that bring visitors flocking to the reserves around the Kruger National Park, the Waterberg area presents a more satisfying wilderness, frontier experience. Here the few lodges blend with a traditional community of horseback cattle mustering, spread over huge undiscovered areas. The fact that there is not much infrastructure just adds to the appeal.

General Information

Tourism in this area is scarcely developed, and you won't find the network of tourist information offices here as elsewhere in the country. You will find the same little "information" signs, but

What to Do and Where to Stay

The **Lapalala Wilderness Area**, still not marked on many maps of South Africa, is one of the foremost conservation areas. It was established in 1981, the brainchild of noted naturalist Clive Walker, a 350 sq km (135 sq mile) private conservation reserve that puts tourism low down on its list of priorities, devoting its energies instead to protecting black rhinos and running outreach programs to local schools. It also has formed an association of other reserves in the immediate area called the **Waterberg Conservancy**, who together control 12,000 sq km (4,600 sq miles) of the northern Waterbergs. A significant advantage is that, though far north in the country, the Waterbergs are also classified as being a non-malarial area.

Horizon Adventures run riding safaris in the Waterbergs, northwest of Johannesburg.

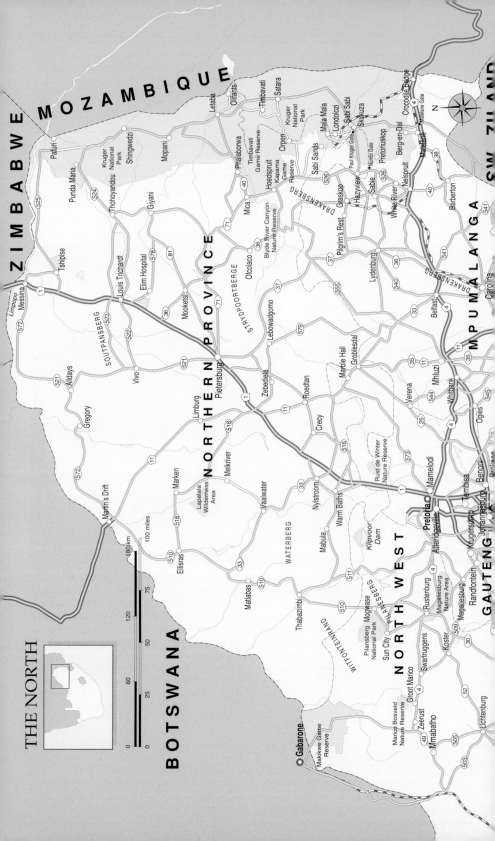

Your choice of lodge will determine the experience. Only a few can match the out-and-out luxury of the private reserves adjoining the Kruger and none can offer such a good chance of spotting the Big Five. However the guides, freed from the duty of ticking off big-game sightings from their client's wish-list can often teach lesser-known and more interesting bush secrets and the bush experience tends to be more rewarding.

Within the Lapalala Wilderness is **Rhino Camp** ☎ (011) 453 7645 FAX (011) 453 7649, Box 645, Bedfordview 2008, R1,400 full board with guiding. This relaxed but luxurious tented camp is set on the edge of the Lapalala River and is a more atmospheric option than staying in the more permanent rondavels of the **Lapalala Lodge** (same contact numbers as above). There are a number of self-catering bush camps sleeping between two and eight people, with a sample price being R196 for Mukwa Camp, sleeping two, with bedding, towels, pots and pans supplied. Guided walking trails offer the best chance to get to know the area and its wildlife, and unlike the national park hikes, which are booked for years in advance, can be undertaken at relatively short notice. Weekend trails start on Friday afternoons and end on Sunday morning, covering 25 km (15.6 miles), while midweek trails run from Monday to Thursday. Accommodation is in tented camps or rustic lodges, all small with between two and eight beds, on the banks of the Lephalala River, with luggage transported separately by vehicle. Per person rates are R620 for the weekend trails and R985 for the four-day midweek trails.

There are a number of camps in the nearby **Welgevonden Reserve** getting close to the standard-setting camps bordering the Kruger National Park, while making the most of their remote setting. One of the best is **Makweti** ☎ (083) 458 6122 FAX (083) 459 1153 E-MAIL makweti@global.co.za, Box 310, Vaalwater 0530, R1,500 to 2,500, thatched and stilted overlooking the Welgevonden Game Reserve, open-sided and taking a maximum of 10 guests in en-suite chalets. It's tastefully furnished with antiques, and dinner is by candlelight. Another is **Sekalala** ☎ (011) 803 4924 FAX (011) 807 4036, Box 3807, Rivonia 2128, R1,600 to R2,000, which is comparable but marginally less nice.

The horseback experience is a key attraction at several lodges. One is **Horizon Horseback Adventures**, a specialist horseback outfit who operate camping safaris in the Lapalala area as well as ranch-based outrides. They offer a more integrated experience, combining an understanding of the natural world with the cattle-farming experience, mustering on horseback and, on Sundays, visiting a local church, getting close to South Africa in a way that could never be dreamed of by the marketing supremos of the tourist industry. Horizon is run as a subsidiary of **Ant's Nest** ☎ (014)

755 3737 FAX (014) 755 3705 E-MAIL tessa@smartnet .co.za, Box 301, Vaalwater 0530, which itself offers an exclusive ranch experience, taking just one group at a time in their own family-run Triple-B ranch and offering a huge variety of game- and horse-based experiences. Costs at Horizon are from US$300 per night in the lodge with horseback safaris lasting for up to eight days, camping overnight, costing in the region of US$200 per person per day. Stays at Ants Nest cost US$430 per night, which allows a minimum of two people to take over the whole lodge, which would sleep a maximum of eight, and covers two people full board including riding and activities. Another operator offering horseback safaris in this area is **Equus Trails** ☎ (011) 788 3923 or (014) 755 2831 FAX (011) 880 8401 E-MAIL equus@equus.co.za WEB SITE www.equus.co.za, 36 Twelfth Avenue, Parktown North 2193. Rates are in the region of R1,300 per person per day, staying in the ranch or R1,600 per day on an eight-night wilderness adventure.

Many of the reserves don't take in day visitors here. However there are less expensive accommodation options. One is the large development, including timeshare, at the **Waterberg Game Reserve's Indabush Lodge** ☎ (083) 630 3615 FAX (083) 640 0174 E-MAIL watberg@iafrica.com WEB SITE www.tmn.co.za/Waterberg, Box 345, Vaalwater 0530, which has two-bed cottages for R415 and beds in their Bapedi Bushcamp available for R75 per person.

How to Get There

This area is not suitable for travelers without their own vehicles. There is little or no public transportation and distances are great. Take the N1 north from Johannesburg to Nylstroom, turning left onto the R33 to Vaalwater. The drive from Johannesburg takes about three hours. At Vaalwater your route will depend on which lodge or reserve you are planning to visit: there are a couple of tourist information signs that might be worth following up though they didn't get me far. A good starting point is the Waterberg Center at Melkrivier (see above), which is 40 km (25 miles) from Vaalwater along the Marken Road, turning left onto a dirt road for just under six kilometers (just under four miles), after which turning right. After 800 m (875 yards) you should see the Rhino Museum and Walker's Wayside restaurant. Alternatively, most of the expensive lodges shown above have airstrips.

THE FAR NORTH

The N1 highway, the "Great North Road" heads up towards Zimbabwe, passing through the towns of Warmbaths, Pietersberg, and Louis Trichardt. To the east is Venda country, formerly a homeland, but most of this area is now farming land, supporting a thin scatter of small stock, sheep, and goats replacing the once-prolific herds of game. Towns established by Voortrekkers heading north now acting as service centers for the surrounding ranches. The road is fast and easy, but the landscape is flat and featureless and with the possible exception of Louis Trichardt, cradled by the tropical Soutpansberg mountains, the predominantly Afrikaner settlements don't present any convincing reasons to stop.

THE TRANSVAAL DRAKENSBERGS

Of all South Africa's spectacular landscapes, the Northern Drakensbergs are among the finest, all too often experienced as a blur through the window as travelers rush through to reach the Kruger National Park. The Blyde River Canyon and Bourke's Luck Potholes, much-photographed for the tourist literature, are among the world's greatest views. There are plenty of other attractions, especially in the area called the Mpumalanga Drakensbergs but known to most South Africans as the Escarpment, where you'll find the restored gold-rush town of Pilgrim's Rest, the mountain town of Sabie, and a scatter of rural manor-house hotels appealing both to overseas visitors and weekending Johannesburgers.

BLYDE RIVER CANYON

From a distance, the Blyde River Canyon is spectacular and beautiful; from close to it just gets better. The Blyde River Nature Reserve extends from the Pinnacle and Gods Window in the south to where the Blyde River Canyon ends at Swadini in the north.

There are a number of principle scenic attractions, which most visitors will have seen on countless postcards and brochures well before they reach the reserve. In the south is the **Pinnacle**, a freestanding quartzite rock pillar rising above a fern-clad ravine and **God's Window** where the vertical cliff of a deep gorge frames the view of the forest and expansive lowveld. In the heart of the reserve **Bourke's Luck Potholes**, where the converging Blyde and Treur rivers have eroded deep, cylindrical shafts into the river's bedrock after aeons of swirling, whirlpool erosion. Nearby a visitor's center explains the geological history of the area, as well as some of the socio-historic features — the canyon was a tourist attraction well before the arrival of European settlers, and implements discovered here date back to the Middle Stone Age, 75,000 years ago. Further north and the **Three Rondavels Viewpoint** offers a famous South African view of the organic mountain shapes and the distant waters of the Blydepoort Dam.

The reserve contains five of the 71 different veld types found in South Africa: northeastern

mountain sourveld, mixed bushveld, lowveld sour bushveld, and lowveld and sourish mixed bushveld. The high summits have montane sour grassland while a few meters along ravines drop through montane forest to riparian forest on the banks of the river and plains of dry brushwood and Protea veld. There's wildlife too: it's shy, so only hikers are likely to see much, but the park is a sanctuary for the rare samango monkey as well as bushbabies and vervets. Predators include civet, leopard, genet, serval, and caracal. Hippo and croc lurk in the rivers and lakes and the most distinctive of the bird species are eagles, buzzards, and falcons.

Most visitors experience the canyon by car. There are a number of drives that take in especially memorable views. The R532 travels from Graskop past God's Window, Bourke's Luck Potholes and the Three Rondavels. The basic route, with stops at the Lisbon and Berlin waterfalls,

covers 79 km (50 miles) out and 50 km (31 miles) back, a total of 129 km (80 miles), taking three hours or so. Alternatively, the way back can be lengthened by a spectacular dirt road that cuts back from Bourke's Luck Potholes and is signposted Vaalhoek, making the trip 29 km (18 miles) longer and reaching Pilgrim's Rest, adding a further 16 km (10 miles) and a whole new dimension of interest to the return journey.

Alternatively, a number of trails head through the reserve. The best known is the Blyderivierspoort Hiking Trail, a 65 km (40.6 mile) route lasting five days with no especially strenuous sections. Well-equipped huts sleeping 30 are available at four points along the way but you will need to carry all food. Getting back by road entails a drive of 150 km (94 miles) so it's best to arrange a lift. Also remember the route ends in the lowveld: malaria country. For further details contact the **Officer in Charge** ((013) 769 6019, P/Bag X431,

Graskop 1270. Places are limited and weekends, especially, often get booked up months in advance.

GRASKOP

The small town of Graskop claims, with 1.5 million travelers passing through each year, to be one of the country's most visited towns. Many, presumably, find themselves wondering why. This is a statistical anomaly, caused by the sheer number of tourist buses that thunder past on their way to the Kruger and the Blyde River Canyon viewpoints. Don't let it influence you into changing your travel plans to fit Graskop onto your itinerary. It might be nearest to the Blyde River Nature Reserve but there's no other convincing reason to stop here, with a couple of low-rise malls offering little more than franchised restaurant chains.

Cattle ranching can make the best of rough or broken ground

Plenty of South Africans will base themselves here to explore the passes and canyons of the area, although Sabie is nicer and Pilgrim's Rest is more interesting.

Graskop dates back to the arrival of Voor-trekkers in 1843, as they tried to forge a southern passage to Delgoa Bay in Portuguese Mozam-bique, and as the route developed it grew in importance. Some scenes described in the seminal South African book *Jock of the Bushveld* took place near here.

General Information

The **Tourist Information** ((013) 767 1833 FAX (013) 767 1855, Spar Center, Pilgrims Road, Box 557, Graskop 1270, 9 AM to 5 PM Monday to Saturday and to 1 PM Sunday, can be helpful. The nearest hospital is at Sabie, and there is no local taxi service. In any case, by taxi the panoramas of the Blyde River Canyon will become very expensive: even from Graskop the headline views are spread over 80 km (50 miles) of road, and with time to walk from each car park to viewpoint will take a minimum of three hours.

Where to Stay

You won't have too much use for a taxi in the town. One of the better small hotels is the **Graskop Hotel** (/FAX (013) 767 1244, at the corner of Main Road and Louis Trichardt, with a variety of rooms from R250. Catering mainly for the domestic South African market, cheaper options including camping is available at the **Summit Lodge** ((013) 767 1058 FAX (013) 767 1895, Mark Street, whose main accommodation consists of thatched rondavels with en-suite facilities for R160, while even less expensive is **Graskop Backpackers Inn** (/FAX (013) 767 1761 E-MAIL graskop@global.co.za, 69 Eeufees Street, R35 in dormitory accommodation.

For meals, **Leonardo's Trattoria** ((013) 767 1078, Louis Trichardt Street, closed Monday, is family-run and is known for its authentic range of Italian cuisine.

How to Get There

Graskop is found at the junction of the R532 and R533, three kilometers (just under two miles) south of the Blyde River Nature Reserve, three hours east of Johannesburg. There is no public transportation.

PILGRIM'S REST

A year after gold was first discovered near Lydenburg, in 1873, Alex "Wheelbarrow" Patterson walked over the mountains to what is now Pilgrim's Creek, pushing all his possessions before him. A wheelbarrow, he asserted, was "cheaper than a horse and won't die of horse-sickness." When he discovered gold in the creek

below Pilgrim's Rest, he sparked off one of the world's largest gold rushes. Within a year he had been joined by 1,500 diggers working 40,000 claims, a huge tented settlement clinging precariously to the slopes. Initially the gold was worked alluvially, panning from the streams, and the first corrugated iron buildings made Pilgrim's Rest into an established center. Through the Anglo-Boer Wars the hills saw some of the most memorable battles, with Boer soldiers camping out in the hills, coming into town to play tennis, but it wasn't until the devaluation of the British pound in 1932 that the town's economy lifted off. Even so, no one expected the gold to last long enough to justify bricks and mortars, and built using corrugated iron structures, prefabricated and shopped in by wagon.

The whole village is a national monument and many buildings have been restored. The high street is lined with red-roofed corrugated iron businesses, including a filling station with 1915 pumps, a Victorian Bar and the Royal Hotel, brimming with Victoriana. Through the day it can get crowded with herding crowds of day-trippers, so it's best to stay the night here, exploring in morning and evening with the chance to catch an elusive breath of period atmosphere.

General Information

The town itself is divided into Uptown, which is old and restored, and Downtown, which isn't. The **Pilgrim's Rest Information Center** ((013) 768 1060 or (013) 768 1471, P/Bag X519, Pilgrim's Rest 1471, 9 AM to 4 PM daily, is immediately opposite the Royal Hotel, on the high street, and sells tickets for the town's museums (R5), all of which are strung along the high street and are open from 9 AM to 1 PM and 1:30 PM to 4 PM.

What to See Do

The museums include the **Dredzen Shop and House Museum**, which is a typical general dealer's store from the 1930s to the 1950s. The **Printing Museum** commemorates the tradition of local newspapers, which were first written and printed here in 1874 and continued to be until the 1950s. And the **House Museum** is a wood and corrugated iron 1913 building characteristic of the village. A private museum is **Allanglade** just to the west of downtown, with guided tours Monday to Saturday at 10:30 AM and 2 PM, which reconstructs the privileged life of the village's rich in the home of an English mine manager. Tickets, available from the Tourist Information Center, cost R20.

The Information Center also sells tickets for **Gold Panning**, one of the best activities in the vicinity. For R5 visitors get to pan for their own nugget in the **Diggings Museum**, Graskop Road,

The Monk's Cowl Valley in the Central Drakensberg, rearing 3,234 m (10,610 ft) above sea level.

an open-air display of old mining equipment and exhibits, with a commentary to explain the realities of trying to wash wealth from the earth. Panning trips take place on the hour, every hour from 10 AM to 3 PM. It is also possible to rent mountain bikes to trail around the hills through **Mountain Bike Trails** ((013) 768 1080, or let a horse take the strain with **Poniekranz Stables** ((013) 786 1211. To come closer to the area's forests there is a two-day trail run by **SAFCOL** ((013) 764 1058 FAX (013) 764 2071, P/Bag X503, Sabie 1260, for groups of up to 16 hikers.

Where to Stay and Eat

By far the best place to stay is in the atmospheric rooms of the **Royal Hotel** ((013) 768 1100 FAX (013) 768 1188, Box 59, Pilgrim's Rest 1290, R530 to R720, a building over 100 years old but with gushing hot water and, in winter, old-fashioned heaters in every room. The bar is a period piece, originally a small church now put to new use. To encourage guests to sample a beer the hotel gives visitors coins, replicas of those printed in the village's own mint, that can be used to buy a drink. They do this so quietly that most guests, like me, only find the coin days later and it's not legal tender anywhere else. Another good accommodation option is the **District Six Miner's Cottages** ((013) 768 1211, Down Town, R180, bookings from 8 AM to 4 PM, a state-run self-catering accommodation imbued with the area's history. Although a good place to stay, book ahead as there's no-one to let you in out of hours. Alternatively, just above the town the **Mount Sheba Country Lodge** ((013) 768 1241 FAX (013) 768 1248, Box 100, Pilgrim's Rest 1290, R900, provides comfortable accommodation in a rural setting, with 25 bedrooms, tennis, and squash courts. There's nowhere, currently, for backpackers.

When it comes to dining the village can be a bit of a disappointment. There are a number of eateries but floods of tourists have done nothing to keep standards up. After the coaches have left only the Diggers Den restaurant, next to the Royal Hotel, stays open and their "Good Old Fish and Chips" were certainly old but not good. In season the Royal Hotel's Peach Tree Inn is a better bet.

How to Get There

There is no public transportation to Pilgrim's Rest — coaches come no nearer than Nelspruit. The nearest airports are at Nelspruit, Hoedspruit and Hazyview, where cars can be rented. From Johannesburg, Pilgrim's Rest is four hours by road. In any case, your own car is especially important in this area, where dramatic drives are such a part of the experience. Pilgrim's Rest is 16 km (10 miles) west of Graskop on R533, 35 km (22 miles) north of Sabie on R532, and 56 km (35 miles) from Lydenburg on R36.

SABIE

The town owes its existence to a party of cheerful picnickers firing off their guns at the rocks. The ricochets revealed a glint of gold prompting the inevitable gold rush, but in the long run timber proved a more durable money-spinner. Arty and crafty, Sabie is at the heart of South Africa's largest forests, unfortunately all pine, dark and drab compared with the variety of the indigenous growth. A short gold rush at the end of the nineteenth century put the town briefly on the map but it hasn't retained its historic heart. However it's not a bad base to explore the Escarpment, although to say it's biggest attraction is a good secondhand bookshop with a huge range of editions of *Jock of the Bushveld* probably damns the town with faint praise.

General Information

There are three tourist information centers, all on Main Street, anxious to make commissions by organizing visitors' accommodation, but the best is by the bookshop: **Sabie Tourism** ((013) 764 3492 FAX (013) 764 2422, 94 Main Street, Box 61, Sabie 1260, 8 AM to 5 PM Monday to Friday and to 1 PM weekends. There are no taxi shuttle services so you'll need a vehicle if you need the **Sabie Hospital** ((013) 764 1222.

What to See and Do

There's not a great deal to do in Sabie; most of the attractions are in driving round the area or hiking to the waterfalls and viewpoints. Historians should head out on the R37 Lydenburg Road, passing through the **Long Tom Pass**, spectacular in its own right but also the scene of years of bitter conflict between British and Boer soldiers. About Sabie's only claim to fame is the unusual **Forestry Museum** ((013) 764 1058, Ford Street, daily from 9 AM to 5 PM, R10, with exhibits relating to the timber industry, and an information center of its own. One of the few worthwhile things to do with a huge forest is to ride through it: the **Fern Tree Park Riding School** ((013) 764 2215 do rides for R35 per hour and lunch rides taking in rock art and a picnic by a the Klipkraal dam for R150 per person.

Where to Stay

Much the most interesting place to stay is out of town, in an old railway station. The **Artists' Café** (/FAX (013) 764 2309, R370 is built in the Hendriksdal Railway Station, with rooms being in the stationmaster's and ticket offices and both first- and second-class waiting rooms. It's on a minor line, and although they say you don't get any unexpected trains, one laden with timber lumbered past within minutes. There's a tiny restaurant, always packed so reserve ahead, which serves Tuscan cuisine, with bits of local art for sale on every wall. The food's not great and the rooms not especially well-endowed, but the owners are charming, the art good, and the atmosphere electric. More sumptuous is the **Hillwatering Country House** ((013) 764 1421 FAX (013) 764 1550, Marula Street, R320, a country home on the outskirts with views of the mountain and a good restaurant.

A step down, in cost, is the **Sabie Vallée Inn** ((013) 764 2182 FAX (013) 764 1362, Tenth Avenue, dinner bed, and breakfast for R320 upwards, conveniently located in the center of town, or the **Sabie Town House** ((013) 764 2292 FAX (013) 764 1988, Power Street, R360. Backpackers have only one option: the **Jock of the Bushveld Caravan Park** ((013) 764 2178 FAX (013) 764 3215, Main Road, R35 camping, R40 dormitory—bedding not supplied. For dining, the **Loggerhead Restaurant** ((013) 764 3341, Main Road, serves lunches and dinners with a particular specialty the Sabie rainbow trout; closed Sunday evening and Monday.

How to Get There

Also four hours from Johannesburg, Sabie is on the R37 beyond the Long Tom Pass. There is no public transportation to Sabie.

THE GATEWAY KRUGER TOWNS

Slide down from the Escarpment and the lowveld stretches out towards the Kruger National Park. Towns here offer cheaper out-of-park accommodation and many also arrange budget game-drives to the park itself. If money is short this is definitely the way to sample the wildlife experience, gaining along the way an insight into country life in South Africa. The northern towns are not especially historic. Although the malarial lowveld was useful for winter grazing, the summer would bring disease and most early settlers would clear off to the hills until the weather cooled. While they don't justify a special trip it is worth slowing down and taking a look around these towns in any case — most travelers hurry through and the locals like those who stop. Phalaborwa is a mining center, with a gate of its own into the park and is best known for its golf course. Don't yawn: where else do you get giraffe and elephant interrupting your game? Hoedspruit is a convenient base from which to reach the Numbi, Paul Kruger and Timbavati gates, and Hazyview is near the Paul Kruger Gate. Meanwhile further south prosperous farming towns have a calm charm of their own and give access to the southern stretches of the park. White River gives good access to Numbi and Nelspruit is within striking distance of the southern gates, Malelane and Crocodile Bridge.

PHALABORWA

The name Phalaborwa, in the local language, means "better than the south," but it isn't really. It only became a town when the phosphate mine was opened in 1957. Since then the town has grown and so has the hole where the phosphates used to be. Now it has South Africa's biggest man-made hole in the ground: two and a half kilometers (just over one and a half miles) wide and one and a half kilometers (just under a mile) long — and still growing.

General Information

The **Tourist Information** ((015) 781 1155 or (082) 955 7683, at the corner of Hendrik von Eck and President Kruger streets, Box 14, Phalaborwa 1390, 9 AM to 5 PM Monday to Friday and to 1 PM Saturday, is very helpful. There's no taxi service locally though local guest houses will run their clients around if required. For medical attention the **Phalaborwa Hospital** ((015) 781 3511, Grosvenor Crescent, has 24-hour casualty service.

What to See and Do

The Tourist Information bureau can arrange night drives into the Kruger which leave from Phalaborwa Gate, also bookable through the local **Park Office** ((015) 781 0027. The usual park entry is R25 per person and R30 per vehicle, while night drives and guided walks are charged at R15 per person and R25 per hour. Other good activities here include going out to see the mine. Booking is essential and tours take place on Fridays only, at 9 AM, or by appointment ((015) 781 2337, free. **Jumbo River Safaris** ((015) 781 6168 run sunrise and sunset cruises on the Olifants River for R50 per person. Golfers should not resist the opportunity of taking a swing at one of the country's leading courses, the **Hans Merensky Country Club** ((015) 781 3931 FAX (015) 781 5309, where wildlife is likely to join in with your game. If such proximity to game is a deterrent, fewer animals play tennis and none play squash, both available here.

Where to Stay and Eat

The Hans Merensky Country Club is also the best place in town to stay or eat, with twin chalets R352 with breakfast. For a more rural experience the **Hippo Lodge Mfubu** (/FAX (015) 781 0412 E-MAIL mfubu@webmail.co.za, R270 to R480 for chalets on the Olifants River, while the **Sefapane Lodge** ((015) 781 7041 FAX (015) 781 7042 E-MAIL sefapane @mweb.co.za, Copper Road, R380 to R460. Finally, the **Impala Protea** ((015) 781 3681 FAX (015) 781 5234 E-MAIL ipinn@satis.co.za, 52 Essenhout Street, R350, is one of the better representatives of this chain, with a lively bar. There is also a good backpackers called **Elephant Walk** (/FAX (015) 781 2758

E-MAIL elephant.walk@nix.xo.za, 30 Anna Scheepers Avenue, R50 backpackers, six-person chalet R480, bed-and-breakfast flatlets R190.

Miners have a high disposable income and there are therefore a good range of restaurants in the town. The Sefapane Lodge has probably the best restaurant in town and **Tiffany's** ((015) 781 2021 or (015) 781 5562, Rooibos Street, is a smart/casual à la carte alternative.

How to Get There

To get to Phalaborwa, two kilometers (just over a mile) from the town center and the Kruger National Park, Phalaborwa Airport receives daily flights from Johannesburg with the major car-rental companies represented. The nearest camp in the Kruger is Letaba, 50 km (31.2 miles) to the east. By road, **Northern Link Transport** ((021) 323 0379 runs coaches to Pretoria, which, by road, takes five hours.

HOEDSPRUIT

Although an important communications hub, Hoedspruit does not have any great appeal, being little more than a spread-out scatter of gun shops and liquor stores. It is, however, right by the entrance to the Kruger Park and is at the heart of several sites of wildlife interest. It's not that easy to get information about the area. The **Central Lowveld Tourist Information Bureau** (/FAX (015) 793 1678, Box 793, Hoedspruit, is based out on a farm and has no drop-in office or indeed opening hours. The **Fort Copieba Motel** ((015) 793 1175 WEB SITE www .hoedspruit.co.za, Main Street, claims to have tourist information but doesn't and there's a further office at **Jumbo Junction**. None get involved in the marketing strategy of the expensive private game reserves and thus are unwilling to help with travel arrangements into the Timbavati, for which you'll need **Eastgate Lodge Transfers** ((015) 793 3678.

Activities in the area concentrate on the wild-life experience. The **Hoedspruit Research and Breeding Center** ((015) 793 1633 FAX (015) 793 1646, Box 1278, Hoedspruit 1380, R40, located 20 km (12.5 miles) south of town, one kilometer (just over half a mile) from Eastgate Airport, open 8 AM to 4 PM daily, R30, breeds cheetah and lion for release into the wild and recently has added a pack of wild dog. This is part of Kapama Lodge, though well away from the wildlife areas where guests do game drives. The **Moholalo Rehabilitation Center** ((015) 795 5236, tours at 9:30 AM and 3 PM (booking essential), R20, looks after sick or injured birds, with a breeding program of its own that extends to animals as large as lion. Accommodation is available.

Where to Stay

There are a couple of upmarket options near town. **Kapama Private Game Reserve** ((012) 804 4840 FAX (012) 804 4842 E-MAIL gentour@iafrica.com

WEBSITE www.kapama.co.za, Box 912-031, Silverton 0127, R2,000, is set in a large private reserve with good game-viewing without the huge expense of the Kruger-bordering lodges. The **Phuza Moya Private Game Reserve** ((015) 793 1971 FAX (015) 793 3313, Box 1669, Hoedspruit 1380, overlooks the confluence between the Blyde and Olifants rivers and costs R1,800 to R2,500, full board with safaris; and the smaller **Kwa-Mbili** ((015) 793 2773 E-MAIL safaris@kwambili.com, Box 1188, Hoedspruit 1380, R1,500 full board, is located 30 km (19 miles) east of town in the Thornybush Reserve. Meanwhile the **Tshukudu Game Lodge** ((015) 793 2476 FAX (015) 793 2078, Box 289, Hoedspruit 1380, 40 km (25 miles) north of town on the R40, organizes morning walks with elephant and hand-reared lion—great for kids. Accommodation here costs R1,500, including game activities. Rather less expensive are the safari tents of **Matumi Game Lodge and Bushcamp** ((015) 793 2452 FAX (015) 973 2743 E-MAIL matumi@global.co.za WEB SITE www.matumi.co.za, Guernsey Road, Box 1483, Hoedspruit 1380, at R240 to R850. On a budget, the best place to stay is out of town, at the **Blue Cottages** (/FAX (015) 795 5144, 29 km (18 miles) on the R527, Box 223, Hoedspruit 1380, with cottages for R200 that sleep two. Better, it is attached to the **Mad Dogz Café** ((015) 795 5425, which is good for all traditional foods and cooks a mean quiche as well as having an unusually good outlet for ethnic crafts: Monsoon. For backpackers, the **Off Beat Safari Camp** (/FAX (015) 793 2422, Box 849, Hoedspruit 1380, is the only choice, with camping available from R30.

How to Get There

To get there, Hoedspruit is served by flights from Johannesburg, and even Cape Town, which arrive at **Eastgate Airport** ((015) 793 3681, 14 km (8.7 miles) south of Hoedspruit. Transfers to the game lodges can be arranged with **Eastgate Lodge Transfers** ((015) 793 3678. By car, Hoedspruit can be reached in five hours from Johannesburg. The best route is inland via Lydenburg, Origstad and the Abel Erasmus Pass. The road running parallel with the Kruger to Hazyview is slow, with carts, cattle, and heavy traffic.

HAZYVIEW

In the midst of huge banana plantations, Hazyview is conveniently located near to the Kruger Park's southwestern gates — just 19 km (12 miles) from Numbi Gate — as well as being quickly reached from the Nelspruit and the N4 highways. A shame then that it isn't more of a town, with an uncomfortable mix of campsites and timeshare establishments with a few luxury lodges.

Generally still, crocs can move suddenly and fast.

There's a **Hazyview Tourism Association**
(/FAX (013) 737 7414, Blue Haze Building, Box 81,
9 AM to 4 PM Monday to Friday and 10 AM to noon
Saturday. They will help with arranging accommodation but little more. There's not a lot to see
here, except perhaps the slight attraction of the
country's only **Tsakani Silk Farm** ((083) 379 5033,
26 km (16 miles) north of Hazyview off the R40,
with guided tours on the hour from 9:30 AM to
2:30 PM Monday to Friday and to noon on Saturday, R40 per person. On the cultural front the
Shangana Cultural Village ((013) 737 7000
FAX (013) 737 7007 E-MAIL shangana@fast.co.za, five
kilometers (just over three miles) north of Hazyview taking a left onto the R535 Graskop Road
where it will be found after four kilometers (two
and a half miles) on left, R50, is a moderately
worthy cultural experience with a reconstructed
village and dancing. Tours are at 9 AM, 10 AM, 11 AM,
3 PM and 4 PM with an evening tour starting at 6 PM
including an African dinner with mopane worms.
The statutory *sangoma* comprehensively failed
an impromptu test — predicting the sex of my
wife's imminent baby — but still charged R50 to
throw his beads and bones before guessing the
answer wrong.

Where to Stay

Perhaps surprisingly there is a sudden array of
luxury accommodation in the area. The smartest
place to stay is undoubtedly the **Blue Mountain
Lodge** ((011) 784 4144 FAX (011) 784 4127 E-MAIL
bluemtnlodge@icon.co.za, Box 101, Kiepersol
1241, R3,520 to R4,400, which offers over-the-top
luxury on the Drakensberg foothills 28 km
(17.5 miles) east of Hazyview and is the first South
African Member of the Small Luxury Hotels of
the World. But the price leaves many guests smart-
ing too. More reasonably, **Highgrove** ((013) 764
1844 FAX (013) 764 1855 E-MAIL highgrove@ns
.lia.net WEB SITE www.highgrove.co.za, White
River Road (R40), Box 46, Kiepersol 1241, is a
"Leading Hotel of the World" with one of the
country's top restaurants. With just eight suites
it is family-run and recreates the ambience of a
Victorian English manor-house, from R1,260
dinner, bed, and breakfast. The other luxury dwelling is Cybele Forest Lodge, listed below under
White River. Nearer into town is **Umbhaba Lodge**
((013) 737 7636 FAX (013) 737 7629 E-MAIL umbhaba
@iafrica.com WEB SITE www.umbhaba.co.za,
Box 1677, Hazyview 1242, R600 to R1,200, on the
outskirts but within range of both park and mou-
tons. Better value at the **Rissington Inn** ((013) 737
7700 FAX (013) 737 7112 E-MAIL rissington@
mweb.co.za, WEB SITE www.rissington.co.za, two
kilometers (just over a mile) south of Hazyview
on the R40, Box 650, Hazyview 1242, R360 to
R580, with perhaps the best à la carte restaurant
outside the private reserves. There's a choice for

backpackers but the best of the bunch is the **Kruger
Park Backpackers** (/FAX (013) 737 7224 E-MAIL
krugback @mweb.co.za, Main Street, Box 214,
Hazyview 1242, R45, with a range of three to four-
night drives into the park on offer.

How to Get There

Hazyview has no public transportation, though
the backpacker lodges will arrange transfers from
Nelspruit or White River (36 km or 22 miles) for
a fee. With your own vehicle Hazyview is four
hours drive from Johannesburg: follow the N4 east
and turn right at Nelspruit on the R537 and then
the R40 to White River, continuing 32 km (20 miles)
to Hazyview.

WHITE RIVER

Very few overseas visitors stay in White River.
City dwellers stay in the larger city of Nelspruit,
20 km (12.5 miles) to the south, while wildlife
hounds race 40 km (25 miles) further north to
Hazyview. Which leaves this farming town un-
fairly neglected. A couple of hotels offer very good
value accommodation and it's a fascinating but
overlooked microcosm of Vaal life. Originally
settled by Voortrekkers, it was swamped by an
English influence when veterans of World War I
bought land grants, blind, and established the area
as a world center of citrus fruits. These days it's
a much underrated base for exploring the Kruger,
within a day's drive of the cities of Johannesburg
and Durban.

White River is in the heart of **Jock of the Bushveld** country, set in a rolling landscape that wit-
nessed the early wagoneers heading from South
Africa's early settlements to the British-free zone
of Portuguese Mozambique's Indian Ocean coast.

There's not a lot to do here. As you'll find if
you reach the **White River Tourism and Publicity Association** ((013) 751 5312, Kruger Park Street,
in the town library and restrained by library hours.
At the point in researching this book I found this
something of a relief: no museums to spend time
on, and no fleecing zoos masquerading as conservation resources. Instead, reasonable and sometimes outstanding hotels manned by owner-
managers not yet jaded by tourists flooding over
from the cities to the Kruger.

Where to Stay and Eat

By far the smartest and best place to stay is **Cybele
Forest Lodge** ((013) 764 1823 FAX (013) 764 1810
E-MAIL cybele@iafrica.com WEB SITE www.cybele
.co.za, R40 Spitzkop exit, just over four kilometers
(about two and a half miles), half way to Hazyview.
This is a converted hunting lodge set in 120 hectares (300 acres) of woodland with stables and
guided walks that consistently wins awards for
its cuisine. Rates are R2,150 dinner, bed, and break-

fast. Less exclusively priced the **Hulala Lakeside Lodge** ((013) 764 1893 FAX (013) 764 1864 E-MAIL hulala@country-escapes.co.za WEB SITE www .country-escapes.co.za, R40 Hazyview Road, running from R730 dinner, bed, and breakfast. It is aimed more at the South African market, surrounded on three sides by a lake for boating, bird watching, and swimming.

Not so much recreating the colonial atmosphere as still in it, the **Karula Hotel** ((013) 751 2277 FAX (013) 750 0413, Box 279, White River, is an atmospheric hotel where period, wood-paneled gloom adds a new depth to the experience of rural South Africa. It's the sort of place where you make little expeditions for bowling or golf and then come back for a game of billiards before dinner — and it's my personal favorite. Rates are R220 including breakfast. In town, the **Gleighnelly Country Lodge** ((013) 751 1100 FAX (013) 751 1200 E-MAIL glenelly@glenelly.co.za WEB SITE www.glenelly .co.za, 34 Alie Van Bergen Street, is not remotely a country club but a newly built hotel with excellent standards of accommodation and friendly management for R180.

The best place in town to eat is **Gianni's** ((013) 751 1727, at the corner of Tom Lawrence and William Lynne streets, with a smart section known for seafood as well as a casual pizza bar, while the **Bag-dad Café** ((013) 751 1177, on R40 by the Numbi Gate turn, is known for its home-baked pies; booking essential for evening meals. Finally the **Timbuctoo** ((013) 751 3353, Paul Kruger Street, does good prawns and game steaks.

How to Get There

Driving, White River is 20 km (12.5 miles) from Nelspruit along the R40, turning right onto the R538. This road continues to Numbi Gate in the Kruger Park, 32 km (20 miles) away. Public transportation to Johannesburg, Pretoria and Nelspruit is provided by **Lowveld Link** ((013) 750 1174, Wednesdays, Fridays, and Sundays.

NELSPRUIT

Briefly the capital of the Transvaal Republic, the modern city of Nelspruit is now the provincial capital of Mpumalanga. It is an important trading center that links South Africa with Mozambique, and most visitors will pass through here, at least, on their way to and from the Kruger. It is at the heart of a fertile area producing mangoes, bananas, avocados and macadamia nuts, and well served by rail and road transportation. Once a conservative Afrikaner town it is rapidly becoming one of the most sophisticated and multiracial cities in the country, with a relaxed, pleasant atmosphere and warm climate. Its wide streets are lined with bougainvillea and jacaranda trees and in season it bursts with color and scent.

General Information

The city center is a compact six by six grid of roads, pierced by the N4 highway, which slows briefly to become Louis Trichardt Street before speeding on to Swaziland and Mozambique. A white-painted pedestrian promenade is at its heart, which is where you'll find the **Tourist Information Center** ((013) 755 1988 FAX (013) 755 1350, Shop 5, the Promenade, Box 5018, Nelspruit 1200, open 8 AM to 5 PM Monday to Friday and 9 AM to 4 PM weekends, which is packed with information about the area and can also help with Kruger Park bookings. For local transport, **Taxi Citibug** ((013) 744 0128 is suitable for travel around town while **Eagle Eye Tours** ((082) 428 4104 runs shuttles to nearby towns. For medical treatment the city has a selection of hospitals but the best for serious problems is **Nelspruit Private Hospital** ((013) 744 7150.

The main attraction is the pleasantly lush gardens of the **Lowveld National Botanical Garden**, three kilometers (just under two miles) out of town on the R40 White River Road, open May to September 8 AM to 5:15 PM and October to April to 4 PM, R20, which houses an important selection of plants with marked trails though tropical rainforest, and the largest collection of cycads in Africa. There's also a steep path following the Crocodile River Gorge: the experience is improved if you remember to pick up the free guide that goes with the trail. Otherwise with not much going on in town local operators have to show a bit of originality to attract your attention. **Balloons Over Africa** (/FAX (013) 751 5409 E-MAIL kevinmv@iafrica.com, Box 2390, White River 1240, float over the surrounding farmlands. And although, being separated from the coast by Mozambique, it might not seem an obvious diving destination **Calypso Dive Charters** ((013) 752 8441 meet between 6:30 PM and 8:30 PM on Tuesdays and Thursdays in their clubhouse at the Municipal Swimming Pool on Tom Lawrence Street. Their operations don't stop at the deep end of the pool. Expeditions to go diving off Mozambique's Indian Ocean coast, two and a half hours away by car, or Sodwana Bay are their main activities.

Where to Stay and Eat

The best option in town is the **Hotel Promenade** ((013) 753 3000 FAX (013) 752 5533 E-MAIL hotprom@ global.co.za, Louis Trichardt Street, R360 with breakfast is centrally located on the main street and next to the pedestrian town center. Four kilometers (two and a half miles) south of town the **Lakeview Country Lodge** ((013) 741 5163 FAX (013) 741 5161, Kaapschehoop Road, Box 20002, West Acres 1211, R350, rents self-catering chalets on the banks of the Nelsloop River. On a more limited budget the **Formule 1** ((013) 741 4490, at the corner of the N4 and Kaapschehoop Road, provides its formulaic accommodation at R145 for up to three people. There are a couple of backpacking options but the best is **Funky Monkey's 102 Back-packers** ((083) 310 4755, 102 Van Wijk Street, R40 in dormitories, which is run by an artist and provides a free beer to every check-in.

Within the Promenade there are a couple of restaurants serving steaks — **Steers** and **Mike's Kitchen**, as well as **Café Mozart** ((013) 752 2637, 56 Promenade Center, Louis Trichardt Street, for quiches and coffee, with evening smart-casual meals best at the Hotel Promenade or the **Villa Italia** ((013) 752 5780, Louis Trichardt Street, nearby.

How to Get There

Nelspruit Airport ((013) 741 1087, Kaapschehoop Road, is at the heart of the transportation system, with all the car rental companies and daily flights to Johannesburg and Durban. A train links the station daily to Komatipoort and Johannesburg/Pretoria, continuing to Maputo on Monday, Wednesday, and Friday. The **Greyhound Bus** ((013) 752 5134 departs from the Joshua Doore Center to Pretoria and Johannesburg daily. By road, Nelspruit is 355 km (222 miles) from Johannesburg along the N4.

NORTHEAST SOUTH AFRICA: PROTECTED LAND

The largest park in South Africa and famous throughout the world, the Kruger National Park is the main draw for many visitors to South Africa. Extending from the Crocodile River in the south up to the Limpopo in the north, it runs for 350 km (219 miles) up the border with Mozambique and is, at its widest, 60 km (37.5 miles) wide. The first area of the park was first proclaimed in 1898, when President Kruger established the southern Sabie River area of the reserve, which is still arguably the best part for wildlife observation. His selection of this area for a national park was not entirely altruistic. Although this section of bush could be used for hunting and grazing in the winter months, tsetse, malaria and bilharzia made short work of settlers who tried to stay on through the summer. The threat of wild animals and tropical diseases did not deter a growing number of "biltong hunters," who, having decimated much of the game from other parts of the country, were moving in to finish off what was left in the Kruger. A police sergeant in Komatipoort was given responsibility for stopping the flood of hunters into the park boundaries. The British authorities expanded the park boundaries in 1903 to the present limits, resisting claims by agricultural and mining lobbies to lift the restrictions. As the only people who wanted to visit the park at this time were hunters and prospectors, public access wasn't permitted and was never a founding principle of the park.

Perhaps unsurprisingly, for this reason conservation as a disinterested principle was not high on the list of priorities, and one MP was famously reported as describing zebra as "donkeys in football shirts." Kruger himself was not a great conservationist, and "never in his life thought about any animal except as biltong," according to a contemporary. And while there was a vague awareness that wildlife conservation was a good thing the concept that wild animals could actually make a contribution through tourism was yet to occur to the world. Wildlife ecotourism was born here in 1923, when South African Railways had the idea of stopping their Pretoria to Lorenço Marques line in the reserve, and obtained permission to let passengers off for guided tours of the bush.

The concept boomed and by 1926 public access to the park was allowed, with entry fees paying to police the borders and to try to distinguish between hunters and tourists. There were no facilities in the park and the first camp was built in Pretoriuskop after publicized incidents of tourists having to overnight in trees while predators stalked hungrily below. In 1947 princesses Elizabeth and Margaret of the United Kingdom stayed in the first luxury lodges and put a visit to the Kruger firmly on most itineraries to South Africa.

Over recent years the park has been growing, almost by stealth. In 1994 the fences came down on the western boundaries, opening up a further 2,000 sq km (about 770 sq miles) of private reserve land to the animals, and current plans are to take the fences down on the eastern border with Mozambique. This would allow some of the seasonal migration routes to be recovered.

THE KRUGER NOW

Surprisingly, the best wildlife experience is generally outside the official park boundaries, in the private reserves on the western borders. Within the park driving off-road, and driving at night, is forbidden, limiting the possibilities for seeing game, who know where the roads are and keep clear. Also, for obvious reasons, getting out of your car is not allowed — though I have seen a Japanese tourist crouching down in front of his car to get a closer shot of a lion in an act of great daring or stupidity. The park accommodation, aimed at the domestic market, tends to be large developments of self-catering chalets, crowded in season and priced to suit the fragile spending power of the rand.

On the eastern borders, however, the private reserves supply the luxury safari experience expected by overseas visitors. Now the fences are down they share the animals of the Kruger but, operating on their own land, they are able to offer guided walks, game-drives in open Landrovers decked with banked seats and fronted by a ranger, perched vulnerably on a jump-seat on the hood.

Night drives introduce a whole new world as the animal night-shift takes over and they can, within reason, blaze new paths into the bush to get close to elusive animals that aren't visible from the beaten track. These reserves are expensive, and so all of them are constantly evolving their lodges, chasing the ideals of luxury and heading continually upmarket. Each new added extra concept that might improve the safari experience is eagerly seized on and followed in a wave by the other private reserves, to such an extent that it is often hard to distinguish one lodge from another.

As the standards of cuisine and en-suite facilities spiral towards an (often inappropriate) luxury there are two main factors which should affect

the safari, rich or professional hunters had plenty of time to wander round Africa with their guns, which was just as well, as stalking and shooting is always a slow process. In the days of the photo-safari and packaged tourism the aim of ticking off the Big Five has become central to many lodges, with rangers becoming quite anxious if they can't fulfil their clients expectations. Even in the most managed reserves the animals are still wild, and even with radio-links between safari vehicles finding the last missing species from the Big Five list is often impossible. Most elusive is the nocturnal — and shy — leopard, which explains why many game-drives last well into the night, flashing 4,000 candlepower floodlights across the bush in

your choice of lodge. One is size. Small is certainly beautiful: the fewer beds make for a more intimate, friendlier and more rewarding experience, and although the larger lodges can moderate their prices they find it hard to avoid a factory, packaged atmosphere and become hotels in the bush. The other factor is the location of the lodge: the Kruger's huge extent contain a variety of habitats and even with a skilled ranger and a four-wheel-drive vehicle different areas lend themselves to different animals.

THE BIG FIVE — AND BEYOND

Many first-time visitors just want to see the Big Five: lion, elephant, rhino, buffalo and leopard. These diverse animals were grouped together by hunters, who considered these the most dangerous animals to stalk and kill. In the early days of

the hope of catching the flash of reflected light from a leopard's eyes.

The key to getting close views of wild animals is their level of habituation. This applies to all animals, but is most noticeable with the leopard, which is the most timid. If they are accustomed to seeing vehicles they gradually lose their fear, and thus Landrovers can get very close to animals who, discounting them as a threat, ignore them completely. Thus they will eat, hunt and even mate while tourists watch and film, and only the humans feel that the animal's privacy is in any way being infringed as radio calls bring in other safari vehicles to share the experience. Most of the Big Five species, confident in their role near the top of the food-chain, are quick to relax. Not so the leopards, which are attacked by lion and often have

This male waterbuck would flee if approached on foot, but is much less nervous of a vehicle.

their kills stolen by hyena. The first lodge to perfect a close relationship with their resident leopard was Londolozi, who regularly tracked and watched leopard in their reserve through the 1970s and 1980s. Even now their Sabi Sands area is the best for catching close sightings of leopard, and is therefore the "best" area for first-time safari hounds to head for. From the security of their vehicle they can take all the photographs they wish.

Stand up and break the vehicle's usual profile, however, and animals can become scared or, recognizing a human, aggressive. This gives a clue to the artificiality of the whole process. While seeing every animal in the Big Five list is a natural ambition, easily sold and generally fullfillable, there is far more to the bush than this. Walking through the bush with an armed ranger won't get you so close to wild animals — it would be very frightening if it did — but it will teach you far more about the plants, insects, bird life, and ecology of the area. And the relentless focus on chasing the Big Five can distract rangers from the smaller pleasures of the bush. Instead of staying to watch a family of mongeese sunbathing and squabbling they will drive on until they find a pride of lion, panting after gorging themselves breathless on their latest kill. Keen birdwatchers, especially, find that the vehicle hurtles right past the creatures they want to see. Four hundred and fifty bird species have been recorded in the park, but animals off the Big Five list, discounted, often get passed by at speed.

Which is where the other areas come in. Further north in the Timbavati district there are still leopard, but because these aren't spotted every day the focus shifts from catching every one of the Big Five. And there are many excellent lodges set in private reserves that don't border the Kruger Park. Many of these don't even have lion — which, according to one ranger at least, "breed like rabbits and eat the merchandise." These reserves tend to provide better value in their accommodation as they miss many of the mass-market tourists and their rangers, freed from the need to clock up the headline species, often have a deeper understanding of and passion for the bush. These private reserves shouldn't be discounted, and if time and finances permit a combination of a headline Big Five lodge and a private reserve slightly off the beaten track is the perfect introduction to Africa's wildlife.

THE KRUGER NATIONAL PARK

In the Kruger itself you'd be lucky to spot all of the Big Five, though the sheer range and variety of the game that you will see from the comfort of your car is reason enough to visit. To reserve lodges and trails, contact the **South African National Parks**, which have offices in Pretoria ((012) 343 1931 FAX (012) 343 0905 E-MAIL reservations@parks-sa.co.za, 643 Leyds Street, Muckleneuk, Box 787 Pretoria, 8 AM to 3:45 PM; and in Cape Town ((021) 422 2810 FAX (021) 422 2810, Box 7400, Roggeland, Cape Town, 9 AM to 4:45 PM, while reservations for Park Board lodges and trails can also be made through **Computicket** ((011) 445 8100. Don't delay in making a reservations as lodges and trails sell out far in advance, and park accommodation must be paid for at least a month in advance.

There are no taxi services that operate within the Kruger but plenty of tour operators (see TAKING A TOUR, page 56 in YOUR CHOICE). It is possible to fly into the park and rent a car, but flights into the park are relatively expensive, as are the local vehicle rental outlets. The airport at Skukuza is a private airstrip for the national parks, scheduled commercial and other emergency flights. All other aircraft that wish to land at Skukuza or any other landing strip in the Kruger National Park require prior permission from the Executive Director ((01311) 6-13611, extensions 2121 and 2124, Kruger National Park, P/Bag X402, Skukuza 1350. Skukuza also has the only ATM machine in the park: withdrawing cash in this bush setting feels truly strange.

For medical facilities there are first-aid posts at Skukuza, Letaba and Satara, but the main medical facility is next to the diplomatic compound in Skukuza.

Entry into the park is charged at R10 per person and R20 per vehicle. Entrance gates and the gates of lodges are closed at night. The exact time the gates will be open varies with the season, ranging from 6 AM to 5:30 PM in the deep winter to 5:30 AM to 6:30 PM in the summer, but check at the gates. No permits will be issued after closing time and the guards will want to be sure you have time to reach your destination camp. Dally at your peril: to arrive late at a rest camp is an offence and you will be fined. In the park the speed limit is 50 kph (31 mph) on the tar roads and 40 kph (25 mph) on dirt tracks. However if you want to see any wildlife you'll have to travel much slower than this.

There are four categories of camp. Main camps have varying levels of facilities, usually including a shop, restaurant, electricity, telephones and gas stations, and are open to day visitors. They can take on a rather suburban atmosphere, especially Skukuza, which, with 6,000 beds is the size of many towns, and within the parks mealtimes are quite regimented: breakfast is served from 7 AM to 9 AM, lunch is from noon to 2 PM, and dinner 6 PM to 9 PM. Bush Lodges are closed to day visitors but can be booked as private lodges by groups of up to 12 people self-catering. For small groups, obviously, this becomes expensive. Bushveld Camps can be reserved and although perfectly comfortable don't have restaurants or shops; and Trail Base Camps can only be visited on a pre-booked trail in the company of a park ranger. All are provided with bedding, towels and soap and have communal cooking facilities, while some have basic crockery and utensils available for rent.

Accommodation is offered in a range of options ranging from hut (one-room chalets, R158), through cottages (bedroom, living room and bathroom, R402) to guest cottages, with two or three bedrooms and at least two bathrooms (up to R774 for the newer and more luxurious options). Prices vary to a limited extent depending on the facilities available and age of the development, but staying in the park itself is far cheaper than in the private reserves outside.

Along its 350 km (219 mile) length the Kruger contains a wide diversity of habitats and varying degrees of accessibility. Largely for this reason the southern district is known to many South Africans as "the circus;" the central region is called "the zoo," and the far north is called "the wilderness." There's an element of truth in this: if you've got time the slow drive all the way up the park is perhaps the best way to experience the changing terrain and atmospheres.

THE CIRCUS

This southern area of the park has the highest concentration of game and is the most accessible area by road. The choice of camps consists of the following options. **Berg-en-Dal** is the most modern of the camps, offering chalets spread out and landscaped, 12 km (7.5 miles) northwest from Malelane Gate. East of here **Crocodile Bridge**, overlooking farmland on the edge of the park, is at Crocodile Bridge Gate and is only really an attractive option if you've arrived too late to proceed further into the park. Thirty-five kilometers (22 miles) north of Crocodile Bridge, **Lower Sabie** is one of the best places for seeing animals, with a number of waterholes in the vicinity. **Pretoriuskop** is reached from Numbi Gate on the eastern park boundary among granite outcrops, tall grass and sicklebush and offers night drives in open trucks as well as some great game-viewing. Finally, **Skukuza**, with an airport and the full facilities of a small town, is 12 km (7.5 miles) to the east of Kruger Gate. The game-viewing is among the best in the park but shared with plenty of other people.

THE ZOO

In the central area the game thins out a little but then so do the crowds. **Orpen** is right by the Orpen Gate, but shaded by trees and already deep in the bush, sheltered by the large Timbavati private land to its west. **Tamboti**, three kilometers (just under two miles) into the park, is one of the Kruger's

more basic campsites, but the restaurant attracts a cult following. **Satara**, 46 km (28.7 miles) into the park along a tar road from Orpen Gate, is the second-largest of the camps but has a far better bush feel. Also the drive to it passes through what is arguably the world's densest lion population. Fifty-two kilometers (32.5 miles) north of Satara is possibly one of the best camps in the park, **Olifants**, overlooking the Olifants Valley with plenty of game and circling raptors. The best rondavels are one to 24, which share superb views over the river. Thirty-four kilometers (21 miles) to the north, **Letaba** is set in mopane shrubland on a curve of the Letaba River, in good elephant country. There is an elephant museum, and views from the restaurant are good. Not, sadly, from the rondavels, but it's one of the best camps in the park for general game.

THE WILDERNESS

In the north the wildlife thins out but the experience is that of huge expanses, wide horizons, and the vastness that is Africa as you cross over the Tropic of Capricorn into open savanna. **Mopani Camp** is 42 km (26.25 miles) north of Letaba, spread out around a dam that provides one of the area's few reliable water-sources. Sixty-two kilometers (39 miles) north again **Shingwedzi** is one of the older camps with brick buildings and whitewash colonial-style bungalows: tatty but friendly, in the words of one pundit. It's a long drive — 71 km (over 44 miles) at regulation speeds, stopping to look at passing game — further north to **Punda Maria**, one of the older camps: duck for low beams. Ancient 1930s buildings all add to this camp's charm. This is really in the wilds, set in varied, thickly overgrown vegetation. Forty-six kilometers (29 miles) further north is a picnic site at **Pafuri**, worth mentioning just because of the kettle kept permanently on the boil for the few who make it up to this northern extremity to reward themselves with a cup of tea. It's a great place to experience the bush near the frontiers with Zimbabwe and Mozambique, though irritating if you forget your teabags. This is also the start-point of daily tours of the Thulamela archaeological site, one of the very few excavated sites of now-dissipated African cultures. These have to be pre-booked through South African National Parks (see above) and a maximum of 15 people are allowed per tour.

WILDERNESS TRAILS

One of the most popular activities in the Kruger are the three-night, two-day Wilderness Trails, where a maximum of eight travel with a ranger on foot through the park from a primitive, but comfortable base camp in the heart of the bush. They are so popular they are often booked up a year in advance, though there is anecdotal evidence that foreign visitors find it easier to obtain a sought-after place on the trails. There are seven different trails. The **Bushman** and the **Wolhunter** leave from Berg-en-Dal and travel through granite hills, dense with San rock art and home to elephant and rhino. The **Metsi-Metsi** runs through undulating savanna and rocky gorges from its starting point at Skukuza. The **Napi** passes through riverine bush with granite hills and departs from Pretoriuskop, while the **Nyalaland** passes the Lanner Gorge in an area of fever tree and baobab forest of the northern park area, departing from Punda Maria. **Olifants** follows the perennial Olifants River at the foothills of the Lebombos from its start-point at Letaba, and the **Sweni** finds Africa on its wildest, starting at Satara. The cost of the bush trails is R1,075 per person per trail. Participants have to make their own way to the start-point and bring their own hats, sunscreen lotion and a powerful torch, and be prepared to walk up to 20 km (12.5 miles) a day. Reservations are through South African National Parks (see above).

HOW TO GET THERE

From KwaZulu-Natal and Johannesburg the most convenient entrance gates are on the southern boundaries of the park, accessible from the N4, Malelane and Crocodile Bridge, 57 km (35.6 miles) apart. Coming from the Blyde River Canyon area, head for the western gates of Orpen, Paul Kruger, and Pretoriuskop. The northern gates of Pafuri, Punda Maria, and Phalaborwa give access to a wilder land where the animals are not so prevalent, but there are plenty of birds and an increasing scatter of baobab trees. Entry at the gates is R10 per person and R20 per vehicle.

THE PRIVATE RESERVES

The private reserves are how most overseas visitors will experience the Kruger's wildlife, especially if they are on any sort of tour. The land on the edge of the park has been parceled off and licensed out to the highest bidders, who then build as many lodges and camps as they can get permission for. Some others rein back the size of their operation but then have to charge more per person to make their sums add up. Area boards police the planning procedure to stop the area becoming too built up but it is easy, driving through, to see the whole area as a suburban housing project on a truly grand scale.

This is not to belittle the wildlife experience. Complicated rules cover access rights and many lodges can offer a private, reserved experience.

And where the lodges do jostle close together you're more likely to enjoy the best sightings, as radio reports from other vehicles lead you to the headline sights and areas of greatest activity. They're not hotels that you can just drift into: they need to be booked up by telephone, often through offices in Johannesburg, and you won't need your car. They operate on a full-board principle, with open Landrovers driven by skilled guides, usually with trackers perched on jumpseats in front, taking game drives in the early morning and evening. Accommodation, whether in tents with the sounds of the wild filtering through the canvas or in concrete lodges offering air-conditioning and satellite television, is rarely less than luxurious.

There are too many lodges to give full details of every last one. Here I will concentrate on my personal favorites and those generally accepted to be leading the field, dividing them into areas. Best for game viewing is probably the Sabi Sands area, that takes a deep chunk out of the southern area of the Kruger National Park and which overflows with game. Further north and the Timbavati district offers very good game-viewing and explores a wilder, less crowded environment. Further north from here and the reserves which look hopeful on the map often turn out to be devoted to hunting, which is better described elsewhere, so this guide will follow with details of lodges concentrating on seeing game rather than shooting it. Glances to the west will take in those private reserves that don't actually border the Kruger but offer good bush experiences. Freed of the costs of prime park-border situations these are significantly less expensive and work much harder to make the most of the bush experience.

THE SABI SANDS

The Sabi Sands area is where the first private game lodges were established, and still offers some of the finest game-viewing experiences. It is also about the most crowded area, in terms of lodges per square kilometer. Leopard sightings, usually the most elusive of the Big Five animals, are most often achieved here, with some lodges managing a sighting five nights out of seven, and this is the place to be if seeing these magnificent animals is your primary goal. However the lodges here are expensive, and after a couple of nights you'll want to move on, either because you've ticked the Big Five off your list and have had enough of wildlife, or because your interest in wildlife extends beyond the headline mammals and you want to learn more.

The original pioneer of wildlife tourism was **Londolozi** ((011) 775 0000 FAX (011) 784 7667 E-MAIL information@ccafrica.com WEB SITE www .ccafrica.com, P/Bag X27, Benmore 2010, still the big cat among safari lodges but now rather bloated with a main lodge accommodating 20 guests and two satellite camps, Bush, with eight twin beds and Tree, with six, trying to blend total luxury with the bush experience. Prices reflect this, starting at US$1200. Singita is another, similarly priced, luxury alternative, which can be contacted at the same phone and address as above.

Just below the top of the market two rival lodges fight it out for second place, with competition famously fierce. **Mala Mala** ((011) 789 2677 FAX (011) 886 4382 WEB SITE www.mala mala.co.za, Box 2575, Randburg 2125, accommodates up to 50 guests in their main lodge in condi-

mweb.co.za WEB SITE www.leopardhills.com, Box 612, Hazyview 1242, from R3,990, set high above a spreading plain. The open-plan rooms here are especially spacious, with views from the huge beds as well as from the claw-footed bath. Rock Lodge at **Ulusaba** ((011) 465 4240 FAX (011) 465 6649 E-MAIL safaris@ulusaba.com, Box 239, Lonehill 2062, is also in an elevated position, while their other lodge, Safari Camp, is set in woodland overlooking a waterhole. Both are luxurious and rates are from R3,250 to, rather frighteningly, R15,600 for their top suite. Although it's not unusual to find family-run lodges, to find family-owned and run lodges is rare: the only one in the Sabi Sands is **Nottens** ((013) 735 5105 FAX (013)

tions of extreme luxury and charges them accordingly: R6,400 including meals and game drives. They also house a further 28 in Kirkman's Camp and 24 in Harry's Camp, where the same game experience in marginally less luxurious surroundings costs R3,500. Their biggest rivals are **Sabi Sabi** ((011) 483 3939 FAX (011) 483 3799 E-MAIL com@sabisabi.com WEB SITE www .sabisabi.com, Box 52665, Saxonwold 2132, just across the estate, who offer luxurious accommodation from R5,250 in three lodges, the best of which is the small eight-bed Selati Lodge. Sabi Sabi are also the people who run **Ranger Training** courses (see TRAIN TO BE A RANGER, page 11 in TOP SPOTS), which cost R4,500 for the three-night program.

Small is beautiful in the Kruger: the smallest lodge in the Sabi Sands area is **Leopard Hills** ((013) 737 6626 FAX (013) 737 6628 E-MAIL leopardh@

735 5970 WEB SITE www.nottens.com, Box 1242, Hazyview 1242, where the owners preside over a nightly dinner-party of no more than 14 people; rates are R1,900.

How to Get There

The Sabi Sands area is reached in four hours by road from Johannesburg or Pretoria via the N12 or N4 highways to Nelspruit and White River and then the R40 to Hazyview. At Hazyview turn right onto the R536 towards the Paul Kruger Gate. The private lodges are on the left after 34 km (21 miles) and are indicated by signs. There is a R30 entrance fee to the Sabi Sands. By air, the nearest airport is Skukuza and your lodge will arrange transfers.

Upmarket safari lodges and camps divide up the private off-Kruger reserves into exclusive concessions.

TIMBAVATI

Just to the north of the Sabi Sands area, Timbavati shares the prolific wildlife, even though the leopard are perhaps marginally less habituated.

Sleeping in a tent is one of the best ways to appreciate the sounds of the bush. Although some camps have tent roofs, there are not that many actual tented camps in the area. One is **Honeyguide** ((011) 341 0282 FAX (011) 341 0281, 10 Bompas Road, Dunkeld West, Box 781959, Sandton 2146, who are inexpensive at R1,800 and also offer a remote and rustic Outpost Camp for R1,000 per night. The emphasis is on the natural experience, with no electricity, and they are in the Manyeleti area between Timbavati and Sabi Sands so the tracks are less crowded with other vehicles. Luxury tents are available at **Tanda Tula** ((021) 794 6500 FAX (021) 794 7605 E-MAIL cuisine @iafrica.com, Box 32, Constantia 7848. This is the sister-establishment of Constantia Uitsig near Cape Town so cuisine is taken especially seriously at this friendly camp. The rates start at R3,000. **Ngala** ((011) 775 0000 FAX (011) 784 7667 E-MAIL information@ccafrica.com WEB SITE www.ccafrica .com, P/Bag X27, Benmore 2010, is another luxury alternative, with a good restaurant but the chalets are a little overshadowed by scrubby trees, at US$900 per night. If these prices are giving you palpitations there is a lower-priced alternative. **Umlani** ((012) 329 3765 FAX (012) 329 6441 E-MAIL umlani@mweb.co.za WEB SITE www.umlani.co.za, Box 26350, Arcadia 0007, has winter specials at R1,500 but its general rates of R2,300 are well below most of its neighbors. It drags rates down by being relatively rustic, unfenced, and using hurricane lamps for lighting rather than electricity — for me, all these things add to the experience. There are just eight reed and thatch chalets, so it's also a relatively small and intimate place. Yet a lower-priced alternative is just nearby, though not actually bordering the Kruger. **Kapama Private Game Reserve** ((012) 804 4840 FAX (012) 804 4842 E-MAIL gentour@iafrica.com WEB SITE www.kapama.co.za, Box 912-031, Silverton 0127, R2,000, might not be quite as luxurious as its more expensive neighbors and leopard sightings are relatively rare, but thanks to being fenced off from the park it is relatively cheaper for the standards of accommodation and guiding. One thing you will find here is cheetah: funds from here go into a cheetah breeding program and a visit is included in your rate.

How to Get There

By road the Timbavati area is five hours from Johannesburg. Take the N4 and turn off at Belfast and drive through Dullstroom, Origstad, Lydenburg and on to Hoedspruit. In Hoedspruit

turn right onto the R40 for eight kilometers (five miles) and turn left at the Timbavati signpost. An entry charge of R30 is payable and the lodges are signposted. By air fly SA Express to Eastgate Airport in Hoedspruit; your camp will arrange transfers. By rail, the Blue Train (see RIDE RESTORED RAILWAYS, page 29 in TOP SPOTS) travels from Pretoria to Hoedspruit. It stops in the middle of nowhere but once again, your lodge will arrange transfers.

THE NORTH AND THE OFF-KRUGER RESERVES

To the north of Timbavati the land bordering the Kruger tends to be given over to private reserves where hunting is the main activity. Whether this is a vital part of conservation or outdated bloodsport is open to endless debate that I won't go into here. However there are some private lodges es-

tablished to the west of the Kruger that deserve a mention. **Garonga** ((011) 804 7595 FAX (011) 802 6503, Makalali Game Reserve, Box 403, Gallo Manor 2052, is set on a far leg of the Makalali Reserve west of the Kruger. This is a lodge that sets new standards in almost every area of its operation. The cuisine is superb, the guiding sensitive and involving, and accommodation is in six half-tent, half chalet dwellings with organic, flowing shapes, and wooden decks overlooking a perennial riverbed where you often see game including lion. Although technically the other lodges in Makalali do have traversing rights over Garonga's part of the reserve, in practice it is too far and you don't see any other vehicles. I don't often go overboard about a lodge but in this case must make an exception. In the low-season rates are R1,900 for two sharing, rising to a peak of R2,950, and they will arrange transportation from Hoedspruit Airport.

Further to the north **Ndazalama Game Reserve** ((015) 307 3065 FAX (015) 307 3066 E-MAIL ndzalama @pixie.co.za, Box 843, Letsitele 0885, is an unusual and enterprising lodge that offers a host of different bush activities. Among these are their bushcraft and survival training courses, in which groups of clients are sent out to fend for themselves in the bush for a period of days. To avoid too high a fatality rate they are accompanied by a ranger who will impart the rudiments of survival, including making fire, traps, useful plants and invertebrates and navigation without instruments. Their five-night survival program costs R2,250. They also operate a lodge (R1,800 per night) and two bush camps (R1,100 per night) and will arrange transportation from Phalaborwa, Hoedspruit, and Tzaneen.

A young lion takes a rest in the middle of a track carved out by four-wheel-drive vehicles.

The Surf Coast

TELL IT TO
THE
GENERATION
FOLLOWING

CENTERED ON THE GATEWAY CITY OF DURBAN, South Africa's Indian Ocean coast is lined by sandy beaches and dramatic headlands, washed by warm waters rolling inshore in surfable breaking waves. For visitors from Europe's cooler climates the year-round warmth and endless days of sun make this part of South Africa a classic vacation destination.

Friendlier than Cape Town and less driven than Johannesburg, Durban is at the heart of a relaxed surf culture where the beach is part of everyday life. With a population of four million growing fast its popularity is shared by countless South Africans. The beaches of the city center are within walking distance of the waterfront hotels, while unspoiled sandy bays line the coast to the north. Head south and a dense ribbon of timeshare developments aimed at the domestic market can offer plenty of entertainment for children but has fewer charms for adults.

Beyond Port Edward there is a dramatic change, as you cross into a former homeland now included in the Eastern Cape Province. Pigs and donkeys appear on the roads, and potholes appear in the tarmac. Now you're in the "Wild Coast," a vibrant region of sheer cliffs and small sheltered bays, with remote villages and a scattering of small, character hotels.

DURBAN

The fastest-growing city in South Africa, Durban has a population of four million, rising rapidly. It is a vibrant, cosmopolitan community that started life as Port Natal, a mangrove-filled lagoon now transformed into South Africa's largest and busiest seaport. First discovered by Vasco da Gama on Christmas day, 1497, and named Port Natal after the Portuguese for Christmas, no permanent landing was made until 1823 when British settlers established a trading outpost, dealing in ivory with the local tribes. Fifteen years later the Voortrekkers arrived and founded Pietermaritzburg, and the Zulus, recognizing correctly what appeared to be a trend of occupation, reacted with violence. After a number of skirmishes and massacres Durban was abandoned, and then resettled by the Boers. For a while Voortrekker and British settlers fought over the site, and in May 1843 Natal was incorporated into the Cape Colony, and Durban started to develop. Sugar was the "Green Gold" that gave the city its wealth, but the Zulus, already irritated by the number of white settlers, were certainly not about to cut cane for their rulers. In 1860 the first Indians were brought in to work in the sugar plantations, indentured for five years, spearheading a wave of immigration that would change the face of the city and indeed the country. At the close of their contracts many opted to stay, establishing the largest Indian community in South Africa.

Of the country's one million Indians, 85% live in the Durban area, bringing their distinctive temples and tastes to this varied city.

The only thing to tarnish Durban's sun-soaked image is crime. The city is not as bad as Johannesburg for street muggings and car-jackings but it is running second. Street boys patrol the city's beaches and are quick to spot any visitor with expensive jewelry. Walking around after dark is not recommended, especially in the city center or along Point Road. Lush trees and poor street-lighting make even smarter suburbs risky for pedestrians, and leaving anything — even a car radio — visible in a parked car frequently results in a broken window and a new 12-volt township trannie.

GENERAL INFORMATION

Durban's townships and suburbs spread over the inland hills but the city center is bounded firmly by the sea and port. Along the "Golden mile" of the sun-soaked beachfront a once-busy highway has been slowed to strolling pace by a number of traffic-calming measures and is lined by a continuous rank of highrise hotels, many with restaurants in the lower levels. All look resolutely out to sea. Behind these monoliths the city center is in a state of some decay, as the large businesses have moved out of town and fast-food outlets, small shops and cheap apartments have filled their often impressive buildings. Like many South African city centers, walking around

LEFT: Durban City Hall, built in the days of the colony of Natal. ABOVE: Imported Indian workers spice up the cuisine of KwaZulu-Natal.

this area is not recommended and is certainly unsafe at night.

The main city roads of West Street and Smith Street run inland, ending two and a half kilometers (one and a half miles) later at the main Indian business quarter. The smartest suburbs spread along leafy tree-lined streets that lattice the ridge running parallel with the coast, in the Berea district. If the beachfront evokes Miami, this ridge is very much San Francisco, with steep streets and abrupt level changes, dotted with many of the city's best restaurants and shops. The port is south of the Golden mile, overlooked by the twin promontories of the Bluff, protected as a nature reserve by a heavy military presence, and the Point. Un-

like Cape Town, the harbor has only scattered development, and much of the waterfront is used as a working port. Various ambitious plans to yuppify the area have so far come to nothing. Should you wish to do so, asking about their waterfront is a good way to put Durbanites off-balance, as they are all frustrated and rather ashamed that nothing ever seems to get done.

Durban has a sophisticated and helpful visitors information service, which is unfortunately renamed, disbanded, and even moved every so often. It is currently run by Tourism KwaZulu-Natal and can be found in the old redbrick railway station at the junction of Commercial and Pine Streets and is open from 8 AM to 4:30 PM weekdays and on weekends from 9 AM to 2 PM. It is called **Tourist Junction** ((031) 304 4934 FAX (031) 304 6196 E-MAIL funinsun@iafrica.com WEB SITE www.durban.org.za, Station Building, 160 Pine Street,

Durban 4001. There is also an office at Durban International Airport in the Domestic Arrivals Hall ((031) 408 1000 FAX (031) 469 3583 which is open from 8 AM to 5 PM weekdays and 9 AM to 2 PM weekends, and another on the beachfront in the Ocean Sports Center, Lower Marine Parade, open from 8 AM to 4:30 PM weekdays and 9 AM to 2 PM weekends. These can offer access to a number of professional bodies, help with tickets for rail, sea and air travel, the booking of tailor-made tours, online reservations for National and Natal Park Board Resorts as well as helping with your accommodation needs.

The best taxi service in town is **Aussie's Taxis** ((031) 309 7888, while also good are **Bunnie Cabs** ((031) 332 2914, **Zippy's** ((031) 202 7067 and **Eagle** ((031) 332 2914.

For private medical attention there are two main clinics within the city which offer 24-hour emergency care and will send out ambulances. **St. Augustine's** ((031) 201 1221 and **Entabeni** ((031) 261 1344. The city's **Emergency Response** ((031) 361 0000 is useful in the event of any other emergency.

WHAT TO SEE AND DO

The tourist board's slogan for Durban is "the city where the fun never sets," and there is plenty to do for all ages and interests. Although the city's favorite activities are often beach and sun-based, there are many sites of historical interest, art events, and areas of great natural beauty.

However, read the average brochure and you'd be forgiven for thinking that the only thing to do in Durban is to take a rickshaw up and down the beachfront. True, the rickshaws are an enduring feature, decorated lavishly with beads and strips of metal and plastic, drawn by locals dressed as tribal chiefs or tramps. But every year the rickshaws seem to travel less fast, less far, and there is so much to do in this cosmopolitan city that taking a rickshaw seems almost to parody its exotic appeal. There are a number of historical features, including the **Vasco da Gama Clock** on Point Road, **Francis Farewell Gardens** with more monuments than any other square in the country, and statues of **John Ross** on the Victoria Embankment and, on the same road at the junction with Gardiner Street, **Dick King**. All these characters played their parts in the development of KwaZulu-Natal.

There are buildings too: **Durban City Hall**, built after the style of the City Hall in Belfast, Northern Ireland. The **Old Station House**, that now houses Tourist Junction, was originally designed for Toronto. The plans were mixed in the post and so it is the only building in South Africa built to withstand five meters (16 ft) of snow. (The Toronto Railway station collapsed in the first bad winter.)

There are also a number of good museums. Perhaps characteristic is the **Time Warp Surfing Museum** in the Ocean Sports Center, 170 Lower Marine Parade, with a collection of boards from the 1930s on, open from Tuesday to Sunday 10 AM to 5 PM. The **Kwa Muhle Museum** ((031) 300 6313, 132 Ordnance Road, powerfully records the history of apartheid; it is small, concise and informative. The **Port Natal Maritime Museum** ((031) 300 6234, Bayend, Aliwal Street, is a vivid reminder of Durban's seafaring tradition, and includes a number of carefully restored boats from the port's working past. For antiques and Africana, the **Killie Campbell Museum** ((031) 253 283, 220 Marriott Road, is one of the best, with

galleries and retail shops, a restaurant as well as a bar overlooking the port. The center also houses a 300-seater cinema and the Zanzi Bar which often has performances by some leading African bands.

There's even more to do where the attraction is just part of the activity. Many of the city's finest attractions are designed to be used, not just visited. Therefore although the **Botanical Gardens** can be visited through the week, they are perhaps best appreciated during the Sunday afternoon sundowner concerts, **Music by the Lake**, where classical music is performed by the city's Natal Philharmonic Orchestra ((031) 369 9404) or one of many professional choirs; performances are advertised on flyers stuck to half the lampposts

a collection of beads, weapons and more than 250 paintings.

There are also a number of art galleries. The **African Art Center** ((031) 304 7915, First Floor, Old Station Building, 160 Pine House, is open from 8:30 AM to 5 PM Monday to Friday and 9 AM to 2 PM Saturdays and promotes and sells original works of art and sculpture from the Zulu and Xhosa traditions. The city's main gallery is the **Durban Art Gallery** ((031) 300 6238, Second Floor, Smith Street, is open from Monday to Saturday from 8:30 AM to 4 PM and Sundays 11 AM to 4 PM. On Sundays a more relaxed art show takes place on the lawns in front of the **Museum of Natural History** on Marine Parade, North Beach, from 9 AM to 4 PM. Perhaps the best of the community art centers is the nonprofit making **Bat Center** ((031) 332 0468, 45 Maritime Place, Small Craft Harbor, Esplanade, which houses a number of art and dance studios,

in the city's smarter areas. Other live cultural offerings can be seen at the **Playhouse Company** ((031) 369 9555 FAX (031) 306 2166, 231 Smith Street, where five theaters are housed behind two fine old colonial façades. Anything from cabaret to opera can be seen here and performances are invariably of a high standard. To listen to African music, make a date on the steps of city hall for Wednesday lunchtime: big names play here as part of a state-funded initiative. During university term times, Wednesday is also the day for evening jazz performances at the university between 5 PM to 6 PM.

Instead of just looking at the port, take a cruise across the sheltered waters. Operators include **Boat Cruises** ((031) 305 4222, whose boat the *Sarie*

OPPOSITE: This Hindu Temple was built by the city's immigrants from India. ABOVE: Rooibos hostel and restaurant in Bat Center.

Marais departs from its mooring near Dick King's statue on harbor cruises at 11 AM and ocean cruises at 3 PM, or the working **Durban Ferry Service** ((031) 304 6091, which ferries workers out to service the ships and wharves.

There are a number of crocodile farms. On the south coast there is **Scottburgh** ((039) 967 1103, on the north coast there's **Umhlanga and Ballito** ((032) 238 8451 or (082) 920 0730, and inland there is **Assagay** ((031) 777 1000. There's a **Snake Park** ((031) 337 6456 FAX (031) 337 3125, Snell Parade, Marine Parade, with daily demonstrations and talks.

Back to the water for the **Sharks Board** ((031) 561 1001 FAX (031) 561 3691, Umhlanga Rocks,

where fascinating talks on sharks are followed by a dissection of the most recent specimen to become entangled in the nets to see who it ate last. Talks take place on Tuesdays, Wednesdays and Thursdays at 9 AM and 2 PM, with another at 2 PM on Sundays. There's also the possibility of going out to watch the boats as they clean up the shark nets. Boat departures leave Tuesday, Wednesday, Thursday at 6:15 AM from the Point Yacht Club Slipway. Groups of four to 10 can fit into the little yellow mini-cat that hurtles out over the waves to see what has been caught overnight; you have to book (and pay) ahead. Often the nets are bare but it's a good way to see in the dawn and get a jump-start on your day. The trip lasts two hours and costs R100; contact Debbie at the Sharks Board for further details. Or see the ocean's greatest fish live at the outstanding aquariums of **Sea World** ((031) 337 3536, 2 West Street, Lower Marine Parade,

where dolphin, seal and penguin shows take place throughout the day.

Meanwhile there are also plenty of parks and gardens, with the **Japanese Gardens** ((031) 563 1333, Tinsley Drive, Durban North, offering a haven of fine delicacy amidst the lush tropical growth. There are also a number of nature reserves that house some of Africa's exotic animals just a few kilometers from the city center. For example, the **Kenneth Stainbank Nature Reserve**, just 14 km (8.75 miles) from the center in the suburb of Yellow Wood Park has duiker, zebra and bushbaby, with 12 km (7.5 miles) of marked trails for a rural wander. Contact Tourist Junction for further details.

BEACHES

From Port Edward in the south to Kosi Bay in the north, KwaZulu-Natal boasts a string of golden beaches, with Durban at its heart. Even in the winter ocean temperatures rarely fall below 18°C (64°F). Ever since shark nets were introduced in 1952 the beaches have been some of the safest in the country. However there can be rip tides, so be sure to bathe in recognized areas, where lifeguards keep an eye on swimmers. These can be spotted by flags in the sand and other bathers, with a notice-board to keep swimmers up-to-date on the local water conditions.

Durban's "Golden mile" is actually six kilometers (three and three-quarter miles) long, and starts in the north with **Blue Lagoon**, popular for its fishing from the pier. Next is **Battery Beach**, uncrowded and known for some serious sunbathers. Head down to **Laguna Beach**, favorite with sports enthusiasts and always on the go with jogging, kite-flying, and jet-skis. North, **Dairy** and **Wedge Beaches** are off the city center, with **Oasis** and **Dune Beaches** the most secluded and unspoiled, ideal for peace and quiet while still close to the city's attractions. **Snake Park Beach** and the **Bay of Plenty** are preferred by surfers, with some of the best waves in the world for a city beach. Nearby attractions are also on hand for children. **South Beach**, **Addington Beach** and **Vetch's Beach** allow dogs, and are also popular for windsurfing, scuba diving, power-boating and parasailing, with the Little Top for children's entertainment during vacation seasons. Last but not least, **Tekweni** is a perfect vacation picnic spot, with grassy areas, paddling pools, and waterslides for children. It is less crowded and calmer than the central beaches and has plenty of parking.

The beaches also extend well beyond Durban city limits. To the south, a series of resorts make up the **Hibiscus Coast** (see THE HIBISCUS COAST, page 218), which includes nearly 50 estuaries and reefs, the most famous of which is Aliwal Shoal. In between are countless lagoons and streams and safe tidal pools. Amanzimtoti is 23 km (14.4 miles) south of Durban, with seven kilometers (nearly four and a half miles) of sand, divided into Pipeline and Inyoni Rocks Beaches, with miniature golf, freshwater pools, and picnic and barbecue facilities. Head on south to Isipingo Beach and Winklespruit, for family caravanning and picnics. To the north of the city is the **Sugar Coast**, starting with Umhlanga Rocks, an upmarket resort with shopping malls patrolled by gold-jangling sunwrinkled Transkei beauties and with small beaches interspersed with rocky areas. At its heart is the **Oyster Box Hotel** (see NORTH COAST BEACHES, page 217), a classic blue-rinse period piece, ideal for a sundowner at least. Further north to Ballito,

45 km (28 miles) from Durban, marks the start of a series of swimming and fishing spots, which just keep getting better all the way to the Tugela River.

SPORTS AND OUTDOOR ACTIVITIES

There are outstanding facilities here for all levels and interests. At water level, there is **canoeing**, with half a dozen clubs specializing in whitewater, flatwater, and long-distance canoeing. **Surfing** is the big event on the Indian Ocean rollers: for information call into the **Ocean Sports Center** ((031) 332 2595 on the waterfront, possibly after calling in for a surfing and weather report at ((031) 408 1442. Classic and barefoot **waterskiing** takes place at Hazelmere Dam, 35 km (22 miles) north of Durban; contact Tourist Junction for further details.

Golfers are spoiled with a huge choice of courses, with perhaps the best being Selborne and San Lameer, but an interesting alternative is the city-center Royal Durban Golf Course, set in the middle of Greyville Racetrack. Contact the **KwaZulu-Natal Golf Union** ((031) 202 7636 for further details. **Horseracing** takes place at least twice a week in the city's two horse-racing courses, at Greyville, in the city, and Clairwood Park, 11 km (just under seven miles) south of the city.

Deep-sea fishing is popular, with rental boats available from the **Isle of Capri** ((031) 337 7751 and the **SA Charter Boats Association** ((031) 301 1115. Rock and surf angling is a huge sport in Durban, with advice and assistance available from the **Natal Coast Angling Union** ((031) 208 1617 or the **Association of Natal and North Coast Anglers** ((031) 51 1333.

Take a hike with one of two associations who regularly organize trips to the Drakensbergs and other reserves, **Mountain Backpackers Club** ((031) 266 3970 and the **Durban Ramblers Hiking Club** ((031) 764 4721.

SHOPPING

With the weak rand, Durban is a shopper's paradise. For traditional crafts you'll find a selection on display along the pavements that line the waterfront in front of the highrise hotels of Marine Parade. Neither price nor choice is likely to be exceptional here. Better head out to the Bat Center or the African Arts Center (see above) for the latest African arts and crafts, or visit the shop attached to the **Natal Society of Arts** ((031) 202 3686 FAX (031) 202 3744, 166/174 Bulwer Road, Glenwood, which has a good selection at reasonable prices. For many visitors the best shopping experience is at the Indian Market at **Victoria Street Market** ((031) 306 4021, housed in a modern building that has stifled some of the old, informal atmosphere but still houses an exotic selection of goods from around the world. Better prices on the quieter and less commercialized first floor, while the ground floor is notable for the stalls and shops selling traditional witchdoctor remedies culled from the surrounding countryside to earnest, beaded traditional healers still practicing their craft in the heart of this essentially modern city.

If the new market is too sanitized, head across raised walkways passing under the toll-road flyover, where more informal traders spread their wares. For antiques, head up to the smart suburb of Berea, and in particular **Florida Road**, where a selection of small and exclusive shops are crammed with fine goods old and new at surprisingly low prices. My favorite is **Colonial Trading** on Clarence Road, or the **Heritage Market** on the

OPPOSITE: The Eastern influence in the Hari Krishna Temple of Understanding. ABOVE: Kids warm up between dips on Marine Parade.

Old Main Road in Hillcrest, where 160 specialty shops sell handmade crafts and antiques in a setting of gazebos, rose gardens and shady walkways.

Increasingly, South Africans prefer to shop in malls. Although fashions change, with the crowds following the newest, currently the smartest in the city is **Musgrave Center** on Musgrave Road, where you'll find the full range of South Africa's midrange designer outlets, bookshops, post offices and supermarkets. Some South Africans claim they just come to the mall for the butternut soup served at **Circus Circus** but the truth is they're there to see and be seen. One of the biggest shopping centers in the country is the **Pavilion** on the N3 highway to Westville, with glazed domes forming a

granted a Royal Appointment in 1860, it now needs some updating but is still hanging on to its five stars. Of its five restaurants the Royal Grill is the one that still wins awards. The **Hilton** ((031) 336 8100 FAX (031) 336 8200, 12–14 Walnut Road, R950 is another top-of-the-range alternative.

Any number of smart new hotels line the city's oceanfront and more stretch endlessly up and down the coast. All provide fairly good value and offer all the air-conditioned en-suite comforts you'd expect from a recently-built resort hotel in the developed world. As such they are rather dull and certainly aren't all about to be listed here. A sample selection includes the **Edward Hotel** ((031) 337 3681 FAX (031) 332 1692, R760 to R960

local landmark. Finally, there's the **Workshop** on the corner of Commercial Road and Aliwal Street, housed in an old railway workshop, with 120 shops and ersatz Victorian barrow stalls on the ground floor.

WHERE TO STAY

As South Africa's prime vacation destination, Durban is long used to entertaining floods of visitors, and there is a good range of quality and mid-range accommodation as well as some good backpacker options.

Perhaps the best — certainly in terms of star ratings — of the city-center hotels is the **Royal Hotel** ((031) 304 0331 FAX (031) 304 5055 E-MAIL theroyal@iafrica.com WEB SITE www.theroyal .co.za, R595, which is sited opposite City Hall and overlooking town gardens and harbor. First

depending on view, well run by Movenpick and located close to the city center and the beach, and the next door **Holiday Inn Marine Parade** ((031) 337 3341 FAX (031) 332 9885, Marine Parade, R438, where all rooms have a sea view. Further north but still on Marine Parade is **Beach Hotel** ((031) 337 5511 FAX (031) 337 5409, 107 Marine Parade, providing good value at R258.

Off the central drag of Marine Parade there are some good options that give more of a flavor of the city. Guest houses include **Ridgeview Lodge** ((031) 202 9777 FAX (031) 201 5587 E-MAIL ridgeview@ inds.co.za WEB SITE www.inds.co.za/ridgeview/, 17 Loudon Road off South Ridge Road, Berea, R440, set in the smartest residential location with distant views over the city and sea. **Essenwood House** (/FAX (031) 207 4547 E-MAIL paddyc@iafrica.com WEB SITE www.wheretostay.co.za/find/essenwood .htm, 630 Essenwood Road, is a luxurious converted

Edwardian plantation manor-house, also overlooking the city, with rooms costing R360.

Bed-and-breakfast establishments are an economical alternative that can give a good insight into the community: contact Durban Tourism's **book-a-bed-ahead (** (031) 304 4934 for further listings. Durban is also lucky to have a **self-catering network (** (083) 626 8470 which will find you accommodation in a private house. Backpackers have less choice in Durban but it is still possible to stay here cheaply. The best alternative is near the fashionable and lively Florida Road in a top residential area, where **Tekweni Backpackers (** (031) 303 1433 FAX (031) 303 4369, 169 Ninth Avenue, Morningside, offers comfortable accommodation, swimming pool and bar with double rooms costing just R95 per night. Nearer to the sea is the **Durban Beach Youth Hostel (** (031) 332 4945 FAX (031) 368 1720, 19 Smith Street, where the sea is just a five-minute walk away even carrying two surfboards. It won't break the bank either: double rooms cost R90 for nonmembers, R70 for members. For backpackers, Durban offers an especially active party scene second only to Cape Town.

WHERE TO EAT

Durban's cuisine, heated by the wave of Indian immigration and stirred by the tropical breeze from the Indian Ocean, is among the finest you'll find anywhere in the continent. Perhaps unsurprisingly, the famous dishes are of Indian descent. **Bunny Chow**, loaves of bread emptied and filled with curry, are a local delicacy. How this tastes depends very much on who's been controlling the spices. Local recommendation is the cheap and cheerful **Sunrise Café** by Parklands Hospital on the junction of Ridge Road and Sydenham Road, with similar offerings at **Patels** in Grey Street and a more refined versions available in the restored plantation setting of the **Congella Hotel (** (031) 205 1082, 497 Sydney Road, Umbilo. The idea of putting curry into bread won't appeal to everyone. If you prefer a more conventional Indian taste try *breyani*, a blend of curry, cloves, ginger and rice soaked overnight in yogurt. To satisfy robust Afrikaner appetites on the move a distinctive solution has been developed as Durban's answer to convenience foods: curry and sometimes chips rolled into a flat *roti* to form the shape of a torpedo and with much the same effect when eaten. Also popular are *patthas*, madumbi leaves spread with a batter of mealie meal, yogurt and spices, rolled and fried. The Grey Street area has a good range of Indian restaurants, including **Manjiras** at 56 Cathedral Road, while the classiest Indian Restaurant in the city is **Gulzar (** (031) 309 4017, 69 Stamford Hill Road, Morningside.

There's more to Durban than Indian food, and the logical specialty, unsurprisingly, is fish. Fresh from the Indian Ocean prawns, crayfish and all types of linefish are served in a number of specialty restaurants. The setting is important, of course. The **New Café Fish (** (031) 301 3102, 31 Yacht Mole, Victoria Embankment, is built on stilts overlooking the harbor. Even better is the small development at King's Battery at the end of Point Road: the **Famous Fish Company (** (031) 368 1060, King's Battery, North Pier, end of Point Road, is at the mouth of the harbor: ships entering port pass meters away from your table to form an atmospheric backdrop to any meal. If you're not feeling fishy, next door is a Brazilian restaurant and if you're not even hungry there's a lively bar with an open ship-viewing deck called **Thirsty's**,

one of Durban's best-known nightspots, which also serves light snacks.

Italian food is well represented in Durban. Best known is the **Roma Revolving Restaurant (** (031) 332 6707, John Ross House, Victoria Embankment, which has a fine reputation for views but less for the cuisine and even less for decor. A smart but surprisingly affordable city-center option is **La Dolce Vita (** (031) 301 8161, Durban Parade, hidden away on the top floor of the Durban Club by the Royal Hotel. Reservations are essential but you don't need to be a member; there's secure parking and the setting and service is superb. For a more casual Italian atmosphere **Guisseppi Trattoria (** (031) 337 0246, Mangrove Beach Center, Somtseu Road, is also good.

OPPOSITE: Overlooked by Durban's highrise oceanview hotels, Waterworld is rich-child friendly. ABOVE: Life's very different for these shanty kids.

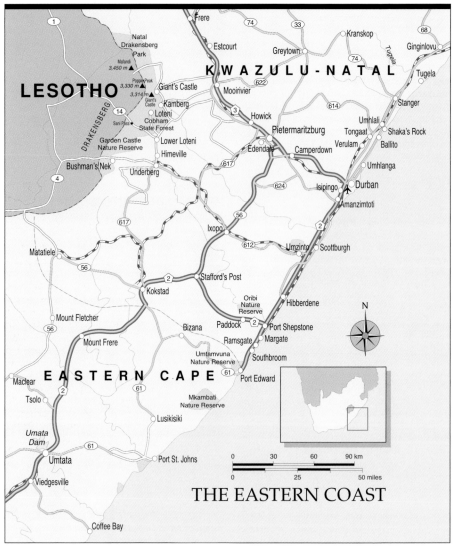

THE EASTERN COAST

NIGHTLIFE

Durban's reputation as a party town is backed by plenty of bars and clubs. Visitors soon get known in a friendly and welcoming atmosphere but hard drinking is the rule so leave some time to work out on the beach or just lie down in a darkened room to recover. This is also another good reason to travel by taxi. Collect a card so you can dial your driver to pick you up as there aren't usually any waiting outside bars or restaurants: they have to be called. As with most South African cities walking after dark is not advisable.

The best bar is possibly **Thirsty's**, King's Battery at the end of Point Road, thanks to its setting right by the narrow entrance to the harbor,

with open decks to enjoy the view. The atmosphere here can heat up quickly and often there's dancing as early as nine. Threats to widen the harbor entrance — demolishing the pub — have so far come to nothing. On the way out, consider a drink at the **Victoria Bar**, marooned in an increasingly dodgy part of Point Road, where the local specialty is the Portuguese drink of *catembe*, cold red wine mixed with cola. It tastes revolting but the locals like it.

Another good bar is **Billy the Bums** on Windermere Road, in a rebuilt mansion with gingerbread ironwork and wide verandas. A range of cocktails are served in a lively atmosphere. The **Horse with No Name** is on Mitchell Crescent, set by the side of Greyville racetrack, especially good when night racing is on and horses thunder past in the floodlights; popular on Tuesday and Friday nights. Alternatively **Legends Café** ((031) 201 0733, shop 221, Musgrave Center, Musgrave Road, is an upmarket bar that stays open until 3 AM, as does the **Bean Bag Bohemia** ((031) 309 6019, 18 Windermere Road, Greyville, known as BBB, a restaurant by day and a lively bar by night, fashionable and popular. Younger drinkers will head down to Marine Parade and **Joe Kools**, a music bar with hot-weather dress and west-coast sounds. The late bars will tend to keep customers by feeding them shots: sharp short schnapps drunk quickly and often. A good venue for this is the small but friendly **Roxy's** ((031) 309 1837, 42 Marriott Road, Greyville, a coffeeshop that doesn't serve much coffee and stays open at least until 4 AM.

Live music tends to be hard to find, not helped by local papers listings almost as single-mindedly as they ignore news. The Sunday papers are more useful than the weekday issues. The Bat Center (see above) is a regular standby, especially on Friday nights, and the Playhouse Company also puts on some performances. If you're lucky enough to be in Durban on a Saturday night, don't miss the all-night competitions of *Isiscatumya* music, a Zulu specialty made world-famous by the Ladysmith Black Mambaza Band. With a frontman leading the tune between eight and 16 singers perform haunting backing vocals in a brilliant expression of African culture. For the last 90 years these choirs have been in constant competition, and everything is up to be judged: fashion, beauty, dancing and, last but not least, singing. These competitions are staged every Saturday night at the Beatrice Street hostel, off Grey Street in the heart of town; they start about 10 PM — just follow the crowds.

On any day of the week a visit to a *shebeen* is an adventure all of itself, only advisable in the company of a professional tour operator. Tourist Junction will be able to suggest someone appropriate. Well-known and established *shebeens* include **All in One**, **Bafuthi's Tavern**, and **Nomalady's Tavern**.

How to Get There

Most visitors to Durban arrive by air at Durban International Airport, 14 km (just under nine miles) south of the city center. Bus services leave every hour from outside the Domestic Terminal. There is a bank and an ATM machine for drawing money on a credit card and most major car-rental companies are represented. Travelers using the train will arrive at the New Durban Station, two kilometers (just over a mile) north of City Hall, where you'll find metered taxis for the short hop into town. Tickets out can be booked either from Tourist Junction (see GENERAL INFORMATION, above) or

direct from **Spoornet** ((031) 361 7609. There are daily services to Durban and weekly runs all the way to Cape Town on the Trans-Oranje: sleepers are available and you won't find many other tourists but if you have two nights to spare it's a great and economical way to travel; first-class tickets are R4,000.

There are a number of travel agencies downtown but none to be especially recommended. The best of them is **Great Escape** ((031) 202 4027 FAX (031) 201 8152 E-MAIL jeanieb@galileosa.co.za, Musgrave Center, Berea, Durban, who are licensed to book student fare flights as well as all other travel services. Intercity Buses arrive at the Motorcoach Terminal attached to the station. By car, Durban is six hours from Johannesburg along a toll highway.

NORTH COAST BEACHES

The north coast beaches above Durban are pleasant and quiet, with miles of banana groves and fields of sugarcane backing uncrowded beaches, gently developed for domestic tourism with little bubbles of upmarket developments. There are two roads up. The coast highway sweeps along the ocean's shore, but the old inner road (the R102) is actually more interesting, passing villages and towns missed by the N2 that owe their existence to agricultural settlement rather than sun-'n'-sand tourism. The first town, 14 km (just under nine miles) north, is **Umhlanga**, home to the Sharks Board, several luxury timeshare and resort developments as well as a wonderful hotel, the **Oyster Box** ((031) 561 2233 FAX (031) 561 4072, a colonial gem of pink wicker and faded antiques, set high over the ocean with the beach a short walk away and with rooms from R420. At the very least it is worth having a beer by the pool while looking down over the sea as blue-rinsed old ladies, faces plastered with makeup, smile nervously and totter from table to sofa.

The road heads north to **Ballito**, 60 km (37.5 miles) north of Durban, a timeshare resort that wouldn't be out of place in Europe's Costas. For tourist information, contact the **Dolphin Coast Publicity Association** ((032) 946 1997, near the BP station by the exit off the N2. Nearby is **Shaka's Rock**, where, it is said, the Zulu King Shaka told cowardly warriors to jump in the sea. Now immersion is more pleasant at **Zimbali Lodge** ((032) 538 1007 FAX (032) 538 1019 E-MAIL kgarratt@sunint.co.za WEB SITE www.suninternational.com, Umhlali, an exclusive lodge just off the M4 charging R1,195 for a double room including breakfast and specializing in a full range of spa and massage treatments.

From here the N2 stays on the coast while the R102 continues through the sugarcane cities of Verulam and Tongaat, settled by early Indian indentured laborers, before **Stanger**, once Shaka's royal kraal and scene of his murder by half-brother Dingane. Stanger is not much considered by the white population but is still a highly significant spiritual base for Zulus, and many Zulu warriors treat it as a place of pilgrimage. A monument to Shaka is in the Victorian garden in the center of town, and a nearby stone is grooved, allegedly by Shaka's sharpening his *assegai* (short Zulu stabbing spear). Far from the Zulu culture is the town's best-known hotel, the **Prince's Grant** ((032) 482 0005 FAX (032) 482 0040 E-MAIL pglodge@saol.com, R930 including breakfast, set in rolling acres with miles of secluded beach, indigenous forest, and sports facilities including a championship golf course.

THE HIBISCUS COAST

For the first 38 kilometers (24 miles) the shore south of Durban, known as the Strelitzia Coast, is quite heavily developed, designed mainly for South Africans fleeing the obvious resorts and ending up with the slightly less obvious. First is **Amanzimtoti**, a name the developers insist came from a complimentary remark Zulu King Shaka made on tasting the river water. Possibly. He probably wouldn't recognize it now. Behind the beach there is a lagoon swarming with canoes and pedaloes, there's a Funland amusement arcade, a main road and factories making chemicals and explosives. Beaches famous for their surf string down the coast in a more-or-less unbroken chain with vacation homes and timeshare flats eagerly watching over the ocean until an intensive burst of development at the busy resort town of Scottburgh. It is one of the oldest of the cities along the coast and does have a certain charm. However, apart from swimming on the netted beach, the most popular tours are of the local rayon factory which seems positively surreal considering that just offshore is the wonderful **Aliwal Shoal**, offering world-class wreck and fish-watching dives even though the water is too cool for much coral. The smartest place to stay is the **Cutty Sark Protea** ((039) 976 1230 FAX (039) 976 2197, Old Main Road, Scottburgh, R460 per double, including breakfast, but there are cheaper alternatives if you self-cater or camp at the nearby Scottburgh Caravan Park.

From here the marketing industry has decided to sell the beaches as the **Hibiscus Coast**. They intend to conjure an image of lush villas festooned with flowers, but all too often the reality is more endless caravans and vacation homes. Still, if you are interested in a stressless break on the beach there are worse places to go. For local travel information contact **Hibiscus Coast Resorts** ((039) 699 2509.

Located 128 km (80 miles) south of Durban is the sprawling industrial town of **Port Shepstone**, best known for being the start of the **Banana Express** ((039) 682 4821, a vintage steam train running every Wednesday and Thursday up to Paddock. Excursions can last just a few hours, or be combined with a guided walk though the spectacular **Oribi Nature Reserve**. Contact the **Hibiscus Coast Publicity Association** ((039) 312 2322 for further details. There are some places to stay: smartest is the bland **Kapenta Bay** ((039) 682 5528 FAX (039) 682 4590, 11–12 Princess Elizabeth Drive, Port Shepstone. KZN Nature Conservation Service have a variety of units within the Oribi reserve itself which cost about R80 per person. It is one of the best of their southern parks.

The main N2 road peels off here, and with it the transportation: all the above resorts are served by a series of coach operators including Baz Bus and Translux.

South from here and you'll be relying on a rental car or a few local bus companies. The resorts continue more thinly on to Margate, Ramsgate, Southbroom and Port Edward, where thankfully the coastal tourist development comes to an end and there's the chance to explore the **Umtamvuna Nature Reserve**, a sandstone gorge that comes alive with flowers in spring, before crossing over into the Eastern Cape and heading on the Wild Coast. There are places to stay: The **Umtamvuna River Lodge** ((039) 303 2313 is best, while there is also the **Llala Cabanas** caravan-based vacation resort with chalets ((039) 309 2729, and if you want there's the African **Mzamba Village** just south of Port Edward selling handicrafts. Unless you've got a boat a dirt road loops back to join the N2 as it heads inland to the undeveloped Xhosa lands of the Eastern Cape.

THE WILD COAST

South of Port Edward the coast is known as the Wild Coast, and for once this is no tourist board hype. The Umtamvuna River marks the start of the old homeland of **Transkei**, traditional home to the Xhosa people and now incorporated into the Eastern Cape Province. On the border the **Wild Coast Resort** ((039) 305 9111 in Port Edward is a casino/country club hangover from the apartheid years, when gambling was only allowed in the homelands, but marks an immediate and unmistakable change of atmosphere: instead of the large-farm discipline of KwaZulu-Natal overgrazed hillsides roll bare, dotted with the small round mud Xhosa huts of subsistence farmers. The tarmac thins into a potholed surface clogged with cattle, donkeys and carts: the N2 in name, but much slower. Drivers who had been averaging 100 kph (63 mph) will drop down to half that speed, held up mainly by slow traffic but also out of caution:

the road is famous for big black pigs straying across the road, especially at night, bringing drivers to a sudden crashing halt.

No property boom has sparked off an ocean-front culture and the main N2 road stays well inland as it continues down towards East London. For visitors, though, the main attractions are on the coast, a good two hours to the east of the main road. Small roads, often dirt, head to a series of sleepy settlements hugging small coves in a beautiful stretch of countryside that first-world South Africa seems to have largely missed. There is no coast road and only hikers can travel along the entire coast, taking between 21 and 24 days to complete the **Wild Coast Hiking Trail** that runs from Port Edward to Kei River mouth. The fact it is such a long way from the main road means that time restrictions generally limit even the most unhurried travelers to visiting just one — or maybe two — of the Wild Coast villages.

The whole area is famous for its *dagga* (marijuana), which means visitors sometimes stay for some time, patching their peaceable lifestyles into a lawless area and positively reveling in the lack of regimentation. Fortunately the offshore waters teem with fish and the land is fertile, so pressures are few. And you would travel far for assistance in case of trouble. To really explore the Wild Coast it is best to use a specialist tour operator, as few people really know their way around this part of South Africa and a four-wheel-drive vehicle is needed to get far off the beaten track. Two such operators are **African Coastal Adventures** (/FAX (043) 748 4550 E-MAIL aca@imaginet.co.za WEB SITE www.africacoast.co.za, Box 595, East London 5200, for an engagingly local Wild Coast experience, and **Amatola Tours** ((043) 743 0472 FAX (043) 722 6914 E-MAIL amatour@gis.co.za, Box 18227,

Theme-park fun lines Durban's waterfront below the hotels of Marine Parade.

Quigney 5211, East London, with programs throughout the Eastern Cape.

There are a host of settlements, some very small, along the coast but the two most interesting — and popular — are Port St. Johns and Coffee Bay.

PORT ST. JOHNS

Heading south from the Kei River mouth, the first town of any note is Port St. Johns. From the N2 most of the road is tar, but the last 18 kilometers (11 miles) are a rugged and unforgiving stretch of dirt, dropping down through the coast through a series of dramatic ravines and gorges. It's the only road into town, and has kept Port St. Johns away from casual visitors and, more importantly, off the casual spoon-fed traveling parties of the Baz Bus backpacker route. Hoteliers may moan but this is perhaps the town's most valuable asset.

The town owes its name to the Portuguese ship *São Jão*, wrecked offshore in the 1500s, leaving its crew to struggle up the coast 700 km (437 miles) to Mozambique and safety; eight survivors made it. Myth has it that one of these survivors was wrecked again at the same place two years later, and faced with the prospect of the long walk home he died of despair.

Perhaps he would have taken a kinder view of his lot if he'd considered staying for a while. The settlement that is now Port St. John's hugs the beautiful gorge of the Mzimvubu River, spilling spectacularly into the ocean through steep, forested cliffs. There's a small town center with a few bars serving drink and conversation in equal measure. The **Museum** on Golf Course Road, open Monday to Friday 10 AM to 5 PM, is a gem. The curator doesn't speak any English but gets very excited when the occasional guest drops in. He'll take you round the exhibits of local tribal life. Some of the musical instruments are quite mystifying, but he'll play them all, loudly, for a long time. There is no admission charge but donations are appreciated.

In such glorious weather the ocean is the main event. **First Beach**, in the town center, is a bit sharky for swimming but fishermen love it, while out of town there are two superb swimming beaches. First Beach stretches from the Post Office and town to the south, while five kilometers (three miles) further is **Second Beach**, with beautiful swimming. Between here and **Third Beach** (great sand, no facilities) you'll find the dramatic coastline wilderness area of **Silaka Nature Reserve**, offering 16 self-catering chalets and hiking huts — paradise for the truly self-sufficient, though during the day you occasionally see tired backpackers rather pathetically begging a day's supply of fish in town before their long walk back to their rural idylls. For information about staying here — or about trekking the coastal route — get in touch with the

Transkei Nature Conservation Division ℂ (047) 532 4322, Box X5002, Umtata.

The area used to be known for its tobacco, but protectionist laws passed in 1906, designed to look after inland white farmers, stopped cultivation. The local farmers switched readily to marijuana and a liberal dope culture still permeates the area.

Arriving in Port St. John's there's no official tourist information and you'll generally have to rely on your hotel to fill you in on the options.

Where to Stay

The oldest hotel is the traditional **Outspan Inn** ℂ (047) 564 1057 WEB SITE www.wildcoast.co.za/ outspan, High Street, R220 including breakfast, located in the heart of the town. Across the river is the **Jetty** ℂ/FAX (047) 564 1072 E-MAIL thejetty@ iphone.co.za WEB SITE www.wildcoast.co.za/ thejetty/, Ferry Point Road, Port St. Johns, R300 for two, including breakfast. This is set between the Mzimbuvu River and the Mount Sullivan Forest Reserve, a little out of town. Towards Second Beach is the **Wild Coast Guest House** ℂ (047) 564 1083, 503 Second Beach Road, Port St. John, R220 for two, including dinner and breakfast. This is great value and has an atmospheric bar built out in the trees and is specially convenient for fishermen: the owner is a keen fisherman. He is not, however, a natural host.

Cheapest of all is **Port St. Johns Backpackers** ℂ (047) 564 1517, % Post Office, Port St. Johns, which is the better of the town's two backpacker lodges. The owner is very helpful and will pick guests up from Umtata, albeit in a very old car. He also arranges a range of alternative and very atmospheric accommodation in the area. For a start, he operates a very basic guest house on Second Beach, the most beach popular for swimming. More popular are overnight stays in the townships with Mama Constance, where for R250 she cooks up a feast. Evenings there are always sociable, with a stream of visitors, and it's a memorable place to stay. Alternatively, if you're prepared to take the local ferry across the river (R1.50) and then walk along the coast for four and a half hours **Franco's Place** is far off the beaten track: small candlelit mud huts by the side of the ocean. Book through Port St. John's Backpackers.

Where to Eat

Perhaps the best menu is at the Outspan Inn, but be warned it is shut Sundays. The Wild Coast Guest House has a good restaurant but often shuts very early if not busy. The Jetty tends to be more lively and also does good meals. The best restaurant of all is **Lily's** ℂ (047) 564 1229, on the way to Second Beach. When Mrs. Mahoney's there you'll enjoy fine fresh seafood with views over the ocean; when she isn't the food is less good, if indeed the restaurant opens at all.

How to Get There

Since the Baz Bus withdrew its service to Port St. Johns the only public transportation is by calling Port St. Johns Backpackers and getting them to pick you up from Umtata — a 95 km (59 miles) trip — free, but you will be expected to stay at the backpacker lodge. With your own car, even a humble saloon, it is easy: the R61 loops to the coast from the N2 in one of South Africa's most spectacular drives; leave plenty of time.

COFFEE BAY

Smaller than Port St. Johns, Coffee Bay has the advantage of a there-and-back tar road from Umtata, and its host of nature reserves and the postcard-famous attractions of the "Hole in the Wall" formation, eroded by the pounding ocean waves, mean it is becoming more and more popular with every passing year.

Village rather than town, Coffee Bay settlement is concentration of dwellings surrounded by scarcely less-populated hills; traditionally the interface between to Xhosa sub-clans: the Pondo to the north and the Bomvana to the south. It's a center for hiking, with the eight-kilometer (five-mile) hike to the Hole in the Wall passing through a number of traditional settlements. This is the starting-point for the popular six-day hike to Port St. Johns. Be warned that a shortage of accommodation on this hike means you'll need to book your place up to 12 months in advance with the Transkei Nature Conservation Division in Umtata (see under PORT ST. JOHNS, above), but the chalets en route are comfortable and cost just R30 per person per night. For accommodation, the **Ocean View Hotel** (/FAX (047) 575 2005, is your only alternative, set on the sea to the north of the main village. Backpackers have more choice, with the best option **Woodhouse Backpackers** (/FAX (047) 575 2029, R40 per person. It is set among the forest and has a ladies-only bar as well as an outside bar and lockup parking but no beds: you are on mattresses here. Alternatively the **Coffee Bay Backpackers** ((047) 575 2005, R40 per person, is traditional favorite but often full. There are minibus taxis running to Coffee Bay from Umtata while the Baz Bus stops at Qunu, Nelson Mandela's home village, 40 km (25 miles) from Coffee Bay, leaving the backpacker lodges to provide a shuttle service on to the coast.

UMTATA

Busy and scruffy administrative center for the Wild Coast Region and once the capital of the Transkei, Umtata does not have any obvious attractions and is best sped through. You might, however, find yourself spending a night here either because you need to arrange access to some of the Wild Coast's national parks or more simply if the slow Transkei roads put you behind schedule. This area is not recommended for driving at night. There is a not-very-useful **Tourist Information Center** ((047) 531 5290 FAX (047) 531 5291, at Leeds Road junction with Owen Road, in the town center. Opening hours are Monday to Friday 9 AM to 4:30 PM. If you are looking for medical attention, the best private hospital is probably **St. Mary's** ((047) 531 2911, 30 Durham Street, Umtata 5100.

Accommodation options include the mainstream **Umtata Protea Hotel** ((047) 531 0721 FAX (047) 531 0083, 36 Sutherland Street, R300 including breakfast, a city-center hotel appealing mainly to businessmen, while **Barbara's Guest House** ((047) 531 1751 FAX (047) 531 1754, 55 Alexandra Road, R160 with breakfast, is central, while other guesthouse signs dot the suburbs. There is no backpackers in Umtata so far.

FURTHER SOUTH

The N2 south of Umtata heads down towards the city of East London, with turnings on the left marking the start of long dirt roads heading off to the coast and a scattering of hotels and resorts in a remote area of great beauty. If you've got time, sights include the **Collywobbles**, an area of undulating, rolling hills whose name acquires a new meaning after driving through the endless twists of minor, often dirt roads, and **Cwebe Nature Reserve**, with dense subtropical forest growing on an unspoiled coastline. The best — indeed only — place to stay here is the privately-run **Haven** ((047) 576 0006 FAX (047) 576 0008, inside the reserve between the forest and the coastal sanddunes. The end of the Wild Coast is marked by the dizzyingly high **Great Kei River Bridge** where a "Whistle Stop" service station houses a very helpful **Tourist Information Center** ((043) 831 1167, open seven days 8:30 AM to 5 PM, which will help with travel advice heading north into the Wild Coast. Those heading south, slowed to the pace of rural life, can pick up some useful orientation here before driving into the urban sprawling speed of East London (see page 152).

Mountains, Wetlands, and Warriors

THERE IS FAR MORE THAN SUN AND SAND to the undiscovered and little-traveled province of KwaZulu-Natal, which contains within its borders all the variety and history of the African continent. From Durban, follow the coast north over the Tugela River towards the Mozambique border and you reach some of the country's most rewarding wilderness areas. Bear inland for the pristine bush of Hluhluwe-Umfolozi National Park, the oldest proclaimed national park in Africa, with a charter dating back to 1895. It has not survived unchallenged though: traditionally it was the hunting preserve of the Zulu kings and twice was deregistered under pressure from neighboring farmers. From 1929 to 1952, a crusade of game extermination was followed to protect local cattle from *nagana*, a disease spread by tsetse fly, and 100,000 head of game were killed. In the 1950s the KZN Nature Conservation Service took over, and their work conserving the white rhino rescued it from the brink of extinction to become the first species ever to be removed from the World Conservation Union's endangered list.

Stay on the coast and you'll reach the five habitats of the St. Lucia Wetlands area, which together comprise the third largest of South Africa's parks, clustered around the hippo-filled waters of South Africa's largest inland waterway, Lake St. Lucia. To the north are papyrus and reed wetlands, inland plains of savanna and thornveld, while offshore are the coral-filled waters of Sodwana Bay, washed by the clear waters of the warm Agulhas current that flows down the coast.

Head inland from Durban and the warm coastal climate cools as you climb through an endless succession of rolling hills, rising gradually to the scenic beauty of the Drakensberg Mountains bordering the inland highlands of Lesotho, protected as the Natal Drakensberg Park. And there is more to KwaZulu-Natal than natural beauty, there's plenty of human interest too. The earliest history is recorded on cave walls: the atmospheric and enigmatic paintings and carvings of the San people date back to the birth of life on the continent, and there are over 600 sites in the Drakensberg Mountains, with more than 22,000 individual paintings. But it is for signs of the more recent past that KwaZulu-Natal is most famous. North of Pietermaritzburg and the rolling emerald hillsides are home to an altogether bloodier history, a wild landscape drenched in colonial blood. Some of the greatest battlefields of the Anglo-Zulu War are found here: Isandlwana, Rorke's Drift, and Ulundi. Knowledgeable local guides are available to explore and explain, with atmospheric lodges scattered among the scenes of some of the greatest acts of resistance ever met by the British in greatest empire days.

Things were only to get worse for the British here: reeling from their Zulu defeats, Natal then saw the start of the Anglo-Boer wars, as the Afrikaner settlers fiercely fought for their heritage. Although the battlefields of this war are spread across the nation, it is in KwaZulu-Natal that they are most clearly commemorated. In time, KwaZulu-Natal was to develop into the heartland of many of this century's great resistance movements, often because the leaders first got into trouble here. Mahatma Gandhi dates his opposition to colonial rule to the day he was thrown off a train in Pietermaritzburg and Nelson Mandela was also arrested in Howick, to start his long stay on Robben Island.

ZULU HEARTLAND

From Stanger the N2 and the R102 roads continue north and cross the Tugela River. While the N2 carries straight on north along the coast the R102 passes through Ginginlovu, scene of one of the most decisive victories in the colonial campaign to destroy the Zulu people and culture. Turn left here on the R66 for the towns of Eshowe and Ulundi and the ancient heart of the Zulu Nation.

The word "Zulu" struck fear into every corner of the British Empire, and even caused a major flutter to the ANC in the run-up to the first postapartheid elections. In fact, the idea of Zulus as national group is fairly recent, dating back to 1825, and their tenure as an imperial nation lasted just 60 years, when they were wiped out at Ulundi by the British forces. In that short time they established a worldwide reputation for great bravery and military prowess. The rise to fame of the Zulu tribal group was caused, to a great extent, by the seemingly trivial development of a short spear.

BACKGROUND

Up until 1800, the Zulus were just one clan among 20 Nguni-speaking chiefdoms in the area, patrilineal family groups grazing their animals, largely in peace. When land disputes did arise they would tend to be solved by the opposing groups lining up some distance from each other and throwing spears. Casualties were relatively rare.

All this changed in a time of upheaval between 1800 and 1830, as the arrival of European settlers to the south squeezed the population and a huge convulsion of aggression took over. The Zulus weren't even a particularly important clan when in 1816 Shaka Zulu took over as the ruler of the Mthethwe coalition of clans. Already a proven General, Shaka made two changes to the strategy of war that were to have far-reaching consequences. First, he replaced the traditional throwing spears with short *assegais*, or stabbing spears; then he instructed his troops in a "horns of the buffalo" tactic to surround their enemies and stab them to death. Territorial skirmishes took on a new

and more conclusive dimension. By 1825 the region from the Tugela River north up to the Pongola River was firmly under the control of Shaka Zulu.

In 1927 Shaka's mother died, and Shaka went off the rails. The entire Zulu Nation started a fanatical killing spree, driving the Matabele north to Zimbabwe and wiping out other clans completely. In 1928 Shaka was killed by his half-brother Dingane, who seized control. The killing continued. By the time of the Boer's Great Trek into Natal much of the land was deserted.

Apart, that is, from the Zulu warriors. The first emissary of the Boer nation was Piet Retief, who led a small group across the Drakensberg Mountains into Zulu territory. In talks with Dingane it was agreed that if Retief could recapture 700 cattle stolen from the Zulus, the Boers would be granted land. Retief trekked across into what is now the Free State, recaptured the cattle from the clan leader — and longtime Zulu foe — Sekonella. Dingane,

however, was not best pleased to see him return with the 700 cattle. Firstly, he suspected the Boers of being wizards. After all, they had recaptured 700 cattle without a drop of blood being spilled in war. Also, they had released Sekonella, who Dingane would much rather have seen killed. This made them wizards he couldn't trust. Retief persuaded Dingane to sign a contract handing over his land, but as the Zulu leader was illiterate its legal validity must be in doubt. In any case, it was never tested. Dingane invited Retief and his entire group to a banquet, at which they were slaughtered.

The main body of Boers, however, was less easily stopped. Under Andreis Pretorius a commando of 464 men in fighting wagons crossed the Buffalo River in 1858 and on December 16 made camp against the banks of a tributary, laagering

The terraced hills of Zululand.

his 450 wagons. When they woke the next day they saw the entire Zulu army sitting on their spears on the other side of the river. The Zulu attack foundered in the riverbed and while the Zulus died in their thousands the Boers suffered no casualties. This miraculous victory is still remembered as a national holiday to the present day. Dingane, disgraced, was forced from office and Andreis Pretorius installed Mpande as ruler. Then Pretorius traveled on to Dingane's kraal, where he claimed to find the body of Piet Retief and claimed also to find a legal document ceding the entire Zulu territories to the Boers.

Meanwhile the British arrived at Durban with territorial claims of their own. After a bloody civil war Cetshwayo took over as leader of the Zulus, building a new capital at Ulundi. Cetshwayo was an anglophile, partly because he didn't care for the Boers, but also because he numbered many British people as personal friends. The British Secretary of State for Native Affairs, Shepstone, had formed a verbal alliance with Cetshwayo against the Boers when, far away in Britain, Disraeli came to power. The British Government, with cable communications only reaching as far as Madeira and then proceeding by boat, didn't really know what was going on in Africa and carte blanche was given over to the colonial powers under Lord Canaervon, fresh from subjecting Canada to colonial rule.

In a shameful series of treacherous maneuvers the British colonial authorities provoked Cetshwayo, who still considered himself an ally of the English, into a conflict. Slight after slight were imposed on the Zulu king, but finally it was decided that the only way of provoking a war was invasion of Zulu territory. A three-pronged attack was mounted, with one of the major columns, under Lord Chelmsford, invading from Pietermaritzburg across the Buffalo River to Rorke's Drift, over 100 km (65 miles) from Cetshwayo's kraal at Ulundi. Of the 4,800 men of this force, the majority were black, poorly equipped and trained, while the senior British officers were either dismally incompetent or wholly unprepared for the conditions of Africa. After winning a skirmish against a minor chief the British forces camped out with their huge trains of oxen set out at Isandlwana, making no attempt to laager into a defensive position. The British forces were divided in a misinformed chase of the Zulu army, but instead the Zulu army found them. The Zulu army attacked — and routed — the British army. The British clawed back some remnants of honor the next day at Rorke's Drift, where a small group of Welsh soldiers defended a field hospital against an overwhelming force of Zulus, but the British Empire had suffered its most major defeat to date.

The Zulus might have won the battle but they were not to win the war. A massive force of sol-

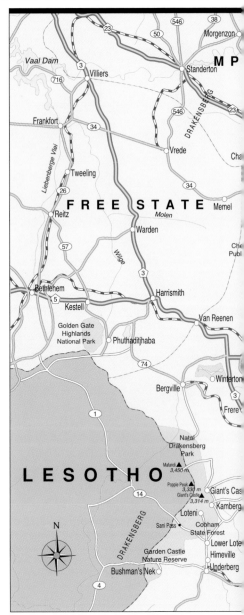

diers were conscripted in the United Kingdom and shipped out. A year later the British would wipe out Cetshwayo's armies and his kraal at Ulundi.

Nervous of a resurgent Zulu nationalism, from that moment the colonial forces systematically stamped out all signs of Zulu's tribal customs, integrating the defeated people into the cash economy so they could help generate a revenue for the crown colony. These days you won't find people in tribal dress wandering round Zululand and the only tribal dancing you're likely to see is in rather structured theme parks — sometimes

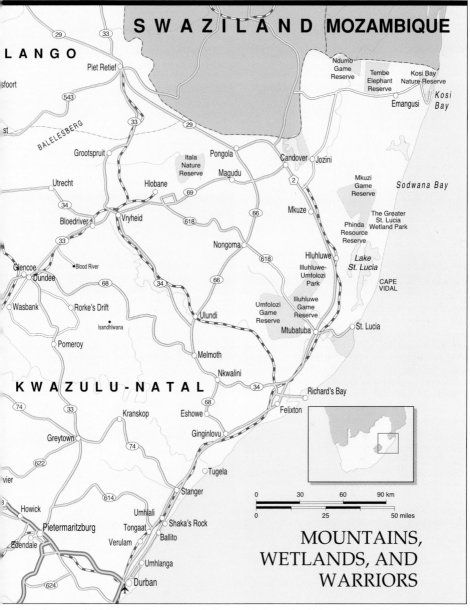

MOUNTAINS,
WETLANDS, AND
WARRIORS

called "Open Air Museums" — constructed using white money and black bit-part actors to appeal to tourists.

Underneath it all the Zulu culture is alive and well. Some community projects can bring you close to the people and since the end of the apartheid regime, power is shifting to the Zulu people. Ancient royal kraals are being rebuilt and new museums set up. For British visitors, at least, to visit these is a small gesture of atonement for a shameful period in our history. Because while Swaziland and Lesotho retain their status as independent kingdoms, the Zulus, most anglophile of all, were robbed of nationhood more than 100 years ago, a colonial act that still carries ramifications into the current political scene today. The Zulu Nation today has a population of some six million, making it the largest of South Africa's black population groups. The Zulu king is Zwelithini Goodwill KaCyprian Bhekuzulu, and his chief minister Mangosuthu Buthelezi, whose early career included acting in the classic film *Zulu*, went on to become the deputy prime minister of South Africa.

ESHOWE

Twenty-two kilometers (nearly 14 miles) inland from Ginginlovu is the town of Eshowe, an often-overlooked sidelight into the Zulu culture. In Zulu Eshowe means "the sound of the wind in the trees," and its hillside setting makes it easy to see how it came by its name.

General Information

Eshowe Tourism and Publicity Association ((035) 474 1141 FAX (035) 474 4733 E-MAIL eshowe@ uthungulu.co.za, at the corner of Osborne and Hutchinson roads, Box 37, Eshowe 3815, open Monday to Friday 7:30 AM to 4 PM and Saturday 9 AM to noon, provides a helpful introduction to the town, but you'll get a more dynamic insight from Graham Chennels, owner of the George Hotel and Zululand Backpackers on Main Street, who will steer you towards the huge array of excursions and adventures he arranges in the area. His hotel details are listed in accommodation below, or visit his WEB SITE www.zululand.co.za/eshowe. A local taxi service is **Mashapi's Tours** ((034) 474 4137.

What to See and Do

Dominating the town, **Fort Nongqai** was built in 1883 to garrison the Natal Native Police. Crenellated and whitewashed, it now houses the **Zululand Historical Museum** ((035) 474 1441, Nongqai Road, open daily 9 AM to 4 PM, no entry fee but donation appreciated, which includes superb collections of Zulu household items, ammonite fossils, and a collection of period furnishings dating back to the first years of settlement. Among the exhibits are many items of furniture belonging to John Dunn, a friend of Cetshwayo, who became the only white Zulu chief and settled down in the area to live with his 49 local wives. The extensive gardens are great for a stroll and two marked trails lead to the Mpushini Falls and through the Dhlinza Nature Reserve, perhaps Natal's most accessible patch of mistbelt forest, teeming with birds and small animals.

Zulu ceramics, beads and basket-ware are starting to be appreciated by the great international art museums, and you can get a good idea of the range and quality available by visiting the **Vukani Museum** ((035) 474 5274 or (035) 474 1254 (curator), Osborne Road, open 9 AM to 1 PM Tuesday to Thursday or by request, R6, where the world's largest collection, with more than 3,000 pieces, is displayed.

Fourteen kilometers (just under nine miles) from Eshowe on the R68 heading towards Melmoth a signposted road turns off to the left with four kilometers (two and a half miles) of dirt remaining to **Shakaland** ((035) 460 0912

FAX (035) 460 0824 E-MAIL shakares@iafrica.com, Normanhurst Farm, Nkwalini, a theme park first built as a set for the 1980s television series *Shaka Zulu*. Now run by the Protea Hotel chain it calls itself an open-air museum but is in fact one of South Africa's largest tribal theme parks, with mud huts, and singing and dancing under the video cameras of coach parties. Tours, which feature a video presentation and rather a lot of traditional dancing, start at 11 AM and 12:30 PM, costing R55 for the tour only, and R85 including a traditional lunch. It is possible to stay overnight here in a traditional beehive hut with en-suite facilities and electric lighting. If you're putting this much time into meeting the Zulus though

you'd be better off traveling to **Simunye** ((035) 450 7103 FAX (035) 450 2534, 46 km (29 miles) from Eshowe off the D246, for a more authentic experience. An overnight stay is the minimum here: travel to a remote community by ox-cart for dancing, an evening meal, and a night spent meeting new friends by candlelight or the relatively modern light of hurricane lamps.

For the highly adventurous Eshowe is birthplace of the little-known sport of "rock sliding," which is marketed as a revival of an ancient Zulu initiation ritual. In shorts and a crash-helmet this consists of sliding, ideally foot-first, down waterfalls between five and fifty meters (16 to 160 ft) high. The operator's claim it is more scary than bungee-jumping, which shouldn't be surprising as it is more dangerous. Rock sliding operates through the summer months on the Manziwayo River west of Eshowe. Contact **Backpack Africa**

((011) 807 0972 E-MAIL animalbru@hotmail.com (to operator Matthew Peckham), or ask at the George Hotel in Eshowe for further details.

Where to Stay and Eat

Best hotel in Eshowe is the **George Hotel** ((035) 474 4919, 40 Main Street, R200, with television and en-suite facilities, and a helpful proprietor, ex-mayor Graham Chennels, who leads tours of the white, colored and black areas of the town and region. The same owner also runs the town's cheapest option just behind the George Hotel: **Zululand Backpackers** ((035) 474 4919 FAX (035) 474 4919 E-MAIL chennels@iafrica.com WEB SITE http://users.iafrica.com/c/ch/chennels, 38 Main

ULUNDI

The town of Ulundi, 105 km (just under 66 miles) north of Eshowe along the R66, is at the heart of the Zulu Nation, with important burial grounds, the site of King Mpande's royal residence and grave, and the half-reconstructed kraal of Cetshwayo. Ulundi is currently co-capital (with Pietermaritzburg) of KwaZulu-Natal, and is constantly rumored to be about to take over as the province's administrative center, a role it seems ill-prepared to fill. Pietermaritzburg, with its imposing colonial buildings and well-established infrastructure, is seen as a relic of the white past,

Street, offers dormitory rooms from R45 per person and rooms from R60. The **Amble Inn** ((035) 474 1300, 116 Main Street, R200, is a small and atmospheric throwback to the colonial days, while to stay near — but not in — Shakaland the **Zulu Nyala Heritage Hotel** ((035) 562 0177 FAX (035) 562 0582 E-MAIL shakazulu@zulu.co.za offers restored comforts in a 1940s plantation mansion for R400 with breakfast.

How to Get There

In your own car, Eshowe is 26 km (16.2 miles) northwest along the R66, reached by turning from the N2 or the R102 at Ginginlovu, three hours northeast from Durban on the coast. The Baz Bus stops at Main Street on its Durban to Johannesburg route and the Translux intercity bus stops outside city hall on its thrice-weekly service from Pretoria/Johannesburg to Richards Bay.

while Ulundi, with its associations with the Zulu past, is seen as a better spiritual symbol of the Zulu Nation. However Ulundi doesn't have the hotels or even housing that would be required from a provincial capital and the civil service, at least, fervently opposes any such move.

There's only one hotel in town, the **Holiday Inn Garden Court Ulundi** ((035) 872 1121 FAX (035) 872 1721, R428 bed only, catering mainly to shuttling civil servants and businessmen. But as there is little to see in the town itself it is hard to find a good reason to stay there. Even the tourist information is not in town, but instead at the area's main attraction, the **KwaZulu Cultural Museum at Ondini** ((035) 870 2050 FAX (035) 870 2054 E-MAIL amafahq@mweb.co.za. Take the airport turnoff

OPPOSITE: Zulu sleeping quarters with food storage just outside. ABOVE: Simunye Village offers a more authentic cultural experience: here, the chief.

from the R66 south of town and follow a dirt road for five kilometers (just over three miles). This major museum of Zulu artifacts and culture is on the site of King Cetshwayo's capital of 1883, razed by the British in the last battle of the Anglo-Zulu War of 1879. Although the royal capital is being rebuilt the plans, so far, outshine the practice, but the museum itself is well worth the visit, with audiovisual presentations and specialist halls packed with cultural displays and insights. The museum is open from 8 AM to 4 PM Monday to Friday and 9 AM to 4 PM on weekends and holidays, admission R5.

Ondini also offers accommodation for tourists, in rather flyblown beehive huts, long on atmosphere but short on comforts. The cost is R160 per couple, and includes dinner and breakfast. Bear in mind that unless you've called ahead the main gates shut at 6 PM. The dirt road past Ondini continues on to Hluhluwe-Umfolozi National Park, 30 km (18.7 miles) west, which makes it a convenient stop for drivers in their own cars on what is already a worthwhile diversion from the coastal N2. By public transportation, access is easiest by air. Ulundi's unlikely administrative importance means it is well served by air, and there is a minibus terminal outside the Holiday Inn linking Vryheid, Johannesburg, and Eshowe. Once in Ulundi you'll need a taxi to get out to Ondini. **Gecko Cabs** ((035) 789 5561 are a reputable local taxi service.

THE NORTHERN PARKS

Past the turn for central Zululand, the N2 curves inland to distance itself from the coastline, with its long, unspoiled beaches rolling back into grassy hills. Richards Bay is 12 km (7.5 miles) to the east of the N2 on the coast but it is hard to see any good reason to deviate that far. Even though it has plentiful facilities backed by a permanent settled population, the fact that the most popular excursion here is a tour of the mineral smelting yards gives a clue as to why. The area is known — by the tourist office at least — for its 400 bird species, but most of these can be found in far nicer surroundings nearby. If you do decide to visit there are plenty of lodges and guest houses. The **Tourist Information Office** ((035) 788 0039 FAX (035) 788 0040 E-MAIL rbtour@uthungulu .co.za WEB SITE www.richardsbay.org.za, the Waterfront, will have further details, and is open 8 AM to 5 PM weekdays. If it is closed there's a lovely guest house overlooking the ocean and harbor called the **Ridge Guest House** ((035) 753 4312 FAX (035) 753 4321 E-MAIL ridge@iafrica .com, 1 Jack's Corner, Meerense, R320 to R480, and full-board backpacker accommodation at the **YMCA** ((035) 753 4086, Box 203, Richards Bay 3900.

Most drivers pass Richards Bay and continue further north on the N2, as the main draw for visitors are the game reserves at Hluhluwe-Umfolozi (pronounced "Shloe-Shloei") to the left of the N2 and St. Lucia to the right. The migrating herds of elephant and impala have gone from the surrounding countryside but within these two reserves careful conservation means there is still plenty to see, especially rhino both black and white but also cheetah, leopard, spotted hyena and wild dog, herbivores including wildebeest, giraffe, hippo, kudu, zebra, and buffalo. Don't even ask about the bird species. Naturalists, particularly, appreciate the self-guided trails and guided trails with armed guards that let visitors explore on foot, and night drives offer the best chance of spotting leopard and other nocturnal animals.

HLUHLUWE-UMFOLOZI NATIONAL PARK

Drive 280 km (175 miles) north of Durban on the N2 and turn left for Hluhluwe-Umfolozi National Park, two of Africa's oldest reserves now linked into a single park. Many people rate this park higher than the Kruger. Certainly it is less-visited, offers a wide range of activities, and is also the only park in KwaZulu-Natal where you are likely to see all the Big Five. Hluhluwe is named after the characteristic thorny climbing lianas that dominate the forests of the area, while Umfolozi derives from the aerial roots of the indigenous fig trees. The park is especially famous for its white rhino. By 1865 only 50 of these were thought to remain in South Africa, all in this small area, and the population is now nearer 2,000, the highest concentration in the world, and many have been relocated to other areas.

The best thing to do here is the four-night, three-day wilderness trail, accompanied by a guide and armed ranger, exploring a designated wilderness area on foot with donkeys carrying your bags. These trails run from March through November: the cost is R1,000 per person, and places on the eight-person groups are often booked out 12 months in advance. There are also shorter hiking routes for weekend visitors, auto trails for those too lazy or sensible to step out of their cars, and short self-guided foot trails with informative booklets. For all access details and hiking arrangements contact the **KZN Nature Conservation Service** ((033) 845 1000 FAX (033) 845 1001, Box 13069, Cascades 3202. Their headquarters are just outside Pietermaritzburg and they also are represented in Durban's Tourist Junction. Although camping spaces can be allocated locally, lodge and chalet reservations have to be made centrally and you can't just turn up in the hope there'll be space. There is an entry fee to the reserve of R8 per person and R30 per vehicle.

Where to Stay

All the accommodation is in the lodges and camps run by the KZN Nature Conservation Service (see contact details above), the very helpful organization that used to be called the Natal Parks Board. Options include **Masinda Lodge**, **Muntulu Bush Lodge**, **Munyawaneni Bush Lodge**, **Gqoyeni Bush Lodge**, and fees are generally in the region of R220 per person in accommodation ranging from two to eight-bed units, generally self-catering, which in South Africa often means with the help of a provided cook. There is also a permanent tented camp called **Safari Camp**, established in 1999, which offers walk-in comforts in 10 tents; two and four-bed configurations cost R240 to R480.

St. Lucia

While Hluhluwe-Umfolozi is to the left of the N2 there is another, equally rewarding reserve which stretches up the coast on the right. It starts around the town of St. Lucia, a vacation resort surrounded by the St. Lucia Reserve and St. Lucia Park, the first of an interlinked chain of reserves and parks that protect much of North Maputaland, ending 80 km (50 miles) up the coast in Sodwana Bay. St. Lucia town itself is crowded and frenetic during public holidays but otherwise a good base for one of South Africa's most rewarding parks. **Tourist Information** ((035) 590 1143, McKenzie Street,

None of the above camps are fenced, which adds to the wilderness experience but don't try going for a stargazing stroll. An exception is the newest, **Hilltop Camp**, which is fenced, allowing guests to walk to the restaurant and bar. Set high on a steep forested slope, it has a collection of rustic thatched designer chalets and traditional rondavels which rival some far more expensive private game-lodges for comfort.

How to Get There

There is no public transportation to Hluhluwe-Umfolozi, though some backpacker lodges will arrange tours. Drivers have to use one of three manned gates. From Ulundi, the dirt road passing Ondini gives access to the Umfolozi section through Cengeni Gate, while two tarred roads lead from the N2 to Mambeni and Memorial Gates in the northern section of the park.

grudgingly offers hotel and tour information, but tend to be most helpful on the more expensive options.

The Greater St. Lucia Wetlands Park is actually made up of several reserves stretching up the coast which, with further planned developments will make this the third-largest protected area within South Africa. Five distinct ecosystems include offshore reefs, Africa's largest river estuary, reed and sedge swamps, thornveld, and open grasslands. Hiking trails are run by the KZN Nature Conservation Service (see below), diving can be arranged with local operators, and boat trips explore the coast. The reserves that make up the Greater Park each have their own special character and attractions and your accommodation choice will be partly dictated by the area you

A lion-sized yawn at the Hluhluwe-Umfolozi National Park in northern KwaZulu-Natal.

choose: most cannot be reached overland from St. Lucia but by separate turnings from the N2.

Where to Stay

In St. Lucia, many tours can be arranged from **Maputaland Lodge** (/FAX (035) 590 1041, 1 Kabeljou Avenue, with swimming pool and restaurant set in a tropical garden, R270 for two with breakfast. A town-center alternative is the **Santa Lucia Guest House** ((035) 590 1151 FAX (013) 590 1467, 30 Pelican Street, two blocks from the high street, provides homely comfort in a great setting for R270 for two, with breakfast. Backpackers are catered to by **St. Lucia's BIB's International Backpackers** (/FAX (035) 590 1360 E-MAIL intback

@mtb.lia.net, McKenzie Street, where dorm rooms cost R45.

Travelers on a budget — or those interested in the peace and beauty of the natural environment — are best advised to take a choice from the KZN Nature Conservation Service properties and campsites. Local contact numbers will handle camping reservations, while for lodges contact **KZN Nature Conservation Service** ((033) 845 1000 FAX (033) 845 1001, Box 13069, Cascades 3202. The most southerly is Mapelane, by the Mfolozi River mouth, with surf-fishing, ski-boating and relatively safe swimming. Log cabins are available and there are camping facilities; contact the **Camp Manager Mapelane** (/FAX (035) 590 1407, Private Bag, St. Lucia Estuary 3936.

In St. Lucia Estuary the Parks Board run cruises on the estuary, spotting hippos and water birds, on the slow-moving *Santa Lucia* ((035) 590 1340 as well as walking trails. On **Fanie's Island** (/FAX (035) 550 1631, Box 1259, Mtubatuba 3935, on the western shore of Lake St. Lucia, they operate a seven-bed cottage and 12 two-bed rest huts perfect for birdwatchers. There are boats for rent but guests are expected to bring their own outboards which is usually a bit of a challenge for international visitors. Other options include **Charters Creek** (two-bed chalets from R115 per person, larger units available), **Mkuzi Game Reserve** (from R280 for a three-bed hut), and **False Bay Park** (four-bed rustic huts from R110). The KZN Nature Conservation Service handles central reservations for all the above lodges and is helpful. Each lodge has camping facilities (even if only a power point) also available on a first come, first served basis: make the arrangements with the officer in charge. Catering is up to you. There is an entry fee of R8 per person to the reserve and R30 per vehicle.

There are a number of more expensive options. **Hluhluwe River Lodge** ((035) 562 0246 FAX (035) 562 0248, Box 105, Hluhluwe 3960, overlooks the Hluhluwe River floodplains and False Bay, with eight log-cabin chalets providing the base for boat cruises, game drives, and walking trails for R1,350 full board. Conservation Corporation operates a deservedly famous set of small luxury lodges in a private reserve in the north of the wetlands in Phinda. **Mountain Lodge** and **Forest Lodge** have now been joined by **Vlei Lodge** and **Rock Lodge** in a seriously upmarket operation that offers one of the country's finest wildlife experiences in total comfort; contact **Conservation Corporation** ((011) 775 0000 FAX (011) 784 7667 E-MAIL information @ccafrica.com WEB SITE www.ccafrica.com, P/Bag X27, Benmore 2010, who don't cut any corners but don't cut any prices either. The very highest standards of service along with game-drives accompanied by skilled guides start with all-inclusive rates from R2,000 per person.

On the western shores of the estuary **Makakatana Bay Lodge** ((035) 550 4189 FAX (035) 550 4425 E-MAIL maklodge@iafrica.com WEB SITE www.makakatana.co.za, Mtubatuba, is a newly established, stilted lodge, and the only private establishment within Lake St. Lucia's proclaimed conservation reserve. Owner-run and managed, this small lodge offers a tranquil and remote setting for R2,000 for two, full board. For luxury tented accommodation on the western edge of Lake St. Lucia, **Falaza** ((035) 562 0319 FAX (035) 562 0739, Box 13, Hluhluwe 3960, consists of 12 tents around a thatched bomas, with excursions, walks, boat cruises, and horseback safaris. Rates are from R1,040 full board. Backpackers will struggle to stay in the heart of the reserves; better to go for **Amazulu Lodge** ((035) 580 1009 FAX (035) 580 4707, 5 Killarney Place, Golfview, Box 453, Kwambonambi 3915, with accommodation a R40 per person and excursions throughout the area's national parks and beyond.

Pass the first turnings for Hluhluwe and St. Lucia and stick on the N2 to turn right for access to **Sodwana Bay**, famous for it's diving and 350 km (219 miles) from Durban: the final 80 km (50 miles) on dirt roads. Underwater visibility is best from May to June, but April to September is broadly the diving season. Although there is no tourist information office, the KZN Nature Conservation Service will be able to help, either through their head office in Pietermaritzburg (see above) or at the entrance gate. They have five-bed self-catering log cabins from R345. For a more comfortable option, two kilometers (just over a mile) before the park gate (five kilometers or three miles before the beach) the **Sodwana Bay Lodge** ((031) 304 5977 FAX (031) 304 8817, R700 for two sharing, full board, also arranges dive packages and nature walks.

Or carry on up the N2 for a further 40 km (25 miles) and pass the northern extent of the Greater St. Lucia Wetlands Park. Here, 10 km (just over six miles) from the road on the right, you'll

dunes to Cape Vidal. Stay on the N2 for a further 10 km (6.25 miles) for the right hand turn to Charters Creek and Fanie's Island, or 20 km (12.5 miles) for the turn for False Bay Park, Phinda, and Sodwana. Although most of the camps are reached by dirt roads they are well maintained and a saloon car is perfectly adequate.

NORTH INTO MAPUTALAND

Turn right off the N2 signposted Jozini and head northeast east for Maputaland, squeezed hard against the border with Mozambique by the mountains of Swaziland. This is a wild area that rewards the adventurous traveler. **Ndumo Game Reserve**

find a further reserve, **Mkuzi**, dominated by Shembe and Mahlangosi Mountains as the montane forest gives way to grasslands and valley bushveld. It is host to an enormous range of game including leopard, white rhino, elephant, and numerous antelope species. Comfortable and reasonably priced self-catering lodges and camps — as well as a permanent tented camp — are provided once more through the KZN Nature Conservation Service (see above for contact information), as well as walks and trails, and a cultural village of the Kwajobe clan.

How to Get There

Drive 280 km (175 miles) along the N2 north of Durban, turn right onto the R618, and the town of St. Lucia is 30 km (19 miles) away on the coast. Turnings to the right reach down into Mapelane, while only a rough dirt road heads left across the

is on the border with Mozambique. Scenically one of South Africa's most beautiful parks it does not have many large predators — they were the first casualties of the war in Mozambique — but plenty of birds and other mammals, although they're likely to be shy. The pans and rivers seethe with crocodiles. In Nyamithi Pan the indigenous tribe used these crocs to detect witches, in the same way as medieval Europeans used dunking stools.

Accommodation is either through the KZN Nature Conservation Service (see above for further details) which is fairly basic, or go seriously upmarket to the five-star luxury of **Ndumo Lodge** ((011) 883 0747 FAX (011) 883 0911 E-MAIL cindyk @sdn.wilderness.co.za, 3 Autumn Road, Box 5219,

OPPOSITE: The wardens at Phinda Reserve are among the country's most professional. ABOVE: In between dances at the Dumazulu village in Maputaland.

Rivonia, with rates from R1,750 to R2,700 full board. Reach it by turning left off the tarmac and travel on dirt for the last 15 km (about nine and a half miles).

Continue eastwards towards the coast to skirt **Tembe Elephant Reserve**, set up as a sanctuary for these large moving feast menus during Mozambique's civil war. Although it does still have elephants, there are certainly easier places to see them. Most travelers who have come this far are heading for the remote beauty of **Kosi Bay Nature Reserve**, a system of lakes and waterways that is mazed by the reed fences of traditional fishermen. For tourist information apply to the **Hluhluwe Tourism Association** ((035) 562 0353 FAX (035) 562

FAX (011) 883 0911 E-MAIL cindyk@sdn.wilderness .co.za, 3 Autumn Road, Box 5219, Rivonia, set against 40 km (25 miles) of untouched beach for strolls, snorkeling, and swimming. The Big Five here are leatherback turtles, palmnut vultures, Buitons skink, lion fish, and Zululand cyclad. Ten thatched tree-house chalets are priced at R1,750 to R2,700 full board.

BACK INTO MPUMALANGA

The N2 highway goes on to skirt the **Pongola Biosphere Reserve**, proclaimed long after the building of a dam planned for irrigation but never used, now an important refuge for elephant, tiger

0351, Box 399, Hluhluwe 3960, or the **KZN Nature Conservation Service** (for contact details see above), who provide camping facilities for R40 per person.

Meanwhile private accommodation is available at the **Kosi Bay Lodge** ((031) 266 4172 FAX (031) 266 9118 Box 499 Kwangwanase 3675, 500 m (about 550 yards) from the lake, with a bar and basic restaurant. The best place to stay here is the **Kosi Forest Camp** ((032) 947 0538 FAX (032) 947 0659 E-MAIL isibindi@iafrica.com, Box 275, Umhlani 4390, with eight bush suites sheltered in the sand forest providing comfortable bases for snorkeling, fly-fishing, turtle tracking, and palm wine tasting. Rates are from R1,060 to R1,680 full board.

A dirt road heading south, back down towards the coast, also heads to the **Maputaland Coastal Forest Reserve** and **Rocktail Lodge** ((011) 883 0747

fish, and millions of birds. There are some good places to stay here. Best perhaps is **Shayamoya** ((034) 435 1110 FAX (035) 435 1008 E-MAIL shaya lodge@saol.com WEB SITE www.shayamoya.com, Box 784, Pongola 3170, set high on a mountain peak in a private reserve. Accommodation is in beautifully finished log cabins with en-suite facilities, dining overlooks the Swaziland Border, and the only thing that mars its tranquil perfection is the distant rumble of traffic from the road far below. There are walking trails with a skilled ranger, the chance of tiger fishing for anglers, and boat trips among the crocs and hippo for photographers and naturalists. Accommodation at Shayamoya costs R850 to R1,030 for two, which includes dinner and breakfast, but travelers on a budget can bed-and-breakfast in a less spectacular setting at the owner's farmhouse for R250. An alternative place to stay here is the **White Elephant Lodge**

(/FAX (034) 435 1117 E-MAIL drheinz@mweb.co.za, Box 792, Pongola 3170, a luxurious tented safari lodge. Walk-in tents cost R1,300 to R1,700. The road sweeps along the mountainous Swaziland border before continuing to Piet Retief in Mpumalanga but there's one last park before the provincial boundary: Itala.

ITALA NATIONAL PARK

Relatively small and one of the youngest of South Africa's national parks, Itala has all the Big Five except lion, in an uncrowded and beautiful landscape of rivers and cliffs. There are self-guided trails and night-drives. The main Parks Board

lodge is a regular award-winner for its accommodation and restaurant: **Ntshondwe Camp** ((034) 907 5239 FAX (034) 907 5303, Box 42, Louwsburg 3150, or book through KZN Nature Conservation (see above). Ntshondwe has a six-bed luxury lodge with swimming pool and conducts night-drives among other game activities. A number of other small self-catering camps are set up in the bush, with a ranger on hand to escort guests on game walks. All are beautifully set. Mhlangeni is set overlooking a stream and contains five two-bed units; with four units Mbizo is smaller, set at the confluence of two rivers; while Thalu has just two twin bedrooms, stunningly set over a large river pool perfect for swimming. Rates are between R190 and R300 depending on whether you self-cater and the size of your group. To get to Itala take the R66 at Pongola for 19 km (12 miles) and then the R69 towards Vryheid: it's all tarmac.

PIETERMARITZBURG

The N3 highway to Pietermaritzburg heads northeast from Durban, carving a fast road through the endless "Thousand Hills" landscape, of mixed wood and farming land rolling huge and unspoiled. Take the minor road to appreciate the sheer scale of the road-building challenge and catch glimpsed sights of small, untouched African villages, but most drivers find the toll road the easier option: for those in a mountain mood the Drakensberg is coming up, bound to dwarf all that comes before.

Pietermaritzburg has something of a reputation as South Africa's most "English" city. Strange then, that it should have been founded by the Voortrekkers in 1838 and named after two of their Boer leaders. It was originally laid out in Cape Dutch style, with thatched roofs, wide streets, and irrigation ditches down every road. The proposed republic of Natalia didn't last long, however, and it was the English, who installed a garrison in 1843, who set the tone. For many years capital of the Colony of Natal it has some fine Victorian residences that remain largely unaltered, and many of the stately buildings could have come straight from England. Its pivotal role in the history of the region is faithfully recorded in museums and monuments.

GENERAL INFORMATION

Pietermaritzburg Tourism ((033) 345 1348 FAX (033) 394 3535 E-MAIL ppa@futurenet.co.za, 177 Commercial Road, 3200, open 8 AM to 5 PM Monday to Friday and 8:30 AM to 12:30 PM Saturday, is housed in the old Police Station building. Exceptionally helpful staff will quickly point visitors in the right direction. Two local taxi companies are **Junior Taxi Service** ((033) 394 5454, 391 Berg Street, and **Wilken Taxis** ((033) 342 3333. For medical emergencies contact **Medi Clinic** ((033) 342 7023, Payn Street, or **Medity** ((033) 342 6773.

WHAT TO SEE AND DO

The highlight sight is the **Natal Museum** ((033) 451 1401 FAX (033) 451 0561 WEB SITE www.nmsa .org.za, 237 Loop Street, 3200 Pietermaritzburg, 9 AM to 4:30 PM Monday to Saturday, entrance R4. This superb museum contains a diverse collection of exhibits including the last wild elephant in Natal (or rather its skeleton), a Hall of African Cultures, and an entire settler street recreated

OPPOSITE: White rhinos have found a new sanctuary in Phinda Reserve. ABOVE: Graceful netting keeps mosquitoes at a safe distance in Pongola.

in painstaking detail. Still worthwhile is the **Voortrekker Museum** ((033) 394 6834 FAX (033) 342 4100, 240 Church Street, also R4, with exhibits dating back to the Boer trek rather swamped by a huge poster rant against apartheid planted incongruously in the middle. In the grounds is an interesting recreation of a Voortrekker general's house.

Opposite the tourist office is the **Tatham Art Gallery** ((033) 342 1804, 60 Commercial Road, open Tuesday to Sunday 10 AM to 6 PM, which is well laid-out with some good South African artists and a surprisingly extensive collection of European art. Upstairs there's a café serving good light meals and cakes on tables and chairs painted by local artists, or on the shady veranda overlooking the busy street. As you stroll around the town, look out for the statue of Queen Victoria who looks down sternly on a crowd of bag vendors. In Church Street there's a statue of Mahatma Gandhi. He traced the embryo of his political philosophy to being thrown off the train here for being the wrong color when he was a young lawyer. There's also the **Macrorie House Museum** ((033) 394 2161, at the junction of Loop and Pine Streets, open Tuesday to Thursday 9 AM to 1 PM and 11 AM to 4 PM Sunday, a two-story Victorian House with furniture and relics from the British settler era.

The town is proud of being the birthplace of author Alan Paton, whose book *Cry, the Beloved Country* was partly filmed at **Natal Railway Museum** ((033) 343 1857, open 8 AM to 4 PM daily, 12 km (seven and a half miles) northeast of the town center in Hilton Station. On the second Sunday of the month one of the local trains fires up to steam to the nearby towns of Howick and Cedera. Just outside Howick is **Queen Elizabeth Park Nature Reserve**, with a network of short walking trails through an area rich with wildlife, at its best in spring. Perhaps it is better known as the headquarters of the KZN Nature Conservation Service, a good source of information and place to book your accommodation before heading out to the province's parks. **Natal Botanical Gardens**, on Sydenham Road, have plants from all over the world, which is not of so much interest to visitors who've come from all over the world, but it also includes a **Zulu Muthi Garden** created with the help of traditional healers and intended to inform viewers and also maintain the ancient healing skills with courses for local traditional healers.

There are two big sporting opportunities in this city. Every June the annual **Comrades Marathon** takes place with runners covering the minor route between Pietermaritzburg and Durban in just a few hours: it's almost a rite of passage for young and fit South Africans, with thousands taking part. Visitors should think twice. It covers

89 km (55.6 miles) of hilly terrain. Scarcely less taxing is the **Duzi Canoe Race** held in January, which follows the Msunduzi tributary and then the Umgeni River to finish up at Durban's Blue Lagoon.

WHERE TO STAY

At the top end of the market accommodation is rather limited. The huge **Karos Capital Towers** ((033) 394 2761 FAX 345 5476, 121 Commercial Road, is continually on the point of closing but hasn't yet. The **Redland Hotel** ((033) 394 3333 FAX (033) 393 3338, 1 George MacFarlane Lane, Wembley, R450, is the best in town. The **Hilton Hotel** ((033) 343 3311 FAX (033) 343 3722, 1 Hilton Avenue, Hilton, R350 double including breakfast, is one of the best hotels in the area but isn't part of the international chain; instead it is in the nearby village of Hilton from which it gets its name.

Then I followed the signs saying "Rooms R199 tonight only" outside the **Protea Imperial Palace** ((033) 342 6551 FAX (033) 342 9796, 224 Loop Street, the rooms cost over twice as much at R440 so I tried — like all the other guests — to make up the extra by overeating at the buffet breakfast. The hotel did, however, have a certain period charm. A better option is the **City Royal Hotel** ((033) 394 7072 FAX (033) 394 7080, 301 Burger Street, R280 a double including breakfast, with reductions on weekends. Cheaper is the **New Hotel Watson** ((033) 342 1604 FAX (033) 345 3124, 62 Church Street, R130 room only, but it's not in a good part of town. Backpackers are better served here, with **Earthwalker Backpackers** ((033) 342 0653 E-MAIL earthwalkers@satweb.co.sa, 150 King Edward Avenue, Scottsville, with rates from R40 per day, while more central is **Sunduzi Backpackers** ((033) 394 0072 FAX (033) 342 2428 E-MAIL Sunduzi @hotmail.com, 140 Berg Street.

WHERE TO EAT

With an active student population at the university, many of the restaurants specialize in cheap but good food. Best restaurant in town is **Da Vinci's** ((033) 345 6632, 117 Commercial Road, with a good Italian menu and which also stays open late with music. **La Provence** ((033) 342 4579, Loop Street, serves French cuisine while **White Mischief** ((033) 342 4579 is recommended for candlelit dinners over game or trout.

HOW TO GET THERE

Only 80 km (50 miles) away, Pietermaritzburg makes an easy day-trip from Durban, or at five hours from Johannesburg, you will want to stay a night at least. While traffic rushes from Durban to Johannesburg along the N3 this city slumbers undisturbed. It is small — and safe — enough to walk around and there is plenty to see, including the Natal Museum, some impressive public buildings, and the lively atmosphere of a university town so it's well worth a stop. If driving, take the middle of three exits from the N3 unless you like getting lost. There are flights from Johannesburg into Oribi Airport but you will then need to get a taxi into the town. In many ways it is easier to fly to Durban Airport, linked by the **Cheetah Shuttle Bus** ((033) 342 2673, 206 Longmarket Street, Pietermaritzburg, twice a day, with other intercity buses dropping passengers at the terminal by the information bureau. Trains tend to run very early in the morning or at night so a better option is either the Translux or Greyhound bus services; book through **Capital Coach** ((033) 345 1348, in the same building as the Publicity Association.

THE MIDLANDS MEANDER

A good way of exploring the Natal Midlands, the area to the west of Pietermaritzburg, is through the "Midlands Meander." Originally a marketing concept linking six art and craft studios, by which they opened their doors to passing guests, this has expanded to include hotels, restaurants, and commercial attractions. Its success has attracted new artists and craftsmen to the area and revitalized communities that previously relied on farming. Now there are more than 100 ports of call, ranging from art studios to country hotels, herb farms, tea gardens, pottery centers, and weaving workshops. A choice of routes marked with road-signs makes it easy to find your way around and promotional literature gives full details of opening times, etc. The concept has been much copied and there are now meandering routes all over South Africa, but the Midlands Meander is still the best, introducing those with their own transportation to little-known parts of the rural countryside.

The Natal Midlands extend from Hilton just outside Pietermaritzburg west to Fort Nottingham and north to Mooi River. Details of the Meander are obtainable throughout the area, or by contacting the **Midlands Meander Committee** ((033) 263 6008 FAX (033) 330 5510 E-MAIL mm@futurenet .co.za WEB SITE www.midlandsmeander.org.za, Box 874, Howick 3290. It's not a route particularly suited to backpackers: not only are most of the establishments on the Meander primarily commercial, they are also well out of the scope of public transportation. However it does take in some charming small family-run hotels known for their cuisine and settings. Well off the beaten track the Midlands Meander does present a good excuse to visit them.

Where to Stay

The best include **Granny Mouse** ((033) 234 4071 FAX (033) 234 4429 on the R103 between Lidgetton and Balgowan, a rural retreat where the interiors are high Victorian with flurries and flounces, and candlelit dinners of traditional English cooking backed by extensive wine cellars. Swimming and croquet are specialties, while riding and tennis are available nearby. Bed with breakfast costs R700. Nearby the **Penny Lane Guest House** ((033) 234 4332 FAX (033) 234 4617 WEB SITE www .zing.co.za/pennylane, 11 km (just under seven miles) on the R103 from the N2, is a small also a good out-of-town choice for visitors to Pietermaritzburg; bed with breakfast rates from

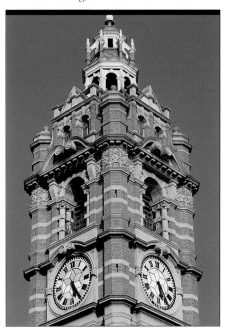

R450. More rural is **Old Halliwell** ((033) 230 2602 FAX (033) 230 3430, on the R114 from the N3, prices from R600 with breakfast, an old wagon-route house dating back to the 1830s, where golf and fishing are the favored day's activities and winter evenings spent around a log fire or enjoying the French cuisine. **Rawdons Hotel** ((033) 263 6044 FAX (033) 263 6048 E-MAIL rawdons@futurest.co.za WEB SITE www.rawdons.co.za, on the Old Main Road, offers accommodation from R600 with breakfast. This is a 81-hectare (200-acre) fly-fishing estate with a resident fly-fishing instructor for those whose idea of fun is pulling out stocked fish from a pond. More to my taste is the fact that Rawdons is also home to a microbrewery with four draught ales on tap.

A walkable city, Pietermaritzburg contains some of South Africa's finest colonial architecture.

THE NATAL DRAKENSBERGS

Confusingly, the mountains from the Eastern Cape to the Blyde River Canyon are all technically part of the Drakensberg Range. In fact, this range of basalt mountains stretch even further, from the Cape to the Limpopo. But to anyone from Kwa-Zulu-Natal the only Drakensbergs worthy of the name are those found in the Natal Drakensberg National Park. This striking range, 200 km (125 miles) in length, forms a natural barrier with the landlocked kingdom of Lesotho and is one of South Africa's most beautiful wilderness areas, with spectacular views, endless hiking trails, and the country's second-largest collection of San rock art. The national park is divided into three main areas: the Southern, Central and Northern 'Bergs.

THE SOUTHERN DRAKENSBERG

The Southern 'Berg is set around the dramatic **Sani Pass**, where a hairpin road switchbacks its way into the remote kingdom of Lesotho, rising up above the towns of Underberg and Himeville. Although not as high as the 'Bergs further north, the Southern Drakensbergs offer some of the best fly-fishing areas in the country and plenty of hikes quite strenuous enough for even the fittest. The most popular activities include hiking on marked trails. Cobham State Forest, Bushman's Nek, and Garden Castle are all south of Sani Pass while Loteni and Kamberg, with its beautiful examples of San rock art, is north. The most popular hike, suiting all levels of fitness, is the five-day, 60 km (37.5 miles) Giant's Cup Trail, running from Sani Pass to Bushman's Nek with camping in KZN lodges en route costing R40 per person per night. Book up to a year in advance with KZN (see contact details below) to secure a place.

For many visitors the area's main appeal is the pervasive influence of Basotho culture spreading over from the mountainous kingdom of Lesotho. There are several local operators who run trips up the Sani Pass and across into Lesotho. This can be done independently (with a passport) but you need a powerful four-wheel-drive to make it. The road climbs 800 m (2,600 ft) in just two kilometers (slightly over a mile). Among the best operators are the **Sani Pass Carriers** ((033) 701 1017, who make daily journeys from the Imperial Hotel in Loop Street, Pietermaritzburg into Lesotho, charging R170 per person, or **Thaba Tours** (/FAX (033) 701 1419 or (082) 824 2916, Box 213, Underberg 3257, who run tours from Underberg for R120, with lunch in the highlands across the border.

Underberg and Himeville

Underberg is the largest town in the area. Their **Tourist Information** ((033) 701 1471 FAX (033) 702 1158 E-MAIL sdpa@futurenet.org.za, Box 300,

Underberg 3257, can provide full details of the local operators, many of whom sport their own signs advertising tourist information but recommending mainly themselves. There's also a 24-hour hospital here: the **Riverview** ((033) 701 1516. In-town accommodation options include the central **Underberg Inn** ((033) 701 1412, High Street, R220 with breakfast, with cheaper dormitory accommodation for backpackers.

Five kilometers (three miles) into the mountains, the smaller village of Himeville also offers last-stop facilities before taking to the hills. **Tourist Information** (/FAX (033) 702 1158, Box 169, Himeville 3256, is open Monday to Friday 9 AM to 4:30 PM, and the **Himeville Arms** ((033) 702 1305, also on Arbuckle Street, R300 with breakfast, is a good place to stay as well as buy a drink.

Where to Stay

Most of the best accommodation, however, is out of town, making the most of the mountain setting. Hikers will want to make use of camps and shelters run by the **KZN Nature Conservation Service** ((033) 845 1000 FAX (033) 845 1001, Box 1306, 9 Cascades 3202. They arrange fairly primitive accommodation in various parts of the park. In Cobham they have caves, at Loteni chalets, and at Kamberg a communal rest camp.

There are smarter options. The **Sani Pass Hotel** ((033) 702 1320 FAX (033) 702 0220 E-MAIL sanipass hotel@futurenet.co.za WEB SITE www.sanipass hotel.co.za, Box 44, Himeville 3256, offers cottages and rooms with a full range of sporting activities available. That they accommodate 200 guests might temper the mountain peace but keeps prices low and the bar and restaurant lively: prices from R640, dinner, bed, and breakfast. Alternatively the **Penwarm Country Lodge** ((033) 701 1777 FAX (033) 701 1341 E-MAIL CapeTownsports@futurenet.co.za WEB SITE www.penwarn.co.za, Box 253, Underberg 3257, manages to keep their prices low in a smaller setting: just five rooms are converted from a 100-year-old sandstone barn, in a 1,300-hectare (3,212-acre) game farm, with prices from R600 full board. There are also a few self-catering chalets and a cave, sleeping two, with gas plates for cooking, a wood-stove for warmth, and a stone bath, set against a private trout dam. Backpacker alternatives include the **Sani Top Backpackers** (/FAX (033) 702 1158, Box 232 Himeville 3256, R340 for dinner, bed, and breakfast, which also offers the highest pub in Africa, perfect for a winter warming drink.

How to Get There

From the N3 take the Underberg turnoff at exit 99 onto the R617. This takes you through Bulwer and on to Underberg and Himeville, the closest

Clear air and still waters at the Champagne Castle in the Central Drakensberg.

villages to the Drakensbergs. By public transportation, the **Sani Pass Carriers** run from Durban three times a week and Pietermaritzburg every day to Underberg, with minibus taxis running on to Himeville. The roads in the area are mainly dirt and can be closed after rain.

THE CENTRAL DRAKENSBERG

The Central Drakensberg, dusted with snow in winter, is bordered to the west by three of the four highest peaks in Africa — Mafadi, Popple Creek, and Giant's Castle. In the south the only roads reaching up to serve small camps are run by the KwaZulu-Natal Nature Conservation Service (see contact details above). For information about travel in the area the central town — and the main source of travel information and supplies — is at Bergville, where the **Drakensberg Tourist Information** ((036) 448 1557 FAX (036) 448 1088 E-MAIL draktour @ls.lia.net WEB SITE www.drakensberg.co.za, Box 325, Bergville 3350, is found. **Giant's Castle** itself is a game reserve, best explored on foot; **Hillside** is a center for horseback riding with outrides lasting hours or days tailored to beginners and experts; **Injasuti** is a hiking center, famed for the rock art in surrounding valleys and caves. Accommodation is generally in campsites or basic self-catering huts, comfortable but little more, booked through KZN in Pietermaritzburg (see above).

There is, however, one hotel in this area that in itself justifies a special visit. **Cleopatra Mountain Farmhouse** ((033) 263 7243 FAX (082) 373 7054 E-MAIL cleo@pmb.lia.net WEB SITE www.cleo mountain.com, Box 17, Balgowan 3275, consists of five bedrooms that combine character and luxury, set around a lake with a restaurant where the cuisine is taken extremely seriously. Owned by Richard and Mouse Poynton, this used to be a fishing hut; until 1962 no women were allowed in. Now it is far more open-minded, and fired by the interior-designing skill of Mouse and the culinary enthusiasm of Richard, it is a great place to stay, privately set on the edge of the national park boundary. Rates are an extremely reasonable R700 for dinner, bed, and breakfast, though this can be increased by excessive reliance on the comprehensive wine cellar. In this spectacular setting, prepare to enjoy some of South Africa's finest Italian-influenced cuisine, and the deserted mountains in the area are perfect for working off the meal, with remote and unmapped examples of San rock art.

The next road west is the R600, which goes through Winterton, on its way to KZN's campsite at Monk's Cowl, passing through a spectacular area known as "Champagne Valley." It's name has its roots far in the past, but is curiously appropriate for the present day, as the road is lined with country lodges and rural retreats where champagne is, indeed, the drink of choice of many guests. It is also home to one of the area's more surprising attractions: the **Drakensberg Boy's Choir** ((036) 468 1012 WEB SITE www.dbcs .kzn.school.za, P/Bag X20, Winterton 3340. This choir tours the world, but when at home at its school near Winterton holds regular concerts on Wednesdays at 3:30 PM (in term time) in the school auditorium — very "Sound of Music."

Where to Stay

The highest hotel is the **Champagne Castle Hotel** ((036) 468 1063 with a range of rondavels, cottages, and family units priced from R600 full board. Further down the slope is **Champagne Sports Resort** ((036) 468 1088 FAX (036) 468 1072 E-MAIL csr@intecom.co.za, P/Bag X9, Winterton 3340, an award-winning leisure resort including an 18-hole golf course and accommodation starting from

R800 for dinner, bed, and breakfast. Just lower, the **Aardmore Ceramic Studio** ((036) 468 1314 FAX (036) 468 1242, Box 1005 Winterton 3340, combines a creative workshop producing world-class ceramics with a friendly, intimate guest farm. Horse-riding, mountain bikes, and walks are mixed with an inspiring, artistic atmosphere with views of Cathkin Peak, Champagne Castle and other mountains; rates are R370 for a rondavel with midweek specials and discounts. Five kilometers (three miles) south of Winterton the **Imani Guest House** (/FAX (036) 488 1265 WEB SITE www.hideaways.co.za/imani, Box 121, Winterton 3340, offers a farmhouse experience in a smaller, more intimate setting for R400 with breakfast. Backpackers can stay well up in the Dragon Peaks at **Inkosana Lodge** (/FAX (036) 468 1202, Box 60, Winterton 3340, with beds from R60 per person, set among 20 hectares (50 acres) of grassland. An added extra here is the screen-printing studio:

sleep under hand-painted duvets then have a go yourself using the lodge's own facilities.

The third road into the Central Drakensbergs heads up towards the Cathedral Peak, and the **Cathedral Peak Hotel** ((036) 468 1063 FAX (036) 468 1306 E-MAIL cph@ls.lia.net WEB SITE www .cathedralpeak.co.za, P/Bag X8, Winterton 3340, with its own golf course as well as helipad for aerial tours of the mountains. Charges are from R720 for a two-person chalet.

How to Get There

The Central Drakensberg can be reached from the N3 Durban to Johannesburg highway. From Johannesburg take the R616; from Durban take the R74 Bergville Road. There is little public transportation to or in the area.

Fishing and hiking are the main activities in the Central Drakensberg's Champagne Valley.

NORTHERN DRAKENSBERG

Perhaps the most photographed feature of the Drakensbergs, the **Amphitheater** is one of the most dramatic views of the northern range, enclosed in the boundaries of the **Royal Natal National Park**. The best way to appreciate this view, where the escarpment tumbles down a sheer edge of rock, is on the six-hour hike from the Tugela Gorge walk. This starts and finishes at Tendele Camp, maintained by the **KZN Nature Conservation Service** ((033) 845 1000 FAX (033) 845 1001, Box 13069, Cascades 3202, which maintains a camp, a selection of comfortable, well-equipped huts with

superb views of the Amphitheater. Cooks will prepare food but you need to bring all supplies; rates are from R180 for a chalet. KZN also subcontract the **Royal Natal National Park Hotel** ((036) 438 6200 FAX (036) 438 6101, P/Bag 4, Mont-Aux-Sources 3353, set within the park boundaries and claiming regal status from a visit in 1947.

A step up in luxury—and expense—will take you to the **Mont-Aux-Sources Hotel** (/FAX (036) 438 6230 E-MAIL mont.aux.sources@movenpick .co.za WEBSITE www.movenpick.co.za, P/Bag 1670, Bergville 3350, a luxurious mountain resort where there are a range of outdoor activities and spa treatments on offer with rates from R580 to R715 per night. In the same area, but rather smaller and less formal, is the **Cavern** ((036) 438 6270 FAX (036) 438 6334, P/Bag X1626, Bergville 3350, with bowls, tennis, riding, and tours of San rock art sites; rates are from R480 full board.

How to Get There

From Durban, take the N3 and then take the R616 towards Bergville, then right on the R74 signed for Jagersrust and travel for a further 30 km (19 miles). From Johannesburg, turn off the N3 at Harrismith and take the N5, then turn onto the R74. There is little or no public transportation to this part of the Drakensberg Range.

THE BATTLEFIELDS

Northeast KwaZulu-Natal is the heartland of battlefield country. It is here that some of the bloodiest conflicts were fought: first between settlers and Zulus, which saw Boers and the British in a fervent and dedicated alliance, and then later the two Anglo-Boer wars which saw them as fervent and dedicated foes. It is also the region that has done most to develop the battlefields to bring history to life for a new generation of visitors.

The area around Dundee is dotted with battlefields: Isandlwana, Rorke's Drift, and Blood River, to name but a few. Around Ladysmith there are more: Spioenkop, Colenso, Vaalkrans, headline-grabbing conflicts from the Boer Wars. All these became household names in Europe around the turn of the nineteenth century, as the new profession of war reportage and the science of photography came together to meet a public demand for information about new and unsuspected corners of the world. News of defeat and glory from the colonial front line were brought back to a hungry audience at home, while British ports were filled with battleships boarding conscripts for the long sea journey south.

There are plenty of individuals and organizations that will show visitors round the battlefields, and they can be found either in the city tourist boards of Durban and Johannesburg, more fully listed in TAKING A TOUR, page 56, or using local guides in the nearest town, usually found through the nearest tourist information office. With your own car it is easy to reach the battlefields, but make sure there's space to squeeze in a local guide, without there will not be much to see beyond a confusing range of mountains and veld and the occasional enigmatic memorial. Local guides can be found through the tourist offices of the major Battlefield towns of Ladysmith (mainly focused on the Boer Wars) and Dundee (Zulu War). The other alternative for self-drivers to immerse themselves in the war experience is to stay in one of the atmospheric — but more expensive — lodges set up in and around the battlefields, most of which employ resident historians to bring the past to life (see RELIVE SOUTH AFRICA'S BATTLES OF BIRTH, page 18 in TOP SPOTS). If you can't find, or don't want, a local guide David Rattray has produced an excellent collection of five audiocassettes which bring the Zulu War's history vividly to life; highly recommended, even at their cost of R300, these can be bought at his lodge, Fugitive's Drift or from the tourist office in Dundee (see DUNDEE AND THE ZULU WAR, page 244). He plans to produce a further series of cassettes for the Boer Wars, and I, for one, hope he does soon. Backpackers or those relying on public transportation will find it very difficult and slow to see around the battlefields and would be best advised to take a tour.

LADYSMITH AND THE BOER WARS

Sited in a gentle valley around the Klippe River, Ladysmith was a British Garrison outpost besieged for 118 days by Boer forces, who pounded the town

and the surrounding battlefields. Without your own transportation the town, spread out across the flat Klippe River Valley, is dauntingly large. A local taxi firm is **Flora's Taxis (** (082) 808 7769.

From the minute you see the artillery guns proudly standing in the main street it is clear that this is a town with a major military past, and to learn more the Tourist Information Office has provide a detailed booklet packed with information on the local buildings of interest, with two itineraries designed to suit visitors on walk-about or drive-about: "edutainement" they call it. Before heading off, of the town's three museums most famous, and best, is the **Ladysmith Siege Museum**, adjoining the town hall, open from 8 AM to

from the surrounding hills from 1899 to 1900. The drawn-out agony of the British troops hit the headlines back in the United Kingdom, even as other European countries warmed to the idea of a handful of farmers pinning down 12,000 arrogant British soldiers. Now it is a city divided in a characteristic way: the white population lives in the plushest part of town, the colored population in their suburbs, while the black population live on the outskirts, if not in shanty satellites 16 km (10 miles) from town. To visit these contact Vusi Dayile (** (036) 631 7081, a guide who will take you on a township tour. For most visitors, however, the first port of call should be the very helpful **Tourist Information Office (** (036) 637 2992 WEB SITE www .Ladysmith.co.za, Town Hall, Murchison Street, open Monday to Friday 8 AM to 4 PM and Saturday to noon, adjoining the museum. They can arrange approved guides to show visitors round the town

4 PM Monday to Friday and to noon Saturday. Inside are dramatic recreations of the Boer hilltop fortifications, period photographs, and armaments. Helpful curators are on hand to explain the importance of the various exhibits. One of the most useful displays is a relief plan of the town and the surrounding hills — emerging blinking into the sunlight the enormity of the scene is clear. Ladysmith is a large town in a huge valley, the hills low against the horizon, and the reality of being pinned down by an incessant, random shelling seems suddenly very real. And to walk up one of the surrounding hills, steep and almost impassable with a scatter of rocky boulders and animal holes, is to realize how invidious was the British position and how hardy the Boer rebels.

OPPOSITE: Zululand's harsh conditions demand a specific type of plant life. ABOVE: The scorched-grass battlefields of Isandlwana.

There are a number of battlefields in the Lady-smith area, including Colenso, Pieters Hill, Elandslaagte, and Vaalkrans, but the most famous of all is Spioenkop. One of the whole war's most costly in British lives, this was a disastrous attempt to relieve the siege of Ladysmith that left 600 British soldiers dead on a small, undefended hilltop 35 km (22 miles) from town. Under cover of mist 2,000 men successfully seized the gently-sloping summit of Spioenkop. Their first problem was that the ground was too hard to properly entrench, but when the mist cleared they found they'd chosen the wrong position to defend: their positions were overlooked by Boer snipers on surrounding hills. Worse, the Boer Mausers outranged the British guns. For a full day the British troops were pinned down by the Boers and picked off, one by one. When darkness fell the survivors fled for their lives, little realizing the Boers had already melted into the hills. This was the last British attempt to use classical battle techniques; from this point on they increasingly adopted the guerrilla tactics of their Boer foes, a strategy which ultimately led to the relief of Ladysmith and, eventually, victory. There are a number of graves and a monument on the hill, but to make much sense of the battle order, a guide is almost essential. I was shown round by **Elizabeth Spire't** ((036) 637 7702, who arrived armed with well-thumbed source books to answer specialized questions. The adjoining land has been declared a nature reserve, so it is possible, with binoculars, to spot rhino from a field drenched with British blood.

Another group of famous local residents who have put Ladysmith on the map are the **Ladysmith Black Mambazo** WEB SITE www.mambazo.com, the choral group who backed Paul Simon on his Graceland album but have also issued plenty, rather better, of their own. These are commemorated in the **Cultural Center and Museum** ((036) 637 2231 or (036) 637 4922, 25 Keate Street, open Monday to Friday 9 AM to 5 PM and Saturday to 1 PM, R5, which has a couple of Zulu houses and a good artifact collection.

Where to Stay and Eat

The best place to stay here is on a farm near the Spioenkop battlefield at the **Three Tree Hill Lodge** ((082) 379 1864, Box 3534, Ladysmith 3370, owned by David Rattray (see RELIVE SOUTH AFRICA'S BATTLES OF BIRTH, page 18 in TOP SPOTS). Accommodation options in Ladysmith include the **Royal Hotel** (/FAX (036) 637 2176, 140 Murchison Street, R380 with breakfast. This hotel was regularly shelled at lunchtime by the Boers because it was a center for colonial conspiracies between Frank (brother of Cecil) Rhodes and Leander Starr Jamieson, and still retains its colonial atmosphere. Now the shells have stopped it's still a recommended place for lunch. Alternatively the **Crown Protea Hotel**

((036) 637 2266 FAX (036) 637 6458, 90 Murchison Street, R400 with breakfast. An alternative resting-place in the town itself is the **Boer and Brit B&B** ((036) 631 2184 FAX (036) 637 3957 E-MAIL diorhc@ls.lia.net, 49 Convent Road, R180 including breakfast, stacked with memorabilia of its own.

If traveling to or from Johannesburg, a spectacular place to stay is 60 km (37.5 miles) along the main N3 to Van Reenen Pass, then seven kilometers (just under four and a half miles) along a dirt road to the right by the Caltex Garage. **Oaklands Country Manor** ((058) 671 0067 FAX (058) 671 0077 E-MAIL oaklands@compuserve .com WEB SITE www.informed~ibis.com/ oaklands/, R500 with breakfast, offers mountain biking, horse riding, and general clean country air. The owner also conducts battlefield tours in full period dress. The cheapest place to stay in the Ladysmith area is **Mambasa Hutted Camp** ((036) 488 1003 FAX (036) 488 1116, off the R600 Winterton Road, whose beehive huts are set on the banks of the Tugela River adjoining Spioenkop Nature Reserve, with canoes and blackwater tubes available for guests use; R45 per person. For a relaxing outdoor experience within sight of Spioenkop **KZN Nature Conservation Service** ((033) 845 1000 FAX (033) 845 1001, Box 13069, Cascades 3202, have self-catering campsites and chalets within the nature reserve with costs from R180.

Restaurants in Ladysmith include Swainson's Restaurant and the Carvery in the Royal Hotel, but also recommended is **Mario's** ((036) 637 2176, Murchison Street, and the **Guinea Fowl Country Restaurant and Pub**, Piazza San Marco, which is the town's most sociable bar.

How to Get There

Ladysmith is on the N11 that turns off from the N3 Durban-Johannesburg highway. By public transportation it is easily reached by train from Durban and Johannesburg but this arrives in the middle of the night and in any case a rental car will be needed to travel around the battlefields themselves. The Greyhound bus stops here between Johannesburg and Durban while the **Translux** ((031) 361 8333 bus stops here between Bloemfontein and Durban. Spioenkop is 35 km (22 miles) west of the town, taking the N11 and crossing the N3, when the road becomes the R616. For air inquiries, call **Ladysmith Airport** ((036) 637 2992.

DUNDEE AND THE ZULU WAR

The town of Dundee, owing its existence to coal deposits exploited since 1880, is most interesting due to its proximity to the battlefields of the Zulu War, but it does have a certain charm all of its own with wide streets and a calm, rural atmosphere.

The **Tourist Information Office** ((034) 212 2121 FAX (034) 212 3856 E-MAIL info@talana.co.za,

Civic Gardens, Victoria Street, open Monday to Friday 9 AM to 4:45 PM, is a helpful source of maps and information and can introduce battlefield guides if required. A kilometer and a half (one mile) from the town center on the Vryheid road, the **Talana Museum** ((034) 212 2654, open Monday to Friday 8 AM to 4 PM, Saturday 10 AM to 4 PM and Sunday noon to 4 PM, admission R5, is the only one in South Africa to be built on an actual battlefield. Having said that, the memories it commemorates have little to do with war. In the eight-hectare (20-acre) grounds the museum includes a life-size model of a section of underground mine, a strange collection of blown glass, and several completely restored settler dwellings, many of which saw

service as dressing stations in the first major battle of the Boer Wars, of Talana. The **Dundee Publicity Association** has a second office here: ((034) 212 2654. Back in town the central **Moth Museum** ((034) 212 1250, at the junction of Wilson and Beaconsfield streets, has one of the best private collections of military memorabilia in the country; viewing by appointment only.

Battle of Blood River, 1838

Certainly one of the most affecting monuments, the Battle of Blood River was a psychological turning-point in the colonization of South Africa. Just after Dingane's massacre of Piet Retief with his band of negotiators, at this battle a huge Zulu *impi* (army) — estimates vary from 4,000 to 15,000 — attacked a Boer contingent of 464 men—and lost. The Boers, under Andries Pretorius, having received reports of a Zulu army nearby, laagered

their wagons in a defensive circle, enclosing their stores and animals. The Zulus, armed with their short stabbing *assegais*, were no match for the Boer marksmen, and after their attack had faltered a horseback commando rode out to massacre any survivors. There were no Boer casualties but 3,000 Zulus died. The successful outcome of this battle assured the Boers that God was on their side.

At the site of the battle there is a laager of oversized wagons cast in bronze, commemorating the Boer victory with stolid confidence. There is little reference to the Zulus who died under superior firepower as they struggled across the river, swamp and *donga* (riverbed). The fighting continued for hours before a reinforcing commando came to the laager's rescue and the victory stands as one of the greatest in the history of world colonial conflicts. The Blood River memorial can be visited from the main battlefield towns. Travel 27 km (17 miles) from Dundee on the R33 (or 45 km/28 miles) from Vryheid and turn off for another 26 km (16 miles) along a dirt track; the monument is well signposted.

Isandlwana and Rorke's Drift

The huge defeat of the British colonial army at Isandlwana sent shockwaves throughout the Empire. After years of maliciously trying to provoke Cetshwayo, the Zulu leader, into open revolt the British forces finally decided to force his hand in 1879 by invading Zulu territory. Three columns of the British attacking force blundered across the Buffalo River in January 1879, sweltering in the hot summer sun, with the aim of driving the Zulu army back towards Ulundi. They had no fear of a native attack; their concern was that the Zulus would not stand to fight. With this as their major concern they made no attempt to fortify their position, and allowed their forces to become split: all of the infantry and most of the guns were set off to chase around the countryside after rumored sightings of the Zulu army. The remaining British forces, including 1000 battle-hardened riflemen and two guns, waited at Isandlwana, in the shade of a sphinx-like hill that eerily echoed the shape of the 24th Regiment's cap badge.

In retrospect, a long litany of misjudgments and strategic errors can be seen, leading up to what was to follow. And the best way to analyze the situation as it happened is overlooking the battlefield itself. Suffice it to say that 20,000 *impis* under Cetshwayo overwhelmed the British forces, taking the camp in just a few hours. Of 800 British soldiers at breakfast on January 22, just 30 lived to tell the tale. This battle forms the basis of the film *Zulu Dawn* — although local historians will take issue with some of the interpretations.

Two Zulu warriors in training with their bows and arrows.

Later on that day a separate engagement took place, immortalized in the in the 1960s' film *Zulu*. The Battle of Rorke's Drift took place as the main British force were already dying at Isandlwana, when an unauthorized Zulu battalion who had missed the main battle disobeyed orders and attacked a Catholic mission commandeered as a field hospital by British Forces just outside Zulu territory. Against overwhelming odds a 126-strong force of British soldiers held out overnight against an attacking army estimated to number 4,500. The next morning the surviving British troops were still able to croak a welcome to relieving forces after a night spent fighting hand-to-hand, room-to-room through the modest, stone-built structure,

off an international industry that has spread to many of South Africa's conflict-torn towns and cities, and his secret is an engaging, melodramatic enthusiasm both for the Zulu people and his country's history. The private reserve that surrounds his lodge includes 17 km (10.6 miles) of river frontage, part of which was crossed by the handful of survivors fleeing the field at Isandlwana and where two officers died trying to protect the Queen's Colors. Guests here can follow the trail and struggle back from the battlefield, reliving the desperate adventure through the rocky landscape, riven by rivers and ravines. This puts a new edge on the battlefield experience as well as the sharpening the appetite for the evening meal, which is

with the hours of darkness lit by flames and embers spilling from the thatch overhead. The original buildings have been rebuilt and house a small museum, open 8 AM to 5 PM, admission free.

More battles were to follow in the course of the campaign to destroy the Zulu empire, most notably Eshowe and Ulundi. However the battles of Rorke's Drift and Isandlwana are the best to visit, not least because of the skilled historians readily available to show who did what, where.

Where to Stay

By far the best place to stay is **Fugitive's Drift** ℂ (034) 642 1843 FAX (034) 642 1843 E-MAIL fugdrift@ dundee.lia.net, which is just a few kilometers from Rorke's Drift. This comfortable, colonial-style lodge is owned and run by David Rattray. This top historian has almost single-handedly promoted battlefield tourism in the area and sparked

lavishly taken on a huge, sociable table amidst exhibits and cuttings dating from the period. Rates are R1,500, full board, with battlefield tours at R250 per person. See RELIVE SOUTH AFRICA'S BATTLES OF BIRTH, page 18 in TOP SPOTS to read more about David Rattray's battlefield experience. Under the same ownership but different management is the **Fugitive's Drift Guest House** (contact through Fugitive's Drift Lodge) which runs lower-priced accommodation by the entrance of the private game reserve and has a much younger atmosphere; they also conduct their own battlefield tours. Alternatively, **Rorke's View Guest House** ℂ (034) 642 1741 Fax (034) 642 1654, Dundee, has views over the battlefield, charges R240 with breakfast, and offers horseback riding and hikes on marked trails.

It takes half an hour to drive from Rorke's Drift to the battlefield at Isandlwana, where the areas only truly upmarket lodge is found. Overlooking the battlefield from the cave where Cetshwayo himself oversaw his troops is **Isandlwana Lodge** ((034) 271 8301 FAX (034) 271 8306 E-MAIL isand@ icon.co.za WEB SITE www.isandlwana.co.za, is a newly-built thatched building molded into the hillside overlooking the wide valley. Rates are R3,000 for dinner, bed, and breakfast, with a proportion going to the local community. This is certainly the most convenient base for Isandlwana. However much depends on the historian talking you through the events of the day, as it is the dramatized account of the battle that brings the scene to life. It requires tremendous acting skills to bring the past to life.

worldonline.co.za, Springvale Farm, Wesselsnek, where bed and breakfast is R150 per night.

There is a greater range of accommodation in Dundee, an hour away, where guests aren't expected to pay for a battlefield location. The **Royal Hotel** ((034) 212 2147 FAX (034) 218 2146, Victoria Street, has comfortable rooms for R500 with breakfast, while an atmospheric farmhouse, surrounded by verandas and flowers is **Thornley** ((034) 212 2738, just beyond the Talana Museum, R200 including breakfast, offers a more personal stay. The backpacker option is the **Environmental** ((034) 212 2215, Tatham Street, with dormitory accommodation and restaurant facilities for 100 people; R40 per person per night.

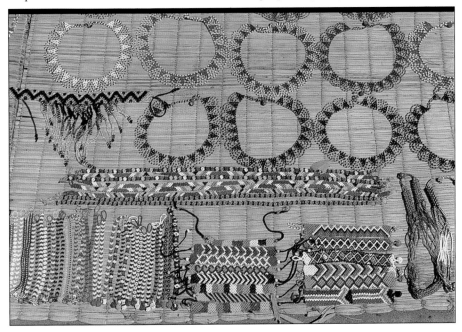

Penny Farthing (/FAX (034) 642 1925 E-MAIL penny@dundee.lia.net WEB SITE www.battlefields .co.za/penny offers farmhouse accommodation for R260 and is 30 km (18.7 miles) south of Dundee, two kilometers (just over a mile) down a farm track off the R33. Meanwhile, blending the military and cultural experience, **Isibindi Lodge** ((032) 947 0538 FAX (032) 947 0659, Umhlali, nine kilometers (just under six miles) from Rorke's Drift, offers atmospheric beehive accommodation in a natural setting between Rorke's Drift and Elandskraal. The experience here includes plenty of game drives and walks around a private nature reserve, whitewater rafting on the Buffalo River, and cultural visits to the local Zulu villages. Rates are from R1,300; most guests love it although some find the price quite steep. A less expensive option is in the nearby village of Elandslaagte for **Umkhamba Leisure Trails** ((034) 651 1392 E-MAIL umkhamba@

How to Get There

Isandlwana is 70 km (43 miles) southeast of Dundee, five kilometers (just over three miles) off the R68 on tarmac roads. Rorke's Drift is 45 km (28 miles) from Dundee and can be reached either from the R33 (turn left after 14 km/just over eight and a half miles) or from the R68 (turn left after 26 km/16.2 miles). Either way, you will have to drive across a certain amount of dirt road, but the scenery is spectacular. If coming from Durban, take care on the R33 through Tugela Ferry: there have been some security problems on this road and it should not be driven after dark. Bear in mind as well that the roads, though generally good, are pitted with occasional potholes which can break axles if taken at speed.

OPPOSITE: A Zulu girl threads and weaves beads into traditional necklaces and bracelets.
ABOVE: The finished products for sale.

Travelers' Tips

GETTING THERE

The national carrier is South African Airways, who fly to South Africa from Australasia, North and South America, and many European cities. Most flights once landed in Johannesburg, but now the more tranquil city of Cape Town sees 80% of new visitors. Durban used to be a third hub, but is now more generally reached after a stopover in Johannesburg. Many other airlines fly to South Africa. British Airways, Virgin Atlantic, and KLM are the best links from America and London; and these and Air France, Lufthansa, KLM, Olympic, Swissair, Emirates, Ethiopian and Sabena all fly regularly from European hubs. From Australasia, Quantas and Air New Zealand fly to South Africa, with Southeast Asian airline companies making the journey less expensively but circuitously.

ARRIVING (AND LEAVING)

Citizens of the United States, Canada, Australia, and New Zealand can stay three months with a valid passport and a return air ticket. Citizens of the European Community can stay six months. African and Eastern European citizens may need a visa, which cannot be obtained at the border and must be purchased in advance. Don't overstay your visa, as you may well be arrested and tried, with a substantial fine the most likely outcome. For extensions the Aliens Control sections at one of the offices of Home Affairs will be helpful if you have evidence of funds. In Johannesburg the office is ((011) 836 3228, 77 Harrison Street, while in Cape Town it is ((021) 462 4970, 56 Barrack Street. The airport tax is generally included in the air ticket.

EMBASSIES AND CONSULATES

FOREIGN EMBASSIES IN SOUTH AFRICA

Australia ((012) 342 3740, 292 Orient Street, Arcadia, Pretoria 0002.
Austria ((011) 883 5739, 60 Trafalgar Place, Sandhurst, Sandton, Johannesburg 2001.
Belgium ((011) 447 6434, Smuts Building, 158 Jan Smuts Avenue, Johannesburg 2001.
Britain ((011) 337 8940, Nineteenth Floor, Sanlam Center, Jeppe & Von Wielligh Street, Johannesburg 2001.
Canada ((012) 342 6923, Arcadia Street, Hatfield, Pretoria 0002; Consulate General (Johannesburg) ((011) 725 159, Kapteijn Street, Johannesburg 2001; Consulate General (Cape Town) ((021) 242 410, 74 Queen Victoria Street, Cape Town 8001.

Denmark ((012) 322 0595, Eighth Floor, Sanlam Center, Andries & Pretorius Street, Pretoria 0002.
France ((011) 334 3468, 35th floor, Carlton, Commissioner Street, Johannesburg 2001.
Germany ((012) 344 3854, 180 Blackwood Street, Pretoria 0002.
Ireland ((012) 342 5062, Tulbagh Park, 1234 Church Street, Arcadia, Pretoria 0002.
Italy ((012) 435 541, 796 George Avenue, Arcadia, Pretoria 0002.
Japan ((012) 342 2100, Second Floor, Sanlam Building, Festival & Arcadia Street, Hatfield, Pretoria 0002.
Netherlands ((012) 344 3910, 825 Arcadia Street, Arcadia, Pretoria 0002.
Portugal ((011) 336 3820, Diamond Corner Building, 68 Eloff Street, Johannesburg 2001.
Sweden ((012) 426 6400, Ninth Floor, Old Mutual Building, 167 Andries Street, Hatfield, Pretoria 0002.
Switzerland ((011) 442 7500, Cradock Heights, 21 Cradock Avenue, Rosebank, Johannesburg 2001.

SOUTH AFRICAN EMBASSIES AND CONSULATES ABROAD

Australia ((02) 233 8188, 8 Light House, Sydney 2001 NSW, and ((06) 273 2424, Rhodes Place, Yarralumla, Canberra ACT 2600.
Austria ((01) 320 64930 FAX (01) 320 67226, Sandgasse 33, A-1190 Vienna.
Belgium and Luxembourg ((02) 285 4400 FAX (02) 285 4402, 26 Rue de la Loi, B7/8, 1040 Brussels.
Canada ((613) 744-0330 FAX (613) 741-1639 E-MAIL rsafrica@sympatico.ca, 15 Sussex Drive, Ottawa, Ontario K1M 1M8, and ((416) 364 0314, Suite 2515, Exchange Tower, Toronto M5X 1ES.
Germany ((030) 825011 FAX (030) 826 6543, Villa Harteneck, Douglasstrasse 9, 14193 Berlin.
Italy ((06) 852541 FAX (06) 852543, Via Tinaro 14, Rome 00198.
The Netherlands ((070) 392 4501 FAX (070) 346 0669, 40 Wassenaarseweg, 2596CJ The Hague, Netherlands.
Spain ((01) 435 6688, Edificio Lista Van der, Calle Claudio Coello 91-6, Cor of J Ortega Y Gasset, Madrid 28006.
Switzerland ((031) 350 1313 FAX (031) 350 1310, 29 Alpenstrasse, 3006 Berne.
United Kingdom ((020) 7451 7299 FAX (020) 7451 7284, South Africa House, Trafalgar Square, London WC2N 5DP.
United States ((202) 232 4400 FAX (202) 265 1607, 3051 Massachusetts Avenue NW, Washington, DC 20008. There are also consulates in Beverley Hills, New York, and Chicago.

The beach is great for strolling but the waters are cold at Llandudno Sandy Bay Beach, near Cape Town.

TOURIST INFORMATION

Small is beautiful with South African tourist organizations: the larger they get the less helpful and more useless they become. Throughout the text the local tourist information bureaus are listed, and these are the people to contact with any queries. Satour, the state-owned tourist bureau, has offices outside South Africa but these often seem allergic to contact by the general public. Politely unhelpful in my experience; however in case this is not universal, the worldwide offices are as follows.

Head Office (South Africa) ((012) 347 0600 FAX (012) 454889, 442 Rigel Avenue South, Erasmusrand 0181, P/Bag X164, Pretoria 0001.

Australia and **New Zealand** ((02) 9261 3424 FAX (02) 9261 3414, Level 6, 285 Clarence Street, Sydney 2000, NSW, Australia.

Austria ((01) 4704 5110 FAX (01) 4704 5114, Stefan-Zweig-Platz 11, A1170, Vienna.

Benelux Countries ((020) 664 6201 FAX (020) 662 9761, Josef Israelskade 48, 1072SB, Amsterdam, Netherlands.

Canada ((416) 283 0563 FAX (416) 283 5465, Suite 2, 4117 Lawrence Avenue East, Scarborough, Ontario M1E 2S2.

France ((01) 45 61 01 97 FAX (01) 45 61 01 96, 61 Rue La Boetie, 75008 Paris.

Germany ((069) 929 1290 E-MAIL info@fra.satour.de, Alemania Haus, An der Hauptwache 11, D-60313 Frankfurt/Main 1, Postfach 101940, Frankfurt 60019.

Italy ((02) 4091 8032 FAX (02) 4801 3233, Via V Monti 8, 20123 Milano.

Israel ((03) 527 2950 FAX (03) 527 1958, Fourteenth Floor, Century Towers, 124 Ibn Gvirol Street, Box 3388, Tel Aviv 61033.

Switzerland ((01) 715 1815 FAX (01) 715 1889, Seestrasse 42, CH 8802 Kilchberg, Zurich.

United Kingdom ((0208) 944 8080 FAX (0208) 944 6705, Numbers 5 and 6 Alt Grove, Wimbledon London SW19 4DZ.

United States (Eastern) ((212) 730 2929 TOLL-FREE (800) 822 5368 FAX (212) 764 1980, 500 Fifth Avenue, 20th Floor, Suite 2040, New York, New York 10110.

United States (Western) ((310) 641 8444 TOLL-FREE (800) 782 9772 FAX (310) 641 5812, Suite 1524, 9841 Airport Boulevard, Los Angeles, California 90045.

GETTING AROUND

Although there is plenty of public transportation between the major cities, public transportation to smaller towns and within cities is hopelessly inadequate and far from safe. A rental car is by far the best way of getting around (see below).

Although people do take local minibus taxis and often report nothing but the most courteous service, it is not recommended, and in cities the terminal buildings are often frequented by armed thieves: Johannesburg's Rotunda is infamous.

Internal flights, on the other hand, are useful, frequent, and relatively inexpensive. The major airlines are SA Airlink and SA Express (divisions of the national carrier South African Airways), Sun Air, Comair (a codeshare partner of British Airways), and Sabena Nationwide. Contact numbers in South Africa are **SA Airlink** ((011) 978 1111; **SA Express** ((011) 978 5569; **Sabena Nationwide** ((011) 390 1660; **Comair** ((011) 441 8600; and **Sun Air** ((011) 923 6400. Air charter is a possibility, especially for groups, as rates are not prohibitive.

Regional coach and bus companies are listed in the text of the touring chapters in their relevant areas. The major long-distance coach companies offer good overnight services between major cities, but can work out to be expensive and inconvenient for shorter journeys. Tickets can be bought through Computicket, with more than 300 branches worldwide, or directly from the companies. The major operators are **Greyhound Citiliner** ((011) 830 1400 FAX (011) 333 5750; **Translux Express** ((011) 774 3333 FAX (011) 488 1357; and **Intercape** ((021) 386 2488 FAX (021) 934 4400.

Backpackers are more likely to travel around using prepaid tickets for the **Baz Bus** ((021) 439 2323 FAX (021) 439 2343 E-MAIL info@bazbus.com, WEB SITE www.bazbus.com, 8 Rosedene Road, Sea Point, Cape Town 8005, which follows a coastal route from the Cape to Durban, and then travels inland on the way to Johannesburg, Pretoria, Mpumalanga, and the Kruger.

Confusion is inevitable when inquiring after taxis. In South Africa "taxi" is taken to refer to one of the minibuses that ferry local Africans on pre-planned routes. Try asking for a "taxi shuttle" to avoid a blank and unhelpful stare in reply. As most South Africans have their own cars, many smaller towns do not have any taxi service at all, and even in the cities taxis don't cruise the streets looking for fares. Call and book a taxi. In inner cities at night, wait until the taxi arrives before leaving the restaurant or club onto the street. Taxis are not especially cheap, but do at least use meters to assess the fare. A 10% tip is expected.

BY CAR

Most white South Africans take car ownership for granted. Apart from links between the major centers, public transportation is not well-developed, so a rental car is almost essential to reach rural areas or to travel around larger towns. In view of the distances between the major cities the best plan is to mix air, coach, or rail travel to cover the big journeys, and then rent a car to get around. There are more than 65 car rental companies in South Africa and the standard of cars provided is, in general, high. The major car-rental companies have desks at most airports and many railway stations around the country, but you can make significant savings by arranging your car-rental through a smaller company, who will often arrange to meet your flight with a vehicle. Further savings can be made by arranging your car-rental before arriving in South Africa. To make designing a flexible itinerary easy many rental companies allow you to pick up your vehicle at one city and drop it off in another with no extra charge.

There are three factors particular to South Africa which should be borne in mind when se-

areas and 120 kph (75 mph) on national roads and highways. On straight, uncrowded roads covering huge distances the temptation to go much faster is almost irresistible, even though you'll inevitably hit a wild animal eventually. Hit a bird and you'll survive, but the big black Transkei pigs will do serious damage to your vehicle at least. Speed and you've also got the police to contend with. There are speed traps, both mechanical and manned, and drivers exceeding 150 kph (93 mph) are liable to arrest. Although it is an offence to warn oncoming drivers of speed traps, many South Africans will flash their lights in warning (thanks).

The wearing of seatbelts is compulsory so belt up: this has the added advantage in Johannesburg

lecting a vehicle. First, don't choose a BMW. In the townships they're known as "Be My Wife," are much sought-after, and are the most commonly car-jacked models. Secondly, choose an air-conditioned vehicle. Air conditioning is not always required by the climate — especially in a Cape winter — but driving round South African cities with the windows down is not safe. Finally, don't skimp and rent a cheap old banger. There are plenty of areas where you don't want to break down. By the same token, check that the spare tire is inflated and there is a jack and lug wrench provided.

Driving licenses must be carried at all times, be printed in English, and include a photograph of the driver. The fact that an estimated 10% of drivers don't possess a license won't stop the police arresting you if they stop you without one. The most common reason to be stopped is speeding. The legal speed limit is 60 kph (37 mph) in urban

of preventing you being jerked out of your car by an attacker. Drunk driving is enforced sporadically but the penalties are severe. The limits are 0.05g/100 ml, with the potential for a fine as well as a six-year prison sentence. The same regulations apply equally if you're riding a bicycle or horse.

Metropolitan roads in urban areas have the prefix "M," while the major national highways have the prefix "N." Although these are sometimes four-lane away from the major centers they thin down to two lanes, one in each direction. It is normal to pull over onto the hard shoulder to let faster vehicles pass: a quick flash of the hazard lights is enough to say "thank you." Regional roads, often very fast and usually deserted but

A tortoise heads for the hills near the Karoo town of Graaf-Reinet.

very occasionally dotted with axle-breaking pot-holes, are identified by an "R" prefix. There are toll roads, signposted in time to let you slip off onto minor roads and travel free, but if you are using the toll road have some money ready. The rate is signposted clearly. At the other end of the scale are the network of dirt roads that provide the only links for many rural areas. While these are usually well-graded, after rain they can become difficult or impassable, and corners should always be taken gently as buildups of loose gravel can cause complications such as skids or rolls.

There are a couple of factors unique to South Africa that might come as a surprise. Firstly, there are plenty of four-way stop junctions where everybody has to give way. Drivers then proceed on a first-come, first-to-go basis. Regulations state that if two drivers arrive at the same time "Common Courtesy" applies to who goes first, which is an interesting legal term. The procedure can be lengthy. Traffic lights are known as "Robots" and offer a number of flashing options: flashing green arrows mean you can turn in that direction; flashing red means you can turn if the way is clear, while steady green arrows indicate you may proceed with caution. Traffic circles are known as "Circles": always yield and give way to vehicles already in the circle. You drive on the left, and it is illegal to park a vehicle on the opposite side of the road facing the oncoming traffic. In general fuel stations do not accept credit cards and only take cash.

Finally, don't get lost, especially in towns. While slowing to ask directions from a pedestrian might be useful in Europe or at home, in South Africa this is usually unhelpful and can conceivably be dangerous. Figure out in advance where you are going and how to get there, and if you do go wrong, pull up in a well-lit shop or gas station to consult the map. It is best not to drive at night for a number of reasons, including wildlife and wild life, which means that it is important to figure out where you'll be spending the night when touring. Personally I like to know by 4 PM where I'll be spending the night when traveling in South Africa, and I carry a portable phone to make sure that I can make arrangements and get directions rather than blundering about in the dark. The drawback is that portable phones, in South Africa, are about the smallest and most valuable possessions available and are frequently stolen. Keep them well out of sight.

There are plenty of car-rental companies. However they vary widely in price and conditions. The minimum age to rent a car is, in most cases, 21. Significant discounts can be obtained by organizing your car-rental before you arrive in South Africa. The big thing to watch out for are mileage charges: unless you'll be staying put for long periods the huge distances in South Africa can make car rental very expensive if you're paying between one or two rand per kilometer on top of all the insurance extras. Travelers used to miles will find kilometers very short.

My personal favorite for rates and service is **Economy Car Hire** ((011) 974 1625 TOLL-FREE 0800 011 257 FAX (011) 974 2827 E-MAIL economy@ brmh.co.za, Box 4008, Edenvale 1610, who keep rates low by saving on service desks. Instead you call them and the car is delivered, often within the hour. Returning the vehicle is simple: either have it picked up or lock the keys in the boot at the airport. Vehicles are new and they offer unlimited mileage if requested. Most car-rental companies also offer itineraries and hotel reservations in combination with inbound tour operators, a useful compromise between taking a tour and traveling fully independently (see TAKING A TOUR, page 56 for further details).

The bigger companies are more likely to have desks at regional airports, though you'll have to pay for this convenience. **Avis** TOLL-FREE 0800 021 111 have more than 100 desks at airports, stations, and hotels nationwide. **Budget** (011) 392 3929 TOLL-FREE 0860 016 622 FAX (011) 392 3900 have fifty offices around South Africa, while **Europcar** ((011) 396 9000 FAX (011) 396 1406 E-MAIL info@europcar .co.za, Box 4613, Kempton Park 1620, have a surprisingly good network, considering South Africa is not, by any stretch of the imagination, in Europe.

Camper travel is popular in South Africa, and there are specialists who rent out motor homes. Based in Johannesburg, **Camper Vacations** (/FAX (011) 392 1051 E-MAIL camvac@iafrica.com, 7–9 Sheri road, Harmelia, Kempton Park 1609, offer a huge range of different vehicles from four-wheel-drives with rooftop tents to lumbering palaces on wheels.

ACCOMMODATION

Standards are high for most types of accommodation. While there are several large luxury hotels, most are working out that small is beautiful at the top end of the market. The national rating system for hotels that was meant to be administered by Satour has fallen into disuse and is no longer a reliable guide to the facilities and standards to expect. Its place has been taken by a veritable flood of associations that try to group the better class of hotels into unified marketing brochures.

There are a number of associations of the better class of hotels. The really top establishments in

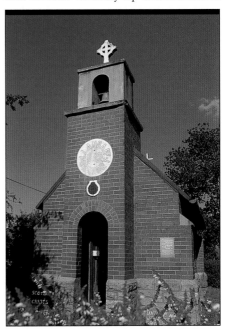

the country, with the finest cuisine and prices to suit, are usually members of the international Relais & Châteaux association, while Chaîne des Rotisseurs membership usually also signifies truly outstanding cuisine, a fact not always reflected in high overnight rates. **Exclusive Getaways CC** ((011) 803 8669 FAX (011) 807 0417 E-MAIL getaways @iafrica.com WEB SITE www.getaways.co.za, 2 Eighth Avenue, Box 5321, Rivonia 2128, have collected a number of very luxurious hotels, usually small, under a central marketing company with a color brochure describing each property.

Portfolio ((011) 880 3414 FAX (011) 788 4802 E-MAIL collection@iafrica.com WEB SITE www .portfoliocollection.co.za, Box 52350, Saxonwold 2132, has two brochures: their "Country Places"

OPPOSITE: Ostriches weed the crops in the Outeniqua Mountains. ABOVE: Van Reenen has the world's smallest Catholic church.

collection concentrates on the smarter country-house hotels and private game reserves while their "Retreats" collection is significantly cheaper; whichever brochure, the emphasis is on small, character accommodation, usually owner-run and managed. The Portfolio brochures are well worth obtaining before traveling around South Africa. Even though Portfolio are a commercial association they do insist on high standards of service and facilities.

Portfolio also list game lodges, but if your interests are in the natural world the **Jackalberry Collection** ((011) 807 7669 FAX (011) 807 7295 E-MAIL reservations@natureworkshop.com WEB SITE www.natureworkshop.com, 10 Wessels Road, Rivonia 2128, keeps the focus on those lodges specializing in the wildlife experience. Game lodges might seem expensive at first, but usually provide full board accommodation, all game drives and activities, and often manage to produce significant luxury in the heart of the bush.

It is usual, however, to tip game rangers (R50 or so if their service has been good).

Local groups of hotels sometimes also band together their marketing efforts. The **Cape Country Routes** (/FAX (021) 887 4626, Box 3200, Matieland 7602, have collected a selection of the better hotels along the garden route. Other associations include **Relais Hotels** ((012) 423 1426 FAX (012) 423 1439 E-MAIL relais@satis.co.za WEB SITE www.relais.co.za, Box 654, Cape Town 8000, with a collection of generally unexceptional hotels; **Leading Independent Hotels of Southern Africa** ((039) 975 1056 FAX (039) 975 1057 E-MAIL info@braddens.co.za WEB SITE www.braddens.co.za, Box 598, Pennington 4184, with a small collection of very fine hotels that usually also feature in the Portfolio Brochures; and **Classic Retreats Southern Africa** (/FAX (021) 790 2603 E-MAIL classics@iafrica.com WEB SITE www.classicretreats.co.za, Box 12158, Mill Street, Cape Town 8010, who have

Dropping down the market a bit, rates tend to be less flexible. **Roger & Kay's Travel Selection** ((021) 715 7130 FAX (021) 712 3340 E-MAIL home accm@iafrica.com WEB SITE www.travelselection .co.za, Box 405, Bergvliet, 7864 Cape Town, is a worthy attempt to form a graded assessment of bed-and-breakfasts and self-catering accommodation nationwide. It is free. Bed-and-breakfasts often provide excellent value but often not much privacy.

Backpackers will find a rainforest of brochures advertising other backpacker lodges racked up in their first lodge reception. There are also a range of booklets that contain full contact numbers and reviews. BUG, currently out of print but with chances of coming back to life, offers objective reviews. The more successful *Jungle* booklet, *Backpack Africa* magazine also provide reviews, generally supplied by the lodge managers. **Hostelling International South Africa** ((021) 424 2511 FAX (021) 424 4119 E-MAIL info@hisa.org.za WEB SITE www.hisa.org.za, 73 St. George's Mall, Box 4402, Cape Town 8000, produces a clear and informative listing with further details online. Most backpacker lodges will offer twin rooms as well as dormitory accommodation.

EATING OUT

The traditional South African diet is a thick porridge made from sorghum or maize, introduced by the Portuguese in the fifteenth century, with thin stews of spinach, beans, tomatoes and onions, with protein from chickens or mopani worms, grasshoppers, ants, and beetles. It's not the sort of food you're likely to be offered these days though, as South African city cuisine steadily ascends to new heights. A few notable hotels and restaurants expect formal dress for evening meals, but in general smart casual will be enough. In rural areas the choice tends to narrow, with plenty of steak houses and fast-food joints serving spicy chicken and other modern staples. It is usually possible to find oases of fine cuisine even in the smaller towns, while many rural restaurants serve traditional Afrikaner classics with considerable panache. Service is not usually included, with 10% tips quite normal, though if the service has not been very good not tipping is also reasonably accepted. One South African specialty is never meant to be eaten in restaurants: biltong can be made out of any sort of meat, spiced or unspiced, and many shops serve their own area's specialty. This can replace lunch for days on the move.

Prices in restaurants are generally reasonable. In one of the chain restaurants you can expect to eat quite well for less than R40, while in the better restaurants a meal with wine is unlikely to exceed

a collection of some of the most expensive and refined accommodation option.

The most comprehensive guide to hotels and bed-and-breakfasts is the *AA Guide*, an unwieldy but comprehensive listing which can be bought in CAN Bookshops in South Africa. The largest chain of mid-market hotels in the country, with member establishments usually aimed at business travelers but often with considerable character, is the **Protea** ((021) 419 5320 FAX (021) 425 2956 E-MAIL uwelcome@protea.co.za WEB SITE www .protea-hotels.co.za, Fifth Floor, Nedbank Foreshore Building, Heerengracht, Cape Town 8001. At around R400 per night these can be found in most towns and cities in South Africa, and can be a good alternative if night falls.

Most hotels in the middle and upper category change their rates significantly depending on season. During low season it is often worth trying to get more of a discount.

Knysna's last elephants are well used to visitors.

R100 a head including wine. The exceptions are the seriously upmarket country house hotels, which aren't always in the country, where prices can creep up. Increased formality generally means an increased figure at the bottom of your bill. If price is a major consideration avoid candlelit and cut-glass settings, and ask to see the menu before sitting down.

BASICS

TIME

There is a single time-band across South Africa: Greenwich Mean Time plus two hours.

ELECTRICITY

Electricity is generally 220–230 volts AC though Pretoria sticks to 250 volts AC, requiring a square-pin grounded socket (as used in the United Kingdom).

WEIGHTS AND MEASURES

Weights and measures are metric: distance is in kilometers and meters, gas in liters, but wine, still, in bottles.

CURRENCY

The unit of currency is the rand, divided into 100 cents, and a mixture of old and new notes and coins are still in circulation. Old and new 1c, 2c, 5c, 10c, 20c, 50c, and R1 coins and R5, R10, R20

and R50 notes are all in use. New R2 and R5 coins and R100 and R200 coins have recently been introduced. The exchange rates at the time of publication were US$1=R6.29, £1=R10.13, 1 euro= R6.24. Although banks will change money they are slow and bureaucratic, and hotel rates are rarely favorable. The best way to get money in South Africa is using a Visa or Mastercard in one of the Automatic Teller Machines (ATMs) that can be found in all major towns — there is even one in the middle of the Kruger National Park. Be alert though: ATMs have, in the past, been targeted by thieves. Credit cards are accepted in most hotels and restaurants, but not in small rural shops or at gas stations. Banking hours are from 9 AM to 3:30 PM, Monday to Friday, and 8:30 AM to 11 AM on Saturdays.

COMMUNICATIONS AND MEDIA

INTERNET

Although South Africans claim they've embraced the Internet with enthusiasm because they're naturally technologically advanced and open-minded about new technology, other reasons are that their telephone service has recently convulsed the country by its haphazard upgrade of the nation's telephone numbers, and the postal service is disastrously inefficient. It's not surprising the Internet is popular. Cybercafés are springing up in all major towns, although access can be relatively expensive; cheaper access is available at many backpacker lodges, where computers are often not in use during the day.

TELEPHONE

Telephone numbers are still being upgraded: the new numbers have three digit codes and seven-digit numbers. All other shorter numbers are subject to change, but often Telkom, the South African Telephone company, won't release details of the new numbers until the last minute, and after they have changed. Dial the old number and you'll get a recorded announcement that will either tell you, curtly, to look up the new number in a telephone book, or blurt out the new number in a mechanical spurt that can take three calls to get down on paper. If a number has changed, call ℂ 1023 for directory inquiries. Be warned that English is not the first language of many of the operators, which can make for frustrating experiences.

For outgoing calls, the telephone boxes, which take cards or coins, work well enough, and are cheaper from 8 PM to 8 AM. Calls made from hotel rooms are invariably marked up substantially. The country code for South Africa is + 27, followed by the telephone number as listed in the text, without dialing the initial 0 of the area code. Portable phones from other countries are also expensive to use in South Africa: it is better to rent one your arrival.

MAIL

The postal service is not good. Letters arrive late or not at all: hence the reliance on box numbers in the mailing addresses featured in this guide. Sometimes it seems easier to save yourself the cost of a stamp and just throw your letter away instead of mailing it. If you have anything to mail it is best to use an office of Postnet, an upstart private rival to the state-owned service, with 160 offices nationwide. In any case, be sure to use the four-figure city code in the address that locates the area within South Africa.

RADIO AND TELEVISION

Radio and television services are good — if you are interested in sports. News and drama are in their infancy, and only sports reporting seems to excel. The same is true to a certain extent of the newspapers, which don't contain much in the way of useful news nor listings. Specific listings magazines published in the major cities are better.

ETIQUETTE

The major etiquette issue in South Africa is race. As the authorities adopt various terms for the black population the words used to define ethnicity quickly acquire pejorative connotations, and new words are constantly being pressed into use to describe established racial stereotypes without giving offense. Thus "Native" and "Kaffir" should on no account be used to describe black people, and for many "Bushman" and "Hottentot," once used all the time are now loaded, and will be seen as offensive. Currently "San" and "Khoikhoi" are acceptable in historical terms. Care should be taken in all matters of race. This is especially true when speaking to white South Africans in bars, as their racial views are, to an outsider, often extreme and offensive. Reasoned discussion in these circumstances is likely to be provocative, and it is best, but not always easy, just to avoid the topic.

HEALTH

Standards of hygiene and health are high in South Africa. The public health system is in crisis, however, with increasing numbers of the country's doctors draining away into practice in Australia and the United States. With the HIV rates in the country it would be a brave person who went to a state hospital for treatment after a serious accident. The private hospitals still maintain high standards but at a price: good travel insurance is a wise precaution as bills can spiral to United States levels.

Although no vaccinations are required for South Africa, polio and tetanus inoculations should be kept up to date, and yellow fever vaccinations are required if you've come from a country where this is endemic. Hepatitis A and typhoid can be contracted from contaminated water, though the risk is remote.

Malaria is more of a problem. The Northern Cape, the Kruger National Park, and some areas of northern KwaZulu-Natal contain a serious malaria risk, especially in the rainy summer. Prophylaxis should be taken and mosquito bites avoided. Rabies is present: beware of strange

animals and see a doctor immediately if bitten. Snakes and scorpions, though present in large numbers in the Kruger, are rarely a problem. If collecting firewood, however, it is wise to knock dry logs before carrying them back. In the mornings, check your shoes — and not with your feet.

Many South Africans, especially in the black population, are HIV positive: in KwaZulu-Natal recent figures from antenatal clinics have run as high as 49%. Prostitution is a pretty charmless business in South Africa so temptation is unlikely, but sexual transmission is the best way of catching AIDS. Getting arrested and sent to prison can also introduce a certain unpredictability to your social life, so don't drink and drive or get involved in drugs.

OPPOSITE: This mailbox looks efficient but the reality is sadly different. ABOVE: A cupola of Port Elisabeth's library.

Most travelers are at more risk from the sun. In the northern latitudes, heat is always of a sub-tropical level, while the southern sun, in the summer, can be unrelenting. A hat is almost essential for many desert hikes, and sunscreen, sunglasses, and plenty of water almost as important. Avoid cheap sunglasses: their apparent shade might miss out the damaging UV radiation and cause even more damage to eyes than going unprotected would.

SECURITY

Crime is a very real problem in South Africa, especially in Johannesburg, with local issues such as car-jacking and mugging covered in the appropriate section (see SECURITY, page 157, under JOHANNESBURG). In city centers the risk is very real: portable phones, especially, are much sought after, and carrying a phone is the most likely way to get into trouble. Cameras or camcorders bring much the same risk, and the most sensible thing to do with expensive jewelry is to leave it at home. On beaches, keep your car keys and cash on your person — there are waterproof wallets for the money and keys that can be pinned to your swimsuit — and look after your passport and driving license at all times. Precautions relating to driving are covered in GETTING AROUND, page 252. While on foot, travel in groups if possible and don't carry too much, and at all times avoid walking in urban areas after dark. Take special care around ATM machines, especially if withdrawing cash: never allow people to crowd around and don't accept help from strangers.

If you have purchased this book because you've been invited to South Africa on a business trip, be warned there have been cases of businessmen being lured over and then kidnapped for ransom, usually by Nigerians. That you have something to read during your imprisonment might be some consolation, but you won't get much sightseeing done.

WHEN TO GO

Broadly speaking, South Africa's seasons are the reverse of those in the Northern Hemisphere. Thus their summer runs from November to February. This is, indeed, a good time for the Cape, although the austral spring and autumn can be good times, with the heat less severe and accommodation easier to find and less expensive.

In the Kruger, however, the austral winter is a good time to visit. The rain falls in the summer, when the weather is hotter, the risk of mosquitoes greater, and the game, hidden by fresh undergrowth and not constrained by thirst, much harder to find. Inland, the temperature is likely to drop at night whatever the season, with frosts common in the winter months. Johannesburg and Pretoria, on their plateau setting, are comfortable year-round, with a dry heat in the day and a bracing chill at night. At sea level, the Durban summer is oppressively hot, the shoulder seasons are humid but warm, and the winter best of all.

WHAT TO TAKE

If game-viewing, take binoculars. These, like most optical items in South Africa, are relatively expensive. When traveling inland be ready for low nighttime temperatures. Game-drives at dawn can be especially cold, and central heating in lodges and hotels is rare. A good set of sunglasses is almost essential for long daytime drives and invaluable for spotting whales, sharks, dolphins, seals, and penguin underwater. If you have time to go shopping during your trip, a good purchase is an extra bag — preferably in Kudu leather — to carry home a new set of purchases. Locally produced goods are generally high quality and very inexpensive.

PHOTOGRAPHY

South Africa is a hugely photogenic place. Colorful townships, splendid hotel and lodge interiors, sweeping views and Africa's famous wildlife all make for spectacular photographs.

However there are local factors which will dictate your choice of camera. First is the chance it will be stolen. If you're taking pictures in a township a small point-and-shoot camera is far less intrusive and much less likely to be stolen. The same is not true if you're taking wildlife: here theft is not a problem. With a 35mm SLR camera you'll want a 300mm lens to take any worthwhile pictures, preferably backed by a really good flash unit for the best game-viewing times of dawn and dusk.

As long as your game-viewing vehicle starts easily, make sure the driver switches off the engine to minimize camera-shake. If you only have a compact camera, just concentrate on enjoying the wildlife experience, preferably with binoculars, and rely on buying postcards to recapture the wildlife experience. Unless a lion climbs on your hood, photographs taken with a wide-angle camera are bound to be a disappointment and tourists notoriously overestimate the power of their flashes to illuminate scenes in the evening and at night.

Africa's landscapes are not easy to capture on film. A graduated filter can help to bring the huge African skies under control and a polarizing filter

will cut down on extraneous light. When taking pictures of people a degree of courtesy is, of course, vital, though in general South Africans are fairly relaxed about having their picture taken as long as it is done with good humor. Locals waiting near tourist areas done up in fancy dress — as they see tribal costume — will probably expect payment for pictures. When taking candid pictures of locals going about their daily life many will ask for a copy of the picture: please don't take their addresses unless you have a real intention of fulfilling your promise.

Film is widely available in South Africa and slide film is less expensive than in Europe. However it is safer to bring your own unless you're confident of having time to find a photographic shop before you start seeing the sights you want to record. Keep films, exposed or unexposed, in the heart of your luggage to protect against extremes of temperature. If staying in air-conditioned rooms, or if driving an air-conditioned car, remember to warm your camera up before trying to use it, or condensation is likely to blur your pictures.

OPPOSITE: A good wind is Cape Town's most reliable climatic feature. ABOVE: Sun City's artificial beach comes complete with artificial waves.

LANGUAGE BASICS

South Africa has 11 official languages. Learning them all is clearly impractical, though a few choice words will certainly help to break the ice. The official languages are: Afrikaans, English, Ndebele (Ndebele), Xhosa (Xhosa), Zulu (Zulu), Sesotho (Southern Sotho), Sesotho sa Leboa (Northern Sotho), Setswana (Tswana), Swati (Swazi), Tshivenda (Venda), and Xitsonga (Tsonga).

Some useful local expressions incorporated into "English" might include:

Africana   All things connected to Africa, now commonly used to refer to books, furniture, paintings, and objets d'art.

Bakkie   A van or light pickup truck, often used for traveling off the beaten track.

Boerekos   Traditional farm-style or country cooking (Boer means farmer).

Bobotie   Traditional Cape dish made from minced meat & spices, covered with a savory egg custard and baked in the oven.

Boma   A fence or enclosure made of wooden posts, traditionally used for corralling cattle now commonly used at safari lodges to shelter dining guests outside.

Braai   A barbecue.

Braaivleis   Meat which has been cooked on an open fire or *braai*.

Bredie   A stew made of meat and vegetables, named after the main vegetable, so tomatoes are used in *tomatiebredie*.

Broekie lace   Ornamental Victorian-style wrought-iron work, often edging verandas or *stoeps*.

Foefie slide   A cable mechanism used to cross a piece of land or stretch of water.

Hartebeeshuisie   A temporary shelter built of wattle and daub: as a comparison a sure way to annoy the host of your luxury faux-rustic lodge.

Koeksisters   A doughnut mixture which is platted, fried, and dipped in syrup.

Koppie   A hillock, either flat-topped or pointed.

Lapa   The courtyard enclosed by a circle of Ndebele huts now used to refer to any outdoor enclosure built of mud or brick.

Pap   The local porridge made from ground maize meal.

Potjie   A heavy iron pot with three legs (usually black), used for cooking over an open fire.

Riempie chairs   Chairs with wooden frames, the seats and backs made from thin strips of softened hide.

Robot   Traffic light.

Rondavel   A circular dwelling, often with a thatched roof.

Rusk   A light dough that is baked until crisp.

Skottelbraai   Originally, the round piece of a plough used to cook on an open fire. Nowadays, a wok-shaped metal pan, usually heated by a gas bottle.

Stoep   Veranda or porch.

Waterblommetjie   A waxy flower that grows in water, eaten as *waterblommetjiebredie*.

WEB SITES

There are countless useful web sites for South Africa, most of which are listed in the text. Even the smallest towns and *dorps* are likely to have their own web sites. Often these can be located by typing "www.placename .co.za." Sometimes these domains have been hijacked by speculators hoping to be able to sell the squatted site back to the community. If so a short vitriolic flame is in order before referring back to one of the major search engines to find the local tourist office's own site.

The bigger local operators such as mweb.co.za and iafrica.com have their own sites, **www.mweb .co.za** and **www.iafrica .com**, with newsy information coming from Cape Town and Johannesburg respectively, and provincial sites can be a rewarding source of links. Catch up with the thinking of the government with the **African National Congress'** Home Page at www.anc .org.za/, who also run a pretty good news service. To find out more about the country in advance the **Transvaal Museum** of Pretoria has a lively site at www-tm.up.ac.za/. To get an idea of the **music** you can expect to find tune in to www.intertainment.co.za/actions/music.htm, with clips from local bands that you can play on your computer. For a magazine-like collection of generally relevant features and links **Epinions** is a good source: their South African page is on www.epinions.com/trvl_Region_ Africa-South_Africa though, as with most things netty, the balance is American. A more **local perspective** is available at za.orientation.com. If crime is your bag take a look at www.saps .co.za/, the site of the **South African Police Service**, which is specially useful if you want to become one.

Perhaps because of poor telecommunication and postal services, South Africans themselves have been keen to adopt the new technology of the Internet, and most commercial operations either have, or are about to, come up with their own sites. There are also a number of umbrella organizations trying to link and prioritize these. On a national level things can start to get unwieldy, but there are several web sites in development which are likely to eclipse the ones available so far. Otherwise, as always with the Internet, the most up-to-date information will be found on the web itself.

Recommended Reading

BEHR, MARK. *The Smell of Apples.* United Kingdom: Abacus, 1995. A small white boy grows up under his military father in 1970s apartheid South Africa.

BRINK, ANDRE. *A Chain of Voices.* Minerva 1995. Eighteenth-century Cape life: slavery and murder brought to life by one of South Africa's most vivid writers. See also *Act of Terror.*

BULL, BARTLE. *Safari: a Chronicle of Adventure.* Penguin, 1988. A fascinating account of the hundred years that opened up Africa and spelled death for the area's wildlife.

COETZEE, J.M. *The Age of Iron.* Penguin, 1995. A white

MOGOTSI, ISAAC. *Alexandra Tales.* Ravan Press, 1995. Family life in Johannesburg's inner-city township of Alexandra.

PAKENHAM, THOMAS. *The Boer War.* 1979; London, Abacus, 1999. The classic account of the historic conflict that shaped South Africa. By the same author *The Scramble for Africa* (London, Abacus, 1992).

PATON, ALAN. *Cry the Beloved Country.* Penguin, 1989. A Natal Pastor comes to Johannesburg to rescue his missing son.

SEPAMLA, SIPHO. *A ride on the Whirlwind.* Readers International, 1984. The riot-swept Soweto of the late 1970s brought vividly to life.

lecturer dying of cancer finds transformation through a tramp who takes up residence in her garden. By the same author *Disgrace, Boyhood; The Life and Times of Michael K, Waiting for the Barbarians,* and others.

GORDIMER, NADINE. *None to Accompany Me.* Penguin, 1996. Worthy white middle-aged South African academic wakes up.

MALAN, RIAN. *My Traitor's Heart.* New York: Random House, 1990. A South African journalist anguishes.

MANDELA, NELSON. *The Long Walk to Freedom.* 1994; London: Abacus, 1996. The definitive political biography, with further editions including the *Illustrated Long Walk to Freedom* (Little Brown) and what should perhaps be called the short walk, the abridged *Long Walk to Freedom* (Macmillan). A classic.

SEROTE, MONGANE WALLY. *To Every Birth its Blood.* United Kingdom: Heinemann. A young township man discovers a political consciousness.

SHREINER, OLIVE. *Story of an African Farm.* 1939; Penguin, 1997. The first-ever South African novel: two sisters in the remote Karoo are swept by the arrival of an Irish traveler.

SPARKS, ALLISTER. *The Mind of South Africa.* London: Mandarin, 1995). The history of South Africa through Boer, black, and British eyes.

SPARKS, ALLISTER. *Tomorrow is Another Country.* South Africa: Struik, 1998. How the Broederbond came to terms with the ANC.

THOMPSON, LEONARD. *A History of South Africa.* Yale University Press, 1996. A concise history of South Africa, best on prehistory though simplistic in the present.

Simplicity and cost define shantytown architecture.

Quick Reference A–Z Guide
to Places and Topics of Interest with
Listed Accommodation, Restaurants and
Useful Telephone Numbers

The symbols Ⓕ FAX, Ⓣ TOLL-FREE, Ⓔ E-MAIL, Ⓦ WEB-SITE refer to additional contact information found in the chapter listings.

Photo Credits

All pictures were taken by Alain Evrard with the exception of the following:

Melissa Shales: Page 11.

Jack Barker: Pages 30, 33, 103, 121, 135, 149 *top*, 185, 243, and 254.

Nik Wheeler: Pages 12, 15, 24, 46 *bottom*, 50, 53, 55, 58, 64, 65, 75, 79, 81, 84 *right*, 85, 86, 89, 92, 93, 95, 96, 99, 101, 155, 170, 179, 181, 182, 194, 199, 206, 207, 208, 209, 210, 212, 215, and 219.